Sociology of the Invisible Hand

STUDIES IN SOCIAL SCIENCES, PHILOSOPHY AND HISTORY OF IDEAS

VOLUME 20

PETER LANG

Adriana Mica / Katarzyna M. Wyrzykowska /
Rafał Wiśniewski / Iwona Zielińska (eds.)

Sociology of the Invisible Hand

PETER LANG

Bibliographic Information published by the Deutsche Nationalbibliothek

The Deutsche Nationalbibliothek lists this publication in the Deutsche Nationalbibliografie; detailed bibliographic data is available in the internet at http://dnb.d-nb.de.

Library of Congress Cataloging-in-Publication Data
A CIP catalog record for this book has been applied for at the Library of Congress.

The publishing of this volume was undertaken as part of the project Paradoks niezamierzonych konsekwencji: Od niewidzialnej ręki do efektów odwrócenia w naukach społecznych [The Paradox of Unintended Consequences: From the Invisible Hand to Perverse Effects in Social Sciences], financed by the National Science Centre, Poland, on the basis of the decision number DEC-2013/09/D/HS6/00242.

ISSN 2196-0151
ISBN 978-3-631-67232-7 (Print)
E-ISBN 978-3-653-06772-9 (E-PDF)
E-ISBN 978-3-631-71043-2 (EPUB)
E-ISBN 978-3-631-71044-9 (MOBI)
DOI 10.3726/978-3-653-06772-9

Peter Lang – Berlin · Bern · Bruxelles · New York ·
Oxford · Warszawa · Wien

This publication has been peer reviewed.

www.peterlang.com

Contents

Acknowledgments

The idea to embark on this collective work came at the intersection of two intellectual endeavors. On the one hand, there was the individual research project run by one member of our team, Adriana Mica. This project, realized under the auspices of the Polish National Science Centre, was determined to draw the theoretical trajectory of the idea of unintended consequences. On the other hand, there was the network-like development of the study of unintended consequences that the four of us, together with other colleagues, started to develop a few years back by way of organizing annual workshops and publications on the topic. This unintended network, supported institutionally by the Polish Sociological Association, the University of Warsaw and affiliated centers, debuted with the intention to formalize the interest and observations regarding the unintended that occur time and again in scientific research, but which are quite implicit to sociology actually.

The first endeavor – the research project – evolved in the direction of a general discussion of the main analytical frames for the study of unintended consequences in sociology, which also includes the invisible hand type of theory. The second endeavor – the unintended consequences network – managed to proliferate by bringing an acute and highly critical input, but also integrative and informal spirit during the debates that we usually organize in May in Warsaw. But what is even more telling, this evidenced a certain level of maturity by publishing the edited collection *Sociology and the Unintended: Robert Merton Revisited* (Adriana Mica, Arkadiusz Pesiert and Jan Winczorek. 2011. Peter Lang). This book, which aimed to redraw the reach of the topic of unintended consequences in sociology, was instantly absorbed in the academia. We took this gratifying element as a sign that it is worth it, and that this is in a sense our opportunity to move forward in our endeavor to articulate sociology of unintended consequences. So we seized this opportunity to systematize the analytical framework that is usually associated with economics but which, at a closer look, emerges to be quite representative of sociology as well. In other words, we embarked on documenting the manifestations, applications and influences of the invisible hand in sociology.

This edited volume is a theoretical concretization of the interest in the unintended that we replenish continuously. But this systematization would not have been realized if it was not for the enthusiastic feedback received from the authors, who are known to be interested in this topic and willing to formalize and institutionalize the study of unintended consequences by contributing to this volume. It is hard to say to what extent the academic cordiality and effective collaboration that the contributors to this volume displayed had anything to do with the fact that the volume set to discuss the topic of the invisible hand. As it is known, the invisible hand is a theme with a great appeal, practically inexhaustible, that it is difficult to say no to. On the other hand, it is also quite challenging. And the amount of pages that were written on the topic render that coming up with something really new is not such an easy task to accomplish. So we owe a big debt of gratitude to the contributors to this volume who took the challenge, to their unmeasurable patience and to their laborious and constant work, not only in these last few months, but also over the years.

These are all scholars known to have dealt, in one way or another, with the metaphor of invisible hand or with the sociological modern take on it, at least once in their academic career. Helmut K. Anheier, Bruna Ingrao, Craig Smith, Emma Tieffenbach and Frederick G. Whelan are longtime analysts and systematizers of the use of the metaphor and its derivatives in economics, science and public policy. Karl-Dieter Opp and Loïc Wacquant are established observers of the phenomena of emergence of norms and of regulation of poverty wherein the metaphor of invisible hand – or visible hands for that matter – plays a key role in the explanatory part. Both Sebastian Giacovelli and Zbigniew Szkop and his colleagues – Rafał Wiśniewski and Marta Sylla – occur as new, but determined learners of the rules of the game of this debate, who also bring in fresh blood in the form of new research sites and theoretical angles. While the three teams composed by Francisco Fernandez de Castro and Raul P. Lejano, Steve McDonald, Scott T. Grether, Kim S. Holland and Hannah McQueen, and by Mikołaj Pawlak and Michał Kotnarowski have proved to be directors of sequels of the modern sociological take on invisible hand-like processes in relation to social capital.

Thus, the positive feedback to the invitation of collaboration was pretty much everything that we, as editors of this volume, could have hoped for in order to cover the subject of the sociology of the invisible hand. This allowed us to illustrate the main analytical streams of study in sociology of the invisible hand (see *Three in One: Invisible Hand-Type Theories in Sociology* [Mica, Wyrzykowska, Zielińska and Wiśniewski in this volume]), as well as to look for shortcomings in the manner in which we tried to articulate the sociology of the invisible hand in our start-up discussion (see *Invisible Hand in Sociology: Where Does It Take Us?* [Mica, Wyrzykowska, Wiśniewski and Zielińska in this volume]). The project turned out to be not only an effective collaboration but also a demanding intellectual challenge, that we would kindly thank again to the contributors to this volume.

It needs to be acknowledged here that on several occasions we reached for theoretical advice and critical overview to the contributors of the volume, and thus extended their engagement with the book through reviewing and commenting of the accompanying texts of *Three in One* and *Sociology of the Invisible Hand: Where Does It Take Us?* In this respect, we are especially grateful to Steve McDonald, Mikołaj Pawlak and Emma Tieffenbach. We are highly indebted to Karl-Dieter Opp and Jocelyn Pixley for embarking the second time around in an edited book project on the unintended consequences with one of the editors of the volume (Adriana Mica). Further, we would also like to express our gratitude to Loïc Wacquant and Frederick G. Whelan for having agreed on the republication of two already existing, but highly relevant, pieces in this volume, as well as for the readiness of Routledge publishing house to put the chapter by Frederick G. Whelan at the disposal of the invisible hand public.

The conceptual realm of the book also benefitted from the research carried out at the British Library in London, UC Berkeley Library, University Library in Warsaw and the National Library of Poland. The invisible hand metaphor goes such a long way back, that an installment to its conceptualization would hardly be conceivable without dedicating dozens of hours spent in the library trying to figure out how does the invisible hand actually work. Without this dedication, the materialization of this edited book would not have been possible.

Adriana Mica, Katarzyna M. Wyrzykowska,
Iwona Zielińska and Rafał Wiśniewski

Three in One: Invisible Hand-Type Theories in Sociology*

In social sciences, the invisible hand mechanism is usually invoked in relation to social institutions that can be shown to be the unintended consequence of juxtaposition of social actions and interactions. Essentially, these actions were not oriented towards producing these institutions to begin with. But due to an intriguing mechanism of aggregation, composition or emergence, the institutions in questions emerged anyway. The invisible hand mechanism is usually associated with the manner in which the economists explain unintended consequences (see Ingrao and Israel 1990; Ingrao 1998; Aydinonat 2008; Tieffenbach 2013; 2016). This is attributed in particular to the authors of Scottish Enlightenment (especially to Adam Smith) (see Smith 2006; 2009), or even earlier to Bernard Mandeville's ideas on public benefits from private vices (see Merton 1936; Elster 1978, 106–108; Ullmann-Margalit 1978; Schneider 1984; 1987; Hirschman 1991, 38–40; Cherkaoui 2005; Campbell 2011, 50–51; Mica 2015).

This strong link with economics notwithstanding, invisible hand accounts have also surfaced in sociology. Generally, the take of sociologists recalls the one of economists. Just that unlike the framing that builds directly on Adam Smith, the sociological theory has its particularity that it focuses on undesirable and perverse outcomes, and that it underlines that the unintended is an outcome of interdependence and/or interaction (see Boudon 1981; 1982 [1977], 255–284). Furthermore, the sociological angle also favors the explanation of invisible hand-like mechanisms as contingent upon social structures and broader processes, and not just as an outcome of aggregation of individual actions.

Despite this visible interest, sociology did not raise the invisible hand to the rank of one of the most important mechanisms. At least not to the extent that economics did. Wherein, as indicated by the subtitle of Aydinonat's (2008) book, the invisible hand became to depict "How Economists Explain Unintended Consequences".

* We would like to express our gratitude for the valuable comments to this start-up discussion given by Mikołaj Pawlak and Emma Tieffenbach.

Certainly, there is a complex of factors that contributed to this rather loose association of the invisible hand with sociology. For one, the high visibility and cumulative knowledge about the model and its subsequent reformulations in economics might have created the perception that the sociological installment, even if it exists, is rather secondary to the mainstream discussion that takes place among economists and political philosophers. But it is also the specificity of the study of invisible hand in sociology, and sociology of unintended consequences in particular, that seems to have contributed to the decreased visibility of the sociological take on the invisible hand processes. In this respect, two characteristics of sociology of the invisible hand stand out.

First, *sociology of the invisible hand is more clearly delineated on paper than in practice*. The study of unintended consequences that result from a complex of individual activities is usually acknowledged as a distinct type of research of unintended consequences related to Smith's invisible hand and Hayek's spontaneous order, as well as to Mandeville's and Popper's articulation of the unintended (see Barry 1982; 1985; Boudon 1990, 119; Zingerle 1998, 180; Mica 2015). Together with the research of unanticipated effects of a singular action that is commonly traced to Merton, this stream is regarded as one of the main modalities of studying the unintended consequences in sociology (see Merton 1936, 896; Giddens 1986 [1984], 13–14; Hirschman 1991; Zingerle 1998, 179; de Zwart 1998, 283–284).[1]

The possibility to demarcate these analytical frames notwithstanding sociology of unintended consequences is a rather fuzzy enterprise. Baert (1991, 203), for instance, indicated the conflation of the diachronic with the synchronic. Hirschman (1991, 35–42) spoke about the conflation of the unintended consequences with the perverse effects, while de Zwart (2015, 283–284) talked about "a habit that stems from mixing up two theoretical traditions: that of 'unintended consequences' from the spontaneous order literature and that of 'unanticipated consequences' following Merton (1936)". He also argued that the confusion of the analytical traditions is one of the factors contributing to the conflation of the "unintended" with the unanticipated consequences. In

1 Certainly, these two framings do not exhaust the modalities of studying the unintended. Sociologists of the unintended are also known to identify themselves, for instance, with the research of mechanisms of reproduction of institutionalized practices (see Giddens 1986 [1984] 13–14), or the analysis of the paradoxical effects of long-term and unplanned processes (see Zingerle 1998, 180). This notwithstanding, the research of the invisible hand-like mechanisms and the study of unanticipated-perverse effects emerge as the dominant analytical frameworks.

addition, we claim, this mixing up has also weakened the perception of sociology of invisible hand mechanisms as a concrete line of study. Should the sociology of the invisible hand have been more clearly defined inside the study of unintended consequences, its chances of being noticed outside would have certainly been bigger (for an analogous phenomenon regarding economic sociology of the unintended, see Mica 2017).

Second, *sociology of the invisible hand rarely presents itself in terms of sociology of the invisible hand explicitly*, but it tends to go under various different names. The following tendency can be observed: when the research of invisible hand-like mechanisms is done very closely, this usually goes under the name of study of mechanisms of aggregation, mechanisms of generation, combination, composition, interdependence, etc. Boudon and Bourricaud (2003 [1982], 124–126) attributed this state of affairs to a certain reservation towards dialectics in sociology. The former author, for instance, talked initially about effects of composition and perverse effects (Boudon 1982 [1977]), ulteriorly about emergent effects (Boudon 1981; see discussion in Lins Hamlin 2002, 48–49) and at a later phase about unintended consequences (Boudon 1990). While Elster (1978) used the concept of counterfinality. Even Cherkaoui (2005), who coined the term of invisible codes, preferred in the actual analysis to talk about emergent effects.

When the research of invisible hand-like mechanisms is undertaken in general, however, this is defined in terms of the study of patterns of interactions, or even of unintended consequences. Giddens (1986 [1984], 13), for instance, distinguished the study of patterns of unintended consequences that result from a "complex of individual activities". While Boudon (1990, 119, 122) talked about the "unintended consequences paradigm" in the sociological analysis "according to which social phenomena should be considered as unintended consequences of individual actions".

Certainly, terms like unintended consequences, emergence and mechanisms depict what the invisible hand is all about in sociology. But the usage of these notions, that – although very much related – are nevertheless distinct from the invisible hand, obscures the identity of these contributions as sociological studies of the invisible hand per se. Thus, the destiny of the sociology of the invisible hand is quite intricate actually. No doubt, this has a distinguishable framework for analyzing the emergent and dialectical effects, and it is linked with the invisible hand tradition in social sciences. Although the contributions to this framework are gaining more and more visibility, these are not explicitly addressed in terms of sociology of the invisible hand, at least not as far as the sociologists are concerned anyway. There are neither "manifest" sociological frames nor distinct methodological approaches that would tag themselves in relation with invisible hand processes directly. But the association occurs indirectly, by pointing to a certain analytical correspondence, intellectual legacy, comparison and – not at all rarely – even to opposition.

Even though sociology of the invisible hand is far from an integrated enterprise, there is a considerable awareness that the type of study advanced by certain sociologists is related to the invisible hand tradition, only depicted by different terms. Although it does not claim to replicate the original line of study, this analytical framework is enmeshed in a general theory of economics or political philosophy inspiration and it usually acknowledges this fact.

1 Sociology – not an invisible hand theory but an invisible hand-type theory

The sociological framework for analyzing the unintended consequences that emerge from aggregation and juxtaposition of individual actions is not an invisible hand theory, but an invisible hand-type theory. It is a framework that claims affinity with the classical invisible hand theory, but does not situate itself in direct relation with this tradition.

This situation was well captured by Zingerle (1998, 180). In an exercise that recalls the work of Merton (1936), Giddens (1986 [1984]) and Hirschman (1991) in this area, he singled out various frames for studying the unintended and unanticipated consequences. Specifically, Zingerle (1998) talked about three instances: (1) when the unit of analysis is the action, (2) when the unit is the group and (3) when the unit embraces the macro level and is difficult to be circumscribed. As known, the invisible hand accounts are usually associated with the third type. Wherein the interest of the researcher is in institutions as outcomes of individual actions that were not intended to produce the institutions as such, but which because of various mechanisms end up bringing about or maintaining these anyway.

And indeed, in the case of the framework that relates to unintended outcomes as macro processes, Zingerle also included the invisible hand as one of the two possible manifestations. He clearly distinguished between (1) the accounts of invisible hand-type and (2) the accounts of paradoxical outcomes of long-term and unplanned social processes. What is even more interesting, when elaborating on the first subcategory, Zingerle made it quite explicit that there are two possibilities when it comes to the invisible hand theories – one, to take the road of the variations of the classical theme associated with economists; and the other, to go with the more modern sociological approaches. Accordingly:

> Here we must place all theories of the "invisible hand" type [...], which are concerned with the summative effects of individual actions, whether they are variations of the classic topic in economic theory from Adam Smith to Carl Menger [...] or of more modern sociological conceptions like that of Boudon (Zingerle 1998, 180).

This brief, but highly condensed, theoretical excerpt confirms the following intuitions. First, the invisible hand-type perspective concerns effects at the macro level that are of an intricate and, at first blush at least, of a paradoxical and ironic origin. This theory does not look at the effects that can be traced to a single event, at the level of various actors, but at the outcomes of processes of interaction, at the level of the social system. It looks at the unintended consequences that result from a complex of individual actions. Actually, the preferred sociological term seems to be interaction, but this is less important in this context. Second, the invisible hand-type theory depicts various mechanisms in relation with this complex of individual actions, such as summation, aggregation, juxtaposition or interplay. Third, the element of summation and aggregation means that there is a place for sociologists in this invisible hand paradigm in social sciences as long as they work along the lines of theories that can be associated with emergence and aggregation mechanisms. Zingerle, as could have been expected, pointed here to Boudon, but one could easily make a more general statement that would further introduce theories such as methodological individualism, game theory, analytical sociology, etc. Thus, *there is not an invisible hand theory in sociology per se, but rather a sociological type of invisible hand theory that has its particularities.*

2 Sociology – not one, but three invisible hand-type theories

As evidenced by Zingerle's (1998) account, the existence of a modern sociological type of invisible hand theory was already put into words, since at least the late 1970s. In essence, this invisible hand-type theory in sociology of unintended consequences is related to the invisible hand theory that was developed in political economy and philosophy from Adam Smith to Carl Menger. But the specificity of the algorithms of aggregation, composition and juxtaposition makes it a very different kind of story. Thus, the sociological account is *related, but different from the invisible hand.*

The effects of aggregation and composition constitute just one of the contexts in which the sociologists relate, albeit not always directly, to the invisible hand metaphor. As the present edited volume shows, the sociological type of invisible hand theories can be found in relation with two other research contexts: *even better than the invisible hand* and *invisible hand, but not of the market*. The former theory – the *even better* – substitutes the invisible hand with other types of mechanisms, which are not always invisible so to say, such as the "hiding hand" (Hirschman 1967); the "invisible elbow" (Tilly 1996); the "grabbing hand" of the government (Shleifer and Vishny 1998) or the "[S]tate's right and left hands" (Bourdieu 1999 [1993], 183). Whereas the latter theory – the *not of the market* – traces mechanisms of the invisible hand, but which are attributed to other instances than the one we are usually accustomed to, such as the "invisible hand of the social capital" (Lin and Ao 2008); the "'[i]nvisible' and [v]isible [h]ands" at work in racial discrimination on the labor market (Royster 2015, 16–36); or even the "invisible hand of data flow" (Harari 2016, 391).

The following section will try to delineate what these three types of approaching the invisible hand in sociology are able to offer.

2.1 Related, but different from the invisible hand

This is the most visible and acknowledged dimension of invisible hand-type explanations in sociology. Includable here are the studies that depict institutions as unintended consequences of individual attitudes and social interactions and that point to specific mechanisms of emergence or maintenance (such as aggregation, composition, feedback, etc.). These studies usually make a point about the correspondence with the invisible hand from political economy, and even acknowledge the original role of Adam Smith's concept in launching this perspective. But they also distance themselves from the invisible hand metaphor by showing that the mechanisms they are commonly depicting are more than simple duplications of the processes discovered by the economists.

The manner in which Boudon started his analysis of the unintended consequences perspective in sociology is illustrative of this type of framing:

> The paradigm according to which social phenomena should be considered as unintended consequences of individual actions has been advocated by many social scientists before and after Merton; by non-sociologists – moral philosophers such as Mandeville [...], economists such as Adam Smith or Hayek [...], philosophers such as Karl Popper [...] – and by sociologists too (Boudon 1990, 119).

As visible in this excerpt, there is a certain autonomy granted to the sociological analysis of social institutions as unintended consequences of social actions. This is neither a sequel to, nor a replication of the political economy incursion into the invisible hand mechanisms, but an autonomous and parallel undertaking run by sociologists, alongside philosophers, economists, etc., within the broader research of unintended consequences.

Sometimes, the sociologists even go into more details and explain the difference between the mechanisms that they investigate and the invisible hand processes. Elster, for instance, discussed the distinction between invisible hand and counterfinality in these terms:

> I submit that whenever we see the invisible hand its mysteries perform, we are dealing with a situation where (i) all the actors have a dominant strategy, and (ii) the outcome that results when all actors use their dominant strategies dominates all other outcomes […]. Counterfinality, by contrast, may obtain when one of these features are lacking […] (Elster 1978, 108).

Thus, as the Boudon and Elster examples indicate, in the *related, but different from the invisible hand* framing, there is clear perception of the manner in which what the sociologists are doing integrates in the broader theoretical context in social sciences. There are also a couple of studies that emerged as classical examples for this stream. First and foremost, there is Weber's (1985 [1905]) *The Protestant Ethic and the Spirit of Capitalism.* Wherein, the German sociologist presented the paradox that the inner-worldly asceticism of the Protestant sects developed a set of values that were compatible with, and legitimative of the ethos of rational capitalism (see Boudon 1990; Cherkaoui 2007; Portes 2000; 2010, 21; Mica 2014). Followed by Merton's (1970 [1938]) study of the dynamics of science as an unintended product of Puritanism (see discussion in Boudon 1990). As well as Schelling's (1978) demonstration of how social and racial segregation developed from attitudes other than segregationist (Aydinonat 2008).

If it comes to the more recent illustrations, as already indicated, these come from the fields of rational choice theory and methodological individualism. These approaches were greatly dominated by the work of Boudon and Elster, which offered a strong base for the study of multiple types such as perverse effects, social contradictions (i.e., counterfinality, suboptimality), etc. (see discussion in Baert 1991; van Parijs 1982). Ulteriorly, with the advance of analytical sociology, the vocabulary of the *related, but different* became more universal. In the sense that this shifted from curious types of outcomes to the study of externalities in economic, political and ecological realms (see secular growth, or overfishing and deforestation in Elster 2007, 304–305), or to the analysis of the invisible codes and generative mechanisms in relation to stratification and social mobility (Cherkaoui 2007).

But it is not only the semantic underpinning that changed, but also the theoretical background. The analytical sociology approach, for instance, takes issue with the rational action framing that supported the debut of this stream, especially as advanced in the work of James Coleman on norms emergence and on Weber's theory of the *Protestant Ethic* (see critique of Cherkaoui 2005, 59–86, 197–223). In this context, an interesting debate is now taking place in the field regarding the further utility of rational choice theory in explaining the emergence of norms. Opp (2015, 203–204), for instance, remarked that rational choice theory has both a narrow and a broader version and that in the latter variety this is perfectly compatible with the cognitivist model put forward by Boudon and Cherkaoui, who were actually targeting the narrow version of the rational choice theory in their critique. On a more general level, and of direct relevance for sociology of invisible hand, Opp argued that the broader version of rational action theory is applicable when trying to understand when do norms emerge spontaneously and when by human design, such as in the case of the non-smoking norm (Opp 2015, 202–203; see 2002).

Importantly, this contemporary sequel of the work initiated in the late 1970s by Boudon and Elster confirms, again, the prominence of Weber and his status as bellwether for sociology of the invisible hand. As mentioned, Cherkaoui (2005) directed a strong criticism against the manner in which rational choice theory, per Coleman, interpreted Weber's Protestant book. But this author, one-time student and close collaborator of Boudon, also brought a systematization of the theme of unintended consequences in the work of the German author. Cherkaoui (2007) reconstructed and systematized the Weberian take on the paradox of unintended consequences in a manner never attended for in sociology of unintended consequences, except perhaps the work of Schneider (1984, 1987) on Mandeville.

Still, irrespective of these theoretical discrepancies, what is common to all these analyses is the focus on institutions understood as unintended consequences of individual attitudes and interactions, or as effects of mechanisms of composition, aggregation and interplay. But, as stated, this analytical frame is not a replication of the original invisible hand research, but more of an analogous sociological endeavor that refers to the approach in economy in terms of an original and related agenda, or as some sort of forerunner in the field of unintended consequences. Elster (1978, 106), for instance, considered that the invisible hand, together with "the ruse of reason" and "alienation", constitutes the "ancestors" of the term of counterfinality in the history of ideas.

Hence, the analysis of mechanisms that are related, but different from the invisible hand, represents a stream of research that does not pretend to have stumbled upon the invisible hand mechanism, in the original sense of the word, beyond economy, in the social life for instance. It just looks into similar social processes, or into phenomena that resemble, but are not identical with the invisible hand. This is maybe why the sociologists do not explicitly employ the invisible hand notion when explaining how they understand the unintended consequences. But they opt instead for notions such as dialectical effects, paradoxes, emergent effects, effects of compositions, fallacies of composition, etc. (perhaps with the exception of Cherkaoui's (2005) "invisible codes", but even he used this term quite episodically, having more commonly opted for the notion of emergent effects).

It may seem paradoxical that a stream that is so close to the invisible hand research in economics goes through all this trouble to establish for itself a distinct identity. Especially in the context in which the sociology of effects of composition and emergence was also at the beginning of developing its own brand. On the other hand, this fact also confirms that the point of reference for sociology of the invisible hand is the broader theory of unintended consequences. This perceives the invisible hand theory as only one of the possible approaches that gives legitimacy to the sociological inquiry without however exhausting it.

2.2 Even better than the invisible hand

In this second manner of framing the invisible hand in sociology, the authors attempt to locate the invisible hand mechanism, but in the course of doing so, they come to realize that the reality is more complex and thus end up substituting or supplementing the invisible hand mechanism with another one. We call this line of theories *even better than the invisible hand* – to paraphrase the title of a popular song launched by the rock band U2 in 1991 – because the main focus here is on mechanisms that present an upgrade to the original approach from economics and political philosophy.

Perhaps, the best way to illustrate this logic is with Tilly's (1996, 593) seminal line: "For the Invisible Hand, let's substitute the Invisible Elbow". As known, Tilly introduced the invisible elbow in order to capture the error-correction mechanisms that render the unintended consequences of social action to be pulled and integrated into ordered and systematic patterns. This is how he envisaged it:

> Coming home from the grocery store, arms overflowing with food-filled bags, you wedge yourself against the doorjamb, somehow free a hand to open the kitchen door, enter the house, then nudge the door closed with your elbow. […] You, your elbow, groceries, and the kitchen have systematic properties that strongly limit the likely consequences of your attempted nudge (Tilly 1996, 593).

Tilly used this example in order to visualize that the errors and unintended consequences are imminent – the grocery bag can be overturned at any moment. But the important thing is the presence of error-correction mechanisms that can be quickly employed – the elbow that would bring the bag in the right position, or preclude the damage to begin with.

The lesson to be learned from the grocery bag story is that the invisible hand is important, if one wishes to understand why the shopping bag did not make it pass the door – "the floor was wet, children left toys just inside the door, the grocery bagger put heavy items on top, or something of the sort" (Tilly 1996, 593). But this is only half of the story. The issue of explaining the social processes that render the reproduction of social structure possible, in spite of (or thanks to) the unintended consequences, is still not addressed. The invisible elbow is more than the invisible hand because it is more comprehensive, and it considers a complex process in which the invisible hand plays a very important role, no doubt, but this is still only one element of a bigger picture.

Sometimes the *even better than the invisible hand* plays out as *something else than the invisible hand*, but in the upshot the underlying idea is the same. Hirschman (1967), for instance, much earlier than Tilly, noticed the limitation of the invisible hand for the analysis of unintended consequences, so he put forward the "principle of the hiding hand". This concept was meant to depict the process by which when undertaking plans of action and exorbitant projects the actors have the tendency to ignore future difficulties that are likely to surface in the course of the endeavor. The hiding hand is basically a mechanism that allows taking risks without however openly engaging in a risky behavior. When introducing it, Hirschman also coquettished with the invisible hand metaphor, after which he predictably opted for altering slightly the original framing, in order to better depict the mechanism he encountered. Although Hirschman did not speak as directly about substitution of terms, it is obvious that he had the same intuition as Tilly ulteriorly did. Accordingly:

> The principle is important enough to deserve a name: since we are apparently on the trail here of some sort of Invisible or Hidden Hand that beneficially hides difficulties from us, I propose "The Hiding Hand" (Hirschman 1967, 13).

Observably, as in the *related but different from the invisible hand*, in the case of the *even better than the invisible hand*, there is also a quite strong connection with the literature on unintended consequences. Thus, Tilly spoke directly to the sociology of unintended consequences by trying to move the focus from the emergence of errors and unintended effects onto the correction and systematization of these. While Hirschman, given that he is known to have been familiar with the unintended consequences literature himself, can be considered to have zoomed in on one of the mechanisms that leads to the ignorance of probable consequences of action.

While the *related but different from the invisible hand* looks at mechanisms that nevertheless resemble the processes used by the economists to explain the unintended consequences of social action, in the case of the *even better than the invisible hand*, the mechanisms are clearly an upgrade of the original process that was observed in the economic domain. The mechanism that the invisible hand gets substituted or upgraded with is "better" in the sense that it brings an addition that is so important as the coining of the term "invisible hand" was initially.

Another feature that distinguishes the *even better than the invisible hand* is that this proves very useful for coining terms that are related to the substantive issue of power. For instance, Auyero (2010a; 2010b), a former student of Tilly, converged the invisible elbow with Bourdieu's perspective on waiting as power game in a study of the protracted delays that are experienced by poor people in the underfunded welfare agencies of Buenos Aires. In this context, the term denotes refined mechanisms by which state agents ensure and reproduce the submission of petitioners by making them wait in the daily encounters between these and the state – "('sit down and wait', 'keep coming' to show your worth)" (Auyero 2010b, 8). The invisible elbows ensure a "subtle production of poor people's compliance" not through force and overt control ("visible fists" and "clandestine kicks"), but through the manipulation of the time, patience and feelings of uncertainty of the people who are in unfavorable situations and are looking for support.

The same slip in the direction of power also occurred in the case of the recent reinterpretations of the principle of the hiding hand. Flyvbjerg and Sunstein (2016) who advanced the term of the malevolent hiding hand brought a considerable challenge. Accordingly, it is rather the malevolent hand that underestimates difficulties and overestimates creativity, that can be observed to operate in the field of planning, and not the benevolent one (per Hirschman), which treats optimistically the difficulties while also having low faith in creativity. These authors reckoned that the malevolent type is driven by ignorance, psychology and, given that it involves a certain degree of manipulation, also by power.

Certainly, power is not the only direction taken in these recent discussions that reactivate the *even better than the invisible hand*. In the case of the hiding hand for example, Anheier's response to the critique formulated by Flyvbjerg and Sunstein (2016) is to reconciliate the two concepts by abstracting them in a broader category of hands that emerge as forms of dealing with lack of information and uncertainty in planning and public policy. Still, in the case when the issue of power becomes too visible, it also becomes observable that the metaphor of the invisible hand is not associated anymore merely with the market, but also denotes the invisible work of power in other domains. Which renders that in certain instances the *even better than the invisible hand* comes very close to the third context in which the metaphor of the invisible hand is used in sociology – i.e., the *invisible hand, but not of the market*.

2.3 The invisible hand, but not of the market

In this line of analysis, the focus is on mechanisms that are clearly in the genre of the invisible hand, yet which are attributed to other instances than the market. Powerful contributions to the development of this approach have been recently made with the conceptualization of the “invisible hand of community” (Lejano and Fernandez de Castro 2014) or the “invisible hand of social capital” in the labor market (Lin and Ao 2008, McDonald and Day 2010; Pawlak and Kotnarowski 2016). Even the notion of “unanticipated gains” (Small 2009), developed in relation to childcare centers, churches, colleges, firms, etc., could be looked at as an example of the invisible hand of practices and structures in the extending of personal networks by enrollment in institutions.

In all these instances, the invisible hand is understood in terms of a cunning, hidden and long-term process. Lin and Ao, the initiators of the notion of invisible hand of social capital, considered:

> Thus, the flow of social credentials or reputation and the flow of job information and influence in routine exchanges constitute ways that social capital exerts effects on attainment in the labor market, beyond the more visible job-search or job-recruiting behavior. These constitute the invisible hand of social capital (Lin and Ao 2008, 113).

This understanding of the invisible hand less in terms of a mechanism and more in terms of a long-term flow manifests quite clearly in some of the contributions to this stream. Harari, for instance, identified that in contemporary society invisible hand processes are linked to the data-processing system, which although unplanned and uncontrollable is perceived by some social actors as working based upon a specific logic. Accordingly:

> No one understands how the global economy functions or where global politics is heading. But no one needs to understand. All you need to do is answer your emails faster – and allow the system to read them. Just as free-market capitalists believe in the invisible hand of the market, so Dataists believe in the invisible hand of the data flow (Harari 2016, 391).

In the case of the analysis of data flow, drawing from the metaphor of the invisible hand of the market pays off because this allows to depict a certain hidden and long-term logic, or a macro movement that although is currently difficult to unravel, in reality it is a more structured process.

The analytical framing of *invisible hand, but not of the market* converges with the understanding encoded in the *related, but different*. Wherein, as we saw, the invisible hand was understood as a sophisticated mechanism that merges social interactions into desirable social institutions. This also converges with the framing typical of the *even better,* in which case the invisible hand occurred as a mechanism that leads to unintended consequences. But there is also a considerable degree of divergence, because in the case of this third stream, especially when the hand is related to power, the theory is infused with a certain deconspiratory flavor.

The attribution of the invisible hand to actors or institutions, which use power to implement their aims, renders the process tricky and "suspicious". This is observable for all the concepts that have been launched: the left hand and right hand of the state (Bourdieu 1999 [1993]), the invisible hand of power (Oleinik 2014), the "invisible" and visible hands at work in racial discrimination on the labor market (Royster 2015), etc.

To take just one example, the concept of the state's left and right hands, that was initially launched by Bourdieu (1999 [1993]), was ulteriorly developed by Wacquant as to also capture the dimension of penal policies. This was accomplished by "inserting the police, the courts, and *the prison as core constituents of the 'Right hand'* of the state, alongside the ministries of the economy and the budget" (Wacquant 2009 [2004], 289). Actually, in this formula, the left hand and right hand model recall the visible fist-invisible elbow logic employed by Auyero (2010a; 2010b): both mechanisms work on behalf of the disciplinary policy, though one of them does so less perceptibly. In addition to the visible fists, the power is shown to be reproduced also through the elbows, i.e., the relatively invisible micro-processes that are putting people in their place, such as manipulation of time, patience and feelings of uncertainty. In the Wacquant interpretation, however, the logic is more of the good cop-bad cop type. What is more, this allows to also research the type of relation between the strategies employed by the hands, as well as the eventual mechanisms of decoupling and conflicts between these (in the manner originally advanced by Bourdieu).

This affinity between the *even better than the invisible hand* and the issue of power explains the attractiveness of these concepts once launched. On the other hand, this process of attribution also renders that the connection with the unintended consequences literature is of a secondary character, and sometimes even lost. These new invisible hand notions realize a brokerage between the unintended consequences literature and their original field of research. Yet, the theoretical input is primarily directed towards the field centered around the instance to which the invisible hand is attributed to. Unfortunately for sociology of unintended consequences, this is not meant as a development to this literature as such.

Tab. 1 depicts in a succinct manner the three approaches to the invisible hand that can be abstracted from sociology. The table shows that these frames can be differentiated when it comes to their scope, meaning attached to the invisible hand, theoretical framework, as well as research sites. Hence, the *related, but different from the invisible hand* looks at mechanisms of aggregation, emergence and juxtaposition of social actions. This frames the invisible hand as a mechanism of emergence, juxtaposition, interdependence, etc., which leads to the occurrence of social institutions as the unintended consequence of a complex of social actions. In terms of theory, the *related, but different* can be traced to sociology of unintended consequences, more particularly to rational choice theory, methodological individualism, analytical sociology, but also to the study of emergence of social norms.

Further, the *even better than the invisible hand* is attracted to mechanisms, processes and instances that occur to be even more "real", "exceptional" or "relevant" than the original process discovered in political philosophy. This stream interprets the invisible hand as a mechanism that leads to social order, in spite of the numerous unintended consequences, or wherein the unintended consequence (at a macro-macro level) is exactly the reproduction of the social order. In terms of theory, it reveals affinity with the sociology of unintended consequences, historical sociology, history of ideas, development economics and state-power theory.

Eventually, the *not only the market* approach is to be found in relation with invisible hand-like operations, but other than that of the market. This type of framing depicts the invisible hand as realizing some sort of finality in the long run – observably, it could hardly be any different from the impersonal, aggregative or error-correction perspective typical of the first two streams than that. In terms of theory, this stream is to be found in political science, social capital theory (job market), inequality theory and state-power theory.

3 The structure of the book

Sociology of the invisible hand emerges less as a concrete sociological paradigm and more like a series of loosely coupled streams of research. These frames derive from sociology of unintended consequences, they claim correspondence with the original study of invisible hand, but they do not define themselves as invisible hand studies, not in the strong sense of the term, that is for sure. Curiously, given that the study of unintended consequences is also a loosely coupled undertaking in its own turn, this correspondence with the tradition of the invisible hand is what renders that various analyses can be linked with the study of the unintended consequences in the first place.

The present edited volume brings together perspectives and types of analysis that illustrate the framing of the invisible hand that is typical of each of these

Tab. 1: Invisiblehand-type theories in sociology

Analytical frame	Scope	Invisible hand	Theory	Illustrations
Related, but different from the invisible hand	Analysis of mechanisms of aggregation, composition, juxtaposition that present alternatives to the invisible hand model	Sophisticated mechanism that merges social interactions into desirable/undesirable social institutions	Sociology of unintended consequences (rational choice theory; methodological individualism; analytical sociology; emergence of norms)	Social institutions as unintended consequences of individual actions; Perverse effects; effects of composition; emergent effects (Boudon 1982 [1977]; 1990); Social contradictions (Elster 1978)
			++ Debate concerning rational choice theory	Effects of emergence; mechanisms; invisible codes; Weber (Cherkaooui 2005; 2007); Emergence of norms (spontaneous vs. by design) (Opp 2002; 2015)
Even better than the invisible hand	Analysis of (additional) mechanisms that lead to the substitution of the invisible hand model	Mechanism that leads to unintended consequences (or social order)	Sociology of unintended consequences (historical sociology; history of idea)	Hiding hand (Hirschman 1967); Benevolent and malevolent hiding hands (Flyvbjerg and Sunstein 2016); Types of hands in response to uncertainty (Anheier 2016);
			Development economics; State-power theory ++ Debate concerning the hiding hand	Invisible elbow (Tilly 1996); Invisible elbow, "visible fists" and "clandestine kicks" as mechanisms of regulating poverty (e.g., via state violence) (Auyero 2010a; 2010b)

(*continued on next page*)

Tab. 1: (*continued*)

Analytical frame	Scope	Invisible hand	Theory	Illustrations
The invisible hand, but not of the market	Analysis of mechanisms that locate the invisible hand model, but in relation to other instances than the market	Cunning, tricky long-term process that realizes a certain finality	Social capital theory (job market); Inequality theory; Sociology of unintended consequences; Political science; Economic theory; State-power theory	Invisible hand of social capital (Lin and Ao 2008; McDonald and Day 2010; Pawlak and Kotnarowski 2016); Social capital and organizational embeddedness (Small 2010 [2009]); Invisible hand of community (Lejano and Fernandez de Castro 2014) Right hand and left hand of the state (Bourdieu 1999 [1993]; Wacquant 2009 [2004]); Invisible hand of power (Oleinik 2014); “Invisible” and visible hands at work in racial discrimination on the labor market (Royster 2015)

three theories in sociology. In the following, the main ideas of the chapters composing the three main parts of the edited book will be presented, as well as the manner in which these advance and complete the picture that has been drawn so far regarding the invisible hand-type theories in sociology.

3.1 Part 1: Related, but Different from the Invisible Hand

The first part of the book offers an insight into the treatment of the invisible hand in the political philosophy and political economy domains where this concept originally flourished, as well as in the economic and sociological fields wherein this develops contemporarily. The contributions illustrate the theoretical and methodological gap between the models of the invisible hand in economics and those in sociology, as well as the points of intersection and overlapping, and even of some misinterpretation.

Craig Smith's chapter is a seemingly quiet piece about the usage of the invisible hand explanation in political philosophy in order to address some issues on the normative, and not just theoretical, side, for a change. It shows that Robert Nozick's response to Rawls's *Theory of Justice* (1972 [1971]) and Friedrich Hayek's critique of socialism and formulation of an alternative political theory incorporate an invisible hand logic to the extent that this concept seems an important player in contemporary debates in political philosophy. As in the case of the forthcoming chapters by Jocelyn Pixley (in this volume) and Frederick G. Whelan (in this volume), the chapter by Smith is embedded in political economy and political philosophy to a great extent. But it also makes a transition towards the sociological discussions of spontaneous order because of its focus on Hayek's work who, as will be indicated in the subsequent chapters in this edited volume, is greatly associated with this concept.

Because of this contrast between the explanatory and normative usage of the invisible hand concept, the chapter indicates that the difference in usage also goes hand in hand with consistent variations also in terms of theoretical cannon, interests and research focus. The definite input of Smith's chapter is that it indicates that the modalities of usage of invisible hand explanations should be systematized. The fact that the invisible hand explanations may be invoked as methodological, explanatory or argumentative tools is an important process. On the other hand, the chapter indicates that confining the usage of the concept within certain limits (explanatory social theory vs. normative philosophy) is not such an easy thing to do either.

Frederick G. Whelan's contribution – a partial reprint from his book on the *Political Thought of Hume and His Contemporaries* (2015, vol. 2) – analyzes the formulation of the spontaneous order argument by Hayek and shows that this is based on two assumptions. First, that the institution that emerges unintentionally is benign. Second, that this is an effect of accumulation, combination or composition of the actions of many individuals. He then abstracts more than forty examples of invisible hand mechanisms from the work of Hume and Adam Smith in order to support the hypothesis that the initial formulation of the unintended consequences thesis was not tied to this assumption of an eventual desirable outcome.

In addition to this comparison between an allegedly benign invisible hand model in economics (per Hayek) and a both benign and perverse invisible hand model in the work of Hume and Smith, Whelan also looks at more recent interpretations of unintended consequences and perverse effects in the work of Boudon and Hirschman. The work of Boudon is shown to be relevant for developing a model of perverse effects that resemble the suboptimal outcomes akin to game theory, as well as for being distinct from the (allegedly) benign invisible hand. While the work of Hirschman is taken up critically in relation with the seminal argument made by this developmental economist that the preoccupation with perversity in social sciences occurred in the eve of the French Revolution, and that this began to look more like a rhetoric of reaction that counteracts social intervention, than a rigorous analysis of it.

Thus, the comparative input of Whelan's chapter for the purposes of this volume is double, if not even triple. First, this indicates that what usually goes as the model of invisible hand is attributed characteristics well beyond the intention of its initial founders. Second, it shows that indeed there is something as a sociological model of unintended consequences that is quite similar yet distinct from what is usually regarded to be the invisible hand mechanism in economics. Third, it challenges the thesis of the shift in the analysis of the unintended consequences from the happy invisible hand perspective to the blurry perversity thesis.

Jocelyn Pixley's chapter makes the argument that the theory of invisible hand, in its various reformulations, has generally refrained from analyzing the social relation of money. Her chapter goes through various formulations of the invisible hand argument, from Adam Smith's depiction to the more recent versions of social and system integration. Pixley's contribution is very well rooted in theory as well as in the reality of distinct episodes of crisis; it discusses, for example, the recent "from below" attempts to control money, such as the Occupy Wall Street from 2011.

It is important to stress that this is not a chapter about sociological models of invisible hand per se, but an analysis of economic models of invisible hand that might benefit from the inclusion of money from the perspective of sociology that is skilled in framing this phenomenon in terms of social relation. This notwithstanding, Pixley's discussion is beneficial for the argument we make about the stream of sociological models of invisible hand that are *similar but not identical with the invisible hand* in two ways. First, this offers a direct window to the economic models. On its basis, we can see how hard these are to digest for the conventional sociological reader, be it even an economic sociologist. Second, this discusses the manner in which the economic models of invisible hand may benefit from the framing of money as a social relation within sociology. Thus, it can be exploited as an opportunity to inverse the power relation between the economic and sociological framings of invisible hand, which usually present the former as the stronger part in social sciences.

Emma Tieffenbach's chapter starts with the classical rivalry between the invisible hand explanations and the intentional design explanations. Her chapter then focuses on the former exclusively in order to make sense of its power of attraction and conviction. To this end, she identifies the various meanings of the invisible hand as well as of the modalities in which the superior explanatory power of this kind of explanations can be accounted for. She makes an impressive theoretical and analytical tour and systematizes in the end no less than eight distinct meanings for the invisible hand (from the lack of foresight to the "spontaneous order"), as well as six arguments for the anti-design plea (from the direct argument to the subjectivist defense).

Eventually, Tieffenbach argues that the explanatory power of the invisible hand explanations lies in the fact that these take the "institutional kinds" more seriously. Meaning that the institutions are not perceived as sole materializations of the purpose and expectations of agents, as it supposedly is the case in the institutional design perspective. Tieffenbach contributes in this way to the debate about the autonomy of social institutions. Although a valuable finding in its own right, the relevance of the chapter is related to other aspects as well. This is one of the not too many attempts in the field of systematizing the invisible hand explanations from the point of view of their semantic stand. Such semantic analysis/interpretation is something new in sociology of the invisible hand and sociology of unintended consequences alike.

Sebastian Giacovelli's chapter can be read as an extension of some of the aspects that were already hinted by Tieffenbach (in this volume). As stated, she argued that the invisible hand is a persuasive narrative or fiction for investigating the "logical structures of social kinds". Giacovelli, however, concentrates on this element of fictionality in exclusivity. Actually, he uses his background in empirical economics, economic sociology and political philosophy in order to approach the invisible hand from a fictionalist point of view entirely. His chapter is instructive in at least two ways. First, it draws the state of the art on fictional entities in social sciences. As it emerges, this is a preoccupation that emerged independently from the invisible hand. Second, it indicates that the invisible hand mechanism has the potential of a strategic site of inquiry in this respect.

Indeed, Giacovelli does a great job of showing that the fiction of the invisible hand had/has real consequences. This influences economic action by way of certain projections and expectations to the point that economy gets infused by invisible hand-kind of logics (such as those associated with the structural adjustment programs of the International Monetary Fund). Thus, Giacovelli's chapter is revealing because it takes the discussion about the invisible hand out of theory and places it into an empirical grounded research site. The invisible hand is not an assumption or a mechanism anymore, but a logic or action vector with real-life consequences.

Karl-Dieter Opp's chapter introduces the two analytical traditions that concretized in the literature regarding the emergence of norms and institutions: the spontaneous order and the institutional design. He analyzes four case studies: table manners, daylight saving time, development of language and the erosion of institutional design under communist rule. Wherein, although there are instances when the process of emergence seems explicable based on one of these models solely, the chapter argues, in fact, a more complicated new model that is based on the idea of concatenation (interdependence) of spontaneous order and design is actually needed. As in the case of Pixley's work (in this volume), Opp's chapter does not directly address the manner in which the invisible hand models in sociology differ from those in economics. This does not contrast the models of spontaneous order in sociology with those in economics even. But it brings an overall reformulation of the spontaneous order model of emergence of norms and institutions that seems attached to sociology and economics alike.

Thus, the importance of this chapter in the context of this book is that it shows that in relation with the idea of spontaneous order, the analytical framings of sociology and economics are not so strictly delimited. On the terrain of the spontaneous order, the phenomenon of *related, but different from* is not so poignant, and there is no visible tendency for the sociological models to delineate their identity. At least as it emerges from Opp's chapter, but also discussed in the case of Whelan's chapter (in this volume), the analytical framings of spontaneous emergence of norms and institutions are not so strictly demarcated across disciplines. This is an interesting element if one takes into account the fact that the spontaneous order argument is a reformulation and generalization of the invisible hand idea actually.

3.2 Part 2: Even Better than the Invisible Hand

The second part of the book presents chapters, which take a somehow critical stand towards the invisible hand framework and offer an imaginative upgrade, or even replacement, of the original model. The contributions come predominantly from sociology, but there is also one instalment that comes from political philosophy and history of science. Although the *even better than the invisible hand* got listed herein as an approach typical of sociology, it seems that such modality of thinking is more widespread in reality.

Helmut Anheier's chapter offers a revision of the principle of the hiding hand and presents a set of theoretical – but empirically testable – propositions that can be applied to the actual infrastructure and development projects. Not only does this chapter clarify the elements involved in the original Hirschman's (1967) hiding hand concept, but it also offers three other types of hands, thus signalizing the limitation of the invisible hand notion and the need to systematize it further.

The chapter thus brings the assumption more down to earth. By taking two dimensions into account – state of knowledge and task complexity – it arrives at four different types of "hands" at work when starting a new project: the "classical" one – the hiding hand, as introduced by Hirschman – and three others: "malevolent hand", "protecting hand" and "passive hand". Each of these has its hypothetical advantages and benefits, as well as disadvantages and costs, and can be employed in a given area according to current needs and opportunities. For instance, in case of emerging problems, such as climate change adaptation, underestimation of a task's complexity might be in fact more functional than total awareness of potential risks ahead, which may prohibit any initiatives altogether.

This systematization serves first and foremost as a theoretical proposition, which could be – and should be – put to empirical testing across various technology and infrastructure projects to specify the extent to which these advantages and limitations materialize. From this perspective, Anheier's proposition may provide a springboard for further theoretical and empirical developments of the workings of invisible hand. Another merit of the chapter is that it shows that the concepts developed as a sequel to the hiding hand should be integrated into a broader family of concepts, and also embedded and bridged with another sociological theory that goes beyond the unintended – "As we have seen, the Principle is part of a family of hands, with three other siblings". This reveals the complexity and interrelations of many concepts involved in the studies of unintended consequences.

Bruna Ingrao's chapter explores the reasons for the seemingly imperishable popularity of the metaphor of the invisible hand, and particularly the paradoxical dominance of the neo-Walrasian imaginary of hidden mechanisms of the market, despite its analytical shortcomings and lack of credibility. The chapter offers a thorough and systematic overview of the literature and discusses the notion of invisible hand in macroeconomics in its association with the theoretical idea of market equilibrium of Walrasian descent, notably the Arrow-Debreu mathematical model. Having presented an elaborate discussion of the use and success of invisible hand imagery in economic theory, often with the help of clever and witty metaphors from art and literature, Ingrao's chapter shows the inadequacy of the use of the term. This analytical concept simply appears as too narrow to explain the intricate and complicated processes that the financial market involves. There is even a hint of frustration that what seems to be a complex process of myriad factors and actors involved is often put down by many authors to an obscure invisible hand explanation.

But frustration leads to innovation. Instead of exploring the mechanisms of invisible hand mechanisms, Ingrao's chapter – somewhat perversely – makes an explicit call for a greater need to research the visible hand(s), rather than clinging to a multiple and often vague meanings of invisibility. To support the argument, the chapter uses a very common example of property markets, highlighting the role of experts ("bodies"), knowledge ("brains"), communication systems ("skills") and networks involved in just a single property operation. These are all too often neglected by those in favor of the invisible hand postulating the equilibrium.

Pixley's chapter concludes that in order to resolve the puzzle of the persistence of the invisible hand metaphor in economics, it is necessary to step back from economics and adopt the sociology of science perspective, as understood by Karl Popper who demanded that science must demonstrate its own fallibility in order to be distinguished from pseudo-science (fallibility criteria). The provocative but well-thought ideas of Pixley's chapter will resonate not only among sociologists of unintended consequences, but also sociologists of scientific knowledge, theoreticians of (more or less strategic) ignorance and economic sociologists alike.

Zbigniew Szkop, Rafał Wiśniewski and *Marta Sylla's* contribution refer to the invisible hand assumption as allocation of resources by the market. Interestingly, when checking Tieffenbach's (in this volume) list of meanings attributed to the invisible hand assumption, this definition is not included. This is probably due to the fact that she is attracted to the general understanding of the invisible hand as mechanisms generating certain institutions via mechanisms of interdependence, aggregation, juxtaposition, etc. Yet the allocation meaning, when the invisible hand is actually attributed to the instance of the market, is also to be spotted in the literature related to economics and public policy. One might even argue that this is its general meaning that got institutionalized in media, and that it also goes hand in hand with another meaning, i.e., the lack of interference.

As Szkop, Wiśniewski and Sylla's chapter shows, this meaning gave quite quickly the possibility of falsification, because as can be inferred from everyday life, the invisible hand of the market, or the allocation of resources by it, does not work perfectly. This is also the general context herein. Szkop, Wiśniewski and Sylla's contribution revise this debate on the terrain of environmental economics and present the Pigou tax as one of the tools devised to ameliorate the deficient allocation of resources within the environmental policy. The strategic case study is the payment for ecosystem services and the implementation of this practice in Costa Rica starting with 1997 in particular.

One of the main conclusions is that in order to be successful in giving a hand to the invisible hand (of the market), there has to be a broader fit of institutional and local factors, and for such a fit there is no universal recipe. Another provocation launched by the chapter is that the invisible hand functions less according to the model of a puppet hand that allocates resources left and right skillfully, but more in terms of a hand-powered crank wherein initial infrastructure, investments and favorable institutional and cultural infrastructure are essential for the invisible hand of the market to work. Thus, although not put in such direct terms, Szkop, Wiśniewski and Sylla's chapter emerges as talking about the invisible hand of institutional and cultural structures that, in the ideal case scenario, creates the conditions for the hand of the market to operate invisibly.

3.3 Part 3: The Invisible Hand, but Not of the Market

The third part of the book gathers contributions that more or less intuitively trace a mechanism that apparently is of the invisible hand kind, just that this is attributable to other instances than the market; in the case of these chapters, to community, social capital and eventually the state.

Francisco Fernandez de Castro and *Raul P. Lejano's* chapter explores a strategic research site in order to account for the relation between micro and macro perspectives on local/regional development and mechanisms of invisible hand. The chapter indicates that projects designed to perform various social functions at the level of the society are inevitably contingent on local informal forms of support, the invisible hand of the community, in order to operate. The chapter illustrates this process by looking at the role of the vocals in the implementation of the conditional Cash Transfer Program in Northern Mexico.

Although developed on different bases (sociology of norms, networks and commons), this contribution can be interpreted as complementary to Wacquant's chapter (in this volume) on the left hand and right hand of the state. Just that Fernandez de Castro and Lejano's chapter addresses what in the model developed by Bourdieu (1999 [1993]) and ulteriorly by Wacquant (2009 [2004]; in this volume) is the left hand of the state, and reveals mechanisms that are more bottom-up. The hand of the market, the multiple hands of the state and the hand/s of the community, the interaction between these actually conditions the reproduction of various processes in the society. As indicated in the conclusion part of the chapter, this interaction is quite slippery. What may seem to be working out just fine in the short run may have dysfunctional effects in the long term.

Steve McDonald, Scott T. Grether, Kim S. Holland and *Hannah McQueen's* chapter investigates the process of serendipitous job finding by applying a reversed approach. That is, it explores job finding not from the point of view of the job offer receivers, but from the angle of the actors who are making or passing on the available offers. The conclusion is that what is commonly being depicted as an unsolicited receiving of job offer is, at least partially, coordinated and structured by patterns of online recruitment activities and constant monitoring of social networking profiles (such as LinkedIn) by HR professionals. Thus, the invisible hand of the social capital on the online job market is not as spontaneous or accidental as it may appear at first blush to be, judging from the notion of surprise that is suggested by the "serendipity" world. But this is structured by strategies of selection reproduced by the HR professionals, and the more or less conscious configuring of the social media profile by job seekers of potentially available job holders.

The merit of the chapter does not only consist in revealing this purposive component, but in exploring it in relation to social change. Thus, the chapter studies the serendipitous process subsequent to the internet revolution and shows how the internet facilitates the appearance of the spontaneous working of the invisible hand of social capital. As in the case of Wacquant's chapter (in this volume), McDonald, Grether, Holland and McQueen's contribution can be seen as pointing that the more a certain group is integrated in the system and enjoys a higher position the more the hand (be it of the market or of the social capital) seems neutral and spontaneous. Hence, the invisible appearance of the market or the social capital is also a matter of social class. The working of the invisible hand of social capital is linked with the phenomenon of social inequality. One more thing, in spite of the general argument that the invisible hand of social capital on the online job market is enabled by the hand of the HR professionals, the chapter by McDonald, Grether, Holland and McQueen does not eliminate the possibility that, indeed, the invisible hand of social capital might be working in the sense that information gets through via the weak ties with no coordination. Accordingly "A lack of conscious intentionality is certain to be more apparent in circumstances where individuals receive unsolicited job finding assistance from their usual social media contacts (as opposed to recruiters for whom job sourcing is an explicit goal)". Thus, the merit of the work, as in the case of the chapters by Anheier (in this volume), Fernandez de Castro and Lejano (in this volume), Ingrao (in this volume), as well as Wacquant (in this volume), is to have approached this topic of the relation between various types of hands.

Mikołaj Pawlak and *Michał Kotnarowski's* chapter refers directly to the connection between the invisible hand and social inequality mentioned above. The analysis of the Polish labor market allows to see that – at least in this particular case – it is the social profile and not the individual characteristics of the actors that contribute to the social inequality. In the sense that participation in networks with resources clearly confers a certain advantage, while the type of education one holds or the type of work (blue or white collar) does not translate automatically in unexpected job offers. Thus, the merit of the paper is to show that some of the processes regarding social inequality that one might consider intuitively valid do not necessarily pertain.

The chapter cross-references with, and resonates very well with, the one authored by McDonald, Grether, Holland and McQueen (in this volume). Both are placed in the same analytical stream actually, and this renders that some of the tensions to be found in the former are also inherent in this one. These two chapters indicate the manner in which the invisible hand of the labor market reproduces social advantage or, as it might be interpreted, it supports social inequality. Yet, there are also some differences. In the case of the chapter by McDonald, Grether, Holland and McQueen, the accent is on the relation between the invisible hand of social capital and other, more or less involved, hands. While, in the case of the chapter by Pawlak and Kotnarowski, the overall approach is to reconstruct the work of the invisible hand of social capital, but less in relation with other hands. Wherein, the invisible hand of social capital is shown to be contingent upon substantive issues such as income, assessment of own material conditions and job satisfaction. The authors indicate that the size of the locality in which the employee resides, human capital and participation in religious practices are not such strong predictors of the manner in which the hand will operate.

Loic Wacquant's chapter argues for a reformulation of the model of the left hand and right hand of the state that was originally coined by Bourdieu in order to show that the multidimensional type of state governing goes beyond the economic domain. Thus, Bourdieu (1999 [1993], 183) operationalized the left hand of the state in relation to social functions (public education, health, welfare, etc.) and the right hand as pertaining to economic disciplining, activization and rhythm setting. In the context of this specific concept, the value of Wacquant's contribution is that it underlines the penal policy element in addition to the invisible hand of the market, or more exactly in a kind of "wedding" with this.

With regard to the purposes of the volume, the value of the chapter is that it confirms, again, that there is not so much the case of discovering another type (of invisible hand), but of also revealing the relation between various types of hands. For instance, Wacquant's chapter is seminal because it shows that what from the outside, or from the perspective of better situated social classes, seems as the invisible hand of the market, is in fact contingent inside, or from the perspective of the disfavored social classes, on an invisible hand, iron fist actually, of penal policy.

Thus, it emerges, the discovering of various hands is not only a matter of theoretical and methodological agenda, but also one that has implications at ideological level. It can also be speculated that certain domains are associated with particular types of hands, and that this is not ad hoc but also influenced by the manner in which these domains are perceived in social sciences and by the lay knowledge. If this is evident, less evident however is the fact that the high visibility of a certain type of hand may go hand in hand with the hiding, ignorance or less visibility of the functioning of others. As underlined by Wacquant, the neo-liberal regime is predominantly presented as a regime embedded in some economic market processes, and less in relation to its penal policies and governance of inequality and social stratification. This fact neutralizes somehow its externalities. Thus, there has to be some more perceptiveness to the fact that the very usage of the invisible hand metaphor, because of its linkage with a macro level positive outcome, also comports this danger of attenuating the visibility of, or reproducing the ignorance or lack of theoretical reaction of, other social processes in the making.

References

Anheier, Helmut K. 2016. "Of Hiding Hands and Other Ways of Coping with Uncertainty: A Commentary." *Social Research* 83: 1005–1010.

Auyero, Javier. 2010a. "Chuck and Pierre at the Welfare Office." *Sociological Forum* 25: 851–860.

Auyero, Javier. 2010b. "Visible Fists, Clandestine Kicks, and Invisible Elbows: Three Forms of Regulating Neoliberal Poverty." *European Review of Latin American and Caribbean Studies* 89: 5–26.

Aydinonat, N. Emrah. 2008. *The Invisible Hand in Economics: How Economists Explain Unintended Social Consequences*. New York: Routledge.

Baert, Patrick. 1991. "Unintended Consequences: A Typology and Examples." *International Sociology* 6: 201–210.

Barry, Norman P. 1982. "The Tradition of Spontaneous Order." In *Literature of Liberty*, vol. V, 7–58. Arlington (VA): Institute for Humane Studies.

Barry, Norman P. 1985. "In Defense of the Invisible Hand." *Cato Journal* 5: 133–148.

Boudon, Raymond. 1981. "Undesired Consequences and Types of Structures of Interdependence." In *Continuities in Structural Inquiry*, edited by Peter M. Blau and Robert K. Merton, 255–284. London: Sage.

Boudon, Raymond. 1982 [1977]. *The Unintended Consequences of Social Action*. London: Macmillan.

Boudon, Raymond. 1990. "The Two Facets of the Unintended Consequences Paradigm." In *Robert Merton: Consensus and Controversy*, edited by Jon Clark, Celia Modgil and Sohan Modgil, 119–127. London, New York, Philadelphia: Falmer Press.

Boudon, Raymond, and Francois Bourricaud. 2003 [1982]. *A Critical Dictionary of Sociology*. London: Routledge/Taylor & Francis e-Library

Bourdieu, Pierre. 1999 [1993]. "The Abdication of the State." In *The Weight of the World: Social Suffering in Contemporary Society*, authored by Pierre Bourdieu et al., 181–188. Cambridge: Polity Press.

Campbell, Colin. 2011. "Limits to Agency: Exploring the Unintended (and Unattended) Consequences of Action." In *Sociology and the Unintended: Robert Merton Revisited*, edited by Adriana Mica, Arkadiusz Peisert and Jan Winczorek, 45–62. Frankfurt am Main: Peter Lang.

Cherkaoui, Mohamed. 2005. *Invisible Codes: Essays on Generative Mechanisms*. Oxford: Bardwell Press.

Cherkaoui, Mohamed. 2007. *Good Intentions: Max Weber and the Paradox of Unintended Consequences*. Oxford: Bardwell Press.

De Zwart, Frank. 2015. "Unintended but Not Unanticipated Consequences." *Theory and Society* 44: 283–297.

Elster, Jon. 1978. *Logic and Society. Contradictions and Possible Worlds*. Chichester and London: John Wiley & Sons.

Elster, Jon. 2007. *Explaining Social Behavior: More Nuts and Bolts for the Social Sciences*. Cambridge: Cambridge University Press.

Flyvbjerg, Bent, and Cass R. Sunstein. 2016. "The Principle of the Malevolent Hiding Hand; or, the Planning Fallacy Writ Large." *Social Research* 83: 979–1004.

Giddens, Anthony. 1986 [1984]. *The Constitution of Society: Outline of the Theory of Structuration*. Cambridge: Polity Press/Oxford: Basil Blackwell.

Harari, Yuval Noah. 2017. *Home Deus: A Brief History of Tomorrow*. London: Harvill Secker.

Hirschman, Albert O. 1967. "The Principle of the Hiding Hand." *The Public Interest* 6: 10–23.

Hirschman, Albert O. 1991. *The Rhetoric of Reaction: Perversity, Futility, Jeopardy*. Cambridge (MA) and London: The Belknap Press of Harvard University Press.

Ingrao, Bruna. 1998. "Invisible Hand." In *The Elgar Companion to Classical Economics*, edited by Heinz D. Kurz and Neri Salvadori, vol. I, A-K, 436–442. Cheltenham: Edward Elgar Publishing.

Ingrao, Bruna, and Giorgio Israel. 1990. *The Invisible Hand: Economic Equilibrium in the History of Science*. Cambridge (MA): MIT Press.

Lejano, Raul, and Francisco Fernandez de Castro. 2014. "Norm, Network, and Commons: The Invisible Hand of Community." *Environmental Science and Policy* 36: 73–85.

Lin, Nan, and Dan Ao. 2008. "The Invisible Hand of Social Capital: An Exploratory Study." In *Social Capital: An International Research Program*, edited by Nan Lin and Bonnie H. Erickson, 107–132. Oxford: Oxford University Press.

Lins Hamlin, Cynthia. 2002. *Beyond Relativism: Raymond Boudon, Cognitive Rationality and Critical Realism*. London and New York: Routledge.

McDonald, Steve, and Jacob C. Day. 2010. "Race, Gender, and the Invisible Hand of Social Capital." *Sociology Compass* 4: 532–543.

Merton, Robert K. 1936. "The Unanticipated Consequences of Purposive Social Action." *American Sociological Review* 1: 894–904.

Merton, Robert K. 1970 [1938]. *Science, Technology and Society in Seventeenth Century England*. New York: Howard Fertig.

Mica, Adriana. 2014. "Weber's 'Essential Paradox of Social Action': What Can Sociology of the Unintended Learn from Public Policy Analysis?" *Profilaktyka Społeczna i Resocjalizacja* 23: 71–95.

Mica, Adriana. 2015. "Unintended Consequences: History of the Concept." In *International Encyclopedia of the Social & Behavioral Sciences*, edited by James D. Wright (editor-in-chief), 2nd edition, vol. 24, 744–749. Oxford: Elsevier.

Mica, Adriana. 2017. "The Unintended Consequences in New Economic Sociology: Why Still Not Taken Seriously?" *Social Science Information* 56: 544–566.

Oleinik, Anto N. 2014. *The Invisible Hand of Power: An Economic Theory of Gate Keeping*. London: Pickering and Chatto.

Opp, Karl-Dieter. 2002. "When Do Norms Emerge by Human Design and When by the Unintended Consequences of Human Action? The Example of the No-smoking Norm." *Rationality and Society* 14: 131–158.

Opp, Karl-Dieter. 2015. "Instrumental, Axiological Rationality and the Explanation of Norms: Cherkaoui's (and Boudon's) Critique of Rational Choice Theory and Its Ability to Explain Norm Emergence." In *Theories and Social Mechanisms: Essays in Honour of Mohamed Cherkaoui*, edited by Gianluca Manzo, vol. I, 183–206. Oxford: The Bardwell Press.

Pawlak, Mikołaj, and Michał Kotnarowski. 2016. "Siła słabych powiązań na rynku pracy w Polsce." *Studia Socjologiczne* 221: 187–215.

Portes, Alejandro. 2000. "The Hidden Abode: Sociology as Analysis of the Unexpected: 1999 Presidential Address." *American Sociological Review* 65: 1–18.

Portes, Alejandro. 2010. *Economic Sociology: A Systematic Inquiry*. Princeton and Oxford: Princeton University Press.

Rawls, John. 1972 [1971]. *A Theory of Justice*. Oxford: Oxford UniversityPress.

Royster, Deirdre A. 2015. *Race and the Invisible Hand: How White Networks Exclude Black Men from Blue-Collar Jobs*. Berkeley, Los Angeles and London: University of California Press.

Schelling, Thomas C. 1978. *Micromotives and Macrobehavior*. London and New York: W. W. Norton.

Schneider, Louis. 1984. *The Grammar of Social Relations: The Major Essays of Louis Schneider*, edited by Jay Weinstein; with a foreword by Robert K. Merton. New Brunswick: Transaction Books.

Schneider, Louis. 1987. *Paradox and Society: The Work of Bernard Mandeville*. New Brunswick: Transaction Books.

Shleifer, Andrei, and Robert W. Vishny. 1998. *The Grabbing Hand: Government Pathologies and Their Cures*. Cambridge (MA) and London: Harvard University Press.

Small, Mario Luis. 2010 [2009]. *Unanticipated Gains: Origins of Network Inequality in Everyday Life*. New York: Oxford University Press.

Smith, Craig. 2006. *Adam Smith's Political Philosophy: The Invisible Hand and Spontaneous Order*. London: Routledge.

Smith, Craig. 2009. "The Scottish Enlightenment, Unintended Consequences, and the Science of Man." *Journal of Scottish Philosophy* 7: 9–28

Tieffenbach, Emma. 2013. "Invisible-hand Explanations: From Blindness to Lack of We-ness." *Social Science Information* 52: 450–470.

Tieffenbach, Emma. 2016. "The Virtual Reality of the Invisible Hand." *Social Science Information* 55: 115–134.

Tilly, Charles. 1996. "Invisible." *Sociological Forum* 11: 589–601.

Ullmann-Margalit, Edna. 1978. "Invisible-Hand Explanations." *Synthese* 39: 236–291.

Van Parijs, Philippe. 1982. "Perverse Effects and Social Contradictions: Analytical Vindication of Dialectics?" *The British Journal of Sociology* 33: 589–603.

Wacquant, Loïc. 2009 [2004]. *Punishing the Poor: The Neoliberal Government of Social Insecurity*. Durham (NC) and London: Duke University Press.

Weber, Max. 1985 [1905]. *The Protestant Ethic and the Spirit of Capitalism*. London: Unwin.

Whelan, Frederick G. 2015. *Political Thought of Hume and His Contemporaries: Enlightenment Projects*, vol. 2. New York and London: Routledge

Zingerle, Arnold. 1998. "The Unanticipated Consequences of Action: Sociological and Ethical Aspects." In *Robert K. Merton & Contemporary Sociology*, edited by Carlo Mongardini and Simonetta Tabboni, 177–186. New Brunswick and London: Transaction Publishers.

Part 1: Related, but Different from the Invisible Hand

Craig Smith

The Invisible Hand and Political Philosophy

Abstract: Invisible-hand style arguments have become a central feature of the work of some of the most important modern political philosophers. This chapter sets out to explore exactly how deeply these arguments have impacted on normative political philosophy. The chapter begins with an examination of the political and methodological implications of Adam Smith's own use of the phrase, before tracing its development in the context of debates about the nature of social justice that arose in response to the seminal work of John Rawls. The response to Rawls's *Theory of Justice* by Friedrich Hayek and Robert Nozick was deeply influenced by invisible-hand arguments, which are put to use to criticise Rawlsian notions of distributive justice. The chapter argues that invisible-hand arguments underpin much of the critical debate in the contemporary discussion of social and distributive justice in post-Rawlsian political philosophy.

Keywords: Adam Smith; invisible hand, Friedrich Hayek, Robert Nozick, social justice

The phrase "the invisible hand" has become one of the most famous and contentious in modern social theory; it seems to have captured the public imagination, and, as Nozick (1974, 18) noted, it has "a certain lovely quality" about it. The essays in this volume all examine different aspects of this particular style of explanation or argument, and taken together they make the case that such arguments lie at the heart of the social sciences as we now understand them. When Popper (1989, 342) observed that the main task of the theoretical social sciences is to "trace the unintended social repercussions of intentional human actions", he was making the case that most social phenomena of interest are produced from unintended consequences. They are, in Ferguson's (1995 [1767], 119) words, "the result of human action, but not the execution of any human design". One consequence of this is that such phenomena, produced as they are by social interaction, do not in any straightforward sense embody the intention of any one individual or a group of individuals. The explanation of events that are the product of deliberative human activity is relatively straightforward: they represent the material of narrative history and biography. But social theory is interested in extending the explanatory scope of science to orders that cannot be attributed to simple models of individual intention > action > intended outcome. This is what Berry (1997, 39) refers to as the "demotion of purposive rationality" that represents one of the main achievements of the early pioneers of subjects such as sociology, political science and economics. In this chapter,

I want to examine the appearance of this particular ramification of invisible-hand arguments in political philosophy. In particular, I want to examine how invisible-hand explanations drawn from explanatory social theory have been put to use as part of normative arguments in the late twentieth- and early twenty-first-century political philosophy concerning the nature of justice.

Adam Smith's use of the phrase "the invisible hand" has entered the public imagination as the preferred nomenclature for the sort of argument with which we are concerned, but it can, in many cases, prove to be misleading. For instance, the term is often believed to invoke some sort of theological explanation or to assert that there is a kind of Panglossian confidence that, left alone, things will work themselves out in the best possible way.[1] In what follows, I want to suggest that the normative application of the invisible hand in contemporary political philosophy is brought to bear in response to a major structural issue that arises in contemporary accounts of justice. My aim then is to demonstrate that the development of invisible-hand explanations in the theoretical social sciences had important consequences for the development of normative political philosophy. In particular, they were put to use in the debate about distributive justice that developed in the wake of Rawls's ground-breaking work.

Perhaps the most straightforward way into our discussion is to examine the famous use of the idea by Adam Smith and use it to make a couple of conceptual clarifications about the form of such arguments and their challenge for normative political philosophy. The second part of the chapter looks at two particular argumentative uses of the invisible hand in the work of two of the most significant figures in the late twentieth-century political philosophy: Hayek and Nozick. Both Hayek and Nozick take the invisible-hand arguments developed in economic and social theory and deploy them in the debate in political philosophy concerning the nature of the central political concept of justice.

1 Adam Smith

I have argued elsewhere (Smith 2006) that the most convincing intellectual lineage for the modern conception of the invisible hand can be traced if we begin with the work of Mandeville. Mandeville's fame rests on his position as a controversialist, but his work also develops a series of insights that would have lasting influence. *The Fable of the Bees: Or, Private Vices, Publick Benefits* (1988 [1705/1714]) – with its famous assertion that:

---

1 See, for example, the discussions in Davis (1983); Martin (1983); Evensky (1993); Rothschild (1994); Otteson (2002).

The Worst of all the Multitude
Did Something for the Common Good (Mandeville 1988, 24),

and argument that morality is socially beneficial, but essentially a form of hypocrisy – provoked a number of indignant replies. Among these was a sophisticated response from Francis Hutcheson (2002 [1728]). Hutcheson was Professor of Moral Philosophy at Glasgow, and through him Mandeville's ideas became part of the common intellectual currency of eighteenth-century Scotland. It is the Scottish Enlightenment that provides us with the first really sophisticated consideration of the phenomenon of unintended consequences. A group of thinkers, including David Hume, Adam Smith, and Adam Ferguson, developed their thinking in the light of Mandeville's legacy. While they did not accept the application that Mandeville made of his ideas to ethics, they nonetheless saw that his depiction of social life in the addenda to the *Fable* captured something important about the reality of social interaction. The problem now became one of the reconciling theoretical explanations that took account of unintended consequences with a moral and political philosophy that maintained an element of normative justification. More specifically: what happens to our notions of responsibility and desert when unintended consequences decouple deliberate intention from distributive outcome.

We can get some purchase on what is at stake here if we look in some detail at the locus classicus of the invisible-hand argument. Adam Smith scholars remain divided on the precise significance of the term "invisible hand"; and while our primary interest for the purpose of this chapter is more conceptual, a brief examination of the actual uses of the term in Smith's work will repay us with some intellectual purchase for our examination of the role of the concept in political philosophy.[2] The phrase occurs on three occasions in the writings of Adam Smith. Each appearance is distinct, but the latter two are sufficiently similar to justify applying the phrase to a single concept.[3]

---

2 For recent examples in Smith scholarship, see Grampp (2000); Harrison (2011); and Heydt (2017).

3 Smith's first use of the term is in his *Essays on Philosophical Subjects* (1980, 49), which was published posthumously but likely composed before his other books, where he refers to the "invisible hand of Jupiter" in connection with the beliefs of polytheistic religions. Smith notes that in primitive societies irregular events are explained in terms of the intervention of an anthropomorphic Deity. The "invisible hand of Jupiter" is not seen to act in the normal course of nature, but rather explains events that run contrary to its expected course. Macfie (1971, 595–598) argues that the latter two uses in *The Theory of Moral Sentiments* (1976a [1759]) and *An Inquiry into the Nature and Causes*

In *The Theory of Moral Sentiments* (1976a [1759]), the invisible hand appears in a section dealing with the effect of utility on the conception of beauty.

> They consume little more than the poor, and in spite of their natural selfishness and rapacity, though they mean only their own conveniency, though the sole end which they propose from the labours of all the thousands whom they employ, be the gratification of their own vain and insatiable desires, they divide with the poor the produce of all their improvements. They are led by an invisible hand to make nearly the same distribution of the necessaries of life, which would have been made, had the earth been divided into equal portions among all of its inhabitants, and thus without intending it, without knowing it, advance the interest of the society, and afford the multiplication of the species (Smith 1976a [1759], 184–185).

The invisible hand here is the mechanism by which a benign outcome, one that is in society's interests in general, can be produced by the self-regarding actions of individuals. The distributive outcome of the interaction of the individuals concerned was not part of the intentions behind their actions. The result is broadly beneficial on a social level since it "advance[s] the interest of society" and "afford[s] the multiplication of the species". The explanation does not depend on any active role for the Deity, and the explanatory thrust of the passage does not rely on a providential plan. While Smith does mention Providence in the following sentence, the reference takes the form of a platitude about the unequal division of property. What Smith does is provide a conceptualised explanation of how exchange leads to a meta-level order that can be assessed, by a favoured normative criterion, as beneficial. We should be very clear here that the explanation offered by Smith is intended to dispel any mysticism about the origin of the beneficial outcome. He explains to us how the process works and then uses the metaphor of the invisible hand as a placeholder that frees him from repeating the exposition.[4]

In *An Inquiry into the Nature and Causes of the Wealth of Nations* (1976b [1776]), the appearance of the invisible hand is again related to the co-ordination of self-regarding action in order to produce benefits for the whole of society. Smith writes:

> By preferring the support of domestick to that of foreign industry, he intends only his own security; and by directing that industry in such a manner as its produce may be of the greatest value, he intends only his own gain, and he is in this, as in many other cases, led by an invisible hand to promote an end which was no part of his intention. Nor is it

---

of the Wealth of Nations (1976b [1776]) refer to the invisible hand of a Christian God that restores the natural order.

4 And, as Kennedy (2008) points out, the invisible hand is not the market in this example.

> always the worse for the society that it was no part of it. By pursuing his own interest he frequently promotes that of the society more effectually than when he really intends to promote it. I have never known much good done by those who affected to trade for the publick good (Smith 1976b [1776], 456).

In this case, the risk aversion of investors explains why they choose to invest close to home. The result of this is that home industries benefit, though this was not part of the intention of the investors. As with Smith's other examples of the role of economic self-interest in historical change, the term "invisible hand" refers to the process, or mechanism, which brings about socially beneficial outcomes from the interaction of self-regarding actors. Here we see an additional argument emerge to underline the point. At the end of the passage, Smith suggests that in contrast to the operation of unintended consequences in this case, the deliberate action of individuals intended to bring about the same beneficial order is less likely to succeed. We should be careful to note that this is not a sweeping claim that unintended order is *always* superior to intended order. Instead, it is the more modest claim that, given Smith's explanation of the particular situation, the process of unintended consequences is more likely to produce the benign order than the affectation of a deliberate desire to attain the same results.

Whether the result is in the distribution of subsistence or in the support of domestic industry, the process is the same: beneficial outcomes are produced as the unintended consequence of the interaction of individuals. In both of these cases, Smith uses the term "invisible hand" in reference to phenomena that he has already explained rather than as a *deus ex machina* to guarantee positive outcomes. In both of these cases, he uses language that indicates that the processes produce benign results through the media of unintended consequences. To say this is not to say that such mechanisms always operate, that they never fail, that they are divinely sanctioned, or that they are associated with any particular set of ideological beliefs.

To be clear: the recognition that certain unintended consequence processes produce beneficial results does not commit Smith to a position that views all unintended consequences as good. For the invisible hand to act as a placeholder for benign unintended consequences, we need to contrast it, not just with orders that result from deliberate action, but also with unintended consequences that produce malign orders. We can see many examples of these in Smith's work as well. In Book V of *An Inquiry into the Nature and Causes of the Wealth of Nations* (1976b [1776]), Smith famously pre-figures the Marxist idea of alienation in his description of the effects of the division of labour on the labouring poor (Smith 1976b, 782). Here we see the malign unintended consequences of the division of labour and trade.

What we see then is a willingness to recognise the reality of a distinction between benign and malign unintended consequences. While the theoretical mechanism of explanation remains the same, the normative assessment of the outcomes differs. But what it has also demonstrated is that the approach takes a particular stance on the separation of explanation and normative justification. What it implies is that the possession of a notion of what one ought to do does not necessarily mean that deliberate pursuit of that goal will generate the desired outcome. The mercantilists claimed that they wanted to increase national wealth and encourage local industry, but Smith's entire point is that this goal is better achieved by leaving individuals to pursue their own economic interest than by deliberately trying to bring about the same. If many (most?) significant social outcomes, both good and bad, are the result of unintended consequences, then what does this do for the idea of responsibility as an element of distributive justice?[5]

It is in this context that I want to examine the place of invisible-hand arguments in political philosophy. I now turn to the place of invisible-hand arguments in some contemporary discussions of the idea of justice. In doing so, I am not making any claims about Adam Smith's own discussion of justice, or indeed about contemporary theories of justice that seek inspiration in Smith's work such as that of Sen (2009). Instead, I want to focus on the conceptual ramifications of accepting an invisible-hand outlook in political philosophy. Late twentieth-century political philosophy is dominated by the work of John Rawls. In his *A Theory of Justice* (1972 [1971]), Rawls revived a discipline that had become moribund in the middle years of the century. Rawls's novelty lay in his development of an innovative modern version of the tradition of social contract theory that he uses to provide an account of social justice. He asks his readers to imagine an "original position" where contractors are behind a "veil of ignorance" about their socio-economic status and are then asked to develop principles of justice that reflect a society that would be acceptable to someone who did not know whether they would be wealthy or poor. Rawls's argument suggests that such actors would agree to an equal distribution of social and political rights, which would then be prioritised over a principle of economic redistribution that recognised both fair equality of opportunity and a desire to maximise the position of the least advantaged. His essential idea being that by screening out morally irrelevant or unfair features such as natural abilities or socio-economic status, actors would settle on a notion of justice as fairness under which they would seek a society

5 For a detailed discussion of this point, see Smith (2009).

characterised by equal rights and the best possible economic settlement for the least advantaged. Under Rawls's system, social and economic inequality is only permissible if it leads to the best possible situation for the least advantaged in society: in other words, he defends an account of justice that prefers a particular pattern of economic distribution.[6]

2 F. A. Hayek

Invisible-hand explanations passed into the mainstream of social science during the twentieth century. They play a particular underpinning role in the basic assumptions of economics and in the social theory developed by economists such as Hayek. This author, along with his friends Popper and Polanyi, developed the invisible-hand approach in a series of writings designed to question much of the prevalent social and political theory of the twentieth century.[7] In the case of Hayek, the idea of spontaneous order becomes central to his criticism of the claims by socialist economists in the 1930s and 1940s that a socialist government could successfully plan an entire economy. Drawing on the arguments of the so-called socialist calculation debate, between von Mises and various socialist economists such as Oskar Lange, Hayek developed an argument that suggested that socialist calculation was impossible because it could not successfully replicate the spontaneous ordering of the price system in a market economy. As a result, the socialist planners would not be able to harness the price signals that efficiently direct investment in their version of an economy run by a central planning Board (Caldwell 2004, 214–220). This led Hayek to develop a theory of the division of knowledge in society that stressed the vital co-ordination role played by evolved institutions such as the rule of law, prices, and markets. In his later career Hayek's attention shifted from pure economics to social theory and political philosophy, but he maintained his interest in spontaneous order arguments.

Almost all of the main elements of Hayek's thought bear some relation to the type of invisible hand, or spontaneous order as he would have it, argument that we have been addressing.[8] Hayek has most often been considered as a thinker

6 For a clear account of the basic form of Rawls's arguments, see Graham (2007).

7 On another front, the same ideas were being deployed in the historical writings of the conservative philosopher Oakeshott (1991). Oakeshott's distinction between civil association and enterprise association was intended to demonstrate that most social institutions are a product of a process of gradual historical evolution.

8 The term "spontaneous order" is first used in this sense in Polanyi's essay collection *The Logic of Liberty* (1951; see Jacobs 1998, 19). The key notion in Polanyi's discussion

with a developed social theory, but a less developed normative philosophy. His spontaneous order is seen as "a methodological tool rather than an ethical postulate" (Gissurarson 1987, 42), as part of a "value-free explanatory system" (Gray 1986, 119–120), or as being "technical rather than value based" (Shearmur 1996, 4).[9] Examples of Hayek's use of this sort of invisible-hand argument can be found in his account of the operation of prices, his discussion of the scientific method, and his description of the evolution of social institutions.[10] But for the purposes of this essay, I want to confine my attention to those explicitly touching on Hayek's political philosophy rather than his economic or social theory. Most of Hayek's argument in this connection lies in his discussion of the concept of social or distributive justice. Hayek's main thrust is that there is something problematic about the idea of distributive justice as it has been practised in normative political philosophy. This problem arises from the "truth" that invisible-hand explanations are a better description of certain social phenomena because the outcomes of such phenomena are not attributable to a specific agent. This social theoretic finding is then deployed to argue that the attribution of justice to social level outcomes is a sort of category error that renders much contemporary political philosophy prey to a fatal conceptual flaw.

For Hayek (1993 [1973-1982], vol. 1, 36–37) order can be exogenous, which is brought about by deliberate command imposed in pursuit of a deliberate design, but equally it may prove to be the result of a spontaneous adjustment that occurs endogenously.[11] The key characteristic of order is that it provides some stability, thus rendering it an appropriate subject matter for examination

---

of spontaneous order is that such orders arise internally, that is to say the order is not imposed by some external agency, but rather represents the formation of an equilibrium by the mutual adjustment of individual "particles" (Polanyi 1951, 155) in reaction to their surroundings.

9 Kley (1994, 3) notes that Hayek does not provide a political philosophy but rather a "distinct body of descriptive and explanatory theory" that may, or may not, lead to the normative conclusions that he wishes to draw from it.

10 There is a large critical literature that accuses Hayek of conflating what he referred to as the "twin" ideas of spontaneous order and evolution: Barry (1982, 11), Gissurarson (1987, 61), Kley (1994, 38–39), and Petsoulas (2001, 17). The accusation is that the mechanism for the emergence of a spontaneous order from mutual adjustment is not the same as the mechanism for the endurance of that order in an evolutionary, survival of the fittest, process. As we will see below, the distinction is also noted by Nozick who nonetheless regards both as types of invisible-hand argument.

11 Hayek (1993 [1973-1982], vol. 1, viii-ix) would later admit that the word is ambiguous, and instead offered the terms "self-generating order" and "self-organising structures".

by social scientists. Spontaneous order refers to a body of explanatory theory concerned with orders that arise endogenously and which its exponents contrast with orders that are externally imposed. Hayek then traces what he calls the anthropomorphic fallacy, a confusion in thought that has persisted since ancient Greece. The dichotomy drawn between "physei" (by nature), on the one hand, and "nomo" (by convention) or "thesei" (by deliberate design), on the other, has misled many of those operating in the social sciences (Hayek 1993 [1973-1982], vol. 1, 20). Hayek then describes how this error leads social thinkers to become constructivist rationalists who conflate "nomo" and "thesei" in such a way as to regard what is not natural as being necessarily the product of deliberate human design. This and allied errors form the basis of Hayek's criticism of socialism as an economic order: with the basic observation being that there is a "synoptic delusion" – "the fiction that all the relevant facts are known to some one mind, and that it is possible to construct from this knowledge of the particulars a desirable social order" (Hayek 1993 [1973-1982], vol. 1, 14). Hayek then connects this observation to his analysis of the efficiency of price signalling and mutual adjustment in a free market system, and this forms the basis of his practical and theoretical criticism of socialism.[12] The invisible-hand analysis provides an instrumental justification for a liberal market society as being best able to harness the epistemic efficiency of mutual adjustment under law in economic exchange.

But it is the specific use of the argument in political philosophy that interests me here. Hayek's claim is that the extended order of society is the product of unintended consequences and, as a result, it becomes "meaningless" (Hayek 1993 [1973-1982], vol. 2, 103) to talk about a society as being just because justice is an attribute of human behaviour. If we use justice in reference to the society as a whole, then we are using it in a sense that is importantly distinct from its use in application to the deliberate acts of particular individuals. If a social order is not the product of the deliberate actions of humans, but is rather created by the mutual interaction and adjustment of a number of individuals, then the term "justice" cannot apply to the end result because there is no specific assignable agent to bear moral responsibility. Without such an actor to whom we may attribute responsibility, the term "justice" is rendered little more than a confusing political slogan.

12 As Lessnoff (1999, 155) notes: "by this stage it is clear that Hayek's social theory is no longer a neutral account of the evolution of human social structures, but is a defence of a particular kind of evolved social structure, one incorporating private property and a market economy".

One response to such an argument is to invoke the jurisprudential distinction between commutative justice and distributive justice (Haakonssen 1982) and then argue that there is a distinct realm of social justice that concerns itself with patterns of distribution of material goods. This is a point that Hayek seems to anticipate when he argues that one can meaningfully refer to justice in the end results of a planned economy that seeks to secure a particular pattern of social justice. In such a system, the government is responsible for the imposition of the pattern and can be considered responsible for the outcomes of the system. But this points to the heart of the issue here. To what extent is it useful to think of actions that are the deliberate outcome of individual actions under the same concept as the outcome of patterns of mutual adjustment that are under the control of no one individual?

When Hayek talks about "rules of just conduct" (Hayek 1993 [1973-1982], vol. 2, 31), he stresses how they facilitate the interaction of individuals in a smooth manner. This order and stability in turn allows individuals to exploit their individualised knowledge and to maximise their opportunities to attain their individual goals, the cumulative overall effect of which is the most efficient practicable management of social resources. Thus cultures that develop stable government, law, and property facilitate the interests of individuals and allow efficient economic and social interaction. Hayek's argument provides an instrumental justification of liberal principles in a broadly utilitarian form.

Hayek is trading on the idea that there is a significant enough conceptual distinction between the regulation of individual behaviour under the rule of law and the pattern of distributive outcomes from such interaction and that it is philosophically misleading to attempt to consider them under the compass of a single concept. This philosophical point is a development of the invisible-hand arguments we outlined earlier in our discussion of Adam Smith. Hayek holds that justice can only be meaningfully understood as a procedural principle in societies that operate through mutual interaction under general rules. The actions of individuals may be just or unjust in reference to general rules, but the final outcomes are attributable to no one individual and, as a result, cannot be considered in terms of justice. Moreover, the idea that one ought to act to provide a desired pattern of outcomes means that one must act in a different fashion towards different individuals. Producing a distributive pattern means treating people unequally, and so in a very different way from the equal treatment demanded by the rule of law.

The challenge to political philosophy is that the use of the term "justice" to apply to both the practice of rule following and the distributive outcomes of human interaction under rules is an intellectual error. As Hayek, somewhat waspishly, puts it: "It would seem as if the conviction that one is arguing in a good cause produced more sloppy thinking and even intellectual dishonesty than perhaps any other cause" (Hayek 1993 [1973-1982], vol. 2, 86). What is interesting about Hayek's thought on this matter is that he does not rule out government action to mitigate the distributive failings of a market system. His aim, rather, is to indicate that these actions are conceptually distinct in their form and effect to an extent that is obscured if we use the term "justice" to apply to them both. For Hayek, the notion of justice can be easily identified as the deliberate infringement of the rules of just conduct by one agent against another. Coercion is used or harm is intentionally brought about. Negligence might be accused and culpability determined. In all of these cases, there are clearly specifiable agents involved and a body of rules that has evolved to ease social interaction. Hayek's point is not that we should not act to relieve the poor; rather it is that it is an intellectual error to think that this activity operates on the same principles as justice.

As he put it: "There is no reason why in a free society government should not assure to all protection against severe deprivation in the form of an assured minimum income, or a floor below which nobody need descend. To enter into such an insurance against extreme misfortune may well be in the interest of all; or it may be felt to be a clear moral duty of all to assist, within the organized community, those who cannot help themselves" (Hayek 1993 [1973-1982], vol. 2, 87). Hayek's argument separates out the normative argument for the rule of law from the empirical argument that the rule of law creates the conditions for an efficient market economy, and, at the same time, it suggests that there are additional moral arguments that the state should act to help the poor – but that the normative basis of these is not the same as that for the rule of law.

In terms of his political philosophy, this leads Hayek to seek a system of government that preserves this distinction. In his idealised constitutional model, he seeks to separate the two houses of Parliament in terms of function (Hayek 1993 [1973-1982], vol. 3, 111–112): an upper house, called the Legislative Assembly, whose purpose is the management of the rules of just conduct, and a lower house, called the Governmental Assembly, which is left in control of providing public policy and services within the legal framework created by the upper house. In effect, this separates reasoning about civil and political justice from reasoning about the provision of social and economic goods in the day-to-day operation of the government. What we see then is that Hayek is using the invisible-hand argument to identify distinct modes of political activity that are, in turn, governed by distinct normative principles. This forms the basis of his critique of twentieth-century political philosophy and also lies behind his plans for an ideal constitutional model. Hayek's argument sets out to disaggregate the management of the rules that govern individual interaction from the provision of services that seek to manage the unintended outcomes of that interaction.

This is interesting because it is treading the same ground as Rawls's influential theory.[13] The animus behind Rawls's work is to provide a theory of justice that is structured around a recognition that we appear to think in terms of both commutative and distributive justice, in terms of consequentialist and deontological modes of moral reasoning. He was concerned that the utilitarian accounts of justice failed to pay sufficient regard to individuals – that they could result in the rights and interests of individuals being sacrificed for collective gains. Rawls's theory provides a lexical prioritising that seeks to ensure that certain basic rights are prioritised before any decision on distribution is made (Rawls 1972 [1971], 43).

His two principles:

> First: "Each person is to have an equal right to the most extensive total system of equal basic liberties compatible with a similar system of liberty for all".
> And Second: "Social and economic inequalities are to be arranged so that they are both: (a) to the greatest benefit of the least advantaged, consistent with the just savings principle, and (b) attached to offices and positions open to all under conditions of fair equality of opportunity" (Rawls 1972 [1971], 302).

are ordered to ensure that distributional concerns do not impinge on the operation of a legal system that protects individual's access to what Rawls calls the basic rights. The same fundamental issue of political philosophy is at the heart of Rawls's discussion of lexical priority as lies at the heart of Hayek's division of upper and lower houses of Parliament, a desire to separate and prioritise distinct elements of what we expect from our political institutions.

3 Robert Nozick

This leads us to another political philosopher who makes extensive use of the invisible hand: Nozick's *Anarchy, State, and Utopia* (1974) is often read as the canonical Libertarian response to Rawls's theory, and invisible-hand arguments

13 Hayek does not directly engage with Rawls's writings, but in an aside he suggests that he sees nothing in them that is incompatible with his own views and indeed suggests that their differences are "more verbal than substantive" (Hayek 1993 [1973-1982], vol.2, xvii). Tomasi (2012, 156–161) has recently argued on this basis for a combination of Hayekian social theory and Rawlsian normative arguments to create a classical liberal account of social justice.

are at the heart of this response. Nozick (1974, 20–21) was familiar with Hayek's work and includes it among the examples he provides of sixteen uses of the sort of argument that he terms "invisible-hand explanations". Nozick uses these examples to indicate a type of argument and to excuse his failure to describe that argument in more detail. He provides nothing much in the way of a conceptual analysis of what these diverse arguments share in common, though he does conclude that invisible-hand arguments can produce both good and bad results (Nozick 1994, 192) and distinguishes between two broad types of invisible-hand explanations that both play a part in his argument: filtering processes and equilibrium processes. Filtering processes rule out certain options while equilibrium processes reflect the mutual adjustment of the elements concerned to local conditions and to each other to produce an unintentional order.

What Nozick does do is make a number of interesting uses of invisible-hand explanations in his argument. Perhaps the most striking of these is his account of the rise of a minimal state that appears in the first volume of *Anarchy, State, and Utopia* (1974, 118–119). Nozick demonstrates how a dominant protective association can gradually arise from the rational actions of individuals living in a Lockean state of nature without a deliberate choice or plan to create one. The invisible-hand explanation shows that once such an association has arisen it is, in a sense, legitimate, as each individual has consented to it by contracting with it to provide protective services (it being rational to seek the service of the dominant association as protection is a special type of good where relative comparison favours the most powerful). Nozick (1974, 30) attaches this to an account of individual rights as "side constraints" on action and determines that such rights would be preserved by the minimal state that evolved from the state of nature. The account shows how, on a conceptual level, a minimal state can arise without infringing the rights of individuals. Nozick's side constraints act as an indication of the inviolability of the individual, but they also act as a filter process. They rule out certain forms of action and make certain types of order more likely. In terms of the state, they make a minimal state that protects individual rights more likely. If we accept that individuals are distinct, that they have value, and that this value involves their capacity to make decisions for themselves, then we are led to a set of moral side constraints on what might legitimately be done to them.

This observation leads us to Nozick's second significant use of invisible-hand explanations. Given the model sketched above, Nozick then goes on to consider the argument for distributive justice put forward by Rawls. Without going into specifics, suffice it to say here that part of Nozick's strategy is to pick away at Rawls's lexical prioritising argument and suggest that the inviolability of individual rights precludes redistribution of property. The argument is centred on the idea that in a free society there is no central distribution of goods (Nozick 1974, 149–150) and that in any effort to redistribute goods we would violate the moral side constraints of individual rights. To illustrate his point Nozick distinguishes two types of justice: historical and end-state (Nozick 1974, 153–155). Historical notions of justice are concerned with the idea that what emerges by just steps from an initially just situation is itself just. End-state notions of justice assess the specific order that has arisen against some normative standard. Both types of principles produce orders, but historical principles tend to be accompanied by invisible-hand explanations. The eventual order is not foreseen by the agents whose actions bring it about. On the other hand, end-state principles tend to focus on the pattern of distribution that arises and determine whether it meets some preferred legitimate pattern. This outlook, the suggestion is, is one that encourages the desire to preserve the favoured pattern through sacrificing the moral side constraints. This, claims Nozick, is why Rawls gets himself into difficult positions when he seeks to separate individuals from their "morally arbitrary" physical and social advantages (Rawls 1972 [1971], 100–102) as part of his justification of the Second (or "Difference") Principle. Moreover, this also indicates an important difference between Hayek and Nozick. Hence, Nozick (1974, 158–159) argues that despite his commitment to invisible-hand arguments Hayek himself falls prey to the urge to provide a patterned account of distributive justice when he attempts to argue that a liberal market order can be understood as producing a pattern of distribution where the position of the average citizen is maximised. As we noted above (Note 13), this may account for the fact that Hayek did not see a significant difference between his position and that of Rawls, but for Nozick it clearly represented a weakness in Hayek's position.

Nozick (1974, 151) calls his own theory the "entitlement theory" and describes it as: "Whatever arises from a just situation by just steps is itself just". The result of such an approach lends itself to invisible-hand arguments precisely because it operates through mutual adjustment under general rules protecting the "side constraints". The use of invisible-hand arguments does not cease there. In his section attacking the consequences of trying to preserve a patterned conception of distributive justice, Nozick observes that liberty upsets patterns. The famous Wilt Chamberlain example is intended to show that even if one intervenes to create a favoured pattern of outcomes, that pattern will be disturbed as soon as you allow individuals even the slightest freedom of choice. The only way to preserve patterns would be for the governing authority to either restrict mutually agreed exchanges between individuals, thus breaching the entitlement notion of justice, or to introduce a remedial taxation system that would result, in Nozick's view, in a breach of the side constraints protecting legitimate property holdings.[14]

Nozick draws on invisible-hand arguments to make another of his points against Rawls. In the "Manna from Heaven" argument (Nozick 1974, 199), he pushes Rawls on the consequences of focussing on end-state patterns. Nozick points out that taking an end-state view of distribution ignores the fact that goods that are distributed are created and are created by individuals. To view all goods as ripe for social distribution, one must accept that those goods are collectively owned in some important sense. As we saw above, Rawls does this through his claim that genetic talent and fortunate upbringing are morally arbitrary. Nozick's challenge is that this runs against important intuitions about desert. There are two significant impacts that arise from this. The first is that it may remove any incentive for an individual to produce if he is aware that he will not be rewarded for his effort, and the second, perhaps more problematic for Rawls, is that distribution under his second (difference) principle takes no account of why someone might be disadvantaged in distributive outcomes. Rawls responds to both of these challenges. The first he believes is covered by the commitment of the actors involved to accept the principles of justice as recounted in the original version of his theory. The second, the so-called Malibu surfer problem – the problem of someone who is least advantaged because they choose to spend all of their time surfing rather than because of some personal or social feature that disadvantages them – Rawls addresses in his later book *Justice as Fairness: A Restatement* (2001, 179), where he argues that by factoring leisure time into the basic goods, he is able to avoid the issue.

The issues of desert that arise from this criticism of Rawls are in themselves examples of unintended consequence arguments and return us to the idea raised by Adam Smith that the deliberate pursuit of a desired distributive pattern may have malign unintended consequences. They also raise once again the problem of exercising judgements of desert in situations of unintentionally generated patterns. This issue has become a major theme in another development in post-Rawlsian political philosophy: Dworkin's (2000, 28–29) attempt to introduce a distinction between undeserved disadvantages and disadvantages that result from our choices. Dworkin's attempt to distinguish between circumstances and choices has led to the development of an influential area of recent political

14 It is also worth noting that Nozick (1974, 158) criticises Hayek for giving in to the temptation to provide a patterned form of justice. This depends on Hayek's observation that free market societies tend to create patterns that reward behaviour that is valued by others (hence the efficiency of competition and choice through the price system).

philosophy, luck egalitarianism, that attempts to develop theories of distributive justice that are sensitive to deserved and undeserved inequalities.[15]

4 Conclusion

My suggestion in this chapter is that invisible-hand arguments have been central to the work of two of the most significant political philosophers of the late twentieth century. The response to Rawls's *A Theory of Justice* (1972 [1971]) by Nozick and Hayek's critique of socialism and formulation of an alternative political theory both give a central role to invisible-hand arguments. Moreover, both of them extend the argument beyond explanatory social theory and into normative philosophy. The invisible hand plays a key role in the argument of each thinker not simply as a "fact" but as an argument against their opponent's position and in favour of their own position. It is partly because Hayek and Nozick's systems can accommodate the reality of invisible-hand phenomena that they judge them to be successful. Both Hayek and Nozick's arguments stress that the pursuit of a particular distributive outcome will come into tension with a desire to protect individual rights. Hayek's use of the concept remains closer to the origins of invisible-hand arguments in social and economic theory, and his political theory is geared towards practical constitutional solutions to the problem. Nozick, on the other hand, offers a more abstract argument that is concerned with illustrating the problems with the form of argument developed by Rawls. Contemporary political philosophy in the Anglophone tradition remains dominated by those exploring the legacy of Rawlsian theory, and to that extent Hayek and Nozick's criticisms remain powerful, but contested. The challenge that invisible-hand explanations provide to contemporary political philosophy is that they raise questions about the background assumptions about responsibility and the deliberate pursuit of distributive justice that are central to contemporary notions of justice. As a result, the invisible hand lies in the background of many of the main debates in contemporary political philosophy.

References

Barry, Norman. 1982. "The Tradition of Spontaneous Order." *Literature of Liberty* 5: 7–58.

Berry, Christopher J. 1997. *Social Theory of the Scottish Enlightenment.* Edinburgh: Edinburgh University Press.

15 For examples of this, see Knight and Stemplowska (2011).

Caldwell, Bruce. 2004. *Hayek's Challenge: An Intellectual Biography of F.A. Hayek*. Chicago: University of Chicago Press.

Davis, John B. 1983. "Smith's Invisible Hand and Hegel's Cunning of Reason." In *Adam Smith: Critical Assessments*, edited by John Cunningham Wood, vol. 6, 300–320. London: Croom Held.

Dworkin, Ronald. 2000. *Sovereign Virtue: The Theory and Practice of Equality*. Cambridge (MA): Harvard University Press.

Evensky, Jerry. 1993. "Ethics and the Invisible Hand." *Journal of Economic Perspectives* 7: 197–205.

Ferguson, Adam. 1995 [1767]. *An Essay on the History of Civil Society*, edited by Fania Oz-Salzberger. Cambridge: Cambridge University Press.

Gissurarson, Hannes H. 1987. *Hayek's Conservative Liberalism*. London: Garland Press.

Graham, Paul. 2007. *Rawls*. Oxford: Oneworld Publications.

Grampp, William D. 2000. "What Did Smith Mean by the Invisible Hand?" *Journal of Political Economy* 108: 441–465.

Gray, John. 1986. *Hayek on Liberty*. Oxford: Basil Blackwell, 2nd edition.

Haakonssen, Knud. 1982. "What Might Properly be Called Natural Jurisprudence." In *The Origins and Nature of the Scottish Enlightenment*, edited by R. H. Campbell and Andrew S. Skinner, 205–225. Edinburgh: John Donald.

Harrison, Peter. 2011. "Adam Smith and the History of the Invisible Hand." *Journal of the History of Ideas* 72: 29–49.

Hayek, F. A. 1993 [1973-1982]. *Law, Legislation and Liberty*, vol. 1-3. London: Routledge.

Heydt, Colin. 2017. "The Problem of Natural Religion in Smith's Moral Thought." *Journal of the History of Ideas* 78: 73–94.

Hutcheson, Francis. 2002 [1728]. *An Essay on the Nature and Conduct of the Passions and Affections, with Illustrations on the Moral Sense*, edited by Aaron Garrett. Indianapolis: Liberty Fund.

Jacobs, Struan. 1998. "Michael Polanyi and Spontaneous Order 1941-1951." *Tradition and Discovery: The Polanyi Society Periodical* XXIV: 14–28.

Kennedy, Gavin. 2008. "Adam Smith and the Invisible Hand: From Metaphor to Myth." Unpublished, revised version of a paper presented to the History of Economics Society Conference, George Mason University, June 2007.

Kley, Roland. 1994. *Hayek's Social and Political Thought*. Oxford: Clarendon.

Knight, Carl, and Zofia Stemplowska. 2011. *Responsibility and Distributive Justice*. Oxford: Oxford University Press.

Lessnoff, Michael. 1999. *Political Philosophers of the Twentieth Century*. Oxford: Blackwell.

Macfie, Alec. 1971. "The Invisible Hand of Jupiter." *Journal of the History of Ideas* 32: 595–599.

Mandeville, Bernard. 1988 [1705/1714]. *The Fable of the Bees: Or Private Vices, Publick Benefits*, edited by Frederick Benjamin Kaye, vol. 1-2. Indianapolis: Liberty Fund.

Martin, David A. 1983. "Economics as Ideology: On Making the 'Invisible Hand' Invisible." In *Adam Smith: Critical Assessments*, edited by John Cunningham Wood, vol. 7, 123–137. London: Croom Held.

Nozick, Robert. 1974. *Anarchy, State, and Utopia*. Oxford: Blackwell.

Nozick, Robert. 1994. "Invisible-Hand Explanations." *American Economic Association Papers and Proceedings*, May: 314–318.

Oakeshott, Michael. 1991. *Rationalism in Politics and Other Essays*. Indianapolis: Liberty Fund.

Otteson, James. 2002. *Adam Smith's Marketplace of Life*. Cambridge: Cambridge University Press.

Petsoulas, Christina. 2001. *Hayek's Liberalism and Its Origins: His Idea of Spontaneous Order and the Scottish Enlightenment*. London: Routledge.

Polanyi, Michael. 1951. *The Logic of Liberty*. London: Routledge.

Popper, Karl. 1989. *Conjectures and Refutations*. London: Routledge.

Rawls, John. 1972 [1971]. *A Theory of Justice*. Oxford: Oxford University Press.

Rawls, John. 2001. *Justice as Fairness: A Restatement*, edited by Erin Kelly. Cambridge (MA): Belknap Press.

Rothschild, Emma. 1994. "Adam Smith and the Invisible Hand." *American Economic Association Papers and Proceedings*, May: 319–322.

Sen, Amartya. 2009. *The Idea of Justice*. London: Allen Lane.

Shearmur, Jeremy. 1996. *Hayek and After: Hayekian Liberalism as a Research Programme*. London: Routledge.

Smith, Adam. 1976a [1759]. *The Theory of Moral Sentiments*, edited by D. D. Raphael and A. L. Macfie. Oxford: Oxford University Press.

Smith, Adam. 1976b [1776]. *An Inquiry into the Nature and Causes of the Wealth of Nations*, edited by R. H. Campbell, A. S. Skinner and W. B. Todd. Oxford: Oxford University Press.

Smith, Adam. 1980 [1795]. *Essays on Philosophical Subjects*, edited by W. P. D. Wightman. Oxford: Oxford University Press.

Smith, Craig. 2006. *Adam Smith's Political Philosophy: The Invisible Hand and Spontaneous Order*. London: Routledge.

Smith, Craig. 2009. "The Scottish Enlightenment, Unintended Consequences, and the Science of Man." *Journal of Scottish Philosophy* 7: 9–28.

Tomasi, John. 2012. *Free Market Fairness*. Princeton: Princeton University Press.

Frederick G. Whelan

"Contrary Effects" and the Reverse Invisible Hand in Hume and Smith*

Abstract: Thinkers of the Scottish Enlightenment are known for explaining social patterns in terms of the unintended consequences of purposive action, especially benign patterns of what Hayek termed "spontaneous order" achieved as if by an invisible hand. These writers, however, also point to negative unintended consequences and even perverse (or contrary) effects, in which actors individually or collectively bring about the opposite of what they desired. This chapter describes numerous examples of such negative and perverse outcomes from Hume's *History of England* and Smith's *Wealth of Nations*. It then considers invisible-hand explanations and perversity in the work of modern social scientists Hayek, Boudon, Merton, and Hirschman.

Keywords: Unintended consequences; perverse effects; David Hume; Adam Smith; Hayek; Hirschman

Abbreviations

E Hume	*Essays Moral, Political, and Literary*
EPM	*Hume, Enquiry Concerning the Principles of Morals*, ed. Beauchamp
H Hume	*The History of England from the Invasion of Julius Caesar to the Revolution in 1688*
Refl Burke	*Reflections on the Revolution in France*, ed. O'Brien
T Hume	*A Treatise of Human Nature*, ed. Norton and Norton, with page numbers to Selby-Bigge edition (references will be given to both NN and SB editions)
WN Smith	*An Inquiry into the Nature and Causes of the Wealth of Nations*

1 Introduction: spontaneous (dis)order

One of the most familiar ideas associated with the social thought of the Scottish Enlightenment is the concept of unforeseen or unanticipated and therefore

---

* This chapter constitutes a partial reprint of chap. 4 from Whelan, Frederick G. 2015. *Political Thought of Hume and His Contemporaries: Enlightenment Projects*, vol. 2. New York and London: Routledge. Certain passages were left out and the reference system was adapted accordingly.

unintended consequences of purposive action and the importance of such consequences in understanding and explaining a variety of social and political patterns and institutions.[1] This theme conflicts with a common interpretation of Enlightenment social thought as promising increasing rational control over events through deliberate design of institutions, on the model provided by the natural sciences and engineering, for the realization of human purposes. The idea occurs frequently in the thought of David Hume and Adam Smith, the subjects of this study, as well as to a lesser degree in Adam Ferguson, Lord Kames, Gilbert Stuart, John Millar, Dugald Stewart, and others.[2] Thus Hume remarks in typical passages that the rules of property, "comprehending the interest of each individual, [are] of course advantageous to the public; tho' [they] be not intended for that purpose by the inventors" (T 3.2.6.6/529); and that Henry VIII's reformation led to "many beneficial consequences; though perhaps neither foreseen nor intended by the persons who had the chief hand in conducting it" (H 3, 207). Ferguson (1995, 119) offers the clearest and oft-quoted general statement: "Mankind, in following the present sense of their minds, [...] arrive at ends which even their imagination could not anticipate; [...] and nations stumble upon establishments, which are indeed the result of human action, but not the execution of any human design".[3]

---

1 Merton (1936, 895) says that every important social thinker has treated "the problem of unanticipated consequences", although the only pre-Scottish thinkers he cites are Machiavelli and Vico. Rousseau should be added: the unanticipated consequences – mostly for the worse – of the casual invention of property are the theme of Part 2 of his *Discourse on Inequality.* The opening of this section is paraphrased by Ferguson (1995, 119). Hayek claims Mandeville as a forerunner of the Scottish theories, but his position is ambiguous because of the role he assigns to "skillful management" by politicians in channeling selfish behavior. See Barry (1982, 16–20), and especially Petsoulas (2001, chap. 3).

2 See references in Hamowy (1989, 25–36).

3 A notable example is the division of labor (Ferguson 1995, 173–175). On Ferguson's contribution, with an emphasis on his providentialism, see Hill (2006, chap. 6). Smith (WN 25) also observes that the division of labor "is not originally the effect of any human wisdom, which foresees and intends that general opulence to which it gives occasion," but rather of individuals' "propensity to truck, barter, and exchange one thing for another". Although the precise origin of the idea of the division of labor is unclear (Hume's *Treatise* 3.2.2 provides an early instance), Hamowy (2005, 36–37) argues that Ferguson was original in drawing out the sociological consequences. Since these include intransigent forms of political inequality, this contradicts the thesis that spontaneously generated orders realize freedom.

The importance of unintended consequences was given special prominence in political theory through writings of F. A. Hayek extending back to the 1950s. Hayek, however, advanced a special interpretation of the larger idea of unintended consequences. Evidently taking Smith's "invisible-hand" passage(s)[4] as paradigmatic, Hayek termed the Scottish contribution the theory of "spontaneous order", signaling the phenomenon of beneficent patterns of complex social order that come about through the actions of many people but without conscious plan, design, or direction on the part either of the participants or anyone else.[5] In Smith's account, individuals acting in a market pursue (and perhaps achieve) their own interest in the most advantageous return on the investment of their capital or labor, and they do so in a rationally self-interested manner, taking account of available information, especially prices and the facts of their local situation. The longer term and cumulative result of their doing so, however, is the promotion of a larger social good or goods, including a balance of domestic over foreign industry,[6] the advancement of the division of

4 That is, principally the famous invisible hand from the *Wealth of Nations* IV.ii.9, but the one from *The Theory of Moral Sentiments* IV.1 (in which the greed of the rich brings about a near-equal division of the necessities of life) has a similar import for present purposes. "Invisible hand" is something of a misnomer, since as usually understood its meaning is that there is *no* directing "hand" behind the scenes.

5 Hayek popularized the concept of "spontaneous order" in *The Constitution of Liberty* (1960, 160). He expressed a preference for the term social "formations" rather than "institutions", a word that might imply that the orders in questions had been consciously "instituted". Hayek had extensively discussed the idea of "apparently purposive" orders, formations, "coherent wholes", or "persistent structures of relationships" that arise without design or the intent of participants earlier in *The Counter-Revolution of Science* (1952, esp. chap. 4 and 8). He offered further context and analysis in "The Results of Human Actions but not of Human Design" (1967) and *Law, Legislation, and Liberty* (1973), vol. I, where he uses the term "constructivist rationalism" to designate the opposed belief that an orderly pattern must have been intelligently designed. See Smith (2006), which despite its title provides a clear analytical exposition of spontaneous order as an approach to social explanation primarily in Hayek, with references to Adam Smith.

6 The specific context of the invisible-hand passage (WN 456) is Smith's contention that under conditions of liberty (as opposed to mercantilist regulation) one would prefer to invest one's resources in domestic rather than foreign industry. This is advantageous in promoting national wealth because domestic commerce stimulates the division of labor more than does foreign. Smith says that the concept applies "in this, as in many other cases", and it can be – and has often been – applied to free market activity in general. The invisible hand does not operate in the manner indicated, of course, when obstructed by politically imposed restrictions. Cf. Fleischacker (2004, 139–142), who

labor, the production of maximal social wealth, and the efficient functioning of the market itself.[7] These are key aspects of the public good, which none of the actors directly foresaw or intended. The market with its self-regulating capacity is a complex social institution that displays a pattern or order, one that serves human interests effectively without the need (as Mandeville emphasized) for public virtue. The order of a market as a whole thus comes about spontaneously as the unintended outcome of the deliberate actions of numerous participants over time. It need not and could not have been – and historically was not in fact – foreseen as a whole, let alone planned or designed, by anyone. Hayek (1979 [1952] 71, 146, 148) went on to observe that other important social institutions could be understood in a similar manner and were in many cases explained in this way by eighteenth-century Scottish theorists: language, systems of moral rules,[8] money, the common law, and constitutional government in England, to name the most important.[9] Crucially, from Hayek's normative perspective, liberty itself, understood as being concretely institutionalized in free markets, legal and moral rules, and limited constitutional government, should be understood similarly in terms of a spontaneous order.[10] Arguments

---

notes the limited textual application but argues that the idea applies broadly in Smith's economic vision.

7 In a highly idiosyncratic interpretation, Rothschild (2001, 177) contends that Smith's reference to the invisible hand was a "mildly ironic joke". If the irony arises from the observation that people in invisible-hand situations do not fully know what they are doing, that is the perfectly serious point of the idea, not a joke. She is also offended that treating the invisible hand seriously implies an unSmithian aloofness and condescension on the part of the "privileged" observer of human conduct (Rothschild 2001, 123–124), but such a position of detachment is involved in all scientific analysis. In this chapter, I treat invisible-hand explanations as part of social science. Smith's intentions are not my topic, but unlike Rothschild I suppose that a "science of man" was among them.

8 *Contra* Hayek, however, the emergence of Humean conventions such as the norms of justice, though spontaneous in the sense of not authoritatively or formally established, would appear to have an intentional component and therefore not count as an invisible-hand phenomenon. The large literature on this is beyond the scope of this study.

9 A telling Hayekian example is a system of footpaths that gradually takes shape in wild country (Hayek 1979 [1952], 70). Such a system would display order but probably not optimal order.

10 Other classical liberals added other free-market-like competitive systems, including those effected by freedom of religion and speech, as in J. S. Mill's "Liberty of Thought and Discussion", which he argues promotes the discovery of truths that are beyond the

having this form have come to be called "invisible-hand explanations" in social theory and philosophy.[11]

The view of such institutions that Hayek emphasizes, with due credit to the Scottish thinkers, takes two forms. Frequently it offers an evolutionary and historical explanation of the development of institutions, with unintended consequences playing a key role along with the idea of gradual adaptation to changing circumstances and an implicit mechanism analogous to natural selection.[12] The other main version of invisible-hand explanation pertains to self-sustaining or self-regulating systems such as the equilibrium model based on a feedback mechanism, such as the price system in a market.[13] Evolutionary variants of the invisible hand explain how orderly patterns emerge and develop from the uncoordinated actions of many individuals without overall design or authoritative direction; equilibrium variants explain how such actions maintain the order in a stable condition without anyone's intention or supervision to

---

grasp of any individual interlocutor. On religious markets, see the discussion of Smith in chap. 6 of vol. 1 of the present work [Editors: Whelan, Frederick G. 2015. *Political Thought of Hume and His Contemporaries: Enlightenment Projects*, vol. 1. New York and London: Routledge].

11 This usage is from Nozick (1974, 18–22), who gives examples of different types. Smith (2006, 14) says that Nozick's usage is non-standard in encompassing both beneficial and pernicious outcomes, whereas for Adam Smith and Hayek "invisible hand arguments refer to the production of benign unintended consequences which manifest themselves as a spontaneous order".

12 In *The Constitution of Liberty* (1960, 160), Hayek refers to a process of "mutual adjustment". He endorses an evolutionary model for social order in "The Results of Human Action" (Hayek 1960, 101) and "Evolution of Rules of Conduct" (Hayek 1960, 77). In assuming the presence of "natural selection" and "adaptive evolution" I follow the interpretations of Gray, *Hayek on Liberty*, chap. 2; Hamowy (1989, 4; *passim*); and Petsoulas (2001). See also Smith (2006, chap. 7, 8). In his account of the Scottish theory, Hamowy (1989, 3) adds two ideas: that complex institutions are "invariably" the outcome of unplanned processes, which is surely too strong a claim; and that the actions that produce the unforeseen results may be habitual as well as conscious and purposive. The concept of perverse effects, the topic of this chapter, logically requires purposive or intentional action.

13 In addition to their function as signals to producers and consumers, Hayek emphasizes the epistemological function of prices, which summarize far more information about variations in supply and demand, costs, and innumerable consumer preferences than any planner could collect and process. Hence overall knowledge-based rationality is generated spontaneously in the system rather than inhering in rational agents, each of whom acts locally or with less complete information.

achieve this result.[14] What is rejected in either version is the rationalist fallacy that orderly, functional, and beneficent institutions must be (or even can be) consciously invented or designed, whether by a classical Legislator, the parties to a social contract, a benevolent autocrat, revolutionary intellectuals, social engineers, order-minded bureaucrats, or some other "directing intelligence".[15]

Two features of Hayek's particular version of the theory of unintended consequences are noteworthy here. The first is that the process, as expressed in the invisible hand with what some have held was a providentalist background, is entirely benign: individuals acting in the market successfully achieve their own local objectives (that is, profit) and at the same time contribute to larger social goods. Second, the unintended outcome is the cumulative, combined, or composite effect of the actions of many individuals.[16] A more comprehensive view of unintended consequences, however, would suggest other possibilities, ones in which the unanticipated effects of actions may be harmful or disappointing in various ways, either compositely or for an actor considered separately:

(a) An actor in a market may fail to achieve his own ends, yet still promote the larger good. Someone may make bad investment decisions, the failure of which will nevertheless send valuable signals to others. More abstractly, all market behavior tends to be self-defeating: whenever a seller enters a market, for example, he increases the supply and thus lowers the price of the commodities he has to offer, to the (unintended) benefit of consumers.[17] The reverse holds true for buyers. In cases like these, the larger goods of market efficiency and creation of value are attained, so that one may still speak – if somewhat less optimistically – of an invisible hand or spontaneous order.

(b) Rational individual actions, however, may combine into social outcomes that are harmful for all involved, thus defeating the goals aimed at and perhaps making everyone worse off. Cases such as the tragedy of the commons provide a

---

14 See Ullmann-Margalit (1997) on evolutionary versus equilibrial explanations, although she unaccountably argues that evolution explains the maintenance of a market.

15 Hamowy (1989, 3).

16 In *The Counter-Revolution of Science* (1979 [1952], 41), Hayek asserts that the aim of social studies in general is "to explain the unintended or undesigned results of the actions of many men" – as opposed to the actions of unitary actors. The theme of composite effects is treated most systematically in chap. 8, "Purposive Social Formations" (Hayek 1979 [1952]). In this work (to which Hamowy oddly does not refer) Hayek (1979 [1952], 146) refers to "spontaneously grown institutions".

17 In "Towards a Rational Theory of Society" (1948, 124), Popper agrees with Hayek on the centrality of unintended consequences for the social sciences.

paradigm for rational choice theory, in which less than optimal outcomes arising from perverse incentives and the interactive effects of the behavior of many actors are a standard subject for analysis. Suboptimal outcomes include ones in which unforeseen costs negate the expected benefits and ones that entirely defeat the actors' aims and make the collectivity of which they are members worse off than it was before, as if by the operation of a malignant or a reverse invisible hand.[18] Controlling behavior (however sensible it may seem at the individual level) to prevent the occurrence of such collective bads, as also to coordinate the provision of public goods, is (for Hayek, following Hume and Smith) the proper function of the state, on the assumption that the competence of the market – or the order that it generates spontaneously – is limited. We shall return to this subject at the end of this chapter.

If we consider simply the actions of individuals and their consequences, without composition effects, we see that:

(c) An individual's action, rationally and correctly calculated to achieve a particular good of his own, may nevertheless have unforeseen and unintended harmful side effects on other individuals, on other values of the actor himself, or on the public at large, as in the economic case of negative externalities. Individuals in such cases are responding to a different form of perverse incentives.

(d) Finally, the action of a particular actor, or the actions of a number of actors, may not only fail to achieve its intended goal, or do so with unexpectedly high costs, but may – perversely – bring about the opposite of what was intended. Actions that are self-defeating through their unintended consequences presumably make actors worse off, whether the actors be individuals, governments, or

18 Pernicious unintended consequences, as in the examples below, undercut the older but now largely discredited providentialist interpretation of Smith's invisible hand. If eighteenth-century thinkers had recognized the prevalence of prisoner's-dilemma situations, would their belief in providence have been shaken? In his *Dialogues Concerning Natural Religion* (1947), Hume of course challenges the design argument with respect to the world as a whole (the claim that the evident order of the world entails an intelligent designer) just as he, Smith, Ferguson, and Hayek challenge necessity-of-design arguments for complex social institutions. But in this work, Hume (1947, 169) also turns the argument around, suggesting that the imperfections of the world might point to an incompetent creator. Neither design nor spontaneity guarantees order, of course. Rothschild (2001, 135) observes that if the order of the universe could exist without God, then perhaps social order could exist without a sovereign – or with a less active one. Smith did not reject sovereigns but thought they should be less active in certain domains (the economy).

compact groups that act jointly for shared objectives, or people acting independently of one another.[19]

The common feature of these four cases is that unintended consequences are negative, in whole or in part, either for the actor himself, for others, or for everyone (the group or society as a whole).[20] Hayek and others who have focused on the invisible hand are correct in noting that the Scottish theorists often point to the beneficial effects of unplanned social processes involving unintended consequences, but they often neglect to observe that these writers also present negative cases as well.[21] This fact is also of course at variance with the implicit providentialism that some have seen in Smith's invisible hand. On the contrary, the assumption here is that these passages are best read in the spirit of social and historical explanation – that is, as contributions to both Enlightenment science and by extension to modern social science; and from the perspective of scientific explanation, the negative cases are as important as the beneficent ones.[22] This chapter deals with the most severe negative case – that of perverse effects, or what Hume and Smith usually refer to as "contrary effects", in which a purposive course of action or policy backfires to produce the reverse of what was intended. A large number of instances of "contrary effects" from Hume and Smith are described in the following section. Humean attempts to explain the occurrence of such effects in terms of fallacious reasoning are examined in the third section, and the concluding section considers some interpretations of this issue in light

19 For an illuminating survey of perverse (or "revenge") effects of contemporary technology in conjunction with policy, see Tenner (1997).

20 In the only similar analysis that I have come across, Rosen (1996, 122–127) distinguishes six kinds of unanticipated consequences in Smith, four of them negative in some way. However, he does not include strictly perverse or composite effects, which are important in what follows. Brennan and Pettit (1993, 204–205) briefly discuss the "invisible backhand", which generates unintended outcomes such as collective-action and free-rider predicaments, which they term "disvalued order" rather than disorder.

21 This applies also to Berry (1997, 40–41).

22 Rothschild argues that the invisible hand is not part of Smith's "system" of thought and that social science explanation in these terms was not among his aims. Her complaint appears to be that invisible-hand explanations ignore (as Smith did not) the intentions and reflections of actors, but such explanations address precisely the *unintended* and thus not consciously grasped consequences of *intentional* action (Rothschild 2001, 136–138, 141–142). I agree with her point that the invisible hand may have had a rhetorical purpose in Smith's campaign to reduce the visible hand of governmental regulation. See also Tieffenbach (2003) for a scientific reading of the Scottish theory in contrast to Hegel's superficially similar teleological and providential concept.

of recent social science. Most of the cases fall in category (d) above; that is, they are straightforward cases of effects that are perverse with respect to an actor's intentions and goals in performing an action or implementing a policy. A few fall in categories (b) and (c), involving actions that appear to be successful from the actor's limited point of view but that are perverse for the group to which the actor belongs or for the actor's successors in a social position.

2 Examples

In this section, I survey some of the more conspicuous cases of perverse effects mentioned by Hume in his *Essays* and *History of England*. The list is supplemented by several instances taken from Smith's *Wealth of Nations* that resemble Hume's and reflect similar patterns of analysis. The cases are somewhat arbitrarily classified as examples of statecraft, in which political figures pursue unsuccessful strategies to secure or advance their power, and public policies enacted by governmental (or in a few cases ecclesiastical) authorities. In every case there is an identifiable actor, whether an individual or a discrete group with a joint purpose, so that it is possible to say that the actors had definite aims that were achieved or – in these cases – frustrated in the outcome of their actions. Depending on how the original aim is specified, these episodes exemplify perversity in the full sense, in that the result is in some respect the opposite of what was intended. Interpretations of recent writers will be considered in the final section.

3 Statecraft

The first two cases, from the earlier Middle Ages, concern dynastic succession and defense against an external aggressor. Though archaic, the political logic of the cases is of interest.

(1) The efforts of kings to safeguard their rule ruins their dynasties. In the era of the seven Anglo-Saxon kingdoms of England, there was no clear royal succession rule for the monarchies, a source of weakness in any regime.[23] The

23 Hume, Montesquieu, and other Enlightenment thinkers sometimes pointed to this deficiency as a source of weakness in oriental monarchies, despite their alleged "despotic" absolutism. One of the conditions of the emergence of strong European states was the acceptance of clear (hereditary) succession rules.

Saxon kings were therefore subject to being challenged by other members of the extended royal family and were "continually agitated with jealousy against all the princes of the blood". To forestall danger they sometimes resorted to killing potential rivals, even though they presumably hoped that the crown would remain in their family indefinitely. The cumulative result of each king's effort to stabilize his throne and his kingdom in this manner was the eventual extinction of the old ruling lines in all the kingdoms except Wessex, which "finally swallowed up all the other Saxon states" and became the basis of a unified English kingdom (H 1, 49, 45).

(2) Trying to appease an enemy with payments encourages continued attacks. King Ethelred, faced with Danish incursions into England, "bribed" them to depart with money payments. "This shameful expedient", Hume remarks, "was attended with the success which might be [but evidently was not] expected". The Danes returned the following year "in hopes of subduing a people, who defended themselves by their money, which invited assailants, instead of their arms, which repelled them" (H 1, 108).

The following, more modern cases concern another dimension of statecraft in early modern monarchies – strategies employed by rulers for dealing with domestic opponents and dissidents.

(3) Keeping dissidents close at hand for surveillance and repression, rather than facilitating their exit, leads to an eventual intensification of opposition.[24] In the 1620s, some of the most zealous Puritans emigrated to New England, relieving political pressure in England. In the 1630s, however, the government's permissive policy was reversed, reflecting both its determination to suppress religious dissent and its fear of disaffection in the colonies. In 1636, a number of emigrant ships were detained by royal order; among those on board, it emerged, were several future leaders of the parliamentary rebellion against Charles I, including Hampden and Cromwell. "The king had afterwards full leisure to repent this exercise of his authority" (H 5, 241–242).[25]

---

24 Cf. Hirschman's analysis of how the possibility of exit reduces "voice" and vice versa in *Exit, Voice, and Loyalty* (1970).

25 Spain and France permitted only undoubted Catholics to emigrate to their American colonies and dealt with their dissident minorities (Jews/*conversos*/Moriscos and Huguenots) by other means. On the whole, England followed the opposite policy, with respect to which the incident cited here is anomalous. The outcome, however, was far worse for the English royal government than for the Spanish or French. It is not clear if this is because the English "exit" policy failed, or because it was not adhered to uniformly, or if the English opposition forces were stronger for other reasons.

(4) Keeping potential dissidents removed from the center of government, on the other hand, can also backfire. Monarchs in early modern Europe frequently worried about opposition from their nobility, whose prestige and material resources made them potentially the king's most dangerous opponents. As Hume notes, a common royal policy was to try to keep the leading nobles at court, where they could be watched and converted into submissive courtiers (a policy that resembles Charles I's effort to keep the Puritans in England). James I, however, followed the opposite strategy of encouraging the English nobility and gentry to reside in their country seats, hoping that dispersal would render them more submissive and less likely to "indulge too curious researches into matters of government". Hume remarks that James lacked a coherent plan for increasing his power; he did worry, though, that the concentration of nobles in London might increase their collective strength. In any case, "the contrary effect soon followed" (H 5, 134). The gentry became wealthier by not dissipating their fortunes at court, and they developed a more independent spirit – the basis of serious subsequent opposition to the crown.

(5) Hostile treatment of suspected or potential political opponents, short of their destruction, converts them into actual opponents, sometimes effective ones. This is a recurrent pattern in the turmoil surrounding the English crown in the later Middle Ages, as Hume recounts it, including Richard II's treatment of Lancaster, Henry VI and the Yorkist faction, and Edward IV and the Tudor claimant. Henry VII (Henry Tudor) became king after defeating the last ruler from the family of York, thus putting an end to the Wars of the Roses. Aware that his own title to the crown was shaky, he distrusted the Yorkist party as former enemies and potential conspirators against him. He therefore lost no chance to "depress" the adherents of the former regime and elevate their opponents. "And while he treated the Yorkists as enemies, he soon rendered them such", provoking them to spread doubts about the validity of his title. Having unified these opponents, Henry lived in fear of them throughout his reign. "By his perpetual attention to depress the partizans of the York family, he had more closely united them into one party, and encreased their desire of [...] taking every advantage, which his oppressive government should give his enemies against him". Hume suggests that "a more enlarged and more benevolent system of policy" would have better served his interest (H 3, 7, 69).

(6) Expulsion of a dissident or dissenting minority weakens rather than strengthens a country. As is well known, Louis XIV expelled the substantial minority of French Protestants (Huguenots) from France in 1685. Hume like other historians comments on the apparent irrationality of this decision in relation to Louis's presumed overriding ambition to increase the strength of France

as the hegemonic power in Europe, since the Huguenots were an industrious community whose departure meant a substantial loss to the French economy. The policy was not perverse, of course, if its goal was simply to attain religious orthodoxy as an independent value; in this case, the policy would have been an expression of what Hume calls Louis's "bigotry", but a successful one. For Hume and others, however, Louis believed that national strength depended on homogeneity of religion in a population living under a uniform central administration, so that the presence of dissidents who claimed special privileges for their unorthodox practices was a source of danger. The Huguenot emigration, however, deprived France of wealth and skills, resources that – in the zero-sum world of mercantilism and power politics – ended up in the camp of Louis's enemies; and the influence of the refugees in their adopted countries stimulated the determination of the international Protestant coalition against France. On this instrumentalist interpretation of his motives, Louis's policy aimed to strengthen his kingdom but perversely weakened it (H 6, 471, 498).

(7) Dignifying a weaker opponent, or publicizing his cause, by openly attacking him can have the effect of strengthening rather than defeating him. Henry VIII (whom Hume describes as impetuous and impolitic) entered the early Reformation controversy by writing a book against Luther in 1521. The unheard-of spectacle of a king publicly disputing with an obscure reformer, however, made the contest "illustrious" and brought Luther "new converts in every part of Europe". This effect was furthered by the fact that the public, which naturally tended to favor the underdog, awarded Luther the victory in the dispute (H 3, 140). The then loyal Catholic Henry received the title "defender of the faith" from the pope, a gratifying side benefit, but his action achieved the opposite of what he directly intended. The papal gesture also had an ironic or perverse outcome, as the title was retained by Henry and his successors when they became the most prominent Protestant rulers in Europe.

(8) Excessive persecution of a noteworthy opponent may backfire. Henry II mounted an intense campaign of legal charges, fines, and confiscations against Thomas Becket, Archbishop of Canterbury. Henry sought to assert royal legal and fiscal authority over the church, while Becket resisted in the name of ecclesiastical privileges and immunities; there was also a personal element in this familiar story in that Henry was particularly aggravated that his former friend and appointee should have turned against him. Henry seems to have mobilized broad public support (such as this could be in the Middle Ages) for his position and succeeded in isolating Becket. However, "the violent and unjust prosecution of Becket, had a natural tendency to turn the public favour on his side, and to make men overlook his former ingratitude towards the king […]

as well as the enormity of these ecclesiastical privileges, of which he affected to be the champion" (H 1, 322). As the last phrase implies, Hume's account up to this point strongly endorses Henry's substantive position against exorbitant clerical "pretensions". Now, however, Hume aligns himself with public opinion in judging that Henry's methods were excessive and unjust. Hume also, however, indicates that Henry miscalculated from a strictly political point of view. He failed to anticipate the shift in public sympathy for Becket as the victim of persecution, as well as the church's reserves of legitimacy and the foreign support to which Becket could appeal. Henry's overconfidence in his proceedings against Becket thus produced a reversal, at least temporarily, in the achievement of his goals – as of course was also the case following Becket's assassination a few years later.

(9) Overreaching or overconfidence on the part of a powerful institution leads to the adoption of self-defeating practices and reduction in its power. Henry II's remote successor in the English variant of the church-state conflict was Henry VIII, who successfully mobilized political support to break decisively with papal authority in the 1530s. Hume implies that one reason for his success was that public opinion had turned (or was guided by the government's policy to turn) more definitively than earlier against perceived abuses by the church or the popes. On this episode, Hume comments: "Thus the authority of the popes, like all exorbitant power, was ruined by the excess of its acquisitions, and by stretching its pretensions beyond what it was possible for any human principles or prepossessions to sustain" (H 3, 206). Henry II's earlier overreaching and its self-defeating consequences were mild by comparison with the perverseness of, to cite one of Hume's main examples, the attempt of the church to extend its wealth and power by selling indulgences (H 3, 137–139).

(10) Leniency in punishing criminals or rebels encourages disorder that in turn leads to greater and irregular violence against them – that is, the opposite of leniency. Conversely, overly severe measures are not enforced, leading to irregular leniency. "Thus, one extreme produces another. In the same manner as excessive severity in the laws is apt to beget great relaxation in their execution; so their excessive lenity naturally produces cruelty and barbarity" ("Of the Populousness of Ancient Nations", E 415). Hume's example pertains only to the former point (excessive leniency). The most severe punishment in the later Roman republic was banishment, even for the most dangerous and traitorous enemies of the republic. Given the high stakes of the party conflicts of the period, it "became necessary" to "draw the sword of private vengeance", leading to a spiral of violence that soon got out of control. This example can also be

characterized as one where a certain (defective) system of law produced rampant illegality. Hume says that the ancient laws "were so absurdly contrived, that they obliged the heads of parties [even notable jurists like Cicero] to have recourse to these extremities". In the converse case, that of sporadic non-enforcement (such as through jury nullification) of what are viewed as overly severe laws, the rule of law in an even-handed manner is frustrated. If the Roman law of banishment is seen as a distinctively republican law, reflecting the republican aversion to imposing harsher or more degrading punishments on citizens, then this is also a case of self-defeating republicanism, since the result was the destruction of the republic through party violence. In a similar vein, the criminal justice system of Anglo-Saxon feudalism, in which each lord had jurisdiction within his territory and could punish robbers without appeal, "must have had a very contrary effect to that which was intended" (H 1, 172). Hume implies that powerful nobles were free to protect as well as to punish criminals, presumably those whose services they found they could use.

The following two examples concern supranational statecraft, including imperial administration and the well-known balance of power in foreign affairs.

(11) Policies enacted by free states to protect their provinces or colonies from official abuses have the effect of worsening conditions there ("That Politics May Be Reduced to a Science", E 19). Echoing ancient commentators, Hume observes that the administration of the Roman republic over its provinces was more abusive than was that of the later emperors. Generalizing this point to include modern cases like Ireland, Hume argues that free states are (paradoxically) always hard on their colonies, since they are responsive to the desire of their citizens (who are represented in the government) to exploit the colonial subjects (who are not). An autocratic ruler could be more even-handed and might find this advantageous. Roman laws designed to prevent provincial oppression backfired, since oppressors now had to extract enough plunder not only to "satisfy their own rapacity" but also to "satisfy" (bribe) their judges and other important people in Rome whose protection they would need. Such laws also invited evasion through collusion or generalized corruption in the governing class, many of whose members could expect to benefit from the empire (even though these same people presumably passed the reform laws as a show of rectitude), and the republican system (according to Cicero himself) lacked the capacity to correct the abuses. This analysis thus points to a paradox about "free" government as well as to a perverse effect of policy. Increased provincial oppression was also an unintended side effect (though evidently not a perverse effect) of the republican practice of frequently rotating governorships among their citizens,

since a governor who knew his term of office would be brief would be more "expeditious" in accumulating wealth.

(12) Smaller states that try to improve their international position by aligning themselves with a powerful, expanding state end up being subjugated by it. Rome's erstwhile allies all wound up as parts of its empire; hoping to remain free and avoid conquest by befriending the conqueror, they "were forging their own chains, while they advanced the conquests of their ally" ("Of the Balance of Power", E 337). What Macedon, Rhodes, the Achaean republics, and the others ought to have done was follow balance-of-power logic, forming coalitions to resist the expanding power and (perhaps counterintuitively) entering contests on the weaker side. The "universal empire" of Rome was facilitated by the fact that the Romans "never met with any such general combination or confederacy against them, as might naturally have been expected" – at least in ages when the logic of balance is better understood. Hume frequently criticizes statesmen who deviate from a foreign policy based on the balance of power.[26] Trying to be a winner by joining the apparent winner can make you a loser.

The following eight cases concern relations between popular grievances and rebellion and governmental policies or responses.

(13) A rebellious disposition in a people is "one chief cause of tyranny in the rulers", who are provoked to more violent repressive measures than they would have used had their subjects been inclined to "submission and obedience". More particularly, the promulgation of doctrines regarding the permissibility of tyrannicide or the assassination of oppressive rulers, "instead of keeping tyrants and usurpers in awe, made them ten times more fierce and unrelenting" ("Of Passive Obedience", E 490), and the practice has historically increased "the jealousy and cruelty of princes" (EPM 11/Enq 180–181). These "ancient maxims" of politics are thus rightly rejected by the modern law of nations and modern opinion on methods of bringing rulers to justice. Hume's claim here anticipates (and may have inspired) Burke's similar argument that "kings will be tyrants from policy when subjects are rebels from principle" (Refl 172). Rebellion, at least if it fails, has the opposite of its intended effect, although some modern revolutionaries have calculated that the heightened tyranny provoked by resistance only makes the overthrow of the regime more probable in the long run. Hume does not reject resistance to oppression altogether but, in view of its dangers, argues

26 See chap. 2 above [Editors: Whelan, Frederick G. 2015. *Political Thought of Hume and His Contemporaries: Enlightenment Projects*, vol. 2. New York and London: Routledge].

that it should be "the last refuge in desperate cases" ("Of Passive Obedience", E 490).[27] Again like Burke, he holds that a political theory should generally teach the rationale of authority and the duty of obedience rather than detailing all the exceptional cases where resistance is justified.

(14) A ruler's attempt to shore up his government through external assistance may intensify internal resistance. Throughout his reign, Charles II covertly accepted subsidies from Louis XIV and adopted a pro-French foreign policy, contrary to the wishes of most of his (anti-Catholic) subjects as well as contrary to balance-of-power logic. Such external financial aid, Charles hoped, would help him increase the strength of the monarchy and make him more independent of parliament; this in turn would lay the groundwork for greater toleration for English Catholics. Instead, however, his subjects became increasingly suspicious of his designs. Their antagonism was directed primarily against Charles' Catholic brother and successor, James II, whom parliament tried to exclude from the throne and later overthrew in 1688. The outcome was a constitutional settlement in which parliamentary predominance and Protestantism were strengthened (H 6, 332–333 and *passim*).

(15) Excessive repression in a conquered country leads to more determined resistance rather than pacification. In 1304, Edward I of England gained control of Scotland, to which he had a feudal claim, after a bitter war. Edward then embarked on a harsh policy, including the abrogation of Scottish law and customs and the destruction of Scottish cultural monuments, with the aim of merging Scotland with England. Most strikingly, he hunted down and executed William Wallace, the "gallant" Scottish leader, in an effort to "overawe the Scots by an example of severity". However, "the barbarous policy of Edward failed of the purpose to which it was directed" (H 2, 135). The Scottish people, "inflamed with resentment", continued their opposition; and Wallace came to be "universally regarded as the champion of Scotland, and the patron of her expiring independency" (H2, 136). Edward's conquest was soon reversed under the leadership of Robert Bruce, who built on these elements to revitalize the national cause. Hume's account suggests that he believed a union of Scotland and England at this early date might have been beneficial to the former from the point of view of the progress of civilization. In this light, Edward's "barbarous" policy seems anomalous as well as misguided and ultimately perverse; presumably Hume thought

27 See chap. 4 in vol. 1 of the present work [Editors: Whelan, Frederick G. 2015. *Political Thought of Hume and His Contemporaries: Enlightenment Projects*, vol. 1. New York and London: Routledge].

other methods would have had a chance of succeeding, although civilized conduct was in short supply, Hume thought, in the early fourteenth century.

(16) In a similar vein, attempted governmental suppression of disorder by the use of insufficient force may provoke more disorder. Elizabeth, always frugal, stationed a thousand troops in Ireland to keep order among the native population, whom Hume describes as "rude" and implacably hostile to the English. "No wonder that such a force, so disproportioned to the object, instead of subduing a mutinous kingdom, served rather to provoke the natives, and to excite those frequent insurrections, which still farther inflamed the animosity between the two nations, and encreased the disorders, to which the Irish were naturally subject" (H 4, 313). In a case like this, the relation between the application of a remedy to a problem and alleviation of the problem is not linear; rather, the use of an insufficient amount of a potentially effective remedy makes the problem worse.

(17) A politician's attempt to win popularity by addressing popular grievances may stimulate complaints beyond his ability to satisfy them, leading to unpopularity or defeat. Around 1549, there were many discontents among the English common people stemming from the dissolution of the monasteries, enclosures, and general economic conditions. The Protector Somerset, who "loved popularity, and pitied the condition of the people, encouraged these complaints by his endeavors to redress them" (H 3, 370). In addition, as regent for the minor Edward VI, Somerset's position as effective ruler was tenuous, and he appears to have been trying to establish a base of support by taking up the popular cause against the interests, as Hume notes, of the gentry and nobility. He issued a proclamation announcing the reexamination of enclosures, whereupon the populace, "meeting with such countenance from government, began to rise in several places, and to commit disorders". When Somerset's commissioners met with resistance from the gentry, the common people, "being impatient for immediate redress, could no longer contain their fury, but sought for a remedy by force of arms". Serious insurrections broke out across the country, leading to opposition to Somerset in the council and eventually his forced resignation. In addition to being a case of a political strategy that backfired, this episode illustrates the analysis of the dangers of reform that is often associated with Tocqueville's account of the origins of the French Revolution: a reform program can be self-defeating if it raises expectations to a level that cannot be satisfied quickly enough, leading the intended beneficiaries to resort to more radical methods and thence (perhaps) to their defeat as well as that of the reforms.

(18) Revolutions result from the people's grievances against the regime in power but lead to even greater oppression on the part of the new regime: "It is seldom, that the people gain any thing by revolutions in government; because the

new settlement, jealous and insecure, must commonly be supported with more expence and severity than the old". Hume's central case here is the Parliamentary rebellion in the 1640s against the government of Charles I, who was held by his enemies to be a tyrant who was trying to eliminate English liberties. The people had been "roused" to arms by ship money (taxation not authorized by parliament) and the star-chamber (a secret inquisitorial court). Now (in 1648), with the king in captivity, parliament itself subdued by force, and a Puritan-led military government in control, "they found themselves loaded with a multiplicity of taxes, formerly unknown; and scarcely an appearance of law and liberty remained in the administration". Even before the military coup, taxes increased eightyfold as a consequence of the revolution, and power fell into the hands of county committees that "could sequester, fine, imprison, and corporally punish, without law or remedy" (H 5, 520, 55–503). Hume's observation anticipates the findings of modern students of revolution.[28] He suggests several explanations: the "insecurity" of the new regime, stemming from its illegitimacy, compels it to be repressive; the disorder (political and, in this case, religious) attending the initial rebellion stimulates more general disorder, which has to be quelled; and the regime is forced to use arbitrary methods to suppress counter-revolutionary opposition in significant sectors of society; and all of these requirements are much more costly than the routine business of government. Those who planned and executed the original rebellion against the king (the presbyterians) "were enraged to find the prize [...] snatched by violence from them" – that is, to have their expectations thwarted in these ways. In sum, Hume concludes, there was "never, in this island [...] a more severe and arbitrary government, than was generally exercised, by the patrons of liberty in both kingdoms" (H 5, 528).

(19) An attempt by a repressive government to orchestrate a show of popular support reinforces its opponents' belief that it is a tyranny. Hume describes the rule of the Duke of Lauderdale, Charles II's minister for Scotland, as being arbitrary and oppressive. Lauderdale summoned an apparently hand-picked assembly at Edinburgh, which "bestowed applause on all [his] administration and [...] expressed the highest contentment and satisfaction". Such complaisance, however, "had the contrary effect in England from what was expected by the contrivers". Opponents of Charles, who were watching Scottish developments suspiciously, concluded from the protestations of contentment that matters were

28 See, for example, Skocpol (1994) on how post-revolutionary regimes are frequently more authoritarian, bureaucratic, extractive, and generally oppressive than those they replaced.

even worse than they had supposed, that "the very voice of liberty was totally suppressed; and that, by the prevalence of tyranny, grievances were so rivetted, that it was become dangerous even to mention them". The absence of any complaints about government is incredible on its face and can be explained only by fear or manipulation. "From the slavery of the neighboring kingdom, they inferred the arbitrary disposition of the king" and the danger to their own liberties (H 6, 331). Insofar as the reassurance of English opinion was the intended objective, Lauderdale's exercise was overdone and hence self-defeating.

(20) Unreasonable resistance to the executive on the part of a representative assembly provokes more arbitrary methods of government by the ruler. Throughout the Tudor and early Stuart period, English monarchs convened parliament primarily to obtain revenue, since the appropriation of taxes was parliament's principal traditional power. With the gradual modernization of society and government during this period, royal requests for revenue steadily increased, and Hume judges them, by and large, to have been reasonable in light of changing circumstances and the increasing wealth of society.[29] Parliament, however, regularly resisted, partly out of stinginess but also from a jealous concern to protect its privileges and to resist royal authority. The frequent result was the resort by monarchs to arbitrary methods of raising or extorting money that actually posed a greater threat to constitutional government, liberty, and the position of parliament itself (and that produced open conflict in the 1640s). Under Henry VII, the "system of feudal law" was corrupted by the king's ministers to raise funds through oppressive fines and confiscations. In this "arbitrary and iniquitous administration", Hume says, the English

> were considerable losers by their ancient privileges, which secured them from all taxation, except such as were imposed by their own consent in parliament. Had the king been impowered to levy general taxes at pleasure, he would naturally have abstained from these oppressive expedients, which destroyed all security in private property (H 3, 67–68).

The "absurd parsimony" of Elizabeth's parliaments led the government to resort to forced loans, grants of monopolies, and debasement of the currency, all contrary to the true interests of the people represented in parliament (H 4, 373–374).

The final two statecraft examples concern inept attempts by rulers either to court popularity or to avoid antagonizing either side in a dispute.

---

29 Another cause of increasing nominal expenditures by government was inflation, which contemporaries could not reconcile with their sense of traditionally fixed obligations (H 5, 39–40).

(21) An oversupply of honors or rewards undermines the attempt to win support through their distribution. On assuming the throne of England, James I sought popularity by bestowing titles and knighthoods profusely on his new subjects. The consequence, however, was that the king, "by his lavish and premature conferring of favours, had failed of obliging the persons, on whom he bestowed them. Titles of all kinds became so common, that they were scarcely marks of distinction" (H 5, 5). Indeed, although the policy indicated the new king's "good nature", it undermined respect for his judgment. For this to qualify fully as a case of perverse effects, the excessive grants of new titles would have to have devalued all titles, including the preexisting ones, leading the king to be hated rather than loved (to use Machiavelli's terminology).[30]

(22) Attempts at compromise can please neither party and have the effect of exacerbating the conflict they were intended to defuse. Henry III became king of France in 1575 in the midst of religious civil wars between the Protestant Huguenots and the militants of the Catholic League. Not only was the country wracked by violence, but the position of the central government was weak, since both religious factions were led by powerful noblemen who had traditional provincial strongholds in addition to the loyalty of the religious zealots. Henry's strategy was to restore the authority of the crown and pacify the country by "acting as an umpire" between the warring parties and working out a compromise settlement based on some form of *de facto* religious toleration. Instead, he came to be distrusted by both sides, "lost the confidence of both, and taught the partizans of each to adhere still more closely to their particular leaders" (H 4, 168). Violence continued, and both the main Catholic leader and Henry himself were subsequently assassinated, as many Protestant leaders already had been. This episode suggests the difficulties of efforts to identify a middle way or compromise policy when conflicts are intense (or indeed, doctrinally non-compromisable): any proposal will antagonize both sides rather than placate them. Indeed, "the king's moderation" itself was "suspicious" to both factions. What Hume emphasizes is that Henry's strategy required him to conceal his own true beliefs, which especially aroused everyone's distrust; indeed, in a situation of religious fanaticism, any suggestion of dissimulation or indifference

---

30 In *The Prince* (any edition, cited by chapter, chap. 17), Machiavelli argues that attempts by a prince to rule by "love", or popularity, such as by conferring material benefits on his subjects, often backfire and produce the opposite effect. It is therefore better for the prince to rule by fear. The similarity between Machiavelli's teaching and the Humean analysis exemplifies the Machiavellianism that pervades Hume's political and historical writings, as documented in Whelan (2004).

about religious issues arouses hostility. It may be, as Hume suggests, that Henry "possessed all the talents of dissimulation" but lacked perseverance and other skills necessary for sustained negotiations. On the other hand, his "artifices" did not stand up well against "the plain, direct, and avowed conduct" of the religious leaders. To the extent that dissimulation is always required in the bargaining leading to a compromise, this may be a common reason for failure or perverse outcomes. This case is disturbing for Hume in that it undercuts his usual counsel of political moderation and compromise, while supporting Machiavelli's advice against the pursuit of middle ways.[31]

4 Policy

The following public policy examples fall into three main categories: population policies; religious laws and practices designed either to promote one religion or church or to suppress dissent from the established religion; and economic regulations, including commerce, taxation, credit, and the public debt.

Policies bearing on population fall under Hume's demographic interests, especially his investigation of the much-debated question of the population of ancient as compared with modern Europe and his interest in China – both prominent topics in Enlightenment thought.

(23) The "barbarous" custom of infanticide increases population pressure and the number of unwanted children in families, the opposite of its ostensible purpose. Hume conjectures that this effect came about through "an odd connexion of causes", both in the ancient world and in contemporary China. "By removing the terrors of too numerous a family, [this practice] would engage many people in marriage; and such is the force of natural affection, that very few, in comparison, would have resolution enough, when it came to the push, to carry into execution their former intentions" ("Of the Populousness of Ancient Nations", E 399).[32]

---

31 Hume frequently recommends and takes a stance as a political moderate, a position that is related both to his "moderate skepticism" in philosophy and his aversion to political or religious fanaticism. In two famous essays, "Of the Original Contract" and "Of Passive Obedience", for example, he criticizes doctrinaire versions of the two opposing English ideologies of his time, seeking common ground. On this issue (though not on the effective uses of dissimulation), Hume diverges from Machiavelli. See Whelan (2004, 133–136).

32 Ferguson (1995, 135) echoes Hume on this point, saying that the permissibility of infanticide, "like many other institutions, has an influence the reverse of what it seemed to portend".

(24) Foundling hospitals such as exist in modern European countries, where Christianity forbids infanticide, have the opposite intent: to preserve the lives of unwanted infants and thereby to promote the state's interest in the growth of a large and healthy population. These institutions too, however, exhibit perverseness when not strictly regulated. "Hospitals for foundlings seem favourable to the increase of numbers, [...] but when they open the door to everyone, without distinction, they have probably a contrary effect, and are pernicious to the state" ("Of the Populousness of Ancient Nations", E 400). One in nine children born in Paris, Hume states, is sent to the hospital, where the level of "health, industry, and morals" is lower than in private families, even though most of these children could have been cared for by their parents. (Other than the reference to "health", Hume does not mention the high mortality reported for foundling hospitals, the most direct evidence of a "contrary effect").[33]

A number of important cases of perverse effects have reference to religious policies and institutions. Many of Hume's examples are drawn from the history of religious conflict in Europe in the preceding two centuries and support the case for toleration.

(25) Religious persecution by state or ecclesiastical authorities intensifies religious dissent and the social disorder arising from religious dissension and sectarianism. Instances of this dynamic in Hume's *History* are numerous. For example, in an early episode of the English Reformation, the Bishop of London bought up and burned all the copies he could find of Tindal's initial English Bible, regarded as especially "dangerous to the established faith". This act not only "gave great scandal to the people" but provided Tindal with money to produce a new and better edition (H 3, 215). Ensuing persecution of Protestantism in the 1520s "served only to diffuse it the more among the people, and to inspire them with horror against the unrelenting persecutors" (H 3, 217). The violent persecution of Protestants during the brief reign of Mary demonstrated "folly" as well as "barbarity", according to Hume. Most observers were appalled at the executions, so that "each martyrdom, therefore, was equivalent to a hundred sermons against popery; and men either avoided such horrid spectacles, or returned from them full of a violent, though secret, indignation against the persecutors" (H 3, 437, 439). Indeed, such persecution "commonly proves ineffectual to the purpose intended; and serves only to make men more obstinate in their persuasions, and

33 In his analysis of population, Hume ("Of the Populousness of Ancient Nations", E 382, 387) draws upon other examples of counterintuitive causation, such as in his claims that plagues do not cause lasting depopulation and that it is not always in the interest of a master to allow propagation among his slaves.

to encrease the number of their proselytes" (H 3, 432–433).[34] The final result was the consolidation of anti-Catholicism in most of the English populace.

Hume observes that even more extensive persecutions in the Netherlands in the same period had the same effect of forwarding rather than checking the "progress of the new opinions" (H 3, 441). The ruler of the low countries in the first half of the sixteenth century, the Emperor Charles V, was a calculating prince, not a religious zealot, Hume suggests, who "purposed to augment his authority under pretence of defending the catholic faith". Nevertheless, his persecutions, "far from answering the purposes intended, had rather served to augment the numbers as well as the zeal of the reformers" (H 4, 152). This in turn brought about the revolt that culminated in the secession of the Netherlands from the Habsburg Empire, a revolt that was itself furthered by the cruelty of the Spanish attempts to suppress it (H 4, 170–172). Charles' acceptance of the doctrine that heresy leads to rebellion, whether genuine or feigned, led him to adopt policies that perversely rendered the doctrine self-fulfilling.

Following the Restoration of the monarchy and the established church in 1660, Charles II attempted to restore religious uniformity, not only in England but also in Scotland, where Calvinism remained strong. "The rigours exercised against the [illicit] conventicles", however, "instead of breaking the spirit of the fanatics, had tended only, as is usual, to render them more obstinate, to encrease the fervour of their zeal, to link them more closely together, and to inflame them against the established hierarchy" (H 6, 328). Charles's ongoing, if less dramatic, efforts to promote Catholicism in England, which he believed offered a stronger support for monarchy, actually undermined his other projects (H 6, 286). This spirit was among the factors that contributed to the Revolution of 1688 and the eventual victory of Presbyterianism in Scotland.

Hume's historical sensibility allows him to set forth the rationale for forcible attempts to impose religious orthodoxy in an era before anyone acknowledged a basic right to liberty of conscience or religious practice. Religious reformers threatened a "total subversion of ancient establishments". The clergy, "who found both their honours and properties at stake, thought they had a right to resist, by every expedient, these dangerous invaders". Rulers usually shared the view that civil order depended on a uniform religious establishment and homogeneity of faith, which were disrupted by heresy. The authorities, however, found

34 In this debate, Hume ironically attributes the argument for toleration to the good man and sincere Catholic, Cardinal Pole, and that for persecution to the "great minister", Stephen Gardiner, who was indifferent toward religious doctrine. The analysis undermines Gardiner's political greatness.

persecution to be a "precarious" remedy, at least when dissent had attained a critical mass, since "enthusiastic zeal" was "inflamed by punishment" and proved "contagious on the compassionate minds of the spectators" (H 3, 282; cf. 4, 19). If persecution to suppress dissent is often a perverse and self-defeating policy, the opposite policy of toleration paradoxically can have this very effect. "Open the door to toleration, mutual hatred relaxes among the sectaries; their attachment to their particular modes of religion decays; the common occupations and pleasures of life succeed to the acrimony of disputation" (H 3, 433). Hume upholds liberty of conscience as part of civil liberty more broadly, even though he is hostile to religious enthusiasm. His defense of a policy of toleration reflects not so much a belief in individual rights as a strategy for moderating the intensity of religious disagreements.[35] If toleration tends to induce religious indifference, this would be an unintended and detrimental effect for its religious advocates, but an intended though indirect and perhaps welcome result from the point of view of a Humean statesman.

(26) Witchcraft, like heresy, is a crime "which commonly encrease[s] by punishment, and never [is] so effectually suppressed as by being totally neglected" (H 4, 62). Elizabethan legislators observed a connection between "fantastical prophecies" and popular rebellions and disorder. Their judgment was not sound, however, in passing a law against "conjurations, enchantments, and witchcraft", the likely effect of which was to promote such superstitions.

(27) Although toleration may dampen the vitality of dissent, a policy of offering pardon to heretics (or perhaps dissidents more generally) may harden their resolve to persist in their offense rather than return to obedience. Several condemned dissenters under Henry VIII rejected a last-minute chance to obtain pardons by recanting, seeing "this offer as a new ornament to their crown of martyrdom" (H 3, 315). Perhaps equally important, Hume notes, the offer was made publicly. This may have been a mistake, as the public circumstances "interested their honour the more to maintain a steady perseverance".

(28) Rationality in religious worship encourages irrational fanaticism. The Protestant reformers rejected what they saw as useless and distracting ceremonies and pursued the apparently reasonable plan of instituting a mode of worship "that borrowed nothing from the senses; but reposed itself entirely on the contemplation of that divine Essence, which discovers itself to the understanding

35 His main strategy, however, combines a complacent established church with toleration, as is discussed in chap. 6 in vol. 1 of the present work [Editors: Whelan, Frederick G. 2015. *Political Thought of Hume and His Contemporaries: Enlightenment Projects*, vol. 1. New York and London: Routledge].

only" (H 5, 68). Human frailty is such, however, that "this species of devotion [...] was observed to occasion great disturbances in the breast, and in many respects to confound all rational principles of conduct and behavior". The rejection of "humaniz[ing]" ceremonies fostered a sullen, obstinate, and anti-social character that Hume regards as typical of Puritanism and that was presumably not intended by the original reformers.

(29) Those who attempt to promote and strengthen an established religion through pious endowments or governmental subsidies end by weakening it. Smith suggests two processes that have this effect. Endowments to support the education of clergymen, such as are commonly found in European countries, cause an oversupply of clergy relative to social need or demand, just as do any policies that artificially increase competition in any trade. This leads to "the church being crowded with people who, in order to get employment, are willing to accept of a much smaller recompence than what such an education would otherwise have entitled them to" (WN 146–147). Underpayment in turn produces a degraded condition among the clergy that is not advantageous to religion. This effect is perverse from the point of view of the intentions of those who seek to enhance religion in this way, not necessarily from the point of view of congregants or consumers of subsidized religion, although the product they get may be inferior.

Second, an endowed clergy, who are under little pressure to attract followers to generate income for themselves, tend to become indolent and lose touch with the people they are supposed to be serving. This is why an established church is often vulnerable to the loss of members to new and more energetic sects.[36] Thus those who seek to support a church by endowing it may ultimately destroy it (WN 788–789). The principal actors in this process may of course be the clergy themselves. Historically, Smith observes, religious and civil conflict have often coincided. The sect "which had the good fortune to be leagued with the

36 Hume defends established or endowed churches precisely in order to "bribe the indolence" of the clergy, as part of a strategy of reducing overall religious enthusiasm in society. If Smith is correct, however, Hume's strategy may fail in the long run, though Hume might still regard it as preferable to sectarian competition under conditions of complete religious liberty. Sectarianism, as the more energetic because more competitive form of religion, seems to win either way in this analysis, the basic terms of which Hume shares with Smith. The secular state also wins, since it is stronger than either an indolent established church or enthusiastic but fragmented sects. See chap. 6 in vol. 1 [Editors: Whelan, Frederick G. 2015. *Political Thought of Hume and His Contemporaries: Enlightenment Projects*, vol. 1. New York and London: Routledge)].

conquering party" naturally expected to share in the spoils of victory. "Their first demand was generally, that [the magistrate] should silence and subdue all their adversaries; and their second, that he should bestow an independent provision in themselves" (WN 792). In the latter demand they pursued their immediate interest in "ease and comfort" while neglecting the long-term detrimental effect this arrangement would have on their authority.

In referring to disequilibria in the supply of and demand for clergy, and in his assumption that a monopolistic or politically protected church will become unresponsive to the religious needs of the people, Smith applies his market model to religious life. The final examples of contrary effects, to which we now turn, pertain directly to economic life and policy, where both Hume and Smith see perverse effects as a frequent occurrence.

(30) Laws restricting the export of commodities deemed vital reduce rather than preserve the supply of these goods. (Promotion of exports, conversely and counterintuitively, increases the domestic supply). Under Henry VII "it was prohibited to export horses; as if that exportation did not encourage the breed, and render them more plentiful in the kingdom" (H 3, 78). Hume and Smith both observe that the French policy prohibiting the export of food in order to prevent famines actually caused food shortages and indeed "the frequent famines, which so much distress that fertile country" ("Of the Balance of Trade", E 309; see also WN 526–527). Hume opens his essay on the balance of trade, which sets forth the advantages of free international trade, with a general statement. Nations that are "ignorant of the nature of commerce" commonly try to prevent the export of things they especially value. "They do not consider, that, in this prohibition, they act directly contrary to their intention; and that the more that is exported of any commodity, the more will be raised at home, of which they themselves will always have the first offer" (E 308). Hume finds such ignorance to have been the rule in the outlook of most governments.

(31) Similarly, price controls designed to keep goods cheap and plentiful have the opposite effect. Again under Henry VII, "in order to promote archery no bows were to be sold at a higher price than six shillings and four-pence. […] The only effect of this regulation must be either that the people would be supplied with bad bows or none at all" (H 3, 78). Political pressure to control the price of food is especially strong during times of shortage; such attempts are "pernicious and destructive", however, worsening the shortage by removing the discipline and conservation, as well as productive incentives, induced by higher prices. "But in reality, the encrease of prices is a necessary consequence of scarcity; and laws, instead of preventing it, only aggravate the evil, by cramping and restraining commerce" (H 2, 177).

(32) Bounties or public subsidies for exports, which are designed to stimulate the export trade and benefit the producers of the exported goods, depress the economy overall and thus damage the position of the intended beneficiaries along with everyone else in the long run. Like its opposite, the restriction on exports mentioned above, this is a political intervention in the economy that backfires. The intent of bounties (such as that on grain in the English Corn Laws) is to make domestic products cheaper and thus more competitive in foreign markets. The effect of this policy, according to Smith, as with all the restrictions of the "mercantile system", is "to force the trade of a country into a channel much less advantageous than that in which it would naturally run of its own accord". Bounties raise the price of the subsidized goods in the home market and thus amount to a double tax on the people – the tax that pays the bounty and the surcharge on the goods when consumed. Higher prices hurt all consumers, but especially the laboring poor, and especially in the case of the corn bounty, since a rise in the price of food pushes all prices up. Since a bounty "diminishes the home, just as much as it extends the foreign market", it does not increase the real income of the producers; in fact, "its final tendency is to stunt and restrain the gradual extension of the home market" and reduce the overall quantity of the product consumed (WN 505–508).

(33) Restrictions on trading with a rival nation, such as are dictated by mercantilism or which arise simply from "jealousy" and "prejudice", aim to damage the rival but hurt one's own producers and consumers just as much.[37] English hostility toward France has led to policies intended to harm that country; as a result, "we lost the FRENCH market for our woollen manufactures", and, forced to buy wine from Spain and Portugal, "we buy worse liquor at a higher price" ("Of the Balance of Trade", E 315). Smith makes the general point more bluntly: "The unjust oppression of the industry of other countries" – often an objective of mercantilism with its zero-sum assumptions – "falls back, if I may say so, upon the heads of the oppressors, and crushes their industry more than it does that of those other countries". Even the attempt to "engross" or monopolize trade with one's colonies fails: after many attempts, the only thing that has been engrossed is the military expense of trying to enforce the policy (WN 627–628).

37 Such policies are strictly perverse only if they fail to harm one's rival (which is presumably not the case, if trade is mutually beneficial), or perhaps if they harm oneself more than the rival. Hume implies but does not say clearly that the latter is the case.

(34) The accumulation of gold and silver makes a country poorer over the long run. Mercantilist thought, seconded by common sense or intuition, equated bullion with wealth and dictated that a country amass as much of it as possible, especially in relation to the quantities held by rival states. Spanish access to American precious metals seemed to promise indefinite wealth and political greatness in the sixteenth century; by the eighteenth century, however, Spain was manifestly poor and weak relative to, say, Britain and the Netherlands. The need to explain this surprising, even paradoxical, fact was a major spur to the development of political economy. The most important point, emphasized repeatedly by both Hume and Smith, was that "industry" or productivity as embodied in the most extensive employment of increasingly specialized labor, not the possession of bullion, was the basis of wealth or prosperity (and indirectly of state power) correctly understood. Wealth in this sense, moreover, was increased by commerce, which stimulated demand for goods and facilitated the division and hence productivity of labor, rather than by mere accumulation or hoarding of any kind. In making these points, Hume and Smith frequently allude to the self-defeating consequences of mercantilist and colonial policies as practiced by Spain. In the first place, gold and silver are commodities and obey the law of supply and demand; hence, the more that is accumulated, the less valuable it becomes, especially where it is concentrated, relative to other goods (WN 219–220). The cheapness of gold and silver, "or what is the same thing, the dearness of all [other] commodities […] discourages both the agriculture and manufactures of Spain and Portugal" (WN 512). Since the major use of the precious metals is as money, its increasing supply has caused gradual, long-term inflation in Europe, which has stimulated production elsewhere, but a more rapid inflation of prices in the countries holding major stocks of bullion has left them in a worsening competitive position. Futile Spanish attempts to prevent the export of silver exacerbated the situation. For Hume, there is no surer way to "scatter our riches" than the "desire of amassing money" through restrictions on the free circulation and exchange of money and goods ("Of the Balance of Trade", E 324).

The sobering but highly instructive story of the rise and fall of Spain resembles another case of historical perversity – or tragedy – on a grand scale that was well known to all. Rome, in its quest for glory, conquered an empire that, especially in Asia, generated wealth that came back to corrode the civic and martial virtues of the Romans themselves, causing first the downfall of the republic and eventually the collapse of the empire. The Roman story was usually framed as a moral discourse of virtue and corruption, while Spanish imperial policy was assessed in the eighteenth century in the perspective of political economy. What the two stories share is the perverse – and of course unanticipated – nature of empire, at least in the long run, undertaken as a means to national greatness.[38]

(35) Politically influential groups that try to engineer economic policy to advance their special interests hurt themselves in the long run by lowering the overall prosperity of the country. This point is a political counterpart to the preceding and is an important component of the political science that accompanies the economic analysis in the *Wealth of Nations*. The Corn Laws and other interventionist or protectionist policies, according to Smith, are not random or neutral in their (intended) impact, as they might be if they simply reflected ignorance of political economy; rather, they are implemented through the special political influence of distinct groups with a conception of their own distinct interests. Thus the Corn Laws (both those offering bounties on exports and those restricting imports) reflected the power of the landlord class in parliament and were designed to increase the landlords' real income.[39] As we have seen, they failed to achieve this result. In fact, the only group that may really have benefited was the corn merchants in the import-export trade, a group the landlords did not set out to assist.

The "country gentlemen" here, in their self-defeating actions, are the victims of the "prejudices" of the mercantilist outlook, a system that understands wealth to arise from exportation rather than from production; they therefore "did not act with that compleat comprehension of their own interest" that is more often found among the commercial classes (WN 514–516). In this, they resemble their medieval predecessors as these appear in Smith's analysis of laws adverse to the rights of tenants. "The proprietors of land were antiently the legislators of every part of Europe. The laws relating to land, therefore, were all calculated for what they supposed the interest of the proprietor". By creating disincentives for tenants to invest in improvement of the land, however, the laws enacted actually "hurt in the long-run the real interest of the landlord" (WN 393). Book III of *The Wealth of Nations* as a whole narrates how medieval landlords acted (rationally) to shore up their privileges to maintain their political power, but in so doing obstructed the development of agriculture and thereby fell behind the growing wealth of the

38 Hume dissents from the classical thesis with respect to the fall of the Roman republic, arguing that its political institutions were inadequate for governing an empire ("Of Refinement in the Arts", E 275–276). See further in chap. 6 below [Editors: Whelan, Frederick G. 2015. *Political Thought of Hume and His Contemporaries: Enlightenment Projects*, vol. 2. New York and London: Routledge].

39 For a list of economic interests and interest groups that influence public policy in *The Wealth of Nations*, sometimes with perverse effects, see Stigler (1975, 238–239).

towns, which eventually challenged their position. Smith comments that "avarice and injustice are both short-sighted". Indeed, in both of these cases as in others that Smith describes, we have an unjust exercise of political power by a privileged group; the power is exercised, however, in a misguided fashion that leads to results that are perverse for the privileged group and generally detrimental for society.

(36) Policies that try to promote one sector of the economy (such as agriculture) by imposing artificial restraints on other sectors (such as manufacturing and commerce) not only fail but depress the favored sector as well. Hume and Smith agree that agriculture and manufacturing, rather than being in conflict (as many thought), are mutually reinforcing. The prospering of manufacturing towns provides a growing market for food, which raises the production and prices of agricultural commodities, increases agricultural employment, and raises the value of land and rents; at the same time, the exchange of manufactured goods for food raises the rural standard of living and stimulates the further development of manufacture. Therefore, systems of political economy "which preferring agriculture to all other employments, in order to promote it, impose restraints upon manufacturing and foreign trade, act contrary to the very end which they propose, and indirectly discourage that very species of industry which they mean to promote" (WN 686). The "inconsistency" or perversity in such policies, Smith remarks, is even more glaring – in his analysis, though not in the prevailing view at the time – than those of the mercantilist system. Hume describes a historical case in the restrictions imposed on apprenticeship and manufacturing under Henry VII. "These absurd limitations proceeded from a desire of promoting husbandry, which however is never more effectually encouraged than by the encrease of manufactures" (H 3, 79).

(37) Excessively high taxes bring in less revenue than would more moderate taxes as a result of their depressive effect on production or consumption. Hume observes that "if the duties on wine were lowered to a third, they would yield much more to the government than at present" as well as allowing people to drink "better and more wholesome liquor" ("Of the Balance of Trade", E 324–325). High taxes thus both defeat the government's revenue-raising purpose in taxing and bring other unfortunate and unintended consequences. This example bears out Hume's observation that in tax policy, we find "what frequently happens in political institutions, that the consequences of things are diametrically opposite to what we should expect on the first appearance" ("Of Taxes", E 347).

(38) An undisciplined public debt, incurred to expand a state's power, ends by undermining it. Like many in eighteenth-century Britain, both within and outside the classical republican discourse, Hume and Smith deplored the apparently

inexorable growth of the relatively novel British debt. The institution of the debt was developed by Whig politicians, financiers, and investors primarily to finance Britain's wars against France, and British victories and imperial acquisitions attained on this basis apparently proved it a great success.[40] A sound system of "public credit" based on the monied class's confidence in the government seemed to be the hallmark of a successful modern state – and a weakness of a monarchy like France. Hume, however, thought that the availability of credit tempted politicians to embark on unnecessary wars and imperial adventures, stirring up dangerous chauvinism in the process. At the same time, the popularity of deferring the costs of such expensive exploits meant that the debt would go on expanding until it became unsupportable and finally ended in a disastrous public bankruptcy. More particularly, seemingly limitless public credit is enjoyed by free governments (like Great Britain), where the confidence of lenders in the government reflects the fact that they enjoy representation in the legislature; the ultimate collapse of the financial system, however, may well lead to the destruction of free institutions themselves ("Of Public Credit", E 349–365).[41] Smith says more moderately that "the practice of funding has gradually enfeebled every state which has adopted it. [...] Is it likely that in Great Britain alone a practice, which has brought either weakness or desolation into every other country, should prove altogether innocent?" (WN 928).

(39) Private credit stimulates investment or consumption and thus economic development, but if it is too "liberal" it can ruin all those involved, both the lenders and the borrowers. Smith describes the career of the Ayr bank, the ostensibly generous lending policy of whose "projectors" was motivated (he implies) by a combination of a private profit motive and Scottish public spiritedness. "The operations of this bank seem to have produced effects quite opposite to those which were intended by the particular persons who planned and directed it. [...] instead of relieving, in reality [they] aggravated in the long-run the distress which those projectors had brought both upon themselves and upon their country" (WN 314–315). The goal had been to make credit available for rapid

40 British "republicans" or "commonwealthmen" opposed the debt along with the corrupt politics, the impact of financial interests, and commercial wars with which they associated it. Hume and Smith stood outside this tradition, but their view of the debt was one point of overlap. The greatest increase in the debt occurred during the Seven Years' War (1756-1763), after Hume's (1752) essay on the subject, but before Smith's remarks in the *Wealth of Nations*. For details, see Laursen and Coolidge (1994).

41 See Hont (1993).

economic development in Scotland; instead, fortunes were lost and development presumably distorted when the bank failed.[42]

(40) The legal prohibition of usury (the charging of rates of interest deemed excessively high in a normative sense) increases the interest rate rather than keeping it down. As Smith explains, people sometimes must borrow money, but no one will lend it at much below its value (as determined by other investment opportunities in the local economy). If the official rate is set at an artificially low level, borrowers will simply have to pay more, since the rate charged will have to cover the risks incurred by the lender in conducting an illegal transaction – "the difficulty and danger of evading the law" – as well as the cost of the money itself (WN 112, 356–357). Here as in other cases, laws that work against economic forces will naturally be evaded, a circumstance that Smith reports in neutral tones. Hence, laws against usury make usury worse.

(41) Alms-giving increases rather than relieves need. Giving alms to beggars, Hume remarks, is "naturally praised; because it seems to carry relief to the distressed and indigent". On a larger view, however, it evidently encourages "idleness and debauchery" and thus the perpetuation of poverty (EPM 11/Enq 180).[43]

(42) Oppression of conquered countries increases the degradation and worsens disorders among the population, thus intensifying the difficulties of colonial government. A number of passages in Hume's *History* allude to the misgovernment of Ireland, a situation exacerbated by what today would be termed ethnic prejudice and the cultural differences between the English and Irish nations. During the reign of Elizabeth, especially, "rapine and insolence inflamed the hatred, which prevailed between the conquerors and the conquered: Want of security among the Irish, introducing despair, nourished still more the sloth, natural to that uncultivated people" (H 4, 311). The disincentives to productive activity contributed to Ireland's inability to generate revenue, and rebellions (such as Tyrone's in this passage) were chronic.

---

42 On this episode, see Phillipson (2010, 206–207).

43 See Chiswick (1989, 9–10) on the consistency of Hume's views on this matter. The perverse nature of indiscriminate charity was to become a more pronounced concern in the 1790s, when it was combined with Malthusian demography. Kames, however, made the same point in *Sketches of the History of Man* (1774, vol. II, 224): "Undistinguished charity to the deserving and undeserving" poor only multiplies the poor.

5 Interpretations

Hume's and Smith's descriptions of numerous cases of perverse effects and their analysis of the faulty reasoning that is responsible may be put in perspective by considering some recent interpretations of these and related phenomena in the work of Boudon, Merton, Hirschman, and Hayek.[44]

Perverse composition effects of collective action. The term "perverse effects" that has been used throughout this chapter as a synonym for what Hume often calls "contrary" effects is borrowed from the work of Boudon.[45] Perverse effects can sometimes be explained in terms of defective reasoning on the part of unitary actors, whether individuals, governments, or compact groups with shared goals. Boudon's version of perverse effects pertains to a different kind of case and provides a different explanation, one in which the perverseness appears in the "effect of composition" of the actions of many individuals acting independently of one another, but in ways that are causally interconnected. Each individual undertakes a line of action rationally calculated to attain some end or satisfy some interest of his own; the combined effect, when many people act in the same way, defeats their purposes and brings about an outcome that worsens their situation or is even directly the opposite of what they intended. Since none foresaw or factored in the actions of the others, this is (like the other cases considered) an example of unanticipated consequences of purposive action (Merton), but of a negative or pernicious type.

Boudon's perverse composition effects are of general theoretical interest for two reasons. First, they closely resemble the suboptimal outcomes that occur in some game-theory models, especially the collective-action problem. In a weak sense, this is true of the positive version of this problem, in which individuals desire to provide themselves with a collective good but fail to do so because of each individual's judgment of his own best course, whether this involves the hope of free-riding or the lack of assurance about the intentions of the others.[46]

---

44 Another candidate would be Rosen (1996), who attempts to connect unintended consequences to false consciousness, on the ground that they involve people's acting against their true interests. Intentions are not the same as interests, however, and they do not help us in the problematic identification of "true" interests.

45 Boudon (1982 [1977], 14) uses "perverse effects" to denote unintended effects that are undesirable and at variance with the actor's objectives, not necessarily in the stricter sense of the opposite of those intentions.

46 Boudon discusses Olson's *Logic of Collective Action* as a contribution to the theory of perverse effects in *Unintended Consequences* (1982 [1977], 29–36).

This is a perverse effect for Boudon but is not strictly an example as the term is used here, since the participants merely fail to acquire a good and remain where they were. Negative collective-action problems – the failure to avoid a collective bad through concerted action – are more on the mark. In the tragedy of the commons (to use the best-known example), each individual intends to fatten his cows and increase his herd by grazing them on the common pasture, but when every eligible person does this, in the absence of authoritative regulation, the common resource is degraded and all the cows starve, leaving the owners below their original baseline. This is a true perverse effect, since each achieves the opposite of what was intended, but one that comes about as a composition effect of many uncoordinated but interdependent decisions.

Second, this version of perverse effects is especially important because it is the direct opposite of Smith's invisible-hand argument, in which it is the combined and unintended result of numerous individual actions in a market that exhibits a beneficial social outcome, one that makes most of the participants and the nation as a whole better off. The individual-actor cases given above show that the Scottish theory of unintended consequences was not always benign, as some commentators have thought. Hayek's influential theory of spontaneous order, however, involves benign composition effects understood as the undesigned products of multiple individual choices without authoritative imposition. This theory is contradicted by the occurrence of negative collective-action situations viewed as the unintended consequence of rational individual choices.

Returning to the eighteenth-century works, the incident of James I's knighthoods (example 21) can be understood, from the viewpoint of the recipients, as a negative composition effect. Each individual reasonably expected to raise his social status by acquiring a knighthood, paying whatever cost this may have involved, but when many pursued the same objective, their goals were defeated. Instead of a collective-action problem, this case is best seen as one involving positional goods, whose value for their possessors depends on their elevation above non-possessors; the value of positional goods like honors or prestige is negated when many acquire them. For James the effect of his policy was perverse, in that his largesse provoked resentment rather than popularity; for the new knights, the effect was at least negative, and perverse if the marginal value of their enhanced position exceeded the price they paid.

This example resembles a case of special interest to Boudon. The expansion of education, both secondary and university, in France in the 1950s-1960s promised upward mobility to many young people from different levels of French society; the net result, however, was disappointment (contributing to the unrest of 1968) when it became apparent that a degree was not as valuable as before, that there were not enough higher social positions to accommodate all who tried to seize this opportunity, and that greater educational equality did not lead to greater social equality. Higher degrees, like knighthoods, are positional goods, valuable through their scarcity. The composition effect of expanded education was a higher cost of improving or even maintaining one's social position. A more general case is the "logic of relative frustration": the efforts of many people to achieve happiness through increased material plenty fail, and may even produce increased dissatisfaction, either because of unpleasant side effects such as competition and envy (as noted by Rousseau), or rising expectations and its corollary, relative deprivation (as noted by Tocqueville), or because the happiness sought proves to be a positional good, or through some other mechanism.[47]

Another case that can be explained as a variant composition effect is that of the foundling hospitals (example 24). The actor who provided these institutions was the government, whose policy objective was to save lives and thereby increase the state's population. If only a few parents of unwanted children had availed themselves of the hospitals, the scheme would have worked. When many did, each following the same individual incentives, the hospitals were swamped and high mortality resulted. This outcome was perverse in relation to the purposes of the government, but it came about through the combined actions of others – people whose behavior was elicited by the government's policy. It was also perverse from the parents' point of view if they hoped and expected that their children would survive.

Two other cases from Hume and Smith may be understood as involving perverse composition effects as well as other possible explanations. The excesses and overreaching of the Church that provoked the Reformation (example 10) may perhaps be seen as reasonable attempts by individual prelates to main appropriate ecclesiastical dignity, yet the overall popular impression, when they all followed this course, was one of extravagance and putative corruption, leading to their downfall. There may also have been a positional-goods effect

47 On education and social mobility, see Boudon, *Unintended Consequence* (1982 [1977], 16–29 and chap. 4); and his *L'inégalité des chances* (1973). The term "logic of relative frustration" and some of these mechanisms are from Boudon (1982 [1977], chap. 5).

here, if the overall level of extravagance was pushed up by each prelate's desire to outdo his peers. In example (12), smaller states seek security in the face of the danger posed by a rising power. Each seeks safety through an alliance with the larger state, with the joint result that they are all less secure than before under the now dominant power. Hume of course argues that the more (collectively) rational course of action would have been to form an opposing, balancing alliance, although doing so would have entailed overcoming the difficulties of collective action.

Perversity through reflexive prediction. A second perspective relates perverse effects to the concept of reflexive prediction in social life. This holds that a prediction of the future behavior of certain actors (or sometimes of an institution), if promulgated, can affect the behavior in question, or the behavior of other actors, causing it to be different from what it would have otherwise been. The prediction, by virtue of its own causal impact on what it purports merely to predict, can then either be self-fulfilling or self-defeating, depending on the motivations elicited by the prediction. The prediction may, through being publicized, become a social fact to which many people respond spontaneously, or it may reflect beliefs held by an influential actor (a government), who makes policies that alter the behavior of others. In either case, reflexive prediction is generally combined with composition effects to produce the perverse outcomes.[48]

A clear and well-known case of a self-fulfilling prediction from modern economic life is the run-on-the-bank phenomenon. If everyone comes to expect – that is, to believe a prediction – that the bank will fail, they will all try to withdraw their money at once, thereby causing the bank to fail.[49] A prediction that might have been false becomes true by virtue of its own causal power. This scenario involves a perverse composition effect as well as a self-fulfilling expectation,

48 The *locus classicus* for this idea is Merton, "The Self-Fulfilling Prophecy" (1949), although he calls it the "Thomas theorem" in recognition of a predecessor. Merton refers to predictions, prophecies, and "definitions of the situation" as equivalent concepts. He treats only self-fulfilling, not self-defeating (or what he terms "suicidal") predictions, and he does not relate the idea to composition or perverse effects. It is clear that Hume understood the logic of a self-fulfilling prophecy. Although it is not a perverse-effects case, Hume narrates the execution of a Scottish heretic who prophesied the downfall of his persecutor and remarks that "This prophecy was probably the immediate cause of the event which it foretold" (H 3, 340).

49 Boudon (1982 [1977], 3) mentions this case as a perverse effect but does not pursue this theme.

since the outcome that is bad for all occurs as the collective result of behavior that is rational for each individual in light of available information, including the prediction. Smith's analysis of the collapse of the Ayr bank (example 39) offers a similar case. Smith provides information on how the crisis developed: in competition with Edinburgh banks, and from a patriotic desire to further Scottish development, the bank extended easy credit to "projectors"; as these would-be entrepreneurs fell increasingly into debt, the bank's position became more and more exposed. Smith does not refer to a run of depositors, but at some point, the bank's creditors lost confidence in its solvency and the bubble burst. Again, the belief that the bank was about to fail was at least the immediate cause of its failure, whatever its prospects might otherwise have been.

Another modern application of the theory of reflexive predictions is central to an explanation of racial or ethnic prejudice and its effects. If members of an "out-group" are believed and expected by the majority to have certain undesirable characteristics, they may acquire or retain these characteristics as a consequence of the prejudicial treatment they receive. Here the prediction is self-fulfilling with respect to the behavior of the out-group, but not because they believe the prediction; rather, the conduct of the in-group, who accept the truth of their own prediction, is the crucial intervening variable.[50] Hume's account of the relations between the English and Irish in the sixteenth century conforms to this analysis (example 42). The English were the dominant group in a conquest regime (an "ill-judged tyranny") and held the Irish in contempt as a nation. Denied legal security, the Irish avoided the English-held cities and

> sheltered themselves in their marshes and forests from the insolence of their inhuman masters. Being treated like wild beasts, they became such; and joining the ardor of revenge to their yet untamed barbarity, they grew every day more intractable and more dangerous (H 4, 311).[51]

---

50 Self-fulfilling prejudice in US race relations is Merton's main practical concern in "The Self-Fulfilling Prophecy" (1949). Blacks were excluded from white-run unions on the grounds that they acted as strike-breakers, lacked collective-bargaining discipline, and accepted low wages, behavior that of course was the effect of their exclusion from the unions. The self-fulfilling prophecy set up an ongoing vicious circle. "In-group" and "out-group" are Merton's terms.

51 In this passage, Hume considers Irish sloth and barbarity only in part the self-confirming effects of English beliefs about and consequent treatment of them. They also reflect the low level of civilizational development in Ireland at that time according to Scottish historiography, an anomaly in Europe that Hume does not explain. A similar self-fulfilling prediction comes from the eighteenth-century British Empire: imperial rulers who accepted the theory of oriental despotism ruled arbitrarily in accordance

A number of other cases may be interpreted as illustrations of perverse effects of reflexive predictions. Both James I and Charles I believed that certain dissidents would prove dangerous to their rule (examples 3, 4); this belief caused them to adopt policies that backfired, provoking or facilitating the dangerous behavior, hence fulfilling the kings' predictions. That they chose opposite strategies brings out a (Humean) complexity in assigning causality (two different causes may produce the same effect) and thereby a difficulty for rulers or policy-makers, whose avoidance of perverse effects depends on correct reasoning.[52] Example (5) has the same structure: mistrustful or hostile treatment of a political rival or a potential opponent out of a prediction (whether true or false) that he will be an enemy may have the effect of converting him into an actual enemy.[53] Similarly, Louis XIV's belief that the Huguenots would endanger the French state led to their expulsion, with the perverse result that they did increase the dangers faced by France by contributing their skills to countries of the anti-French coalition (example 6). A popular belief that the ruler is or is becoming a tyrant causes him to become one, or more of one, as he takes forceful measures to guard against rebellion and tyrannicide (example 13). In premodern monarchies, opponents of the king were deemed and treated as rebels, who in turn anticipated the worst from the ruler in a vicious circle of self-fulfilling expectations.[54] In the movement of international relations, small states can predict that a more powerful state is growing stronger and thus more dangerous, and they may accordingly seek

---

with its maxims, thereby promoting despotic habits and institutions in Asia. See Whelan (1996, 244).

52 Reflexivity poses a difficulty for social science that aspires to predict human phenomena, as well as for policy-makers who utilize such predictions. At another level, science, which predicts the future course of events, is opposed by policy, which seeks to alter it.

53 Paradigm cases of self-fulfilling predictions, like the run on the bank, involve a number of people whose behavior is changed by the prediction, and thus usually a composition effect. The cases in this paragraph involve a self-fulfilling belief on the part of a single actor (a ruler or government), although this brings about a collective effect. Merton (1949, 423) observes that a self-fulfilling prophecy can occur within a single person (a student's examination anxiety) or between two parties (two nations whose assessments of each other's intentions lead to war).

54 Sabl, *Hume's Politics* (2012, chap. 3), argues that this dynamic was resolved only by the growth of constitutionalism, which restrained the king's power in predictable ways. Benign and system-stabilizing self-fulfilling predictions attended the emergence of limited government and a loyal opposition.

protection – if they neglect balance-of-power logic – by becoming its allies, thus fulfilling the prediction by adding to its power (example 12).

Finally, we should recall that reflexive prediction may take the negative form of self-defeating predictions: a prediction, when disseminated or embodied in a policy, may create incentives that cause people to act in ways that invalidate the prediction or frustrate the policy based on it. Hume and Smith provide a number of cases in which actors, mainly rulers, bring about perverse effects through this mechanism. In the case of religious persecution (example 25), the policy of persecution entails a prediction that sufficiently harsh repression will cause heresy to disappear. Although this may be true, Hume suggests, in "the first beginnings of heresy" (H 3, 432), this prediction is self-defeating once the number of heretics has reached a critical mass, both because persecution hardens the resolve of the heretics and because it arouses the sympathy of onlookers in their favor, and the net effect is the contrary of what was intended. The psychological processes at work here would appear perverse in another sense – that is, irrationally obstinate – to the official agents of persecution.

When persecution of witches has the effect of increasing the incidence of witchcraft (example 26), the logic is similar, although the cessation of persecution does not normally cause religious dissent to die out, as Hume says it does in the case of witches. With witchcraft, however, reflexive prediction may play a causal role even without persecution. If people widely believe in witchcraft and expect evil spells to be cast, some individuals will conform to this expectation by casting such spells, and occasional misfortunes will confirm the truth of the belief in many people's minds.

The motivating prediction made by benefactors that their endowments will strengthen charitable institutions is self-defeating insofar as it induces complacency and inefficiency in the institutions' operations (example 29). Inept interference in the marketplace, finally, is based on erroneous predictions reflecting ignorance of political economy. Thus prohibitions on the export of horses or grain appear naively to be means toward assuring more of these commodities in the kingdom, while capping the price of bows is expected to make them available to more people (examples 30, 31). The less obvious market feedback relation between demand and prices on the one hand and levels of production on the other, which shape the incentives of market actors, render these predictions self-defeating and the policy effects perverse.

Alleged perversity as ideology. In a third perspective, Hirschman has discussed "the *perversity thesis* or thesis of the perverse effect" as a recurrent feature of what he terms the "rhetoric of reaction".[55] Ever since the French Revolution and Burke's impressively prophetic argument that the radical quest for liberty and

55 Hirschman (1991, 7).

equality would culminate instead in terror and tyranny, reactionary or conservative thinkers are said frequently to have deployed the notion of perverse effects to oppose attempts at social reform.[56] The perversity thesis, according to Hirschman, holds that "any purposive action to improve some feature of the political, social, or economic order only serves to exacerbate the condition one wishes to remedy", or more precisely, that purportedly progressive reforms "will produce, via a chain of unintended consequences, the *exact contrary* of the objective being proclaimed and pursued".[57]

A notable feature of Hirschman's book is that he makes no effort to assess the substance or validity of any particular example of a perverse-effects argument, but rather confines himself to its pervasiveness and effectiveness in conservative rhetoric. By calling the idea "rhetoric", however, he implicitly denies its analytic uses and force. This is problematic for Burke, who applies such an argument to revolution but not to reform in general,[58] which he explicitly approves, and doubly problematic for such relatively detached thinkers as Hume and Smith. Hirschman concedes, however, that the effectiveness of the rhetoric stemmed originally from the dramatic fulfillment of Burke's warnings about the Revolution: rhetorical claims would be empty if they lacked any empirical support.[59] Nevertheless, Hirschman treats the perversity theme exclusively

---

56 Hirschman protests that he uses the term "reactionary" in its literal, neutral sense, or as merely synonymous with conservative. He doth protest too much; however, his protests indicate his obvious awareness of the word's contentiousness.

57 Hirschman (1991, 7, 11). Well before Hirschman, Barry pointed to "anti-rationalist conservatism", which he also traced to Burke and found in Oakeshott, as "*the* conservative argument". Barry endorses a limited version of the theory in *Political Argument* ([1990 (1965)], 56–57).

58 A perversity argument is not even generally true of Burke's analysis of revolution in his *Reflections on the Revolution in France* (1968), which contains a defense of the English Revolution of 1688 as a counterpart to the critique of the French Revolution.

59 If Hayek is correct that a free society must evolve as a spontaneous order, then Burke was correct to view the revolutionary attempt to design and impose liberty on France as both a misguided form of rationalism and an essentially authoritarian project from the outset. In addition to the perverse-effects analysis, Burke's critique of the revolutionary "metaphysicians" may be compared with Elster's (1989, 17) notion of "hyperrationality", the failure to attain an end through utilizing means that are superficially rational but actually incompatible with the objective, or "the irrational belief in the omnipotence of reason". See also Tieffenbach (2002) who contrasts Burke's view of evolved institutions as a "spontaneous order" with the "methodical anarchy" (Burke's term) inherent in the revolution. *Contra* Hirschman, however, she argues that this

as part of an ideological response to reform movements on the part of their opponents in the post-Burkean world. As we have seen, Hume and Smith attribute perverse effects in some cases to ideological thinking on the part of political actors (including revolutionaries), and there is of course no reason why the invocation of perverse effects could not form part of a counter-ideological reaction or critique. In treating it as he does, it is clear that Hirschman doubts the validity of the perverse-effects argument in many or most cases, especially since it has become (he says) a cliché of conservatism. The more general idea of unintended consequences of action, which was "magisterially" elaborated during the Scottish Enlightenment, has been a major contribution to social science, but the inordinate focus on the special case of perverse effects tells us more about the political motives of certain thinkers than about the social world.[60]

One difficulty with Hirschman's argument in light of the findings of this chapter is his claim that the perversity thesis dates only from the French Revolution. He grants that Burke was probably influenced by earlier Scottish theorists, but says that prior to the Revolution, the concept of unintended consequences appeared only in "invisible-hand" arguments, in which self-interested and local actions combine to yield unforeseen benign social outcomes.[61] The rhetorical brilliance of Burke, de Maistre, and their successors lay in their inverting this argument into the perversity thesis. In a subsequent essay, Hirschman repeats this historical claim (which is important to his perception of the perversity thesis as inherently reactionary) even more strongly: "It was only with the experience of the French Revolution that the idea of unintended consequences [...] came to stand for a process in the course of which well-intentioned human actions have an undesirable or disastrous social outcome".[62] The cases from Hume and Smith that

outcome was not, for Burke, a perverse effect of a benevolent intervention but rather the result of a malignant conspiracy (Tieffenbach 2002, 198).

60 Hirschman (1991, 35–36; and also 1995, 50). Hirschman says that the perversity thesis is invoked so regularly by conservatives that it is unlikely that it could be pertinent in so many cases. To this one might respond that neither Burke nor anyone else (except maybe De Maistre) has held that *all* political interventions aiming at reform will backfire. In accusing conservatives of exaggerating the frequency of perverse effects, Hirschman exaggerates the frequency of their use of this rhetorical device. Further, this charge of an automatic response clearly has no relevance to Hume and Smith: as we have seen, they provide quite a few examples of perversity, but they also point to beneficial unintended consequences as well as other kinds of explanations of historical processes.

61 All of Hirschman's references to Smith are to this effect; he does not cite Hume.

62 Hirschman (1995, 47).

have been surveyed here surely compel a backdating of the origins of this kind of social analysis. The appearance of such arguments in the middle of the eighteenth century, moreover, prior to the polarizing experience of the French Revolution, would seem to force us to reject Hirschman's claim that the theory of unintended consequences underwent a seismic shift, from an assumption of usually positive to usually negative outcomes, as an ideological consequence of that upheaval. In fact, the Scottish Enlightenment theorists drew upon variations of unintended consequences in their quest for social and historical understanding. They did not deploy their theories to support a single-minded attitude to history and change, either optimistic or pessimistic.[63]

Once we see that arguments about perverse effects go back (at least) to Hume and Smith, another problem emerges from Hirschman's treatment of such arguments as reactionary and as having a politically conservative orientation. Hume and Smith do not seem to have been reacting against anything comparable to the reform movements that Hirschman sees as provoking modern conservatives. Hume's uses of the idea cover a wide diversity of cases and occur mostly in his *History*, where they extend from episodes in Anglo-Saxon England (in which Hume can scarcely have had a polemical interest) to his own time. The recognition of the perversity in various misguided policies in many of his examples, however, would appear to serve long-term progressive or liberal reform. Smith more consistently writes in opposition to certain practices, such as mercantilist policies and educational endowments, but his perspective is generally that of an analytic and reasonably detached economic historian, as when he surveys the effects of the Spanish bullionist policy over several centuries. Perverse effects, like the more general conception of unanticipated consequences, are primarily a contribution to historical understanding and social science. However, if Hume and Smith may generally be said to be reacting against something in their use of perverse effects, it is not newly proposed reforms but long-established policies and institutions, or policies based on long-established beliefs, as well as illiberal practices such as religious persecution and arbitrary restrictions on free trade. This stance seems to be, if anything, more reformist or progressive than conservative, much less "reactionary" in the modern sense of the word. "In

63 As we shall see below, Hume and Smith sometimes employ the argument as part of their advocacy of reform of established practices. The Scottish discovery of unintended consequences may have prepared the way for Hirschman's reactionaries, but this was not the Scots' intent. Indeed, we might say that the later reactionary use of the perversity thesis was itself a perverse effect of the introduction of this theory for mostly progressive purposes by Hume and Smith.

the conduct of public affairs", Hume says, "nothing can be of more use than to improve, by practice, the method of reasoning on these [political and economic] subjects, which of all others are the most important" ("Of Interest", E 304). By identifying the errors of reasoning that lead to perverse results, Hume in particular seems to be attempting to improve the quality of political thinking so that statesmen will be better able to foresee the consequences of their policies, an accomplishment that could lead to more successful reform efforts.

If we examine the cases cited in this chapter in light of Hirschman's argument, we get the following results. Several of the Hume-Smith applications of the perversity thesis indeed seem conservative in the common modern sense of the word. These include those that point to the self-defeating character of leniency in the punishment of criminals (example 10),[64] of attempts to reform provincial administration (example 11), of popular rebelliousness and revolutionary doctrines (example 13), of attempted suppression of insurgency with inadequate force (example 16), of attempts to remedy popular grievances (example 17), of overly rationalistic approaches to religious worship (example 28) and, as with Burke, of revolution itself (example 20).[65] A larger number of cases, however, can readily be characterized as reflecting a liberal orientation. These include those that point to perverse effects stemming from governmental attempts to suppress political dissidents (examples 3, 4), from hostile treatment or persecution of political opponents (examples 5, 8), from the expulsion of a non-conforming minority from a state (example 6), from attacks by a ruler on an apparently vulnerable would-be reformer (example 7), from excessive repression in a conquered country and the attempt to stamp out local customs (example 15), from the attempt by a repressive regime to manipulate a show of popular support (example 21), from religious persecution in all of its forms (example 25), and from the criminalization of a misguided but harmless – or imaginary – activity like witchcraft (example 26). Some cases are impossible to classify on the liberal-conservative spectrum. The more interesting of these concern the dangers of appeasement (example 2) and of political compromise (example 19), the risks of not maintaining the balance of power (example 12), stubborn resistance by a

64 However, example (10) also includes the reverse of this – the pitfalls of excessive severity – and this works both ways ideologically.

65 Hume's argument in example (20) that the people (including participants) rarely gain by revolution, and that important (short-term) results of the English civil war were the opposite of what was aimed at, is similar to Burke. Indeed, anti-revolutionaries in France cited this part of Hume's *History* to this effect during the Revolution (Bongie 1965, 100).

legislature to policies proposed by the executive (example 22),[66] the paradoxical consequences of infanticide (example 23) and foundling hospitals (example 24), which both liberals and conservatives would presumably deplore, and the political temptations and perils of an unrestrained public debt (example 38).

Most important for an assessment of Hirschman's claim, perhaps, are the cases involving criticisms of economic policy. Hirschman himself remarks that the perverse-effects doctrine seems especially strong in the economic realm, where it is tied to the idea of a self-regulating market, any political interference with which is bound (according to the theory that Hume and Smith pioneered) to produce worse outcomes than the "beneficent equilibrating processes" of the market.[67] As Smith puts it, any "extraordinary" encouragements or restraints on the disposition of the capital of society "is in reality subversive of the great purpose which it means to promote. It retards, instead of accelerating, the progress of the society towards real wealth and greatness" (WN 687). Cases that fit this pattern include those involving export controls (example 30), price controls (example 31), export subsidies (example 32), bullionism (example 34), and politically determined preferential treatment for one sector of the economy over others (example 36). Related cases that draw upon the same mode of economic analysis would include the criticism of religious and educational endowments (example 29), criticism of the use of trade policy to punish rival nations (example 33), the failure to implement a "supply-side" approach to fiscal policy (example 37), and the attacks on usury laws (example 40) and alms-giving (example 41).[68] Both Hume and Smith

66 Hume thought, in the case cited, that the royal tax requests represented enlightened policy and that parliament was a bastion of conservative prejudice, but these roles could of course be reversed.

67 Hirschman (1991, 27).

68 In retrospect, the alms-giving case, with its modern analogues in welfare policy, constitutes a particularly important issue for perverse-effects and perverse-incentives arguments, or in today's terms, moral hazard. In example (41), Hume refers to private alms-giving rather than public systems of provision for the poor. He refers only briefly to the beginnings of poor relief (H 4, 380) with no indication of its effects. Hirschman describes the growing opposition, after Hume's lifetime, to the traditional Poor Law on similar grounds to those Hume mentions for alms-giving – that it perversely encouraged idleness and hence greater poverty. The much harsher New Poor Law of 1834 was designed to avoid this effect, but was soon denounced for its own unintended pernicious consequences (Hirschman, 1991, 30–31). This episode does not serve Hirschman's argument well; however, the old Poor Law was tied to the traditional social order and was opposed on perversity grounds by liberals, not conservatives, who believed themselves to be engaged in rational and progressive policy-making. The

aim the perverse-effect conclusions that derive from such economic analysis at established customs, institutions, and policies that may be said to represent the status quo and therefore a conservative outlook on society and policy. The new political economy that they enunciate, with its sometimes counterintuitive and seemingly radical conclusions, represents the (classical) liberal position in this domain, which was a self-consciously reforming and progressive doctrine in the eighteenth century. A liberal political orientation is most apparent in example (35), where Smith criticizes the Corn Laws as the product of the pernicious influence of the entrenched landlord class in parliament – although of course Smith also criticizes the protectionist political agenda of merchants and manufacturers elsewhere.

All in all, the Hume-Smith use of the perverse-effects argument seems ideologically multivalent and hence, in effect, neutral, comprising as it does cases of both a conservative and liberal bearing, as well as some that are unclassifiable in these terms and others that reflect a doctrine (classical political economy) whose political bearing has shifted with time. It is true that Hume often expresses a cautiously conservative (or as he would say, "moderate") approach to political practice, given the dangers of presumptuous political rationalism and more generally the fallibility of human reasoning, which is importantly evidenced by the frequency of unforeseen and perverse consequences of action. Nevertheless, the reasonable conclusion is that the perversity theme in Hume's and Smith's writings is neither "rhetoric", nor ideology, nor expressive of a generally reactionary or conservative orientation, but rather a mode of analysis that they employed, often with plausibility, as social and moral philosophers.

6 Conclusion

Hayek and the invisible hand. It has not been the aim of this study to deny the common view that socially benign unanticipated consequences, invisible-hand explanations, and processes generating spontaneous order are conspicuous among the social theorists of the Scottish Enlightenment. Smith's equilibrium model of a market is no doubt the best example, while his (and Ferguson's) account of the emergence of the division of labor, in which the uncoordinated decisions of many individuals to pursue specialized occupations bring about a functional and efficient system of production and exchange, provides a good example of the evolutionary variant of the idea. Along the same lines,

---

modern neoconservative critique of social policies points not only to moral hazard but also to their corrosive effects on traditional institutions like the family and community.

Hume adds that "a happy concurrence of causes in human affairs [...] checks [without intention by participants] the growth of trade and riches, and hinders them from being confined entirely to one people", since the manufacturing head start enjoyed by one country is offset by the lower price of labor in others ("Of Money", E 283). Hume's argument that manufacturing gradually migrates from high-wage to low-wage countries set off a long-running "rich countries – poor countries" debate, but from Hume's Scottish vantage point the equalization of prosperity is a benign invisible-hand effect.[69]

Both Smith and Hume also provide concrete historical examples of social and political significance. For Smith, "A revolution of the greatest importance to the publick happiness, was in this manner brought about by two different orders of people, who had not the least intention to serve the publick". These were the great medieval proprietors, whose power declined as they developed a taste for consuming luxury goods, and the merchants and artificers who satisfied this demand. "Neither of them had either knowledge or foresight of that great revolution which the folly of the one, and the industry of the other, was gradually bringing about" (WN, 422). The most noteworthy example of undesigned order in Hume's work is the development of the English constitution, the main overall theme of his *History of England*. In Hume's narrative, the ultimate outcome, which he praises as a system of liberty and balance, was decidedly not foreseen or intended by any of the key participants – turbulent barons and arbitrary kings; religious reformers, fanatical Puritans, and Tudor and Stuart absolutists; original-contract Whigs and divine-right Tories – who drove the historical process.[70] The emergence of what Hume terms the "rules of justice" may be understood as a piecemeal and indirect process comparable to the evolution of the common law[71]; and balancing a large state on general laws, Hume adds, "is a

69 For discussion of this controversy, see Hont (1983).

70 On the English constitution as an unplanned "plan of liberty", see H 2, 525, and 4, 355n. On the point that it could not have been foreseen by the various protagonists, see "Of the Coalition of Parties" (E 495). See generally Whelan (2004, 97–100). Hume occasionally expresses concern about the future of the constitution; Ferguson (1995, 210) suggests more bluntly, in an anti-Hayekian spirit, that liberty can be self-defeating, since its attainment can lead to a decline in the virtues that were necessary to achieve and sustain it.

71 "Tis self-love which is their real origin; and as the self-love of one person is naturally contrary to that of another, these several interested persons are oblig'd to adjust themselves after such a manner as to concur in some system of conduct and behaviour. This system, therefore, comprehending the interest of each individual, is of course

work of so great difficulty, that no human genius, however comprehensive, is able, by the mere dint of reason and reflection, to effect it [by design]" ("Of the Rise and Progress of the Arts and Sciences", E 124). We have here four of the most important social formations that Hayek interprets as spontaneous orders rather than products of "constructivist rationalism".[72] The rejection by Scottish writers of both founding Lawgivers and social contracts – two forms of intelligent design – in favor of historical accounts of the origins of property and government also accords with this interpretation.

What this chapter has indicated, rather, is the degree to which Hume and Smith recognize the possibility of unintended consequences of purposive action that are detrimental and even perverse with respect to the intentions of the actors and sometimes harmful for society at large. The invisible hand is not always benign, as is assumed in most treatments of the subject. The Scottish emphasis on unintended consequences is often praised as a contribution to Enlightenment and to modern social science. From a scientific point of view, however, both the positive and the negative versions are equally valuable in explaining various observed patterns and outcomes of action, whether these may be described as orderly or otherwise.

One kind of case is perfectly compatible with Hayek's interpretation. Political interventions in trade (whether by governments or interest groups), which meet with perverse and socially detrimental results, also represent misguided attempts to interfere with the spontaneous order of the market, or to obstruct the beneficent invisible hand in that sphere. Negative consequences are the expected outcome of such violations of the theory's normative prescriptions. A similar argument can be made about attempts to impose religious uniformity through persecution, at least if one holds that improvement in religion is the natural outcome of denominational diversity and competition, as Smith did (Hume demurred but of course did not defend persecution).[73] Of course, Hume's view is that persecution tends to backfire; in this case, persecution is perverse for the persecutor but unintentionally beneficial for society at large, assuming that religious reformation via dissent from orthodoxy is socially valuable. Demography offers a more complex topic. For most of the later eighteenth century, it was believed that population

---

advantageous to the public; tho' it be not intended for that purpose by the inventors" (T 3.2.6.6/529).

72 Hayek (1969, 336), among other places.

73 See chap. 6 in vol. 1 of the present work [Editors: Whelan, Frederick G. 2015. *Political Thought of Hume and His Contemporaries: Enlightenment Projects*, vol. 1. New York and London: Routledge].

would naturally increase along with economic growth – the desirable pattern – and that political attempts to regulate it were pointless or perverse: population studies revealed a case of spontaneous order. When the prevailing view shifted to a concern about overpopulation in the 1790s, the newly discovered Malthusian equilibrium appeared as a case of spontaneous disorder or misery – one that was so strong as to be resistant to political amelioration.

Malthusian population theory (which is beyond the scope of this chapter[74]) presents a direct challenge to the theory of spontaneous order, since the independent and reasonable procreative decisions of numerous people, largely in the lower classes, combine to create a situation that is worse for each (lower wages) and bad for society (general poverty and perhaps famine). This analysis resembles that in the case of Hume's foundling hospitals (example 24), which provided an extra incentive for childbearing by the poor; as in the tragedy of the commons, the hospitals were a common resource that collapsed through overuse, exacerbating rather than solving a social problem. The downfall of the Ayr bank (example 39) offers a similar case of a reverse invisible hand, especially if its ruin damaged regional development in addition to the bank's borrowers and creditors. Finally, a national debt that grows incrementally until it reaches a tipping point and causes a public bankruptcy (as Hume worries may happen in Great Britain, in example 38) is also a perverse composition effect among the class of politicians who approve public borrowing with the intention of strengthening the state.

The confidence in the prevalence of spontaneous orders brought about by invisible-hand mechanisms, which Hayek claims to share with the eighteenth-century forerunners, is for him the basis of a classical-liberal and anti-authoritarian political doctrine. It opposes the naive (or for Hayek, misguidedly "rationalist") view that apparent order must have been deliberately designed for the purpose it serves, and that stable and beneficent social patterns and institutions must be imposed and maintained by an intelligent political authority. Invisible-hand processes, in the market and elsewhere, remove the need for government supervision and planning in large areas. May such a view be attributed to Hume and Smith to the same degree as to Hayek, whose embrace of spontaneous order and liberty is more comprehensive and doctrinaire?[75]

---

74 See chap. 5 below [Editors: Whelan, Frederick G. 2015. *Political Thought of Hume and His Contemporaries: Enlightenment Projects*, vol. 2. New York and London: Routledge].

75 Hume (1932, vol. I, 111) referred to himself as a "sceptical Whig", a term that connotes much of what is meant by "classical liberal" applied retroactively to the eighteenth century. Hayek preferred the designation "Old Whig" for himself in view of the changes in the meaning of liberalism. Hayek's close affinity to Hume is expressed in his "Legal

In addition to the perverse effects of economic regulations and religious persecution, many of Hume's examples concern inept attempts by rulers to maintain their power and deal with opponents. Hayek might regard such episodes with disdain, as pathologies to be expected from systems of political power that exceed what is necessary in a world where spontaneous order would otherwise prevail. As a political thinker, however, especially in his *History*, Hume is far more interested in analyzing the concrete politics of governmental formation and maintenance and the strategies and tactics that seem inescapable at this "Machiavellian" level of analysis, which Hayek ignores. Hume's skeptical political interest (and sympathy) might be particularly engaged by situations (such as in examples 3 and 4) where two opposite and plausible courses of action both carry risks and may lead to perverse (perhaps fatal) consequences for rulers. Such situations – though usually with less-than-deadly risks – are not uncommon in political life, and successful decision-makers must be skillful in negotiating them.

At a more abstract level, all agree that the spontaneous order of the market cannot in fact (as a truly orderly system) be completely spontaneous. (Other systems of order, however, such as language and morality, are self-correcting and need no – or much less – external support). The market requires certain background conditions in the form of clear rules defining property rights, their transmissibility, and the forms and limits of valid contracts – what Hume terms the "rules of justice" and Hayek simply calls general laws. And the rules of property and contract must be applied and enforced, and private force and fraud prevented. These are the main functions of government for Hume in the *Treatise*, whereas the "administration of justice" and defense stand side by side as the first tasks (and hence expenses) of the sovereign for Smith. Both the rules of justice and, to some degree, forms of government may develop spontaneously, in that their final and systematic character was not a matter of conscious design at earlier stages, although surely some political institutions are consciously constructed.

For Hayek, the analysis of the market order as spontaneous and benign implies a policy preference for laissez-faire or non-interference by government beyond provision of background conditions. Hume and Smith agree with this position to a point, both in their criticism of specific anti-market controls (examples 30, 31) as well as in Smith's critique of more comprehensive ideologies of state control of the economy for political purposes, especially mercantilism (33, 34). On the other hand, Smith is well aware that economic classes and special interest

---

and Political Philosophy of David Hume" (1969), with emphasis on the evolution of social practices and institutions.

groups will try to exert political influence to gain protectionist policies in their own favor. This is true of landlords who seek agricultural price supports, import restrictions, and bounties on exports (examples 35, 36) as well as of merchants, who seek analogous protection and of whom Smith famously says that they seldom meet together "but the conversation ends in a conspiracy against the public, or in some contrivance to raise prices" (WN 145). That these efforts are often perverse in the long run, as the examples indicate, does not negate the challenge they pose for the invisible hand. A system of economic freedom combined with political representation results not in a market spontaneously ordered to the public good, but one distorted by the rent-seeking of successful political groups. *Contra* Hayek, and going beyond anything Smith explicitly says, the market requires supervision and intervention by government to prevent collusion and monopoly, and the objective of such efforts is a matter of conscious design authoritatively imposed.

Once government has been established for these basic functions, it is soon realized that it can raise revenue and organize the resources of society for other useful purposes, especially the provision of public works that would not otherwise exist and that in many cases further promote commerce. "Thus bridges are built; harbours open'd; ramparts rais'd; canals form'd; fleets equip'd; and armies disciplin'd; every where, by the care of government (T 3.2.7.8/539) – a point in which Smith and Hayek concur.[76] Since public works and public goods more generally must be provided by the authority of government, however, it follows that they must be designed, whether well or badly; and when they work out to serve the purposes for which they are intended, this is most likely attributable to intelligent design, possibly to lucky side effects, but not to an invisible hand.[77]

76 Defense, justice, and public works comprise parts I-III of Book V of *The Wealth of Nations* (Smith 1981 [1776]). See Hayek (1969, 360). Hamowy (1989, 21) gives a long list of governmental functions from the *Wealth of Nations* – mainly public goods, taxation to finance them, and monetary policy – but it is unclear if he believes Hayek agrees. Public goods provision by the state is legitimate even for libertarians. Hayek is not explicit on the point that this need reflects a case of market failure, that is, spontaneous disorder. For Hayek (1973, vol. I, 139–140), most of the actual business of modern governments is "measures of policy" aimed at particular groups, not public goods at all.

77 Spontaneous-order theory implies that there are three kinds of goods: private goods supplied by the market to buyers, public goods supplied by the state and financed by taxes, and other large-scale public goods such as language, morality, and the market itself that develop or evolve on their own.

Finally, there is one important kind of case indicated by Hume and Smith that Hayek neglects – the remedy that can be provided by authority for negative or perverse composition effects of the uncoordinated actions of many people. Hume's case is the collective-action problem in which a thousand persons, unlike two, find it impossible to drain a meadow, both because they cannot "concert so complicated a design" and because "each seeks a pretext to free himself of the trouble". Authority, however, can solve both the transaction and the free-rider problems. Government "obliges men to make such conventions [for mutual interest], and forces them to seek their own advantage, by a concurrence in some common end or purpose" (T 3.2.7.8/538). Smith's case concerns the need for the state to provide a public good of a different sort, namely education, especially of a civic and cultural nature for the working class. This program is (morally) necessary to counteract the narrowing and degrading effects of the division of labor, which, when allowed to proceed (spontaneously), makes most laboring people "as stupid and ignorant as it is possible for a human creature to become" (WN 782). Since the division of labor is a favorite example of an invisible-hand process for all of the authors discussed here, and since Smith himself viewed it as a key to productivity, its ultimate perversity, both for the individuals involved and for the quality of their society, and the dire need for corrective policies are deeply problematic both for Smith and for Hayek.[78]

Hayek sought to recruit Hume and the other Scottish Enlightenment writers to the cause of liberty (and opposition to social and economic planning by states) that he grounded in his enthusiasm for evolved orders and the invisible hand.[79] There is some plausibility in this project, but it conflicts both with the frequency of perverse effects noticed by the Scots and with Hume's numerous statements to the effect that "liberty is the perfection of civil society; but still authority must be acknowledged essential to its very existence" ("Of the Origin of Government", E 41).[80] Hume's authority is not the rationalist and designing type that Hayek

---

78 Barry (1982, 22) is unusual in recognizing that, *contra* Hayek, the invisible was not always benign for Smith and Ferguson. For both, economic progress through the free market came with negative side effects or at the cost of civic virtue and full human development.

79 Hayek's enthusiasm for social evolution, which seems to have grown over the course of his career, appears to overlook the phenomenon of evolutionary dead ends, in which organisms and institutions lock onto developmental paths that ultimately prove maladaptive. Most species, after all, are extinct.

80 Hayek (1969, 354) essentially misquotes this passage by omitting the second half.

excoriated in its twentieth-century manifestations, but he along with Smith recognize the necessity and a role for government well beyond what Hayek often suggests.

References

Barry, Brian. 1990 [1965]. *Political Argument*, reissue of 1965 edition with new introduction. Berkeley: University of California Press.

Barry, Norman. 1982. "The Tradition of Spontaneous Order." *Literature of Liberty* 5: 7–58.

Berry, Christopher J. 1997. *Social Theory of the Scottish Enlightenment*. Edinburgh: Edinburgh University Press.

Bongie, Laurence L. 1965. *David Hume: Prophet of the Counter-revolution*. Oxford: Clarendon Press.

Boudon, Raymond. 1973. *L'inégalité des chances: la mobilité sociale dans les sociétés industrielles*. Paris: Armand Cokin.

Boudon, Raymond. 1977. *Effets pervers et ordre social*. Paris: Presses Universitaires de France.

Boudon, Raymond. 1982 [1977]. *The Unintended Consequences of Social Action*. New York: St. Martin's.

Brennan, Geoffrey, and Philip Pettit. 1993. "Hands Invisible and Intangible." *Synhese* 94: 191–225.

Burke, Edmund. 1968. *Reflections on the Revolution in France*, edited and with an Introduction by Conor Cruise O'Brien. Harmondsworth: Penguin.

Chiswick, Harvey. 1989. "David Hume and the Common People." In *The 'Science of Man' in the Scottish Enlightenment*, edited by Peter Jones. Edinburgh: Edinburgh University Press.

Elster, Jon. 1989. *Solomonic Judgements: Studies in the Limitations of Rationality*. Cambridge: Cambridge University Press.

Ferguson, Adam. 1995. *An Essay on the History of Civil Society*, edited by Fania Oz-Salzberger. Cambridge: Cambridge University Press.

Fleischacker, Samuel. 2004. *On Adam Smith's Wealth of Nations: A Philosophical Companion*. Princeton: Princeton University Press.

Hamowy, Ronald. 1989. *The Scottish Enlightenment and the Theory of Spontaneous Order*. Carbondale: Southern Illinois University Press (reprinted in Hamowy, Ronald. 2005. *The Political Sociology of Freedom: Adam Ferguson and F. A. Hayek*. Cheltenham: Edward Elgar, chap. 3).

Hamowy, Ronald. 2005. *The Political Sociology of Freedom: Adam Ferguson and F. A. Hayek*. Cheltenham: Edward Elgar.

Hayek, Friedrich August von. 1960. *The Constitution of Liberty*. Chicago: University of Chicago Press.

Hayek, Friedrich August von. 1967. "The Results of Human Action but Not of Human Design." In his *Studies in Philosophy, Politics, and Economics*, chap. 6. Chicago: University of Chicago Press.

Hayek, Friedrich August von. 1969. "The Legal and Political Philosophy of David Hume." In *Hume: A Collection of Critical Essays*, edited by V. C. Chappell. Garden City (NY): Doubleday (reprinted in Hayek, Friedrich August von. 1967. *Studies in Philosophy, Politics, and Economics*, chap. 7. Chicago: University of Chicago Press).

Hayek, Friedrich August von. 1973. *Law, Legislation, and Liberty*, vol. I: *Rules and Order*. Chicago: University of Chicago Press.

Hayek, Friedrich August von. 1979 [1952]. *The Counter-Revolution of Science: Studies on the Abuse of Reason*. Indianapolis: Liberty Press.

Hill, Lisa. 2006. *The Passionate Society: The Social, Moral, and Political Thought of Adam Ferguson*. Dordrecht: Springer.

Hirschman, Albert O. 1970. *Exit, Voice, and Loyalty: Responses to Decline in Firms, Organizations, and States*. Cambridge: Harvard University Press.

Hirschman, Albert O. 1991. *The Rhetoric of Reaction: Perversity, Futility, and Jeopardy*. Cambridge: Harvard University Press.

Hirschman, Albert O. 1995. *A Propensity to Self-Subversion*. Cambridge: Harvard University Press.

Hont, Istvan. 1983. "The 'Rich Country–Poor Country' Debate in Classical Scottish Political Economy." In *Wealth and Virtue: The Shaping of Political Economy in the Scottish Enlightenment*, edited by Istvan Hont and Michael Ignatieff, 271-316. Cambridge: Cambridge University Press.

Hont, István. 1993. "The Rhapsody of Public Debt: David Hume and Voluntary State Suicide." In *Political Discourse in Early Modern Britain*, edited by Nicholas Phillipson and Quentin Skinner. Cambridge: Cambridge University Press.

Hume, David. 1932. *The Letters of David Hume*, edited by John Young Thomson Greig. Oxford: Clarendon Press.

Hume, David. 1947. *Dialogues Concerning Natural Religion*, edited by Norman Kemp Smith. Indianapolis: Bobbs-Merrill.

Hume, David. 1978. *A Treatise of Human Nature*, edited by Sir Lewis Amherst Selby-Bigge, first baronet, revised by P. H. Nidditch. Oxford: Clarendon Press.

Hume, David. 1983. *The History of England from the Invasion of Julius Caesar to the Revolution in 1688*, six volumes. Indianapolis: Liberty Classics.

Hume, David. 1987. *Essays Moral, Political, and Literary*, edited by Eugene F. Miller, revised edition. Indianapolis: Liberty Classics.

Hume, David. 1998. *An Enquiry Concerning the Principles of Morals*, edited by Tom L. Beauchamp. Oxford: Clarendon Press.

Kames, Henry Home, Lord. 1774. *Sketches of the History of Man*. Edinburgh: Creech.

Laursen, John Christian, and Greg Coolidge. 1994. "David Hume and Public Debt: Crying Wolf?" *Hume Studies* 20: 143–149.

Machiavelli (any edition, cited by chapter). *The Prince*.

Merton, Robert K. 1936. "The Unanticipated Consequences of Purposive Social Action." *American Sociological Review* 1: 894–904.

Merton, Robert K. 1949. "The Self-Fulfilling Prophecy." In *Social Theory and Social Structure*, chap. XI. Glencoe: The Free Press.

Nozick, Robert. 1974. *Anarchy, State, and Utopia*. New York: Basic Books.

Petsoulas, Christina. 2001. *Hayek's Liberalism and Its Origins: His Idea of Spontaneous Order and the Scottish Enlightenment*. London: Routledge.

Phillipson, Nicholas. 2010. *Adam Smith: An Enlightened Life*. New Haven: Yale University Press.

Popper, Karl R. 1963. "Towards a Rational Theory of Society." In his *Conjectures and Refutations: The Growth of Scientific Knowledge*. London: Routledge and Kegan Paul.

Rosen, Michael. 1996. *On Voluntary Servitude: False Consciousness and the Theory of Ideology*. Cambridge: Harvard University Press.

Rothschild, Emma. 2001. *Economic Sentiments: Adam Smith, Condorcet, and the Enlightenment*. Cambridge: Harvard University Press.

Sabl, Andrew. 2012. *Hume's Politics: Coordination and Crisis in the History of England*. Princeton: Princeton University Press.

Skocpol, Theda. 1994. *Social Revolutions in the Modern World*. Cambridge: Cambridge University Press.

Smith, Adam (1981 [1776]). *An Inquiry into the Nature and Causes of the Wealth of Nations*, two volumes continuously paginated. Indianapolis: Liberty Classics.

Smith, Craig. 2006. *Adam Smith's Political Philosophy: The Invisible Hand and Spontaneous Order*. Abingdon: Routledge.

Stigler, George J. 1975. "Smith's Travels on the Ship of State." In *Essays on Adam Smith*, edited by Andrew S. Skinner and Thomas Wilson. Oxford: Clarendon Press.

Tenner, Edward. 1997. *When Things Bite Back: Technology and the Revenge of Unintended Consequences*. New York: Vintage.

Tieffenbach, Emma. 2002. "La philosophie de l'histoire d'Edmund Burke (1729-1797): de l'ordre spontané à l'anarchie méthodique." In Annales Benjamin Constant 26: 177–205.

Tieffenbach, Emma. 2003. "De la main invisible à la Ruse de la Raison: traduction romantique d'une idée des lumières." In *Dénouement des Lumičres et Invention Romantique*, edited by Giovanni Bardazzi and Alain Grosrichard. Geneva: Droz.

Ullmann-Margalit, Edna. 1997. "The Invisible Hand and the Cunning of Reason." *Social Research* 64: 181–198.

Whelan, Frederick G. 1996. *Edmund Burke and India: Political Morality and Empire*. Pittsburgh: University of Pittsburgh Press.

Whelan, Frederick G. 2004. *Hume and Machiavelli: Political Realism and Liberal Thought*. Lanham: Lexington Books.

Jocelyn Pixley

Money versus System Integration Concepts

Abstract: This chapter looks beyond the invisible hand metaphor to related debates on whether social and system integration is an automatic result. Some analysts of Smith suggest that no automatic link can be found; by the mid-twentieth century, sociology explored prospects for harmony by stressing possible tensions between the two levels of integration (e.g. "system and lifeworld" tensions). However, my concern is that neither concept (invisible hand or integration) incorporates money as a social relation. The result is that major systemic conflicts over the production of money are neglected; conflicts that, evidence shows, compromise the chances of social integration as well. Such omissions of social level conflicts over money's value (or its stability and so on) that play their own role, although affected by the relative control over money by private banks or by nation-states, limit analysis. Macro concepts are weakened if money is assumed as a mere addition, given that its order or disorder can produce tendencies to inflation or savage deflation. These tendencies can overwhelm any other harmony achieved at social and system levels (households, labour markets and production of goods and services) to the point where dangers of disintegration and depression are apparent.

Keywords: Social integration; system integration; theories of money; banking sectors; money's disorders

Whichever way one looks at "the invisible hand" thesis – with praise, doubts, rejection or reconstruction from it – the thesis rarely tries to explain money, but nor do recent uses of terms such as "system integration". An attempt to do so, under methodological individualism tied to one version of the invisible hand, lands onto the turf not of sociology but of libertarian economists such as Hayek and his bizarre cybernetics. That, in turn, partly came from pre-Smith "contract" theories of a society "held together by a natural identity of interests" in the interdependence of exchange, the newly arising division of labour and an assumed motivation of self-interest. There is nothing in this (a kind of automatic social glue), which largely became twentieth-century neoclassical economics as Ingham (1996, 253) argues, that appeals to sociology.

Extreme individualism was not a driver in Adam Smith's works, nor in other ways to analyse an impersonal social order, such as in these concepts that separate social from system integration (my focus). Such distinctions are touched on in this chapter, which moves on to see if plausible theories of money have a place in these distinctions. The social nature of money is mostly neglected in Smith (as stressed in Schumpeter 1954) we see, and in recent approaches to social order. The problem with money, I conclude, is its double nature as a social relation that is primarily responsible for "systemic" order, harmony, capitalist dynamism, and inclusive or integrating economic development, and as well for disruptions, interminable disorder and social-systemic disintegration at worst. In other words, the conflicts in money's relations over its "value" may well override those in capital-labour conflicts (to an extent), as analysed in the labour theory of value. Finally, there is a reminder that one cannot reduce either social order or disorder to capitalism's driving conflicts and occasional harmony. Calhoun (1992) restated the classic sociological argument that modernity comprises far more than "a capitalist economy" or "modernization". What about money then?

Modern "capitalist-state" money has been aptly described as "a space of exception" (Mann 2013), the implications of which upset the optimistic invisible hand model. Let me start with an intriguing example. We know that the 2011 Occupy Wall Street movement made the obvious point about the unseemly wealth of the "one per cent". But a more inscrutable banner had this, crudely termed analysis: "Screw opportunistic disinflation. It's a dual mandate". What on earth did it mean? The *Financial Times* journalist explained that it referred to the US Federal Reserve System's "other goal that supposedly aims for full employment, in addition to low inflation".[1] He missed the point of what retrieving this ideal entails.

The dual mandate became a mid-twentieth-century ideal, briefly, when central banks, having formerly aimed to control only money's inflations always to great social distress, were directed, as well, to prevent savage deflations that created such high unemployment. That is, their interest rates must not be "too high" for "too long" as to increase joblessness. Central banks alone cannot create employment but need to work jointly with the state's fiscal arms and, more distantly with private banks if possible, to foster investment in long-term job-creating enterprises. However, corporate firms and the banking system are concerned only with bottom-line profits: they regularly externalize the costs to

1 Luce (2011). The fact that Luce had to interpret the slogan for *FT* readers, just to say "Occupy" people are educated, is relevant itself, in that money is not defined as clearly as any other economic/social relation, perhaps due to the underlying conflicts involved. Full employment seemed dead and buried after the 1970s, for example. In Bryan's (2010) work on the "anchor" metaphor, translated to "the believability of the safeness of US treasury bonds compared to myriad forms of credit money", one can see money's social fragility. Another (interminable) metaphor is an inverted pyramid, which is hardly social either, although suggests money rests on shaky bases (Morris 2008).

people, the environment and social renewal. Finance sectors want certainty of "stable money" via low wages and not over their own asset inflations, which disinflation with Quantitative Easing further fostered; small business also demand low wages, counterproductively to businesses as a whole. Disinflation is not a source of social integration. The Occupy movement, rightly then, accused the Fed of ignoring its full employment mandate as did Treasuries and private banks.

This example takes me (rather grimly) to Polanyi (1957 [1944]) and his critique of the "fictitious" commodities of land, labour and money as they were treated during the "great transformation". It is much loved in sociology and sometimes heterodox economics. Yet, many have bypassed his argument that, under the sway of harsh nineteenth-century capitalist change, money was incorrectly treated as a commodity as much as labour and land. As well, in Polanyi's broader argument often missed was that instead of social structures "embedded" in personal relations of hierarchy or reciprocity, the great transformation involved "embedding" newly impersonal market forms of stratification, and class relations of not only labour-capital but also creditors-debtors-states. Therefore, Polanyi's hopes in 1944 that "de-commodification" might bring lasting improvement are qualified with his embedding thesis (albeit including countermovements against despoliation of land, and positive challenges of unions). That is, today money is again mistreated as a commodity, as is land and labour.

1 The split between sociology and economics

Unfortunately, economic sociology did not take up Polanyi's challenge on money readily. And economists, however decent like the Keynesians, rarely joined sociologists in mutual shared work. Financial promoters of money, as "commodity" again, were ably assisted by a rising neoclassical economics of which sociology played no part. That emerged from the split in the German social sciences in the 1900s, with Weber and Schumpeter defending the historical method and the Austrians and "marginalists" an individualist method. In the 1930s, Talcott Parsons, as Moss (1999, 552) describes, also ceded theories of money to economics in "the nefarious deal" with the marginalist economic theory put forward by Lionel Robbins, into an "ominous détente" that constituted sociology as the "science of leftovers". That lost the new sociological components of Schumpeter and Keynes. Collins early on railed against this loss of money as an obvious social relation: The split, not to Parsons whose "functionalism is the sociological counterpart of neoclassical general equilibrium theory", left money as the *social* phenomenon that it is, but about which "there is virtually no sociological analysis", said Collins (1986, 11–12). Ingham continued berating the split, although so far, the simplicities of the neoclassical reduction of money to a commodity, water and so on are less criticized than the claims that financial markets are "efficient".[2]

Thus, neoclassical views that play down money are now rather like Monty Python's "Dead Parrot": the last decades have seen the failure of its medicine as rising disaffection takes over. Bankers and politicians grimly maintain the Dead Parrot is "alive" despite four decades of financial crises across the capitalist world. On the one hand, for recently former Soviet states, the market in all things, including capitalist-state money, seemed fine. On the other, many sociologists took up "rational actor" market models, against which the main sociological defence was to use Polanyi's concept of embeddedness, but via omitting the creditor-debtor class relations of money, and their dangers. Granovetter (1985; cf. Ingham 1996) was one who made thoughtful interventions, but thought one could leave rates of "inflation" or forces of "supply and demand" to technocratic control. Granovetter disputes what he takes to be Polanyi's argument as an "over-socialized conception of man". This is an incorrect category shift. He insists that "the overlay of social relations on *what may begin in purely economic transactions* plays a crucial role" (Granovetter 1985, 498 [emphasis added]). While correct to argue that instrumental/rational behaviour "aims not only at economic goals but also at sociability, approval, status, and power" (Granovetter 1985, 506), Granovetter misses that "purely economic transactions" and "goals" *are* social relations.[3]

Inflation-deflation are conflicts over money's production and its "value": here the approaches of Ingham and, say, Keynes meet. The (capitalist) class relations of modest inflation are those where the producers of goods and services (debtors) and the labour forces they employ oppose deflationary class relations of those private actors who hold the state's debt and who guarantee (ever more reluctantly) the creation of bank-money. "Rentiers" and entire financial sectors make profits from high interest rates, low wages (high wages detract from dividends) and a reserve army of labour to keep wage inflation ever lower. These stipulations,

2 To show there are indeed exceptions to this split, the late Professor Moss, editor of *American Journal of Economics and Sociology*, drew on the Austrian (Hayek) and partly the Henry George traditions, and attended many International Sociology Association meetings. Moss was a very generous and inclusive scholar. However, a social movement story that moves beyond cryptic slogans (cited above) is yet to develop; the GFC showed catastrophic inefficiencies, but public debates on money's social nature as debt are still in the obscurity of academia.

3 This segment partly draws on my article Pixley (2010).

combined with massively reduced government money creation (save for wars, and for rescuing bank-money, funnily enough), provide "certainty" and enhanced profits for the groups who merely produce money: banks et al. There is a tendency (Minsky 1992) for banks to create money not for careful production but for speculative or at worst Ponzi corporate positions. As the level of unpayable loan servicing rises, banks run the danger of insolvency, bank recalls, defaults and eventually global financial crises (GFC). Minsky was an economist drawing on Keynes and Schumpeter. So too, economists like Panić, who points out that industrial and financial global corporations, merely by holding financial assets in numerous currencies, can switch funds at short notice. This can increase inflation or unemployment "to the point at which they threaten the social fabric and political stability of a country" (Panić 2003, 170).

So, economists do meet sociological analysis (somewhat). For example, Goldthorpe (1978, 208) argued the experience of rising inflation in the 1970s was best seen as an expression of conflict over income distribution, eased not through greater democratic participation but through further inflation. Although these conflicts over the value of money (and employer prerogatives) were resolved in favour of *rentiers*, which Hirsch (1978) argued at the time would seriously undermine the democratic process, in my view the (income-regressive) anti-inflation medicine of the lash of unemployment was less bitter for many, than before the 1930s: social security eased the strain; worse was the so-called democratization of debt. That is, conflicts changed character. As well, economist Forder (2014) also met sociology in his marvellous debunking of the distortions of Milton Friedman who accused post-war full employment economists of being inflationary.[4] That was not true.

2 Money

Money is created by states and private banks and, in what became a fusion of these two moneys via the early seventeenth-century central banks, became as Ingham (2004, 126–133) shows, a symbiosis of "state-capitalist money". In his *History of Economic Analysis* (1954, 321), Schumpeter argued the idea that banks manufacture money could sound frightening. The credit theory is counterintuitive, silenced and cause for unease (space of exception), yet he like others put money at the centre of capitalism's development and the world's social-economic relations.

4 This was under the label "Phillips Curve" whereas the entire post-war era of high employment came with very low inflation: the 2% CPI that the ECB is longing to get up to, with present EU rates hovering below 1% (i.e. deflationary).

In discussing how the deposit-creating loan was consolidated in Amsterdam after the Renaissance Italian bankers, Galbraith (1975, 18) said: "The process by which banks create money is so simple that the mind is repelled". These processes, that banks and central banks simply deposit loans (not the reverse), hint at a larger problem of this production of state-capitalist money than only being counterintuitive, to a normative deficit and social dilemma about integration (or about invisible hand harmony).

Schumpeter's magnificent history devotes much space to Adam Smith; above all, to his approach to barter and money, and Smith's insistence on the saver having a major role, compared to the thinking that "saving is sterile and a disturber", just like Keynes's views. Schumpeter did not give the saver a large role either, because only a *fraction* of loans is based on savings, the bulk are deposited loans. They create new, (taxpayer)-backed money we use as cash. Smith's work in many respects was aimed at analysing modern national wealth, as opposed to old mercantilist "visible hand" policies of military power. Back then, even exports were regarded as a loss of resources that could give more power to an enemy nation.[5] Still, Schumpeter saw money as the dynamic source of capitalist development. He hoped that this was at last acknowledged (or "visible") before he died in 1950, although he had long warned (1934 [1911]) of banking tendencies to "destruction without function". (He also assumed that no one would retain the "split").

Schumpeter suggests that Smith's "invisible hand" thesis came from "the principle of Natural Liberty", which for Smith gave a *policy* of laissez faire, and as well, "the analytic proposition that free interaction of individuals produces not chaos but an orderly pattern that is logically determined: he never distinguished the two clearly", said Schumpeter (1954, 184–186). However, contemporary scholars of Smith (on whom I have little expertise), such as my colleague Peter McCarthy, take issue with the prominence that was later given to Smith's comment. First, McCarthy argues "the invisible hand" was part of an older "*doux-commerce* thesis" proposing civilizing results but second, Smith's *Wealth of Nations* hardly shares that notion. To the opposite of "*douceur*" was the "self-destruction" thesis proposing that a capitalist society (or others) tended to undermine "the moral foundations" on which (any) society rests. And this latter constitutes the main

5 Polanyi (1957 [1944]) also discussed in Pixley (2010); Schumpeter (1954, 287) on the sterile "saver"; fractional reserve banking is the practice of creating money on debt-credit relations; Ingham (2008, 7–8) on mercantilism (or plunder), which may be President Trump's apparent position against Chinese imports. This is not the topic herein, only to distinguish the so-called invisible from the visible mercantile hand.

"part of [Smith's] sustained critique of commercial society", McCarthy says, citing vivid examples. From Polanyi's conception, one could say that norms of opportunism and a logic of money not as means to an end, but the (only) end, became embedded to transform old forms of distribution (reciprocity and hierarchy).

Schumpeter agrees (with a backhander at Smith's luck of being "in sympathy with the humors of his time"). Details he cites include Smith's denigration of "'slothful' landlords", conspiracies of employers, "merchants" who happily let "clerks [...] do all the work" and "the poor laborers" who support everyone else into "luxury". Concerning *laissez faire*, McCarthy is openly ambivalent about whether Smith's "markets" foster, or "require" sympathy, saying the latter is most emphasized in the Austrian school of economics' "spontaneous-order theory". Indeed, Hayek aimed to remake the world on this "spontaneity" from the 1920s onwards, in a methodological individualism belied in Smith's class divisions. With Hayek, even the "Prince" is an individual (wicked social democratic state), and the "invisible hand" requires obedience to "natural" market norms that bring unequal outcomes, even disorder, but are "just" and "efficient": Hayek claimed opportunism is unjustly denigrated. That twentieth-century corporations and monopoly were ignored went with Hayek's view that money creation must be left to market individuals, a "de-nationalized" money, self-regulated. Orléan (2014) argues the sociological idea of money as a social fact, universal need, and objective desire was a "monstrosity" to Hayek.[6]

Hirschman, like McCarthy, is ambivalent about Smith on the "invisible hand", pointing to his awareness of unintended consequences, whereas in Hayek and others, Hirschman argues that as capitalism came to "triumph" all these views of the "invisible hand" of self-interest's "restraints" created a problem. In effect, self-interest is "earnestly" expected, and *intended* to have the desirable effects "that

---

6 Schumpeter (1954, 184–186) on Smith, noting the other "humor" was free trade aka-*laissez faire*, a hallmark of orthodox economics. Hirschman (1977, 104) suggests Smith was less prone to *laissez faire* than orthodoxy then and now. He also says Schumpeter's loathings are a "mystery", likewise to me: e.g. why did he oppose Smith but not Hayek? McCarthy's terrific work on Smith includes a co-authored contribution, Pixley, McCarthy and Wilson (2014, 314–316), and in Hill and McCarthy (2004), among his other scholarly works. The 1960s re-popularization of "invisible hand" is too often directly attributed to Smith, e.g. in Ingham (2008, 7–14). Schumpeter and Ingham are, however, fairer in their criticisms of Smith's view of money. On opportunism, see Hayek (1945); and Hayek is discussed/cited from multiple sources in Pixley (2011; 2014); as well, Orléan (2014, 159) draws on Durkheim, Simmel and Simiand to criticize Hayek; also see Giannini (2011) on the "Prince" as "a fatuous" concept of Hayek.

then wholly fail to materialize". Self-interest does not repress or clamp down on other passions like lust for power; thus, Hirschman's own thesis is not about unintended consequences, but lack of desired outcomes. Moreover, Hirschman has little doubt that Smith was aware of the "fallacy of composition": that is, self-interested actions of individuals do not aggregate but, in the wider social whole, can undermine that self-interest, for good or ill.[7]

Probably Schumpeter's sharpest, more cogent criticism of Smith's sophisticated approach was about saving. This has the most relevance for my theme. Adam Smith gave savers a crucial part in the creation of new industry: "parsimony and not industry is the immediate cause of the increase of capital". Schumpeter said not one economist who "swallowed" this "looked askance at that word 'immediately' " or that in depressed conditions, saving (parsimony, thrift) will diminish economic activity, since "what is saved is not spent". This is a fallacy of composition of individuals each saving, that collectively, unintendedly, furthers recession.

Generally, orthodoxy's casting of money as a "neutral veil" over the "real" of market exchanges in goods and services was (and is) criticized in heterodoxy, including Keynes's. Schumpeter rightly said the "essential features of the capitalist process" in fact depend upon the "veil". That is, money is the driver, no mere veil, and ideas that the features of money can be "represented by a barter-economy model", he said, must be abandoned. Furthermore, admitting that Smith's focus on "an efficient banking system" and that serious "monetary disorders" and even "conspicuous disturbances" are accepted in most "neutral money" views like Smith's, Schumpeter emphasized that these very same monetary processes "act in even the most normal course of economic life". That was evident in the ultimately disruptive expansion of business and household debt between the 1990s up to 2007's crash. He also showed how Marx accepted Smith's (also Ricardo's *ad nauseam*) views. In contrast, the saver's role is minor, even if some of these thrifty do actively direct their savings to investment. As with Quantitative Easing after the GFC, which deposited billions of state-created moneys into bank reserves, there was no "immediate" investment in, or loans to, enterprises and job creation. QE repeated Smith's error. Banks complained of lack of demand for such long-term loans (individuals and small firms were saving, cutting back their earlier debts, enduring bank foreclosures!),

7 Hirschman (1977, 131), on his own thesis (and partly Smith's he said) that "interests" failed "abysmally" to "tame passions"; Hirschman (1977, 134) on what he calls Hayek's "caricature" of "the invisible hand".

and, given businesses are anyway expensive (involving fixed investment and so on), banks turned QE to cheap short-term asset bubbles instead. The "Occupy" slogan of the "dual mandate" was largely correct.[8]

3 Social integration and system integration

Moving on from these useful scholarly positions on Smith's work, one of the reconstructions or transformations of the impersonal "invisible hand" thesis on social order (or disorder) was the mid-twentieth-century debate on social integration and system integration. Why are these models important? One cannot derive impersonal complex economic and political relations directly from person-to-person relations. If one subscribes to methodological individualism, none of the problems just mentioned, like fallacy of composition, indirect links, failure of "self-interest" to tame other vices and impersonal processes, has an entry point. "Society" is reduced to an aggregate of (self-seeking) individuals, for which in the face of global forces and conflicts that intrude or probably govern everyone's lives, systemic concepts are surely preferable. However, none give an adequate conceptualization of money either, or its link to full employment. It is to me a tragedy of excellent contemporary sociology to miss the full nature of the attack on full employment (FE) and wages since the 1970s, and today's obvious rise in disaffection from the years of stagnant employment and low wage inflation, when in fact that attack on FE was framed through direct links to money's systemic and social importance, for good and for ill. This connection is not made.

One who mentioned money was Lockwood (1964) in his introduction of the distinction as an answer to what he called Parsons' "normative functionalism", coincidentally as Parsons declared money of little concern to sociology. In the 1964 volume to which Lockwood contributed, there are also references to Smith's "invisible hand" and even Mandeville's "private vices, public virtues" dichotomy. Lockwood opens out this duality of social and system integration to much

---

8 The above two paragraphs: see Schumpeter (1954, 325–326) on parsimony and "thrift" and also Blinder (2013, 355); Schumpeter (1954, 277–278) on banks in Smith; and Schumpeter (1954, 290) on Marx. Reflation and QE transfers to banks' central bank accounts did not automatically go to bank-money creation on socially productive loans (as central banks assumed) but on far cheaper asset bubbles. The point is not that the Fed's "dual mandate" creates employment, but that Treasuries had saved banks, not the households and small businesses weighed down with debt after the GFC. Bernanke (2013, 88–90) on banks, repeats Smith. Instead of fiscal stimulus, job retraining, etc., most Treasuries chose austerity.

greater complexity. His schema is devoted to showing that social integration, such as conflictual or harmonious labour-capital class relations, are not necessarily related to high or low degrees of *system* integration between the "parts", such as tensions from "overproduction". No fallacy of composition appears in this model. As important, he rightly refuses to "narrow down" the problems of system integration such as "contradictions", dysfunctions or "tensions" to "industrial production" alone, and includes other "subsystems" subject to "incompatibility", if not actions of "vested interests" that potentially create more social order *or* "a vicious circle of social disintegration" (Lockwood 1964, 250–252). Thus, he cited Weber about how a continuing "pure bureaucratic administration" required "a developed money economy" as its "normal precondition" with "a stable system of taxation" (Lockwood 1964, 253–254). A tax crisis (systemic) was possible too, then, said Lockwood; but "a money economy" was not mentioned. However, Weber discussed at length what he called a "memorable alliance" between London merchant-financiers and the British crown, through the creation of the Bank of England in 1694, which put a brake on the crown's power to default, much to the Tories' disgust for being "republican". More to the point, Weber (1981 [1927], 337) also said "mobile capital" thereupon could "play off nation-states". Surely this alliance or deal amounted to a system "problem" as well, and as Galbraith remarked, its "repellent" nature was due to how, when the Bank of England lent to the crown (for war finance), it also lent out the crown's "security" to repay via taxes, in notes to other merchants that doubled the money.

Ingham develops Weber's *en passant* comments from the *General Economic History*: in this new lending - in effect the creation of modern money - was the "alliance". States would rule and "merchant classes" would make money (Weber 1981 [1927], 264–265; Ingham 2008, 32–34). In *Economy and Society* (1978 [1922]) Weber said:

> at the beginning of modern history, the various countries engaged in the struggle for power needed ever more capital for political reasons and because of the expanding money economy. This resulted in that *memorable alliance* between rising states and the sought-after and privileged capitalist powers that was a major factor in creating modern capitalism [...] (Weber 1978 [1922], 353 [emphasis added]; this translation is based on the 1956 fourth German edition).

Weber (1978 [1922], 354) stresses that this "novel structure of emergent modern capitalism [...] was unknown to Antiquity and in the long run profited greatly from state protection". (You can say that again.) In this emergent structural alliance, positions are created not necessarily for "persons" with specific backgrounds in common (e.g. Oxford or Harvard), or *necessarily* with definite power from other sources (e.g. ownership), but for officials, managers or professionals of "mobile capital". Corporate (banking) officials are able to "dictate the conditions" to states on which they support them (Weber 1981 [1927], 337) with loans at a price, or rather with deposited loans at bankers' chosen interest rate. Managers must act the part (Hughes 1937; Lyman and Scott 1969), make money, compete yet collectively defend private money-creation's official-legal power of disposition. If not, their bank boards will sack them: it is impersonal and indirect.[9]

My argument is that a one-sided "integration" in today's "social whole" *through money* is tenuous, but that this problem is very hard to criticize. Money has no agreed "normative definition" or mode of justification (see later); moreover, indignation – about the US/UK financial crisis of 2007, for example – is difficult when so few know that money consists in debt. With unemployment or norms against labour market exploitation of children, indignation at contraventions is readily available. In contrast, with money, a central social institution and complex social relation, to (some) sociologists, historians and heterodox economists, there is silence. In orthodox economics, its "troubles" only *reflect* order and disorder – "elsewhere", despite the evidence that money is inherently troublesome. Banks are mere "middlemen" not money-creators, innocently "allocating" savers' resources "efficiently". But to heterodox views, money *creates* order and disorder. If it is mysterious, a promise into the unknowable future, it might be an institution that cannot be a lasting source of social integration; if it is a systemic problem of bank-state money creation, mobile capital's ability to "play off" nation-states surely must be included. Yet in its inescapable nature, we must "believe" in it.[10] What kind of "imagined" community is possible in one-sided relations to the financial sector and to those states mostly interested in war finance? I mention this because banking sectors often lend for, and make profits from, war finance.

Habermas (1975) indeed included the costs of war in a long list of "burdens" of the state's costs since the "class compromise" (of the 1940s), in which the state "altered the determinants of the realization process" – meaning that the labour theory of value was tempered (systemically) for democratic legitimation through a "reactive crisis avoidance". This neglects that states actively want war finance!

---

9 This paragraph is drawn from Pixley (2013).

10 In Russia in the 1990s, businesses did not "believe" in state management of the rouble (the IMF neglected it) and took to barter or surrogate currencies – social chaos was the result (Woodruff 1999). When the US army conquered Iraq, people burned dinars in the street; only the US dollar was "trusted" (Ingham 2004). To Orléan (2014), money is social desire and need.

He said of the early 1970s, this "crisis cycle" was "replaced by inflation and a permanent crisis in public finances" (Habermas 1975, 61). His text makes sad reading given forty years of hindsight, since he searched for collective discursive ways that might stave off "disturbances in system integration" that "endanger" "social integration" or what he calls "the lifeworld" (Habermas 1975, 3–4).[11] Unfortunately, if anything, Habermas has a "quantity" view of money, or even monetarist approach so popularized by Milton Friedman (1968; not that monetarism proved workable). Quantity views hold that only states create money and if "too much" is created, it ends in "inflation".

That those deciding that "too much" state money was being created, say to spend on employment and the welfare state (pitiful in the USA), also happened to be rentiers, banks and the financial sector (which also create money), become lost from view. Inflation is inimical to their "vested interests" since it reduces the value of their "loans". Banks create money too, and if firms and people demand loans, cash in hand and purchasing power, money expands. And these loans can be serviced if the expenditure is on successful (taxable) job-creating or job-maintaining ventures. But, bank-money for asset inflations or currency speculation can be created in this way too (say on housing bubbles). Up to a point (but not to mass bankruptcies), low economic activity to deflation is also lucrative to finance since the debt (and its interest) grows in value. Also, oligopolistic firms and large "cartels", notably OPEC in 1973, can raise prices (as they did), and unions can demand higher wages, as they did in the 1970s' corporate sector, which was raising prices in a wage-price spiral. Further "systemic" problems arose, then, not about state money "solely" being inflationary but from collective action or more systemic action.

By the 1980s, as Kalecki (1943) suggested, employers finally revolted against full employment for its lack of discipline on workers, and progressive taxes also came under attack. Taxes are more (and less) important than either Lockwood- or Habermas-type approaches give due. States spend money into existence and taxes retire that debt if inflationary pressures occur. It is not a matter of taxes

11 His theory of communicative action was Habermas's considered response; this 1975 (5–6, his emphases) text is his challenge to Parsons and particularly Niklas Luhmann's systems theory, which "transform *questions of validity* into *questions of behaviour*". That is, Habermas challenged how the "system" rules the whole show to Luhmann, and, as Schumpeter (1954) also charged of Adam Smith, Luhmann's "system" relies on simple stimuli-response behavioural changes, imposed from the top down in Luhmann's case, but not so in Smith's except via exploitation, from which, Schumpeter claimed, Marx could do a far better job with his labour theory of value.

paying "directly" for specific goods and services from the state but of taxes servicing the National Debt if needed, since the state can always borrow from the capitalist banking system (thus, governments search for AAA credit ratings, meaningless as they proved after 2007). However, like state debt with its much more reliable taxes than bank advances, bank liabilities also need to be "retired", interest paid and at least some of bank loans paid back. As we knew after 2007, banks had built up liabilities that were never likely to be paid back (UK and USA notably), and the state (taxpayers) were dragged in to rescue banks.

To my mind, Habermas was correct about a democratic *legitimation crisis* and a great deal of protest of many kinds that came from below during the 1970s and the 1980s. Disaffection re-emerged also in key elections of 2016, amidst a return of demagoguery: one cannot say, at the time of writing, if disintegrating features may be further exacerbated. More relevant to Habermas's analysis at that time was the sight of British police charging in lines over the Yorkshire moors to put down the miners and their unions. Indeed, the end of FE took major campaigns, via appealing to the sainted "saver", the pensioners and of course wealthy on unearned incomes to "fight inflation first", and to castigate "greedy unions".

Even if the "social integration-system integration" analysis is somewhat useful, when conflicts over money are not a major subset of "system", analysis can get side tracked. Paul Volcker, the US Fed Chair basically stopped the American economy in 1980, in effect tearing up the "dual mandate" of the dominant central bank, which only shares FE as a remit with the Reserve Bank of Australia. Other central banks (Bank of England, Bundesbank and in no way, the ECB) did not even have that democratic "burden" to tear up. Yet some governments controlled price-wage spirals with agreed controls and social wages (e.g. in Australia called the Accord; in Germany with corporatism; and in Sweden, too).

Later, the global finance sector could do what it wanted, which was largely to make socially useless profits on "the certainty" of low economic activity, low wages and a reserve army of labour. To critics, that was not only cruel but also the consumer debt was unsustainable, systemically: they were silenced. Not only this, the state deficit data also shows that except for huge state debts in the Second World War, the major occasion that governments created heavy debts was in bailing out the financial sector after 2008. And far from this state deficit creating inflation, many countries are veering to deflation. So much, then, for the "quantity" theory of money.[12]

---

12 Schularick (2014) on debt levels; former RBA Governor, Fraser (1996) on how banking prefers "low economic activity". Hayek did not share the "quantity" theory, but liked depressions (cleansing) as, e.g. US Treasurer Mellon said in 1929 – "liquidate labour,

The problem then is that "the invisible hand" thesis, or even the complex far-flung "system integration" with its "tensions", does not quite capture the argument that money is "a space of exception". Very few people, bankers and certainly political leaders included, have any idea that banks create money. Monetarism lives to misguide as ever (but even among some central bankers who know better, since they also create money), and, when recently "neo-liberalism" came under attack, it was often of those even prepared to use the nuclear "answer", rather than from any revival of social democracy. Nevertheless, banks and financial sectors have never been less popular, not that the current elite demagogues are likely to control them. And one most unfortunate diagnosis of Habermas (1975, 28) in rejecting Luhmann's idea of "contradiction" (rightly to me) was this. Contradiction "should not obscure the difference between the logic of self-regulated systems and the logic of ordinary language communication". But from the systemic "logic" (of even Habermas, but who poses resistance from the lifeworld against Luhmann), I suppose one could say that after 2008 governments validated the (false) "self-regulatory" claims of the finance sector, but only at the cost of state debt, their ludicrous turn to "austerity" and great social distress. Where is any logic or self-regulation in such a system?

Would it make a difference if money were included in systemic models? Honneth (2010), who partially continues with a "system integration-social integration (forms of recognition)" model, suggests the "appropriate" norms for the "handling of central coordination problems" are formed by "practical experience" of what is superior and sensible for "central functional areas of society". A misapplication would be a "moral regression" (Honneth 2010, 387). Yet money is not included (again) and what indeed has been "sensible" for money's "coordination"? Financial markets did not "self-regulate" any more than banks. My point is that with money, "regression" is the "norm" and yet it's a dominant "coordination mechanism". With money, appropriate norms have rarely applied because "practical experience" – in seeking "sensible" social purposes of bank-money creation – tends historically to be short-lived.

For example, back in the 1890s–1900s, some argued that the Bank of England was unable to prevent the banking reserves that it held from banks using it as "cash".[13] Moral and practical justifications rest on two functions: first, banks

liquidate banks, liquidate industry and farming", sounding a bit Stalinist; Mellon cited in Bernanke (2013) who called him "harsh".

13 Withers (1918 [1909]) (editor of *The Economist*) on the BoE's lack of control. The history of democratic agreements is pretty depressing: William Gladstone, nineteenth-century British PM and economic liberal, talked bleakly about the "money power" putting the state into subservience; Jefferson too. Government bonds were an attempt to diminish

fund the investment and creative development of economic life (for a profit, i.e. interest, and with a by-product as it were of taxable employment for states). Second, state-licensed private banks, acting as an arm of the state, are supposed to maintain the payments system. These functional roles of money in production and not only in consumption rely on trust, mutual obligations and contracts of banks, to keep deposits freely available or "at call", and of borrowers to service interest payments and not default. Whereas Simmel (1990, 176) warned, "money is the reification of exchange among people, the embodiment of a pure function", in 2008 it was patently clear that banks and the whole finance sector had reneged on these two morally justifiable functions. And they have done so before, yet what was "sensible" (in understanding money from heterodox views) had again been scotched by banks, governments and aided by harsh orthodox views. At the time of writing, none had apologized or admitted to responsibility for the GFC.

The credit theory is counterintuitive and rather repugnant. Banking practices show that "savers" do not "directly" fund economic development, the banks are supposed to take these dangers by extending loans (e.g., to business ventures), which are deposited. In an interesting book of Beckert (2016, 285) on "imagined futures", the credit-debt theory of money is acknowledged, unlike so many sociologists, and he mainly refers to the "demonic" and "eternal process of capitalist renewal". Beckert knows that by 1933, capitalism nearly died, and to be fair, my chapter herein is focused on "disintegration" and no signs of renewal are evident.

The shareowner and money fund models also "fund" investment on imagined futures, but hardly conducive to renewal. Also, trading is usually on dangerous leverage and, with High Frequency Trading, often for only a millionth of a second. Pension funds (the "savers") face "legally" rigged markets. Also, today's banks gain profits from "services" to other finance institutions. Given loans create deposits, then the "saver" who deposits has a minor functional role (in tiny fractional reserves for banks) since many or most deposits are loans. Banks "manufacture" money on future promises; loans are their assets for the profit stream from interest payments, whereas deposits are their liabilities: the more loans, the more profits, on a model of borrowing short and lending long, so credit inflation and bust is regular due to unpredictable collapse of trust, in terms of the problem of time passing in credit expansion.

---

this subservience by borrowing directly from "the public". Jump to say, Alessandri and Haldane (2009), entitled "Banking on the State" and Haldane (2010).

It means that in all the juggling of short- and long-term debts and credits, banking is built on a lie or at best a shaky promise, that all deposits can be redeemed all at once: that is in fact a bank run (on its liabilities). A further "secret" is that banks do not want all loans to be repaid: money would disappear, along with their profits. Some are morally outraged at banks trying to prevent clients from paying off their credit cards too quickly. True, the traditional role of a lending officer was to hope for the borrower's success (Wray 2010) – this is the "imagined future" that entails caution and renewal: or "relationship banking" as it was practised in Europe, so that advances are paid off eventually. The same applies to state money: at the extreme of collapse, all money disappears if state budgets are in surplus via spending cuts and large tax hauls, and banks at the same time have all loans repaid. Banks took to lending to each other overnight, so that the central bank did not, and could not scrutinize their "books" before lending to banks as a "last resort" at high rates. These market institutions such as the London Interbank Offered Rate (LIBOR) were later rigged during the GFC: banks cheated on each other (not unusual). Whatever control is applied tends to be evaded particularly in large finance centres (Gibson 2009; Gibson and Tsakalotos 2006).

Disorder in money can "unmask" some of these ways of understanding money, but that is still socially problematic. This is due to the difficulties facing the public in trying to criticize the institution of money in an *effective and democratic way*. If money is still a mystery, one cannot "recognise the situation" (Honneth 2010, 387) with a "critical capacity" from a plural set of "repertoires of evaluation" of one's own and others' actions (Wagner 1999, 346). These sociological debates about Boltanski's approach to a theory of value cannot be developed here. Boltanski (2011; and elsewhere) argues, for example, that a market evaluation of "worthiness" based on how much money is made is usually thought inapplicable to raising children or to an engineer's professional values. Such a transposition of norms is readily regarded as inequitable. In contrast, the "empire of value" – money – as Orléan (2014) puts it, is not considered. Here, to me, lie the conceptual problems of system and social integration from the lack of possible equivalence or inclusiveness of evaluation, or of potentially peaceful public critique, regarding the mystery of money.[14] That is, after the financial crisis, the

14 Boltanski and Thévenot (2006 [1991]; 1999) try to argue that there are a plurality of "worlds" in which people, not god-like intellectuals (only), understand the norms pertaining to many of these worlds, and "therefore" are capable of their own social critique, even indignation, from the principles of value or valuation of each "world", be it "creative" in the worth of artistic inspiration from a "garret" or very differently a

only semi-accurate recourse for nearly everyone's indignation was to accuse bank officials of greed (FCIC 2011). This ignores that different money-class groups prefer deflation or inflation of money's value. Ironies abound, including the anti-wage inflation strategies since the 1970s, said to be in the interests of "savers" whereas inflation is in the interests of borrowers (Krippner 2011). While ever more people borrow from banks and save in pension funds, they are often the same people and are used instrumentally in both cases. Another irony is that Hayek and Keynes came to similar conclusions about money as credit, but their political recipes were poles apart (Schumpeter 1954, 1120–1121) – the market and the state; inequality versus equality.

With social integration, then, the link between money's social forces that conflict, to the potential for purchasing power, comes through the opportunities for paid employment. When deflationary forces win (temporarily given banks' other, ultimately unsustainable options), there is economic stagnation and social exclusion. In social contexts of financial sector dominance and mobile capital "dictating the terms" to the state, the unemployed are blamed as are unions in merely asking for a living wage. The double standards leave the excluded unrecognized, stigmatized, isolated, unable to contribute to the social whole and thus deprived of a strong avenue to a sense of citizenship and mutual belonging in workplaces. As well, mass reduction of purchasing power results in systemic stagnation. These are concrete and visible relations, not the distant forces that decide not to invest and choose to fight (only one, wage) inflation that could be and has been moderated by consensus (say in corporatism, worker participation on boards and public agreements in parliaments). The Occupy movement was just as correct to point to the "one per cent", then, as the "dual mandate" (Pixley 1993; 1997).

Major actors appear to have no better critical capacities about money than populations; when still PM in the UK, Gordon Brown did liken money to a sewerage infrastructure – when the sewer is blocked, emergency action is required. (The metaphor is appealing but not so accurate). Disorder in the institution of money raises fear and anger, but the *targets* after 2009 moved, often inaccurately onto many states. Those who preferred deflation did not favour state spending, even amidst distress from lack of long-term investment. Some governments had earlier pushed for relieving their responsibilities onto a financial sector claimed

---

"market" worth of "money" and lots of it, as proof of "worthiness" (or not). See also Wagner (1999) and Boltanski (2011).

to be perfect, and some but not all central banks feted financial markets or were ordered to do so. But money remains "a space of exception".

My final link in talking about "manufacturing money" is to large scale, indirect types of integration or "invisible hand" accounts of order, which is increasingly top-down in many spheres of life. I despair that any normative grounds for critique are developing or if money can ever have "inclusive" types of evaluation. A little-known article by Calhoun (1992, 205) put out a challenge to sociology to seek theories of society more appropriate than "capitalism" or "post-industrial society"; in effect, to "improve our understanding of social integration" as it is too often neglected.

Calhoun (1992, 206) argues that those functionalist accounts of integration, and Habermas's distinction of social integration/lifeworld and system integration/system, the latter cybernetically defined with a "disintegrative effect on the lifeworld", neglect definite social relations.[15] In modernity, personal direct relations do not account for either *patterns* of relations between members of populations or coordination and organization of social action/public life. As we know, primary and secondary "direct" relations are compartmentalized, but as he says, "indirect" social relationships are growing; their scale and importance ever increasing: that is, there is an *extension of social integration on a very wide scale* (also Pixley 1999). These relations are highly mediated, by markets, administrative organizations (states and corporations) and information technology.

Our use of credit cards, employment applications, purchases of goods and services, all provide data subject for reanalysis by corporations and governments. Rates of inflation, unemployment, public debt and consumer price indexes are reanalysed for purposes good or ill. Does Calhoun here see "rates" are social relations? I agree though, with the extraordinary growth in corporations and bureaucracies, which consequently increases the social interactions between individuals and corporations and between corporations (Calhoun 1992, 211).

Instead of the individualism that is often counterposed to reified concepts like "the economy" and the "market", Calhoun urges that we consider "the corporation" and administrative organizations to be distinctive, as social entity and cultural artefact. Manifestly, the relations of "natural persons" to corporations are completely asymmetric and typically unequal. That does not mean these social relations are excluded from the banner of "integration", but it does mean the underrepresentation of natural persons vis-à-vis the corporation

15 Calhoun never pursued this further, and like Boltanski and others, see above, nor did he pretend to include money relations, though he recently has been.

gives it huge advantages. And yet, there are relational aspects that contribute to integration.

The key concept is indirect, mediated relationships, ever further subject to manipulation. Calhoun urges much more study of "concrete social relations", which he takes from Weber as "the probability that the actions of one person will influence the course of action of another". Despite Calhoun's reference to credit cards and inflation, social relations of money *per se* are not mentioned in his paper. Nevertheless, his formulation is useful to show the ways that natural persons are, under Calhoun's argument, socially integrated in indirect relations of "mutual determination" with the corporations and bureaucracies. I hope that this shows also that top-down corporate manipulation is more reactive than "planned", as response to the last disaster only of yesterday.

For example, after the 1970s inflationary years, central banks took on egregious types of objectification of populations, which is largely forgotten already. Their euphemisms set in, about the *certainties of low wage inflation (mass unemployment)* in policies like the NAIRU, operational to this day. The human degradation hidden in this acronym is a "Non-Accelerating Inflation Rate of Unemployment". They ignored bank-money's creative and destructive roles in economic activity and central bank uselessness in deflation. They descended into giving "credibility" to the market, and defined it as "managerial competence" or essential for financial sector "confidence". They worried endlessly about self-fulfilling prophecies that, in this anxiety of doing nothing whatsoever to control banks, also became self-fulfilling prophecies.[16]

After banking's widespread sale of debts to households for some decades, eventually to people with no hope of servicing let alone repaying loans that banks alleged had been "securitized" safely, yet one more collapse over 400 years of monetary disorders took place starting in 2007. And, as events turned out, the aggregate of these debtors did influence the course of action of the "other", namely of the entire financial system.

As we know, this was no intended social movement but lone Americans – perhaps gulled or enticed into a predatory loan – who simply broke that relation. Mortgages were abandoned, house keys thrown into the gutter. It had a shocking "influence" on the finance sector. It is a kind of negative proof that the concrete relations that we all have with the finance sector are an indirect form of social

16 I interviewed some who, I feel, thought that these technocratic duties were not to be questioned, or not to me. Yet in US Federal Reserve (FOMC) transcripts, there are dissident and critical views in these meetings, and other records of dissidents (Pixley 2004; Fraser 1996).

integration into a disintegration at the general level. These people did not *mean* to create a global financial crisis and now, we see, ever further disorder created by this sector as governments, taxpayers and populations suffer and divisiveness rises. The sector behaved as though aloof from society, as though money was not a social relation but a "thing" that banks could create solely in reference to the sector (yet secretly via government bailouts; or the US prison system, with a *quarter* of the world's prisoners: Western 2006). Creditors cannot exist without debtors and the community (i.e. governments and taxpayers) that validates their manufacture of money. When the CEO of Goldman Sachs said at the time, banks are "doing god's work", the judgement that some indeterminate kind of abuse took place seems appropriate. But this major social relation of immense global proportions cannot be wished away by theoretical decree; that decree is part of the problem.

After the collapse of the credit-money inflation in 2008, more critical views emerged among so-called experts. This has not extended to politicians. Nevertheless, BoE senior officials showed that for over a hundred years, the UK private banking sector assets (its loans) stayed much the same as a percent of GDP, at 50%. That is, lending was in line with general economic activity. Assets then grew to 500%, most spectacularly from 1982 to 2007. At the same time, and against old norms of credit expansion, banks also took on more dangers, with capital and liquidity ratios declining (Alessandri and Haldane 2009). A similar pattern occurred in the USA, with "assets" of stocks, bonds, loans, mortgages, though not including derivatives, which is estimated at possibly 1000% of global GDP (Morris 2008, xii). This ratio of credit piled on top of real output, as Morris says, makes a huge and "wobbly" inverted pyramid, which seems ever more dangerous. Then it turned out that the large French, Swiss and German banks were in a similar position. Moreover, those political leaders who do demand a return of jobs to "rustbelts" most recently, via anti-migrant divide and rule, and futile (dangerous) mercantilism, leave the idea of full employment as a brake on banking's preference for deflation, as a dirty secret "forgotten" in the long bank-money inflation. In 2017, the idea banks might be controlled seems further from sight.[17]

Without a renewal of social democracy, the Keynesian "moment" when many placed trust in the democratic state to defend full employment may not return.

---

17 Admati and Hellwig (2013). Demagoguery is less studied in Nigel Farage's "England first" campaigns (than Trump), although he is a financier engaged in *global* deals that further undermine the UK's economy!

Recall the US Congress standoff in 2011 against a Democrat President. Weisberg (2011, 7) said a "lesson" from those Tea Party Congress members who "clearly desired default" is that "America now regards its most solemn financial obligations as flexible commitments". He suggests that "whatever their motivations, there is something sad about desperate Americans looking to a party that lacks any inclination to alleviate their misery". Despite this, I remain hopeful for social democracy, and who knows?

4 Conclusion

There are critiques from other types of evaluation than the "market", such as responsible and socially creative bank-money production that Schumpeter championed. But criticisms are hugely complicated, in looking at arrangements that formerly seemed "to work" (as if by an invisible hand) but only as a buildup to a disaster, and at the problem of complete lack of consensus about money. Increased purchasing power through paid work on a living wage is desperately needed for social integration and means of recognition; taxable employment is essential for systemic state spending and servicing bank advances, but that remains ignored. The "invisible hand" or system integration rarely proves that way if money is included, yet analysis is weakened without concepts such as these. Things look grim if governments only agree to provide further "certainty" to the global financial sector: this is the demand from its so-called lobbyists despite the "systemic" problems of unintended consequences already in evidence from the GFC and many before. Similarly, governments that pursue (nuclear) war finance at a rising scary rate, along with major tax cutbacks, only throw themselves into greater dependency on borrowing: not only misunderstanding but losing any broader views of money's direct and indirect relationships. Is money a vast "sub-system" with ever larger impacts, or such a "space of exception" that analyses cannot accommodate money? Whatever one decides, the outlook for any inclusive forms of social integration and constructive critiques that might drive a movement for even limited form of democratic controls over money "from below" is still bleak, despite the lonely attempts of the "Occupy" movement back in 2011.

References

Admati, Anat R., and Martin Hellwig. 2013. *The Bankers' New Clothes: What's Wrong with Banking and What to Do About It*. Princeton University Press.

Alessandri, Piergiorgio, and Andrew S. Haldane. 2009. "Banking on the State." Bank of England. Paper presented at the Federal Reserve Bank of Chicago conference on "The International Financial Crisis: Have the Rules of Finance

Changed?" Chicago, September 25, 2009. Accessed November 16, 2017. http://www.bankofengland.co.uk/publications/speeches/2009/speech409.pdf.

Beckert, Jens. 2016. *Imagined Futures: Fictional Expectations and Capitalist Dynamics*. Cambridge (MA): Harvard University Press.

Bernanke, Ben S. 2013. *The Federal Reserve and the Financial Crisis*. Princeton University Press.

Blinder, Alan S. 2013. *After the Music Stopped: The Financial Crisis, the Response, and the Work Ahead*. New York: Penguin Books.

Boltanski, Luc. 2011. *On Critique*. Cambridge: Polity.

Boltanski, Luc, and Laurent Thévenot. 1999. "The Sociology of Critical Capacity." *European Journal of Social Theory* 2: 359–377.

Boltanski, Luc, and Laurent Thévenot. 2006 [1991]. *On Justification: Economies of Worth*. Princeton University Press.

Bryan, Dick. 2010. "The Duality of Labour and the Financial Crisis." *The Economic and Labour Relations Review* 20: 49–60.

Calhoun, Craig. 1992. "The Infrastructure of Modernity." In *Social Change and Modernity*, edited by Hans Haferkamp and Neil J. Smelser, 205–236. Berkeley: University of California Press.

Collins, Randall. 1986. *Weberian Sociological Theory*. Cambridge University Press.

FCIC [Financial Crisis Inquiry Commission]. 2011. *The Financial Crisis Inquiry Report*. Final Report of the National Commission on the Causes of the Financial and Economic Crisis in the United States, Washington (DC): U.S. Government Printing Office.

Forder, James. 2014. *Macroeconomics and the Phillips Curve Myth*. Oxford: Oxford University Press.

Fraser, Bernard William. 1996. *Collected Speeches: B. W. Fraser, Governor Reserve Bank of Australia 1989–1996*, vol 1-2. Sydney: Reserve Bank of Australia.

Friedman, Milton. 1968. "The Role of Monetary Policy." *The American Economic Review* LVIII: 1–17.

Galbraith, John Kenneth. 1975. *Money: Whence It Came, Where It Went*. Boston: Houghton Mifflin.

Giannini, Curzio. 2011. *The Age of Central Banks*. Cheltenham: Edward Elgar.

Gibson, Heather D. 2009. "Competition, Innovation and Financial Crises: A Perspective on the Current Financial Market Turmoil." *Open Economic Review* 21: 151–157.

Gibson, Heather, and Euclid Tsakalotos. 2006. "Narrowing the Options: The Macroeconomic and Financial Framework for EU Enlargement." In *Growth and Economic Development: Essays in Honour of A. P. Thirlwall*, edited by Philip Arestis, John McCombie and Roger Vickerman, chap. 11. Cheltenham: Edward Elgar.

Goldthorpe, John H. 1978. "The Current Inflation: Towards a Sociological Account." In *The Political Economy of Inflation*, edited by Fred Hirsch and John H. Goldthorpe, 186–214. London: Martin Robertson.

Granovetter, Mark. 1985. "Economic Action and Social Structure: The Problem of Embeddedness." *American Journal of Sociology* 91: 481–510.

Habermas, Jürgen 1975. *Legitimation Crisis*. Boston: Beacon Press.

Haldane, Andrew. 2010. "The Contribution of the Financial Sector: Miracle or Mirage?" Paper presented at the Future of Finance Conference, London, July 14, 2010, 1–38. The LSE Report: London School of Economics.

Hayek, Friedrich August. 1945. "The Use of Knowledge in Society." *American Economic Review* XXXV: 519–530.

Hill, Lisa, and Peter McCarthy. 2004. "On Friendship and *Necessitudo* in Adam Smith." *History of the Human Sciences* 17: 1–16.

Hirsch, Fred. 1978. "The Ideological Underlay of Inflation." *The Political Economy of Inflation*, edited Fred Hirsch and John H. Goldthorpe, 263–284. London: Martin Robertson.

Hirschman, Albert O. 1997 [1977]. *The Passions and the Interests*. Princeton University Press.

Honneth, Axel. 2010. "Dissolution of the Social: On the Social Theory of Boltanski and Thévenot." *Constellations* 17: 376–389.

Hughes, Everett C. 1937. "Institutional Office and the Person." *American Journal of Sociology* 43: 404–413.

Ingham, Geoffrey. 1996. "Some Recent Changes in the Relationship between Economics and Sociology." *Cambridge Journal of Economics* 20: 243–275.

Ingham, Geoffrey. 2004. *The Nature of Money*. Cambridge: Polity Press.

Ingham, Geoffrey. 2008. *Capitalism*. Cambridge: Polity Press.

Kalecki, M. 1943. "Political Aspects of Full Employment." *Political Quarterly* 14: 322–330.

Krippner, Greta R. 2011 *Capitalizing on Crisis: The Political Origins of the Rise of Finance*. Cambridge (MA): Harvard University Press.

Lockwood, David. 1964. "Social Integration and System Integration." In *Explorations in Social Change*, edited by George K. Zollschan and Walter Hirsch, 244–257. London: Routledge and Kegan Paul.

Luce, Edward. 2011. "Why America Is Embracing Protest." *Financial Times*, 31 October: 9. Accessed August 10, 2017. https://www.ft.com/content/242bd162-0152-11e1-b177-00144feabdc0.

Lyman, Stanford M., and Marvin B. Scott. 1969. "Coolness in Everyday Life." In *Sociology and Everyday Life*, edited by Marcello Truzzi, 143–157. Englewood Cliffs: Prentice-Hall.

Mann, Geoff. 2013. "The Monetary Exception: Labour, Distribution and Money in Capitalism." *Capital and Class* 37: 197–216.

Minsky, H. 1992. "The Financial Instability Hypothesis." *The Jerome Levy Economics Institute*, Working Paper No 74. Annandale-on-Hudson: Bard College.

Morris, Charles R. 2008. *The Trillion Dollar Meltdown*. New York: Public Affairs.

Moss, Larry. 1999. "Editor's Introduction." *American Journal of Economics and Sociology* 58: 551–558.

Orléan, André. 2014. *The Empire of Value: A New Foundation for Economics*. Cambridge (MA): MIT Press Books.

Panić, Milivoje. 2003. *Globalization and National Economic Welfare*. Houndmills: Palgrave.

Pixley, Jocelyn F. 1993. *Citizenship and Employment: Investigating Post-Industrial Options*. Cambridge University Press.

Pixley, Jocelyn F. 1997. "Employment and Social Identity." In *European Citizenship and Social Exclusion*, edited by Maurice Roche and Rik van Berkel, 119–134. Aldershot: Ashgate.

Pixley, Jocelyn F. 1999. "Impersonal Trust in Global Mediating Organisations." *Sociological Perspectives* 42: 647–671.

Pixley, Jocelyn F. 2004. *Emotions in Finance: Distrust and Uncertainty in Global Markets*. Cambridge University Press.

Pixley, Jocelyn F. 2010. "Decency in Anglo-American Financial Centres?" *Thesis Eleven* 101: 63–71.

Pixley, Jocelyn F. 2011. "Sociology of Uncertainty." In *Sociology and the Unintended: Robert Merton Revisited*, edited by Adriana Mica, Arkadiusz Peisert and Jan Winczorek, 89–111. Frankfurt am Main: Peter Lang Publishers.

Pixley, Jocelyn F. 2013. "Geoffrey Ingham's Theory, Money's Conflicts and Social Change." In *Financial Crises and the Nature of Capitalist Money: Mutual Developments from the Challenge of Geoffrey Ingham*, edited by Jocelyn Pixley and G. C. Harcourt, 273–299. London: Palgrave Macmillan.

Pixley, Jocelyn F. 2014. "Uncertainty: The Curate's Egg in Financial Economics." *British Journal of Sociology* 65: 200–224.

Pixley, Jocelyn, Peter McCarthy, and Shaun Wilson. 2014. "The Economy and Emotions." In *Handbook of the Sociology of Emotions*, vol II, edited by Jan E. Stets and Jonathan H. Turner, 307–333. New York: Springer.

Polanyi, Karl. 1957 [1944]. *The Great Transformation*. Boston: Beacon Press.

Schularick, Moritz. 2014. "Public and Private Debt: 'The Historical Record (1870-2010).'" *German Economic Review* 15: 191–207.

Schumpeter, Joseph A. 1934 [1911]. *The Theory of Economic Development*. New Brunswick: Transaction Publishers.

Schumpeter, Joseph A. 1954. *History of Economic Analysis*. New York: Oxford University Press.

Simmel, Georg. 1990 [1907]. *The Philosophy of Money*. London: Routledge.

Wagner, Peter. 1999. "After Justification: Repertoires of Evaluation and the Sociology of Modernity." *European Journal of Social Theory* 2: 341–357.

Weber, Max. 1978 [1922]. *Economy and Society*, edited by Guenther Roth and Claus Wittich. Berkeley: University of California.

Weber, Max. 1981 [1927]. *General Economic History*. New Brunswick: Transaction Books Inc.

Weisberg, Jacob. 2011. "Washington's Appetite for Self-Destruction." *FT*, August 5, 2017, 7.

Western, Bruce. 2006. *Punishment and Inequality in America*. New York: Russell Sage Foundation.

Withers, Hartley. 1918 [1909]. *The Meaning of Money*. London: John Murray.

Woodruff, David. 1999. *Money Unmade: Barter and the Fate of Russian Capitalism*. Ithaca: Cornell University Press.

Wray, Randall. 2010. "What Should Banks Do? A Minskyan Analysis." *Public Policy Brief* 115. Levy Economics Institute of Bard College.

Emma Tieffenbach

The Explanatory Power(s) of Unintended Consequences

Abstract: Commentators on invisible-hand explanations often stress their distinctive explanatory virtue. They claim in particular that one provides a greater insight about the nature of a certain social outcome when one supposes that those who contribute to that outcome do not intend it. But commentators also tend to avoid offering a precise account of the nature of the related explanatory gain. An explication is missing, and it is the goal of the present chapter to supply it. Because the notion of unintended consequences is highly ambiguous, its multiple (often conflated and tacit) meanings are preliminarily distinguished. The chapter then critically reconstructs several arguments in support of the explanatory power of unintended consequences thus disambiguated. It finally points to another understanding of the merit of unintended consequences: the point of re-describing an intended social outcome as an unintended one, I submit, is to acknowledge those social aspects that exist independently from what we or some legal authority, decide, accept or believe to be the case.

Keywords: Invisible-hand explanations (IHE); intentional-design explanations (IDE); unintended consequences; explanatory power; mind-independent entities

To offer an invisible-hand explanation (hereafter IHE) is to think of the various choices that, over several successive stages, many individuals would have to make for a certain social outcome to obtain, *without the latter figuring among these individuals' objectives*. The italic restriction in this definition is crucial. For the success of an IHE centrally depends on whether it dispenses with an intention to produce the outcome to be explained on the part of those who bring it into being. IHE conflict with the more standard, intentional-design explanations[1] (hereafter IDE) of the same outcomes, which assume just the opposite: that these outcomes could not realize were it not for certain human intentions.

The point of an IHE may occasionally be to supplement the IDE that initially suggests itself. More often, however, IHE are intended to be preferred to the latter. As Tuomela phrases it:

1 Ullmann-Margalit (1978). IDE are also termed "straightforward explanations" (Nozick 1974), "direct explanations" (Wray 2000), "intentional explanations" (Elster 1983) or "explanations from design" (Vermeule 2010).

> What an invisible hand explanation typically does is the following. It replaces an easily forthcoming and initially plausible explanation according to which the *explanandum* is the product of intentional design with a rival account according to which it is brought about via a process involving the separate actions of many individuals who are supposed to be minding (only) their own business unaware of and hence not intending to bring about the ultimate overall outcome (Tuomela 1984, 451).

Likewise, Nozick defines IHE as defeating the IDE that initially suggested itself:

> [Invisible-hand explanations] show how some overall pattern or design, which one would have thought had to be produced by an individual's or group's successful attempt to realize the pattern, *instead* was produced and maintained by a process that in no way had the overall pattern or design "in mind" (Nozick 1974, 18 [emphasis added]).

Showing that individuals need not after all pursue an outcome for reaching it is inherently rewarding. Still, many commentators do not (officially) approach IHE as a mind game. Rather, the value of converting intended phenomena into unintended ones, it is usually claimed, is to provide a finer understanding of these phenomena. Nozick claims, for example, that IHE "yield greater understanding than do explanations of [the same social patterns] as brought about by design as the object of people's intentions [and that] it therefore is no surprise that there are more satisfying" (Nozick 1974, 19). Likewise, Ullmann-Margalit holds "'good' invisible-hand explanations [to] yield substantial understanding of, and provide considerable insight into, the nature of the social patterns and institutions explained" (Ullmann-Margalit 1978, 277). She relates the "explanatory import" of IHE to an "element of reduction" in them. That is, these explanations are about a social pattern arising "through a process involving the actions of individuals who do not have it mind" (Ullmann-Margalit 1978, 277). In short, IHE carry more illumination, and this is why they are to be preferred over their intentional-design rivals.

A century earlier, Menger expressed similar confidence in the explicatory power of unintended consequences. He offered an "organic explanation" (Menger 1985 [1883], 145), *aka* IHE, of money that purposefully avoids to construe it as the intended result of an "express agreement" or a "legislative act" (Menger 1985 [1883], 154). Only by depicting money as the "unintended result, as the unplanned outcome of specific efforts of members of a society", Menger claimed, will "the origin of money […] truly be brought to our *full understanding*" (Menger 1985 [1883], 136 [emphasis added]).

Let us call such a defence of IHE the "anti-design plea", which I define as follows:

> **The anti-design plea:** It is because IHE show that individuals can produce a social outcome S without intending S, or have S in mind, that they have greater explanatory power than an IDE of S.

Commentators agree on IHE having more explicatory value than their intentional-design rivals. But they also tend to avoid any precise claims about the explicatory benefit that is thus provided. They leave it at one's guess the explanatory gain of assuming, while offering an explanation of S, that those who contribute to S are not aware of S, let alone intend S. What is it that we get to know about S that is concealed when S is featured as intended? An explanation is missing, and it is the goal of the present chapter to supply it.

On the proposed account, IHE are thought experiments that can be used to investigate the logical structure of the social reality. They provide insightful answers to questions such as "What distinguishes money from barter?", "Could a State exist unbeknownst to those It protects?", "Could property rules arise without being decreed nor agreed upon?", etc. The merit of IHE, I argue, is to sort out those aspects of social entities that are grounded in our choices, and those that stand independent from our will or knowledge (see Thomasson 2003). Here is how I shall proceed. The first section puts flesh on what I have so far too abstractly referred to as IHE. Here I retell a few "stories" commonly labelled as such. The second section disambiguates the notion of unintended consequences. The multiple, often conflated, meanings that that notion currently has in the literature are spelled out in this section. The proposed clarification will prove useful when, in the subsequent section, several arguments in support of the explanatory power of unintended consequences are critically reviewed. The fourth section presents a more promising way of understanding that explanatory power. The point of re-describing an intended social outcome as an unintended one, I show in this conclusive part, is to offer a conception of social reality that acknowledges those institutional aspects that exist independently from what we, or some legal authority decides, accepts and believes to be the case – those mind-independent features that would remain concealed were we to rely on an IDE for understanding them.

1 Invisible-hand stories: a few examples

Since Nozick (1974, 8) first coined the term, the notion of IHE has been used to refer to a wide variety of economic models, experiments and historical narratives. While not exhausting the range of application, the following examples are often invoked for illustrating the notion:

- **Hume's explanation of the origin of property rules**: Absent any property rules governing who owns what, people acquire their goods by stealing them (Hume 1896 [1739], book III, part ii, sect. 2). Being more profitable in the long run, the rule "Don't steal unless others steal" progressively inspired an increasing number of persons. This is how property rules evolved, that is, without anyone mutually promising to follow them. Surely, an initial agreement could have taken place. But such an exchange of promises is too remote to have any direct effect on those who were not part of the agreement. The rules of the stability of possessions are therefore not the product of, and are conceptually independent from, a mutual consent to refrain from stealing one another's good. These rules evolved and were not implemented.

- **Smith's account of the prosperity of English industries**: English entrepreneurs prefer to not invest abroad, where trades rules are neither clear not efficiently enforced (Smith 1904 [1776], book IV, chap. 2). While the English industries greatly benefit from the typical entrepreneur's aversion to the risks of investing abroad, that desirable effect is not part of the English investor's goal, who "intends only his own gain, and he is in this, as in many other cases, led by an invisible hand to promote an end which was no part of his intention" (Smith 1904, book IV, chap. 2, § 9). Smith further argues that the prosperity of English industries is often better served when it is no one's goal. "By pursuing his own interest [the entrepreneur] frequently promotes that of the society more effectually than when he really intends to promote it" (Smith 1904, book IV, chap. 2, § 9).
- **Nozick's explanation of minimal State**: In the State of nature, people interact without any political authority supervising them (Nozick 1974). They are equipped with rights, which they defend against aggressors by punishing them or by obtaining compensation from them. People may also transfer their right and find it advantageous to transfer the right to protect them to some specialized protective agencies. Non-competitive protective private agencies get eliminated, until one of them offers its service to all individuals living in one unified geographical. This monopolistic agency is a State, although only a "minimal" one given its limited prerogative. As Nozick (1974, 132) stresses, "no one, as they buy protection services from their local protective agency, has in mind anything so grand" as the institution of a State. Still, a State is what people bring about by all joining the agency – and not, *Pace* Locke, by " 'agreeing with other men to join and unite into a community,' consenting 'to make one community or government' (*Theory of Government.* sect. 95), compacting to make up a commonwealth (sec. 99)" (Nozick 1974, 132).
- **Menger's "organic" explanation of money**: Money is commonly conceived as whichever thing (wheat, barley grain, etc.) States accept in payment of taxes (Ingham 2004). Against such view, Menger claims that money is the "unintended result of historical development" (Menger 1985 [1883], 130). By this he means that "money is not a State institution" (Menger 1892, 51), nor the

result of a "conscious common will of society directed toward establishing [it]" (Menger 1985 [1883], 173). According to Menger, money evolves from the barter system and a recognition of its inconveniencies: barters depend on a "double coincidence of wants" (Jevons 1876, chap. 1, § 5) that limits their happening. A solution is to acquire a few, highly saleable, even if useless goods. The point is to increase the odds of finding someone willing to give, in exchange of these intermediary goods, the goods one wants. The more a certain good is chosen as an intermediate good, the more its salability increases, the more it will henceforth be chosen as an intermediate good. Until a small number of goods, sometimes only one, are used as such. Money is just one of these goods.

- **Lewis's theory of convention**: Conventions are solutions to coordination dilemma (Lewis 1969). For example, deciding which side of the road we should drive on, assigning to a good the function of a medium of exchange, figuring who should call back when a phone conversation has been interrupted. In each case, everyone has an interest in doing whatever everyone else does, but face multiple solutions. One may resolve the dilemma with the help of external coordination cues: fines from the highway patrol to whoever does not drive on the correct side. Lewis objects that forming the right sort of mutual expectations plays a more crucial role than such external incentives. Mutual expectations, he further argues, are formed when certain options "stand out uniqueness in some conspicuous respect" (Lewis 1969, 35). In the Commonwealth, the option "drive on the left" is salient enough to cause mutual expectations as to which side to drive on. Conventions need not be decreed for existing.
- **Schelling's checkerboard city:** In this game, residents are played by dimes and pennies, spread at random over a chessboard, with some squares left empty (Schelling 1978). Dimes and pennies prefer living in a non-segregated environment, in which at least one-third of their neighbours is of the same (social, ethnic or cultural) type as themselves. They can move from square to square until they reach the nearest empty square at which their preferences are satisfied. Moving the pieces according to the stipulated motives results in dimes and pennies entirely segregated from one another. Residential segregation is the unintended consequence of the residents' choices to live in mixt neighbourhood.
- **Keller's theory of linguistic changes**: Gallantry urges men to "choose expressions that tend to belong to a higher level of style or social standing rather than a lower one" (Keller 1994, 73). Sometimes, however, it is not obvious which level of style words belong to. The rule, in the latter case, is to

> minimize risk. Speakers will "choose an expression that is a notch too high rather than too low" (Keller 1994, 73). If everyone believes that "Dame" is more gallant than "Frau", then "Dame" is more gallant than Frau. As the rule diffuses, it becomes normal to use Dame, whereas using Frau starts sounding slightly discourteous. Ultimately, the same fate will happen to "Dame". Pejoration of terms is the unintended effect of all speakers' willingness to use stylish and gallant words (Keller 1994, 44).

As already noted, the success of an IHE depends in part on whether it persuasively describes its *Explanandum* as one no one has in mind or intends. How do the explanations here outlined fare in this respect? The impression could be that some of them fall short of such expectation. Let us consider a few reasons why. First, one could suspect that some of the explanations *complement*, rather than truly *supplant* the IDE that initially suggests itself. Consider in this regard Menger's account of money. As Menger admits, a full understanding of the money system may require both types of explanation. For, even if "[the State] is not responsible for the existence of the money-character of the good", still it is often "responsible for a significant improvement of its money-character" (Menger 2007 [1871], 262). In particular, States may play a role in "the full establishment" of the money system by making "legally binding" the use of a particular currency (Menger 2007 [1871], 262). So an IHE of the *emergence* of the money system can very well be combined with an IDE of its *maintenance*.[2] Here are some other ways explanations of the intentional-design type and of invisible-hand type may complement each other:

- The State may not be responsible for the fact that many agents will prefer using a certain good as a medium of exchange. Still it will ensure *via* a decree that all agents abide by that existing rule. An IHE of the broad, informal use of a thing as a medium of exchange is here combined with an IDE of that thing becoming legal tender.
- Alternatively, the State may not be responsible for the fact that everyone's preferences converge *à la Menger* on a restricted range of money-commodity. Still, it will ensure that they henceforth use only one of these commodities as a medium of exchange. An IHE of the use of few goods as a medium

2 What about the opposite combination of an IDE of the emergence of money with an invisible-hand account of its maintenance? Menger would object to such combination; one may conjecture that it misguidedly construes money as being a creation of a state.

of exchange is here combined with an IDE of the use of *a single* good as a medium of exchange.

- Finally, the State may not be responsible for the fact that many agents prefer using a single good as money. Still, it will ensure *via* a decree that they all must use *one particular* good as such. An IHE of the ongoing use of a thing as a medium of exchange is, in this case, combined with an IDE of the obligation to use, say, note bills as a medium of exchange.

In each case, the IHE is not to be preferred to the IDE because it does not conflict, but complements the latter.

The impression that the initially forthcoming IDE has not been really challenged may be explained still differently. Some of the IHE just listed may be objected for accounting for an embryonic variety of the institution to be explained, rather than the full-blown version of the institution. Consider again Menger's account of money. One may object to that account that money is *not* just any good that is universally used as a medium of exchange. For the possession of money comes with a range of obligations, permissions and licenses, which Menger's account leaves explained. For example, no one could be obligated to accept without question the intermediary good that plays the role of money in Menger's story. Nor does possessing a few of intermediary goods confer the *right* to the purchase of anything. Real money differs from these intermediary goods in Menger's story in both respects. There are certain things, like refusing the demanded amount of money in exchange of something put on sale, which one is not licensed to do with real money. In Menger's story, there is nothing wrong with not using as a medium of exchange the good that is commonly used as such within one's group. So while the use of real money is governed by various norms, the sort of commodity-money that invisible-handedly arises from the barter system has none of these normative dimensions (Tieffenbach 2010). Because it misses crucial, normative properties of money, one may object to Menger's IHE of money that it is not the perfect substitute to the more standard IDE of the same outcome that it is supposed to be.

Finally, some IHE may be criticized for depicting agents as too close to aiming at the outcome to be explained. This may constitute still another reason why they appear to fail to truly defy the IDE of the same outcome. Gaus objects to Nozick's explanation on that ground. According to Gaus, it is not entirely obvious that the rise of a minimal State is not among the goal of the dominant protective agency. This is because "the actions and reasoning of the dominant protective agency in prohibiting unauthorized enforcement by independents is too close to aiming at [the minimal State] to constitute a satisfying invisible hand explanation of [the minimal State]" (Gaus 2011, 122). The attempt to gain a monopoly on the authorization of coercion is not truly different from aiming at a minimal State. So the transition from an ultra-minimal State to a minimal State seems more intended than what it would need to be for qualifying as an invisible-hand transition. The participants have in mind something too close to a State as what the monopolistic protective agency amounts to. But then one will be tempted to ask: "How familiar with the full notion of State should individuals be for the story to remain of the invisible-hand type?" Difficulty to answer this question indicates that there might not be a clear-cut dividing line between IHE and their rivals.

Let us suppose however that an IHE avoids the shortcomings or ambiguities just listed. Still, one may justifiably ask: why *prefer* it to an IDE of the same about? To address this question, I will review various arguments in favour of the distinctive, explanatory value of unintended consequence in the following section. To prepare the discussion, the next section disambiguates the wide range of meanings that this notion currently has received in the literature.

1.1 The various meanings of unintended consequences

As a constraint, an IHE depicts individuals who do not intend to bring about the social pattern that is to be explained. While this constraint is consensually followed and recognized in the literature, there is not any consistent standard for how to label it. One common formulation is to refer to invisible-hand outcomes as "unintended consequences", with some further qualifications (cf. Ullmann-Margalit 1978; Aydinonat 2008, chap. 2). Alternatively, the participants of invisible-hand stories are said to be "minding (only) their own business" Tuomela 1984, 451), or not having "the overall pattern in mind" (Nozick 1974, 18). Whichever expression is used, the general idea is that individuals fail to understand what is going on and it is in this sense that the process in which they participate is invisible to them. To avoid confusion due to multiple wordings, I will refer to the "unintended consequence assumption",[3] which I define as follows:

> **The unintended consequence assumption:** Individuals act in the way that is required for some social pattern to emerge, without yet intending it, nor even have it in mind.

3 That term is broad enough to encompass most of the meanings reviewed in this section. Its merit is thus to lexically unify the various formulations used in the literature under one single wording.

Besides receiving variable formulations, the unintended consequence assumption also happens to be understood in a great variety of ways.[4] There is obviously more than one way a social outcome may elude those who bring it about. This section reviews the most important possibilities. The next section will discuss the explanatory value of unintended consequences on any of these meanings.

1.1.1 The "lack of foresight" meaning

One obvious sense in which agents may not have the outcome in mind, let alone intend it, is that they do not foresee it. In the literature, "unintended" and "unanticipated" are often used equivocally. Ullmann-Margalit (1978, 278) defines invisible-hand outcomes as those individuals "neither foresee […] nor intend to bring […] about". For Anomaly and Brennan (2014, 263), an invisible-hand outcome is "surprising, unforeseen, or unpredictable by those who produce it". Unintended consequences are in this case unanticipated ones.

In Menger's account of money, the barterers do not have anything like the emergence of a money system as the remote effect of their individual strategy to ascribe to some goods the function of serving as a medium of exchange. Likewise, the sense in which linguistic changes are, in Keller's analysis, unintended also points to that meaning. None of the speakers, in Keller's analysis of the pejoration of expressions, presumably predicts that *Dame* will undergo the same pejoration that *Frau* has endured.

However, whether short-sightedness plays a crucial role in IHE is questionable. To be relevant, short-sightedness would have to determine individual choices: that the participants of invisible-hand process would have acted differently, had they anticipated the effect of their action. But, in the cases above,

---

4 For the sake of clarity, I shall stress the difference between:

(1) The variety of *terms* and *expressions* that, in the literature, are used to refer to the unintendedness of the invisible-hand outcomes. In this chapter, I refer to the "unintended consequence assumption" in order to avoid the multiple formula displayed in the literature. The merit of that term is to lexically unify the terms used in the literature under one single wording.
(2) The variety of *meanings*, listed in this section, ascribed to the unintended consequence assumption.

In the literature, no systematic connection obviously stands between wordings and meanings.

such correct recognition does not play any obvious role. To recognize the future pejoration of any words used with the intention to distinguish themselves does not provide a reason to not use these words. Knowing that everyone using something as a medium of exchange results in the emergence of the money system does not make the choice to use something as a medium of exchange in the first place less advisable. Because short-sightedness does not impact on individual's choices, that particular sense in which an outcome is dubbed "unintended" can be disregarded in the remaining part of the discussion (see also Aydinonat 2008, 80).

1.1.2 The "lack of decree" meaning

The participants of an invisible-hand process may not intend the outcome to be explained in another sense: no central authority has made it obligatory to act in the way required for that outcome to occur. IHE based on those assumptions are meant to dispense with a legislative act (be it a decree, an enactment, etc.) or any other intervention from a central authority. Unintended consequences have now the sense of non-legislated ones.

Unintended consequences explicitly take that meaning in Menger's organic explanations of money. According to Menger (2007 [1871], 261, 130), it is in virtue of being "an invention of the state [nor] the product of a legislative act" that money can be rightfully construed as the "unintended result of historical development".

1.1.3 The "profit-motive" meaning

On some other meaning, unintended consequences are those that benefit many although caused by choices made for personal benefit. The point of an IHE is in this case to dispense with altruistic motivations. This meaning is in Elster's definition of invisible-hand consequences as good-for-all outcomes resulting from good-for-me choices:

> A person acts in order to benefit. In doing so, he also affects other people (and often himself) in a secondary way. Typically, the secondary impact, whether negative or positive, is quite small compared with the primary, intended benefit. Yet when everybody acts in this way, each person becomes the target of many small benefits (Elster 1989, 97; see also Williams 2002, 33).

Unintended consequences are here conceived as effects that are profitable to a larger number than to those who produce them and primarily benefit from them. The weak version of that thesis conceives altruism as causally inefficient. The strong version conceives altruism as not only irrelevant, but counter-productive

(Lynch and Walsh 2003, 44). Smith (1904) has in mind the latter variant when he claims to "have never known much good done by those who affected to trade for the public good" (1904, book 4, chap. II, § 4).

1.1.4 The "lack of agreement" meaning

Still alternatively, invisible-hand explainers may intend to dispense with a binding agreement when they refer to the outcome to be explained as unintended. The point of the IHE is in this case to show that the outcome can perfectly be the effect of many non-concerted choices.

Menger has this other particular sense[5] in mind when he claims that money is "not the product of an agreement on the part of economizing men" (Menger 1985 [1883], 262). Likewise, Nozick introduces his IHE of State by contrasting it with a Lockean social pact. He defends his IHE precisely for dispensing with the " 'agreement,' or 'mutual consent' ", which Locke considered to be central to the establishment (and justification) of a government (Nozick 1974, 18).

1.1.5 The "lack of theoretical knowledge" meaning

The notion of unintended consequences may further refer to those social patterns that *theoretically* elude those who contribute to their occurrence. Mäki's analysis of "Austrian explanations" (*aka* IHE) appeals to that particular meaning. Austrian explanations, according to Mäki (1990a, 337), are "theoretical redescriptions meant to replace the superficial 'phenomenological' or 'empirical' description of intentional-design explanation". The redescription thus provided is a form of "ontological microreduction" by which complex phenomena are identified with their various basic constituents (Mäki 1990a, 321–323). Such a reduction, Mäki (1990a, 325–326) argues, will in effect turn an apparently intended social outcome into what it "essentially" is, that is, an unintended one. Mäki (1990a, 326) approaches Menger's explanation as showing that "it is part of the essence of money that it is a spontaneous outgrowth of an unplanned process of individual interaction" (see also Vernon 1979).

---

5 The following quote illustrates the variety of meanings, listed in this section, that Menger does not care distinguishing: "as *each* economizing individual becomes increasingly more aware of his economic interest, he is led by *his interest, without any agreement, without legislative compulsion and even without regard to the public interest,* to give his commodities in exchange for the other, more saleable, commodities, even if he does not need them for any immediate consumption purpose" (Menger, 2007 [1771], 260.

Similarly, Rothschild defines the unintended consequences of IHE as theoretical constructions that are not available to those who bring them about. As she writes, "the disembodied hand is invisible to its millions of petty subjects, but it is visible to 'us': to theorists" (Rothshild 2001, 124). Rothschild also complains about the related elitism of "presuppos[ing] the existence of a theorist (if not of a reformer), who sees more than any ordinary individual can". She finds the idea "un-Smithian" (Rothshild 2001, 124; see Aydinonat 2006 for a critical discussion).

1.1.6 The "lack of we-ness" meaning

Unintended consequences may occasionally mean something else, that is, consequences produced by agents acting individually rather than collectively. The latter distinction can be grasped by means of Tuomela's (2013) collective acceptance account of social practices. Tuomela distinguishes between two modes of attitudes, intentions, actions or beliefs, namely the "I-mode" and "we-mode". He defines the I-mode attitudes as "private ones, to which the person having it is only privately committed" (Tuomela 2001). In contrast, the we-mode is at work when agents hold attitudes "qua group members". The choice of using something as money, according to Tuomela, illustrates the we-mode. Any kind of physical entity can become money in virtue of the members of the collective in question accepting it as money (Tuomela 2013, chap. IV). In other words, for something to become money, individuals need to collectively accept it as such.

As I have argued elsewhere (Tieffenbach 2013), Menger's account of money may be approached as showing that the I-mode suffices for money to emerge out of the barter system. Only the high saleability of a certain good is relevant for ascribing that thing the function of a medium of exchange. Nor is the we-mode required for individuals to converge on a few number of commodity-monies. The self-reinforcing nature of the choice to use highly saleable good – the more a good is used as money, the more saleable it is, and the more it is likely to be used as money – suffices for obtaining such a convergence (Menger [1892], 131). Aydinonat (2008, 25 [emphasis added] also refers to this particular meaning when he qualifies the "unintended consequences" that pertain to the invisible hand as those produced by individuals who "do not pursue the same end collectively (that is, [when] collective intentionality is excluded)".

1.1.7 The "lack of any sense of the aggregate shape of things" meaning

Unintended consequences sometimes are macro-regularities that supervene on individual's choices. Individuals display a lack of sense of the way everyone's choices aggregate into a significant overall social pattern. It is then by switching to some higher level of description that unintended effects are obtained.

Thomasson's (2003, 606) analysis of "unintended social entities" illustrates such an account. By that category, she means "large scale social facts or those involving statistical generalizations over social facts (e.g., the fact that we are in a recession, or that 70% of Americans support the death penalty) that depend on certain mental states (regarding money and financial transactions, regarding the death penalty), but not on any intentional states regarding recessions or statistical generalizations" (Thomasson 2003, 606). For example, racism and gender discrimination "depend on the existence of certain sets of beliefs and intentional behaviors" (Thomasson 2003, 606): racism would not occur if individuals did not believe that certain groups of agents are superior than others and acted accordingly. But racism, as Thomasson (2003, 606) notes, "may exist without the existence of any beliefs that are themselves about racism". Racism may well, and often does, prevail in certain groups independently from agents having any belief regarding such prevalence. It belongs to the class of "unintended social entities" for the reason that it exists "without anyone having any thoughts at all about [it]" (Thomasson 2003, 551).

In the same vein, Gerrans (2005, 67–68) defines "unintended consequences" as "macro-regularities, discernible at the social level" that result from the "explicitly represented intentions of agents pursuing their own short-term micro-level agendas in their individual transactions". One example he gives is "patriarchal social structures". As Gerrans (2005, 67) notes, "the agents involved do not self-attribute [the] intention [to reproduce the regularities interpreted as patriarchal social structure] as they patronize, belittle and discriminate against their female colleagues". And yet they do contribute to the maintenance of patriarchal social structures by acting in the aforementioned manners. Macro-regularities are unintended in the sense of being the aggregative result of many micro-behaviours made by agents who do not intend to contribute to these macro-regularities.

1.1.8 The "spontaneous order" meaning

Hayek's idea of "spontaneous orders" points to one further conception of unintended consequences. Hayek recalls that social orders have long been viewed as either the products of deliberate human interventions or existing independently of human acts. But that dichotomy, Hayek argues, masked the category of "spontaneous orders": regularities that are obtained in virtue of human actions, but not of human intentions. It is Hayek's (1979, 155) view that, once discovered, spontaneous orders became the scope of theoretical social sciences, leaving constructed orders and natural phenomena the target of psychology and natural sciences, respectively. Popper (1963, 124) similarly conceives "the characteristic problems of the social sciences" as "aris[ing] only out of our wish to know the unintended consequences, and more especially the unwanted consequences which may arise if we do certain things [...]". For Hayek and Popper, consequences are unintended if they are the *explananda* of social sciences.

2 Arguments for the anti-design plea

Invisible-hand stories are usually praised for having distinctively superior explanatory import, and they would not have such a power, it is often further claimed, if it were not for the unintended consequence assumption on which they rest. But the explanatory merit of that assumption, in whichever of the eight listed meanings, is less than obvious. I now turn to arguments in support of this claim and show why each fails to be entirely persuasive. A more promising basis for the explanatory power of unintended consequences is suggested in the final section.

2.1 The direct argument

Let us start with the last sense of unintended consequence reviewed above, that is, the *spontaneous order* sense. *If* the scope of theoretical social sciences only comprises unintended consequences, *then* it is methodologically required to assume that all social outcomes are unintended. The problem is that the explanatory relevance of unintended consequences is here built into the very definition of theoretical social science. The explanatory relevance is therefore presupposed, rather than properly explicated.

2.2 The argument of realisticness

Consider now the *lack of foresight, lack of theoretical knowledge* and the *lack of altruism* meanings of the unintended consequence assumption. The point of basing an explanation on any of these assumptions could be to provide a truthful, realist, if somewhat bleak, account of the social realm. The Scottish Enlightenments are notorious proponents of such a down-to-earth understanding of human psychology. Smith's (2009, 11) historical overview of the notion of unintended consequences stresses a related concern for "accurate description of the empirical reality of social life, and that this is supported by the historical record". If the point is to provide a realistic, truthful and documented description of social reality, Smith (2009, 14) argues, that entails a rejection of "social contracts theories, Great Legislator (TMS) myths or divine right arguments". Keller also praises the unintended consequences assumption, especially under the *lack of altruism* meaning, for providing more realistic explanations. Because "the assumption that ape-men are selfish and gluttonous is [...] more realistic than the assumption that they are helpful and unselfish, one should use this option" (Keller 1994, 30).

However, to praise the notion of unintended consequences on account of its truthfulness is to partly miss the point. For it amounts to considerably restrict the scope of IHE to those rather rare cases where they happen to be historically true. Consider Menger's story. Historical cases of money that best incarnate such an account include bread serving as a medium of exchange in prisons of WWII war camp,[6] the use of packs of Marlboros in Moscow in 1990, or cowry-monies used by the Ojibway. However fascinating these examples of commodity-monies are, they remain the exceptions rather than the rule (Graeber 2011). So to claim, in view of the limited number of cases, that the unintended consequence assumption offers the prospect of empirically more accurate explanations sounds preposterous. In fact, if historical accuracy were the criterion by which the merit of IDE and IHE are to be respectively assessed, IDE would undoubtedly fare better.

2.3 The conjectural defence

IHE are often referred to as conjectural accounts justified by lack of historical evidence. For example, Aydinonat (2008, 28) treats Menger's account of money as "a conjecture about the way in which money could have emerged". Conjectures are justified, he argued, when "it is usually not possible to have enough information about the motives of the individuals" (Aydinonat 2008, 89). Likewise, Keller (1994, 35) argues that it is because "in many cases the truth value of propositions about the motives of actions cannot be verified or falsified, due to either technical or psychological reasons" that it is justified to assume agents' motives do not align with the consequences of their actions. Consistent with such view is Keller's conception of IHEs as exemplifying Steward's (1858 [1811]) idea of conjectural history (Barry 1982; Keller 1994, 35; Aydinonat 2008). As Höpfl (1978, 20) defines it, conjectural history is "simply a *faute de mieux*, a way of filling out the lacunae in the documentary record". The idea is that, absent any data about agents' true motives, it is methodologically advisable to suppose a mismatch between agents' intentions and the result of their actions.

---

6 Cf. Levy (1979, chap. 8).

However, one may object to such a construal in two ways. Firstly, the lack of evidence and the associated need to conjecture does not by themselves give any priority to the speculation that agents do not intend the outcome to be explained over the view that they do intend that outcome. Secondly, if the outcome to be explained were conjectured as unintended, the explanatory merit of such conjectures would not be entirely independent from its ability to get the fact right. This is because conjectures aim at truth. Conjectures are like guessing: their explanatory worth increases when proved right, and diminishes when proved wrong. So if IHE were conjectures, they would remain vulnerable to empirical falsifications (Roy Sorensen 2013, 38). However, so goes the argument, IHE are not subjected to the same fate. Whether they are supported with (or, for that matter, contradicted by) empirical evidence does not impact on their explanatory merit. As Nozick (1974, 8–9) puts it, IHE "pack explanatory punch and illumination, even if incorrect". Aydinonat agrees:

> [I]nvisible-hand explanations are valuable independently from their truth for they *explicate* the process that may have brought about the social phenomenon at hand (Ullmann-Margalit 1978). This suggests that these models are valuable even if they are false, or even if they do not get the facts right (Aydinonat 2008, 6).

Rather than conjectures, it is more correct to view the unintendedness of the outcome to be explained as an assumption. For assumptions need not be factually true, nor backed by empirical considerations and are not affected by how things turn out to be.

2.4 The parsimony defence

On an alternative account, what is at stake is rather parsimony. To describe an outcome as unintended is to dispense with a wide range of intentional states, such as altruistic motives, theoretical knowledge, agreements, decrees, collective intentions or a sense of the aggregate shape of things. The resulting parsimony is often stressed as a valuable feature of IHE. Vanberg (1989, 149) praises Menger's organic explanation of money for "rest[ing] on very parsimonious assumptions concerning the process that eventually leads to the institution in question". Likewise, Miller (2002, 17) stresses the way explanations "economize on information (no one needs to grasp the whole picture in order for the outcome to occur) and also often on moral motivation (self-interest can be turned to public advantage, as in Smith's account of the market)". The explanatory power of unintended consequences is then the value of explaining a lot by a little. IHE are to be preferred to their rivals on the principle that the fewer the number of assumptions an explanation depends on, the better.

Mäki (2009) proposes an analysis of parsimony that conceives its merits in terms of the unified picture of the reality thus delivered. The success of IHE may be assessed accordingly. To show that money, States, private property linguistic changes could be the unplanned outcome of many self-centred choices, is to show what is common to all of them, beyond their apparent disparities. A unified picture of these apparently unconnected social phenomena is thus provided.

But parsimony may alternatively be justified on ontological scepticism, the principle being that non-existent entities serve no explanatory point. Discovering that certain entities that were initially thought of as existed, actually do not exist, is arguably a reason for neglecting them. Such an ontological scepticism, however, cannot support the choice to frame the outcome to explain as an unintended one. For nobody can seriously deny the existence and causal power of legislative acts, agreements, we-intentions and altruistic motives.

Parsimony may alternatively be justified on account of the superfluity of the factors that it counsels to neglect. Consider Lewis' explanation of the convention to drive off a certain side of the road. As Lewis stresses, a different explanation would appeal to fines from the highway patrol. While such explanation would qualify as an IDE, it would also point to a superfluous explanatory factor. This is because, Lewis argues, what decisively dictates the drivers' choice is what they expect other drivers will do. If I expect others to drive on the left side, my reason to also drive on the left side is stronger than the reason to drive on the right side given by a fine. As Lewis (1969, 45, 48) concludes, "the punishments are superfluous if they agree with our convention, are outweighed if they go against it, are not decisive either way". So the unintended consequence assumption ought to be favoured in view of the shallow motives it urges to neglect.

One may however object to that argument that it too hastily assumes that decree and governmental sanction always weigh less on our choice than mutual expectations. If the English driving code offers the example of a redundant, easily superseded, reason to drive on the left side, it is because of the unusual trade-off between the risk of a car accident, on the one hand, and the risk of being fined, on the other. Surely the high cost of the former certainly tits the balance *in this case* for disregarding the English driving code. But legal sanctions do not always weight less on our choices than others' expected choices. Sometimes, the expected cost of transgressing the law exceeds the benefit of compliance, so that obeying the law presents itself as a more pressing option. The choice of a currency may be such case. In the French penal code, the issue of alternative currencies is penalized with five years of prison and a fine. So, even if I expect most of my economic partners to accept forged money instead of fiat money, still it does remain in my interest to use the latter. The point is that decrees or agreements may only be contextually or contingently redundant sources of motivations, and therefore negligible explanatory factors. But there is no *a priori* reason to believe that decrees (or for that matter, initial agreements) always are superseded by our mutual expectations regarding individual choices. The search for more parsimony does not adequately explain the explanatory superiority of unintended consequences.

2.5 The stability defence

At face value, IHE are about the origin of institutions: they usually start with the description of an initial state of nature, followed by a succession of steps during which institutional arrangements progressively, albeit unintentionally, get shaped. The explanatory import of that description, it is sometimes argued, is *not* to cast light on the genesis of these institutional arrangements. Rather, its virtue is to reveal the robustness of these arrangements: why they prevail and are likely to remain in many different societies.

This account is based on an "even more so" kind of argument that goes as follows. To suppose no one intended a certain outcome is to postulate a range of rather inauspicious antecedent conditions: that individuals cannot meet and reach voluntary agreements (under the *lack of agreement* meaning), that they cannot act jointly (under the *lack of we-ness* meaning), that they do not master the relevant institutional concepts (under the *lack of knowledge* meaning). Invisible-hand accounts show, however, that these unfavourable conditions do not prevent the institutions from taking place and show in this manner why these institutions are high in stability: why they actually prevail and remain in many different societies (Pettit 2007).

According to Ullmann-Margalit, Schelling's checkerboard city can be interpreted accordingly:

> if we learn from the model how an extreme and stable pattern of residential segregation tends to emerge rapidly in a situation where the participating individuals have only minor and moderate racial or segregationist preferences, then a fortiori we should expect to find segregated residences in the real world, where racial sentiments run high (Ullmann-Margalit 2010, 81).

One worry with this argument concerns the questionable relevance of the information that is provided. Resilience is arguably a crucial information to learn when, as an institutional designer, one plans to implement, or get insight on a new, unexperienced institutional arrangement (consider Universal Basic Income as a case in point). But the related information will not prove as relevant with respect to already proven, long-lasting institutions, such as Money, States, property rules and residential segregations. We do not need Nozick's account of States, Menger's organic explanation of money and Schelling's checkerboard city in order to discover that States, money and residential segregations are highly stable institutional patterns (Rosenberg 1995, 161). For this is something we can confidently suppose, given the actual, wide prevalence of these institutions across the world.

2.6 The subjectivist defence

Consider now the *lack of theoretical knowledge* or the *lack of aggregate shape of things* meanings of the unintended consequence assumption. To assume either one or the other is justified on the ground that it amounts to *no more than* taking the perspective of the individuals, thus avoiding to postulate anything beyond individual's subjective perspective. For example, the merit of Nozick's explanation is to avoid confusing the individual's intention (to join private protection agencies) with the theoretical reconstructions given of them (the establishment of a minimal State). The explanatory merit of unintended consequences is here construed as an exemplification of Hayek's methodological subjectivism. According to Hayek, individuals' choices are rarely determined by "holistic concepts" such as "society", "economic system", "capitalism" and "imperialism". It is thus more advisory to "systematically start from the concepts which guide individuals in their actions and not from the results of their theorizing about their actions" (Hayek 1942, 286). But such an understanding of the unintended consequence assumption may not withstand close scrutiny. Whereas methodological subjectivism prescribes that reference be made to individual's intentions, and nothing beyond, it does *not* further require that agent's intentions dis-align with the outcome to be explained. At best, a methodological individualist places its followers in a favourable position to eventually discover that what motivate agents may not be the holistic concepts by which the aggregate outcome of their action can be theoretically described. But, methodological individualism does not commit its followers to reach that conclusion in particular, nor to assume anything of the kind – in the way invisible-hand explainers do, as a constraint.

3 The true explanatory worth of the unintended consequences assumption

None of the arguments reviewed so far in support of the explanatory power of unintended consequences has proved entirely immune from objection. To be sure, the merit of that assumption has been substantiated in various ways. But none of the proposed *rationale*, I have argued, offer a decisive reason to believe that explanations, such as IHE, that are grounded on such assumption yield greater understanding of social reality. Let us now turn to a more conclusive argument.

My contention is that IHE are narratives (hence their fictional outlook) that can be used to investigate the logical structures of social kinds. While IDE could be used for the same exploratory purpose (and in fact have been used as such), IHE are better suited for this task than their intentional-design rivals. In particular, IHE are finer devices for laying bare the *nature* and *mode of existence* of social kinds.

Consider first the question "What is the nature of money?", and suppose that one would have to rely on an IDE of the rise of the money system for getting an answer to it. That explanation could take various forms. Anthropologists typically define money as that which States started to accept in payment of taxes (Ingham 2004). Contractualist thinkers, on their side, approach money as that which individuals consent to exchange against perishable goods (Locke 1967, 318–319. While varying as to *who* (the central bank, the State, property owners) is the ultimate designer of money, these accounts all qualify as IDEs.

Relying on one of these two theories for knowing what money is, however, would not lead us very far. For these theories inform of the conditions under which money, *about which it does not say anything substantial,* exists. They lay bare what it takes for the property of moneyhood to be exemplified, but offers no insight about the nature of money (see Massin 2011, 92–96; Massin 2017 for a general presentation of that distinction). The explanation reveals what it takes for money to exist, and points to various intentional states as determining the extension of the concept of money. But someone entirely unacquainted with the nature of money would not gain much or learn much about that institution by being told that money is any entity that is prescribed to be used as such. At best, that person would learn that there are certain persons who, by the very act of prescribing the use of a certain entity as money, have the power to fix the things exemplifying the remaining mysterious property of moneyhood. The explicatory import of IDE is, in short, restricted to the conditions of exemplification of institutional properties, leaving it at one's guess what the entity that such property qualifies is.

Menger already stressed this shortcoming of IDE. In the analysis he offers of "organic" (*aka* invisible-hand) and "pragmatic" theories, *aka* IDEs, Menger (1985 [1883], book III, 129–159) points to an important restriction in the latter's explicatory import. As he argues, a pragmatic explanation of money will typically be in terms of "legal dispensation", thus referring to "causes lying outside the sphere of individual considerations". Pragmatic explanations do not elucidate the reasons agents have, apart from these legal dispensations, for using something as a medium of exchange. This is why they are less satisfactory, according to Menger.

Likewise, Nozick (1974, 14) argues that a "direct explanation" (*aka* IDE) is one that accounts for a social pattern "in terms of the desires, wants, beliefs, and so on, of individuals, directed toward realizing" that pattern and that "within such explanations will appear descriptions of the pattern, at least within quotation marks, as objects of belief and desire". Unless one is already acquainted with the social pattern to be explained, that explanation will not provide much information about the social pattern. By contrast, it is because an IHE "minimizes the use of notions constituting the phenomena to be explained" (Nozick 1974, 14) that it "carries important explanatory illumination" (Nozick 1974, 8; see also Ullmann-Margalit 1978, 277; Williams 2002, 34). In sum, IHE are to be preferred to IDE for the reason that they do not display the circularity to which the latter fall prey. Its greater explicatory import can be explicated accordingly.

Consider next the following, uncontroversial definition of a State:

State^{def}= A State is a single protective entity that is dominant over a geographical territory.

Let us then ask, "What makes that definition true?", and suppose again that one were first to count on an IDE, such as Hobbes contractual explanation of government, for an answer to that question. According to Hobbes (1909 [1651]), government originates in agreement among individuals who consent to give to a central authority the right to protect them against potential aggressors. Based on such an explanation, the answer to the above question will be that what makes it true that a State is a single protective entity is that people agreed to confer to States such a function.

But surely that cannot be so. What makes a State the sort of protective entity that it is, endowed with the sort of duty, obligations and rights that it has, has certainly nothing to do with what people may contingently agree to. It is false to say that people agreed *that* a State to be a single protective entity that is dominant over a geographical territory because what follow "*that*" is true by definition of any State, even of those that people did not agree to have as their only protector. States are authoritative, non-biological persons *by definition* – and not in virtue of what people agree to. Surely, agreements can sometimes make it true of *a* certain particular State that *It* dominates over *a* particular geographical territory. But agreements are contingent acts and therefore cannot ground the a-temporal truth of any definitional proposition.

The explicatory virtue of Nozick's IHE of State is to sort out what pertains to agreements and what is true independently from the latter (Zaibert 2004).

It shows that the truth of a proposition defining what a social kind is, such as a State, has nothing to do with anyone holding it true. And it makes such a point by describing a process during which a protective agency evolves as something equivalent to a State, unbeknownst to those who willingly join that agency. In other words, States are single protective entities regardless of what individuals who benefit from such protection happen to believe, or agree to.

Still one may insist, a private protective agency could not be an instance of a State if its clients had no knowledge of what a State is. But, here again, Nozicks' story may be used as refuting this view. State beneficiaries do not need to master the concept of State for making choices that ultimately bring one into being. Those who join the private agency that ultimately performs the function of a State may not even realize that they have left the State of nature. (Likewise, Menger's story shows that something can serve as money – and in fact be nothing less than money – even if no one, among its competent users, knows anything about the concept of money).

In sum, IHE convey a certain view of institutional reality that is more independent from our will and representations than what intentional-design accounts could ever suggest, given their insistence on institutional kinds being what they are in virtue of we intending them to be what they are.

4 Conclusion

I have argued that the explicatory import of unintended consequences is to provide more insights into the nature and mode of existence of institutional kinds than their intentional-design rivals. I have argued, in particular, that the point of an IHE is to challenge the view that social reality is composed of entities that are what they are in virtue of people individually or collectively believing, agreeing or accepting them to be what they are. The opposite view, sometimes described as the "self-referentiality" of social kinds (Searle 1995, 33–34) happens to be more popular in social ontology. While that conflicting view comes up in various forms, the central idea is that facts about the existence of social entities are grounded on shared representations among those who are concerned by these facts. The point of invisible-hand stories is to offer ground for a more realistic, mind-independent view about the mode of existence of social kinds. Their merit is to show that individuals' intentional states (individual's beliefs, attitudes, intentions) neither entirely nor infallibly determine the extension of social kinds. And they support such a conclusion by showing that things like money, States and property rules may evolve and fully come into being unbeknownst from those who contribute, by their actions, to their emergence.

References

Anomaly, Jonny, and GeoffreyBrennan. 2014. “Social Norms, the Invisible Hand, and the Law.” *University of Queensland Law Journal* 33: 263–283.

Aydinonat, Emrah. 2006. “Is the Invisible Hand Un-Smithian? A Comment on Rothschild.” *Economics Bulletin* 2: 1–9.

Aydinonat, Emrah. 2008. *The Invisible Hand in Economics: How Economists Explain Unintended Social Consequences*. INEM Advances in Economic Methodology. London: Routledge.

Barry, Norman. 1982. “The Tradition of Spontaneous Order.” *Literature of Liberty* 5: 1–58. Arlington (VA): Institute for Humane Studies.

Elster, Jon. 1983. *Explaining Technical Change*. Cambridge: Cambridge University Press.

Elster, Jon. 1989. *Nuts and Bolts for the Social Sciences*. Cambridge: Cambridge University Press.

Gaus, Gerald. 2011. “Explanation, Justification, and Emergent Properties: An Essay on Nozickean Metatheory.” In *The Cambridge Companion to Nozick's “Anarchy, State, and Utopia”*, edited by Ralf M. Bader and John Meadowcroft, 116–144. Cambridge University Press.

Gerrans, Philip. 2005. “Tacit Knowledge, Rule Following and Pierre Bourdieu's Philosophy of Social Science.” *Anthropological Theory* 5. Accessed October 17, 2017. http://journals.sagepub.com/doi/pdf/10.1177/1463499605050869.

Graeber, David. 2011. *Debt: The First 5000 Years*. New York: Melville House Publishing.

Hayek, Friedrich A. 1942. “Scientism and the Study of Society”, part I. *Economica* 9: 267–291.

Hayek, Friedrich A. 1979. *Law, Legislation and Liberty: Vol. 3, the Political Economy of Free People*. Chicago: University of Chicago Press.

Hobbes, Thomas. 1909 [1651]. *Leviathan; Or, the Matter, Form and Power of a Commonwealth, Ecclesiastical and Civil*. Oxford: Clarendon Press. Accessed October 16, 2017: https://archive.org/details/hobbessleviathan00hobbuoft.

Höpfl, H. M. 1978. “From Savage to Scotsman: Conjectural History in the Scottish Enlightenment.” *Journal of British Studies* 17: 19–40.

Hume, David. 1896 [1739]. *A Treatise of Human Nature*, reprinted from the original edition in three volumes and edited, with an analytical index, by L.A. Selby-Bigge. Oxford: Clarendon Press. Accessed October 16, 2017. http://oll.libertyfund.org/titles/342.

Ingham, Geoffrey. 2004. *The Nature of Money*. Cambridge: Polity Press.

Jevons, William Stanley. 1876. *Money and the Mechanism of Exchange*. Library of Economics and Liberty. Accessed October 16, 2017 from the World Wide Web. http://www.econlib.org/library/YPDBooks/Jevons/jvnMME1.html

Keller, Rudi. 1994. *On Language Change: The Invisible Hand in Language*. London and New York: Routledge.

Levy, Primo. 1979. *If This Is a Man and The Truce*. Harmondsworth: Penguin modern Classic.

Lewis, David. 1969. *Convention: A Philosophical Study*. Cambridge (MA): Harvard University Press.

Locke, John. 1967. *Two Tracts on Government*. Cambridge: Cambridge University Press.

Lynch, Tony, and Adrian Walsh. 2003. "The Mandevillean Conceit and the Profit-Motive." *Philosophy* 78: 43–62.

Mäki, Uskali. 1990a. "Scientific Realism and Austrian Explanation." *Review of Political Economy* 2: 310–344.

Mäki, Uskali. 2009. "Economic Imperialism: Concept and Constraints." *Philosophy of the Social Sciences* 39: 351–380.

Massin, Olivier. 2011. *On pleasures*. PhD dissertation. University of Geneva. Accessed October 15, 2017. https://philpapers.org/rec/MASOP.

Massin, Olivier. 2017. *The Metaphysics of Ownership: A Reinachian Account*. Axiomathes 27 (5): 577-600.

Menger, Carl. 1892. "On the Origins of Money." *Economic Journal* 2: 239–255.

Menger, Carl. 1985 [1883]. *Investigations into the Method of the Social Sciences with Special Reference to Economics*. New York and London: New York University Press.

Menger, Carl. 2007 [1871]. *Principles of Economics*. Auburn (Alabama): Ludwig von Mises Institute.

Miller, David. 2002. "The Justification of Political Authority." In *Robert Nozick*, edited by David Schmidtz, 10–33. Cambridge: Cambridge University Press.

Nozick, Robert. 1974. *Anarchy, State and Utopia*. Oxford: Blackwell, Basic Books.

Pettit, Philip. 2007. "Resilience as the Explanandum of Social Theory." In *Political Contingency: Studying the Unexpected, the Accidental, and the Unforeseen*, edited by Ian Shapiro and Sonu Bedi, 79–96. New York: New York University Press.

Popper, Karl. 1963. *Conjectures and Refutations: The Growth of Scientific Knowledge*. Florence (KY): Routledge/Taylor and Francis Group.

Rosenberg, Alexander. 1995. *Philosophy of Social Science*. Boulder: Westview Press/Harper Collins, 3rd revised edition.

Rothschild, Emma. 2001. *Economic Sentiments, Adam Smith, Condorcet, and the Enlightenment*. Cambridge and London: Harvard University Press.

Schelling, Thomas C. 1978. *Micromotives and Microbehavior*. New York and London: W. W. Norton & Company.

Searle, John R. 1995. *The Construction of Social Reality*. New York: Free Press.

Smith, Adam. 1904 [1776]. *An Inquiry into the Nature and Causes of the Wealth of Nations*, edited by Edwin Cannan. London: Methuen. Accessed October 16, 2017: http://www.econlib.org/library/Smith/smWN.html

Smith, Craig. 2009. "The Scottish Enlightenment, Unintended Consequences and the Science of Man." *Journal of Scottish Philosophy* 7: 9–28.

Sorensen Roy. 2013. "Veridical Idealizations." In *Thought Experiments in Science, Philosophy, and the Arts*, edited by Melanie Frappier, Letitia Meynell and James Robert Brown, chap. 2. New York: Routledge.

Stewart, Dugald. 1858 [1811]. "Biographical Memoirs of Adam Smith, L.L.D., of William Robertson, D. D. and of Thomas Reid, D. D. Read before the Royal Society of Edinburgh. Now collected into one volume, with some additional notes." In *Collected Works*, vol. X. Edinburgh.

Thomasson, Amy. 2003. "Foundation for a Social Ontology." *ProtoSociology* 18: 269–290.

Tieffenbach, Emma. 2010. "Searle and Menger on Money." *Philosophy of the Social Sciences* 40: 191–212.

Tieffenbach, Emma. 2013. "Invisible-Hand Explanation: From Blindness to Lack of We-ness." *Social Science Information* 52: 450–470.

Tuomela, Raimo. 1984. *A Theory of Social Action*. Dordrecht, Boston and Lancaster: D. Reidel Publishing Company.

Tuomela, Raimo. 2001. "Collective Intentionality and Social Agents." Paper invited for the AI conference IMF, May 21-23, 2017. Toulouse. Accessed on October 16, 2017. http://www.helsinki.fi/tint/tuomela/materials/toulouse.html.

Tuomela, Raimo. 2013. *Social Ontology: Collective Intentionality and Group Agents*. Oxford: Oxford University Press.

Ullmann-Margalit, Edna. 1978. "Invisible-Hand Explanations." *Synthese* 39: 263–291.

Ullmann-Margalit, Edna. 2010. "The Invisible Hand Viewed and Reviewed. Book Review of *The Invisible Hand in Economics: How Economists Explain*

Unintended Social Consequences, by N. Emrah Aydinonat, London and New York: Routledge." *Journal of Economic Methodology* 17: 77–92

Vanberg, Viktor. 1989. "Carl Menger's Evolutionary and John R. Commons' Collective Action Approach to Institutions: A Comparison." *Review of Political Economy* 3: 334–360.

Vermeule, Adrien. 2010. "The Invisible Hand in Legal and Political Theory." *Virginia Law Review* 96: 1417–1452.

Vernon, Richard. 1979. "Unintended Consequences." *Political Theory* 7: 57–73.

Williams, Bernard. 2002. *Truth and Truthfulness*. Princeton (NJ): Princeton University Press.

Wray, Brad W. 2000. "Invisible Hands and the Success of Science." *Philosophy of Science* 67: 163–175.

Zaibert, Leo. 2004. "Toward Meta-Politics." *The Quarterly Journal of Austrian economics* 7: 113–128.

Sebastian Giacovelli*

The "Invisible Hand": A Fiction with Real Consequences

> *"[...] he proclaimed the mystical principle of the 'invisible hand': that each individual in pursuing his own selfish good was led, as if by an invisible hand, to achieve the best good of all, so that any interference with free competition by government was almost certain to be injurious. This unguarded conclusion has done almost as much harm as good in the past century and a half, especially since too often it is all that some of our leading citizens remember, 30 years later, of their college course in economics" (Samuelson 1948, 36).*

Abstract: In the chapter presented, the fictional character of the "invisible hand" and its real consequences are central. Beginning by discussing the current debate in economic sociology about fiction, and especially the fictional character of economics, a heuristics is proposed to analyse the fictional character of the "invisible hand". The assumption is that if actors mix up fiction with something like a precise prescription of daily life or some kind of instructions for economic action and tend to dogmatize what was once a fiction by their inventors, a fiction like the "invisible hand" has real consequences. And, on top of that, its fictional character also seeks to explain, while the idea behind the "invisible hand" has not already disappeared: While hypotheses can fail because of the empirical reality, fiction is immune to reality. Likewise, its social impact is not to be underestimated. In this sense, the chapter illustrates its social impact on economics and on the economy, focusing on the logic underpinning the structural adjustment programme of the International Monetary Fund (IMF). On a heuristic and an empirical level, this chapter brings together various, until now, unconnected approaches; and these have to be brought together to understand the functionality and long range of the "invisible hand".

Keywords: Fiction; expectations; social consequences; economics; IMF

---

* I would like to thank the editors and reviewers of this volume, as well as my colleagues at Institute of Sociology of Justus Liebig University in Giessen for their comments on previous versions of this chapter.

1 Introduction

Adam Ferguson, coeval with Adam Smith and David Hume and located in the same Scottish tradition as Adam Smith and John Millar, with a special focus on the relationship between the division of labour and prosperity, brought an idea into being that seems to be forever linked with the understanding of societies and particularly of markets. Beyond the individual there is nothing that evolves by intentional human action: "Nations stumble about upon establishments, which are indeed the result of human action, but not the execution of any human design" (Ferguson 1767, 187).

Order, in Ferguson's understanding, can be characterized as: "undirected, unintentional, gradual, inevitable and generated at the efficient or individuo-psychic level" (Hill 2006, 103). He was not the first to formulate a theory of spontaneous order. Ferguson was in good company, with Montesquieu, David Hume, Adam Smith, Thomas Reid, Gilbert Stuart, William Robertson and John Millar. But his approach was the "most exhaustive, systematic and explicit statement to date of the way in which social patterns, order and progress emerge spontaneously from the seemingly random, private actions of individuals through time" (Hill 2006, 101). But, even if he described it adequately, he never used the term "spontaneous order". This should be credited to Michael Polanyi, in 1950, almost 200 years later, while Friedrich A. von Hayek popularized it in 1960 (Hill 2006, 102).

Smith (1976 [1776], 26–27), who also applies the metaphor of the "invisible hand", suggests that, as the following quote highlights, the general interest somehow benefits from actors' self-interest – and not from altruism, love or anything comparable: "It is not from the benevolence of the butcher, the brewer, or the baker, that we expect our dinner, but from their regard to their own interest. We address ourselves, not to their humanity but to their self-love, and never talk to them of our necessities but of their advantages".

Regarding this, two observations lend the figure of the "invisible hand" an outstanding role in economic theory: First, the fact that the metaphor of the "invisible hand" was not only differently interpreted by a series of authors, even Smith himself made no coherent interpretation of the term (see *Impact on economics*, in this chapter). And second, this ubiquitous figure seems to be highly compatible at any time in history, while scholars likewise are still asking themselves what this figure really means (cf. Ullmann-Margalit 1978; Grampp 2000; Pohoryles 2015).[1] That this figure has such an impressive influence, particularly

1 Or, they disagree with the understanding of unintendedness in general, as for instance Tieffenbach (2013, 465) concludes, "that precluding the existence of designers, be it

in economics, may be partly explained by the dominance of micro-perspective analogues to mainstream economics. But concerning the range of attempts to explain what Ferguson and Smith really meant, this prompts a different hypothesis. The chapter presented explains instead the apparent timeless claim of the validity of the indistinct term "invisible hand" by its *fictional character*. Therefore, this chapter expands the discussion in economic sociology by combining the current debate about fictionality (see *Economics as a fictional genre*, in this chapter) with Ferguson's as well as Smith's prominent figure of the "invisible hand".[2] The idea is that this "invisible hand" can be interpreted as a *fiction with real consequences*, especially if actors mix up the fiction of the inventors with something like a precise prescription of daily life or, even worse, a kind of instruction for economic action and tend to dogmatize what was once a fiction by their inventors.

By addressing "invisible hand" as a *fiction with real consequences* on a heuristical and also an empirical level, this chapter brings various, until now, unconnected approaches together – and, this is one main concern of this contribution: they have to be brought together to understand its functionality and its long range. Obviously, some economists not only (mis-)use the fictional figure of the "invisible hand" as a hypothesis (cf. Vaihinger 1924; Aydinonat 2008). Furthermore, others, like McCloskey (exemplarily: 1985; 1990; 1994) or recently Akerlof and Shiller (2016), emphasize the storytelling quality of economics, which still omits to point to its fictional core as a crucial characteristic. It seems useful to understand economic approaches addressing future events as purely fiction, because it points to the core character of their approaches and does not resist specifying the form that economics takes. This approach is also convincing as regards the still viable reinterpretation of the "invisible hand" (cf. Ullmann-Margalit 1978; Rothschild 1994; Mäki 2002; Aydinonat 2008; Tieffenbach 2013; Pohoryles 2015). Fictionality, especially, is considered to have an ambiguous character (see *Economics as a fictional genre*, in this chapter). It explains far better the potential of steady reinterpretation as an explanation for the understanding that economic approaches still depend on a framing story that fills gaps in, for instance, neoclassical formulas. In other words, understanding the "invisible hand" as a

an external ruler or a group of agents acting jointly to produce some outcome is not sufficient to ensure the unintendedness of the outcome to be explained". Concerning various interpretations of unintended social consequences, see also Aydinonat (2008).

2 These thoughts represent, likewise, a link to the emerging research field of the sociology of economic thinking.

fiction pushes the finger deeper into the wound, as if pointing solely to the form in which economic approaches are presented.

In the presented chapter, the long-running discussion about the "invisible hand" is situated within the current discussion in economic sociology, which does not stop discussing its fictional character but, rather, pins down its real, in the sense of empirically observable, consequences. By doing so, this chapter connects the general discussion about economics as fiction with studies about structurally shaping the power of institutions like the International Monetary Fund (IMF), as demonstrated later on. While authors like Peet (2009) or Stiglitz (2012) are wondering about the victory march of a specific logic, and explaining it by its neoclassically shaped market design, which is favourable only for a specific social group, the presented approach reveals why such logics are able to be applied in such different surroundings. In a way, this chapter brings the "invisible hand" into play; it brings the philosophy of economics, the sociology of economic thinking, economic sociology, the academic debate about modelling and social studies of finance into a vital discussion – and thus a transdisciplinary discussion is campaigned for, which is essential to avoid misinterpretations of the "invisible hand" (cf. Reichspfarrer and Sulz 2015, 62–64).[3]

For that purpose, I unfurl in a first step the heuristic perspective that is not located in economics, but seizes the current discussion in economic sociology about the role of fictions, not only in the economy, in order to understand economic theory as fiction. To clarify this argument, particularly Esposito's (2007) view on fictionality and Beckert's (2013; 2016) "fictional expectations", these will be adduced, because they make valuable contributions to our topic. But, even if Esposito's and Beckert's approaches offer useful insights regarding the role of fictionality in economy and economics, they lack a deeper understanding of the formative power of the "invisible hand". And it is Vaihinger's (1924) "Philosophy of the 'as if'" that not only helps in filling this gap, but also sensitizes us to the relation of fiction, hypothesis and dogma. To gain an appropriate heuristic, their contributions will be brought together in my synthesis, as prominent fictions, like the "invisible hand", are powerful in part because of their importance concerning coordinating action by shaping expectations and, therefore, communication and action. But, moreover, due to the fictional character of the "invisible hand", it turns out to be immune to reality, while hypotheses can fail because of the empirical reality (*Economics as a fictional genre*, in this chapter). Besides this conceptional refinement, in a second step, the impact on economics

3 Reichspfarrer and Sulz (2015) focus solely on Smith's interpretation of "invisible hand".

and also on the economy is discussed based on a few illustrations – in the latter case using the example of the structural adjustment programmes (SAPs) of the IMF. These illustrations serve to clarify perfectly the ambiguous structure and resulting scope for interpretation of the "invisible hand"-fiction on the one hand, and most notably its shaping power on the other hand (*The "Invisible hand" as consequential fiction*, in this chapter). To complete this chapter, six key findings concerning the usage of a fiction-based analysis of the "invisible hand" are formulated; these underline this figure as a tool for understanding the functionality of economic theory and powerful fictions (*Drawing a lesson from the "invisible hand": Fictionality and its social impact*, in this chapter).

2 Economics as a fictional genre

Before discussing the social impact of the "invisible hand"-fiction, we have to clarify the terms "fiction" and, as its counterpart, "hypothesis", and also their relation to economics. To this end, we pay attention to the current debate about fictions and "as if"-logics in economic sociology, and we combine these thoughts with an interpretation of economics as a fiction in the following. These preliminary considerations allow us to discuss the "invisible hand" as fiction, which – and this is the topic of the part on *The "invisible hand" as a fictional genre* – can then be analysed concerning its real, in the sense of social, consequences.

Exemplarily, from the point of view of Beckert (2016, 9, 61ff.), whose recent publications revolve around the concept of fictional expectations, actors, confronted with uncertainty, organize their activities and orient them towards imagined future states, in the sense of mental representations and the emotions associated with them. Accordingly, "Given fundamental uncertainty, the expectations substituting for the unachievable calculation-based anticipation of future states are not based on observable facts but on contingent assumptions about future developments that are unavoidable and can only 'pretend' to describe a future reality and must suggest decisions based on nothing more than 'as-if' assumptions about the future" (Beckert 2013, 226; 2016, 74). The clue here is that these expectations are imaginations that guide the actors' behaviour, *as if* these expectations actually describe future states (Beckert 2016; cf. Giacovelli 2016a). He evidently derives this as-if logic from literary theory, citing, e.g., Iser (1993, 12–13; cf. Searle 1975; Beckert 2016, 225 fn8), who describes the same logic regarding fictional texts: "it (fictional texts, SG) turns the whole of the world organized in the text into an 'as-if' construction".[4]

4 Not that far from this debate, Courtemanche's (2011) study explores the relation between the "invisible hand" and British fiction between 1818 and 1860.

Another reference is an ethnographic study about international collaterals conducted by Riles (2010; 2011). According to Riles, the truth content of fictional expectations only lasts conditionally. In this view, expectations are understood as "placeholders" in the decision-making process (Riles 2010, 9). Even if general sociology is short on content concerning the imaginative character of expectations, there is at least Luhmann (1976) and Koselleck (2004), who highlight the aspect that perceptions of the future go together with ideas about political utopias.

Therewith, *fictionality* is already addressed: Also, Esposito (2007) interrelates future expectations with fiction. She expands Luhmann's assumption of a "doubling of reality" to the idea of a pluralism of realities. In addition to the horizontal segmentation in different lifeworlds (Husserl 2007 [1936]), subsystems (James 1890) or units of meaning (Schütz 1932), thus in addition to phenomenological and psychological perspectives, she assumes a pluralism of realities due to the relationship between real reality and fictional reality. And this segmentation proceeds vertically. The latter applies to probability calculations. Just as fiction is not a lie, although the things and events it deals with are untrue, a probability calculation understands imperfect knowledge not as an error, but as an area with own rules (Esposito 2007, 21). In common with the current debate, Esposito establishes a connection to fictional literature. She compares the consequences of technologies, such as probability calculations with fictional literature, to the extent that, despite their fictional basis, they have real consequences (Esposito 2007, 11, 61).

That said, both Esposito (2007, 86–95) and Beckert (2013; 2016) also understand economics as such a fictional genre with real consequences, in other words, as a social fact that shapes action (Durkheim 1982 [1895], 50–59). For Vaihinger (1924), theories in general and economic theories in particular have the task of simplifying reality; for that reason alone, it is not possible to represent reality in detail. But this *does not prevent* us applying models when building our expectations of the future. He discusses theorizing in different disciplines considering economics, too, with the concern of this chapter adequately matching the example of Smith's (cf. Vaihinger 1924, 20) assumption that "all human actions, and particularly those of a business and politico-economical nature could be looked upon *as if* their driving force lay in but one single factor – egoism". According to Vaihinger (1924, 24), Smith was convinced that he was dealing *with nothing but a fiction*. And even if he succeeded in "bringing the whole of political economy into an ordered system", his assumption has great value as fiction, but it is "positively ruinous as hypothesis or dogma" (Vaihinger 1924, 24). It is beyond question that it is not possible to prove this empirically – aside from the fact that the egoism assumption has to be immediately abandoned if one actor behaves unselfishly (Vaihinger 1924, 24). And this is the salient point: According to Vaihinger (1924, 24, 268–269), the difference between fiction and hypothesis lies in the possibility of a phenomenon being *empirically verifiable* in its connection to reality. The idea of a God is a perfect example – at least from an agnostic point of view: In this sense, God could be understood as something fictive, which was never, is not and will never be empirically observable. Nonetheless, this idea guides the actions of men, *as if* God were real. And we are also reminded of Thomas' theorem, which says: "if men define situations as real, they are real in their consequences" (Thomas and Thomas 1928, 571–572; Merton 1995).

But if economic theory is not only contingent but also distant from empirical reality: What makes it credible? To answer this question, we only have to glance at the comprehensive research done by sociologists, historians, philosophers, anthropologists and economists themselves. McCloskey (1985; 1994), Mirowski (1994) and Morgan (2012) are proponents of an approach that explains the credibility of economic theories with the storytelling qualities of their authors.[5] McCloskey's (1990, 9) well-known statement is exemplary for this branch of research: "Plainly and routinely, ninety per cent of what economists do is such storytelling. Yet even in the other ten per cent, in the part more obviously dominated by models and metaphors, the economist tells stories". Referring to Morgan, Beckert points out that it is this storytelling that gives economic theory meaning. In other words, the meaning of a model does not result "from its mathematical formulae", but *from narrations that link it to reality* (Beckert 2016, 254).[6] And, at the same time, these stories have to regard specific conventions; for instance, even if they are fictional, it would be regarded as inappropriate if they appeared as science fiction–like stories (cf. Ullmann-Margalit 1978, 271).

A final aspect we have to consider is the observation that economists tend to assume that economic actors are embedded in a kind of fixed reality, omitting

---

5 An aspect missing from this debate is the situation of being without an alternative. Particularly, taking notice of a phenomenon for the first time, there is possibly at first solely only one explanation, which is not utterly satisfying, but at the moment has no alternative.

6 This applies especially for temporal ambiguities in models, which allow various interpretations, but are, likewise, unavoidable should these findings be used for practical considerations regarding economic life (Giacovelli and Langenohl 2016c, 48–49).

their ability to interpret their environment. This is, according to Mirowski (1991, 578), due to the tendency of – especially neoclassical informed – economists to "imitate physicists and their models". Its obverse can be found in literary fiction, where author and reader agree on a reality that obviously differs from the real reality. For Esposito (2007, 88; Luhmann 1996a), who distinguishes "real reality" and "fictional reality", based on a Luhmannian "doubling of reality", but in the sense of a "pluralism of reality", the problem does not result in mathematical constructions, but in mixing them up with "real reality". Even if her main focus is the interdependence between fiction and reality, with a special focus on temporality, her analogy to Beckert's crystal ball is,[7] unsurprisingly, a probability calculation with underlying quantitative data. And her conclusion, rooted in systems theory, is that a mirror is thus for the purpose of (self-)observation, but not a window on the world (Esposito 2007, 89); that is why she talks about the fiction of probability (Esposito 2007, 91).

Besides a range of observations, Esposito repeatedly refers to the discussion of two crucial issues in economics, which she ties to probability calculations. But the clue of the chapter is what seems to be most useful for discussing the invisible hand as a fiction. Esposito's focus is on the relationship between "real reality" and "fictional reality", and discussing solely that type of economics, which is based on probability calculations, but excludes, e.g., neoclassical economics. According to Esposito, the reality of markets consists of forecasts, statistics and models. But, these cannot be understood as information in the proper sense, but rather as a system generating second-order information. Therefore, Esposito interprets them as fictions and not as the immediate reality. From her perspective, this type of information cannot be imagined in models but, nevertheless, these models are useful, because they reveal their particular nature: The self-generated uncertainty, based on imperfect information, is doomed to remain uncertain (2007, 86–95). These thoughts help to understand the substantial difference between fiction and hypothesis, even if Esposito mainly focuses on the relation of fiction and reality in a daily-life manner.

Even though hypothesis and fiction are able to shape action (Esposito 2007, 61, 86–95), fictions have the unique feature of non-refutability, because they are located in "fictional reality" and not in "real reality". Therefore, they will not enter the empirical reality. Coming back to Vaihinger, the type of economics Esposito

---

7 That is why Beckert (2016, 247) uses the illustration of a crystal ball: not assuming that it shows us the future, but while trying to see the future reflecting our vision of the future.

describes can be first understood as an idea or archetype.[8] But, there seems to be an inconsistency between the two positions when Esposito comprehends the probability-based economics of all economic streams to be a fiction: particularly statistics-based economics, e.g. econometrics, is based on the formation of a hypothesis, and starts due to its inductive method coming from empirical observation. That means that especially this kind of economics will not be understood as fictive in the sense of Vaihinger. In Vaihinger's aforementioned understanding, neoclassic economics would have been a more convincing example. Because neoclassics with its deductive-nomological foundation does not run the risk of failure because of empirical reality, this is the merit of an ideology (cf. Giacovelli 2016b).

In contrast, Esposito (2007, 7–12) conceptualizes non-observability not on the basis of the difference between inductive and deductive method, but on confusing forecasts based on probability calculations ("fictional reality") with the future presence ("real reality"). In the present, the future is not directly observable – so any offer to observe the future has to be fictional. Here, she also locates the aspect of circularity, referring to Keynes, based on the expectation concept: Expectations, which are considered as the engine and reference of market orientation, are themselves driven by expectations - expectations about future prices that depend on current trade decisions. That means, referring to the future, that expectations depend only on themselves or, in other words: "the present is determined by the future and vice versa" (Esposito 2011, 88; Keynes 1965 [1936]). And circularity clarifies even better the function of an imagined future for the present. Models, Esposito describes, are fictional and still useful, because these shared fictions at least offer shared orientation, even if uncertain events remain uncertain.

Thinking one step further, the question of why, for instance, neoclassical thinking still survives, despite all the progress in economics, is now easy to answer: Because neoclassical assumptions *cannot be proven by reality*. Such fictions gather strength by not becoming reality; thus, they cannot be banished

8 Following Kantian terminology, Schiller points out that plant or animal archetypes can never be found in any experience, and to which no empirical being can ever correspond, neither in the past nor in the future. They represent an idea. That is why they can be assumed to be valid hypotheses. Along these lines, Schiller recognizes the meaning in Goethe's assertion that "all plant and animal species were to be regarded *as if* they had been formed according to the standard of an animal or plant-archetype", and it goes on to say that "Goethe's animal archetype is a schematic fiction, whereas the Darwinian theory of evolution is an hypothesis" (Vaihinger 1924, 267).

by empirical analysis, particularly not if they are directed towards the future. With Esposito, it is all the more understandable how fictional theories can be seen as potent, in the sense of socially formative, survival artists.

Drawing a line from Esposito back to Vaihinger, there is first a substantial difference concerning progress in science, as already mentioned. While Vaihinger (1924, 1–15) explains scientific progress as the progress of heuristics, Esposito (2007, 68–73) and Beckert (2016, 245–268) favour the contingency of theories as an explanation attempt. But, regarding the difference between fiction and hypothesis, Vaihinger's view can be maintained, but in a refined version: Both hypotheses and fictions are able to shape action.[9] On that point, we agree. But with Esposito we can assume that fictions are more potent than hypotheses, because *hypotheses can fail because of empirical reality, whereas fictions are immune to reality* – that is, concerning their verifiability *by*, but obviously not in view of, their shaping power *of* reality (cf. Giacovelli 2018 forthcoming).

3 The "invisible hand" as consequential fiction

In discussing the fictionality and social impact of the "invisible hand", we have to consider that the term "invisible" is actually used by Ferguson (1767, 138) only once in his work, concerning "invisible agents, that are supposed to guide all precarious events to which human foresight cannot extend". And Smith, with whom the metaphor is even more commonly strongly associated, uses the term only three times in his complete works. Keeping this in mind, clarifying the question of how this fiction was able to become so prominent seems to be all the more necessary. For this purpose, we apply the considerations above and focus on the role of ambiguities and scope for interpretation pointing to its impact on economics and the economy.

3.1 Impact on economics: triumph march, ambiguities and scope of interpretation

Beginning with the impact on economics, the triumph march of logics behind the "invisible hand" is obvious and well documented – especially in this volume. But, what economists nowadays call a "pillar of capitalism" (Jahan and Mahmud 2015, 44) was once quite progressive. It was "progressive in that it questioned the authority of the landowning nobility, the grand merchants and the monarchical

9 Especially as the difference between fiction and hypothesis is academic and not observable in everyday life (cf. Vaihinger 1924, 269).

state, with their conservative ideas of divine rights, family values, feudal loyalties and patriotic duties" (Peet 2009, 5; cf. Blaug 1978, 37–38). The idea that *something* magically transforms private interest into public virtue, in the sense of an efficiently organized, growing economy capable of providing benefits for everyone, was situated in a time when governments intervened directly to guide the development of national economies in the interests of the accumulation of state power and strengthening the position of entrepreneurs (Peet 2009, 4–5; cf. Mäki 1990).[10]

In his works, Smith mentions the "invisible hand" only three times. But, as already worked out by many scholars, the figure of the "invisible hand" offers wide scope for interpretation.[11] These varieties of interpretation can be distinguished in the interpretations made by Ferguson or Smith themselves, and those ones by their intellectual offspring. The basic assumption presented here is that a wide scope of interpretation offers a wide reach of application in economics – and also in the economy (see next part; cf. Giacovelli 2016b).

Taking Smithian interpretations of the invisible hand as an example, the following three versions of interpretation were the only ones made (cf. Rothschild 1994) – ipso facto, these are the only three times Smith mentions this figure himself. Here, Rothschild (1994, 319; cf. Smith 1980 [1795], 49) points out that his first use, in Smith's "History of Astronomy", is obviously sardonic, when he interprets people in polytheistic societies as being credulous, that is those "who ascribe 'the irregular events of nature,' such as thunder and storms, to 'intelligent though invisible beings – to gods, demons, witches, genii, fairies'. They do not ascribe divine support to 'the ordinary course of things': 'nor was the invisible hand of Jupiter ever apprehended to be employed in those matters'". The second time this figure was used was in *The Theory of Moral Sentiments* (1976 [1759]). Here again, Rothschild identifies a sardonic usage, but with a different notion. Smith describes some wealthy proprietors as quite unconcerned with "humanity" or "justice", and in "their natural selfishness and rapacity", they are

10 Keynes already points to the relevance of circumstances as new approaches were situated. Particularly, when Keynes (1965 [1936], 32–34; cf. Stiglitz 2012) explains Ricardo's triumph not solely by its theoretical conviction, but with social interest groups, it is exactly those broader surroundings that provide political and economic support for specific concepts.

11 Strictly speaking, such ambiguous figures lead economics away from a clear and distinct language. While science usually tries hard to avoid ambiguities, the question arises of whether metaphors, like the "invisible hand", lead science in the direction of poetics (cf. Eco 1976, 263).

only interested in satisfying "their own vain and insatiable desires". These people employ thousands of poor workers to produce luxury commodities: "They are led by an invisible hand to […] without intending it, without knowing it, advance the interest of the society" (Rothschild 1994, 319; cf. Smith 1976 [1759], 184). And the third time Smith uses this figure is to be found in *An Inquiry into the Nature and Causes of the Wealth of Nations* (1976 [1776]), arguing against restrictions on imports in international trade and domestic merchants, who are solely interested in their domestic industries and "upon many occasions intimidate the legislature". From Smith's point of view, "(e)very individual is continually exerting himself to find out the most advantageous employment for whatever capital he can command […] and he is in this, as in many other cases, led by an invisible hand to promote an end which was no part of his intention" (Smith 1976 [1776], 453–471; cf. Rothschild 1994, 319). So, there are three usages with three different notions – what they have in common is that they are placed in sardonic wording. People who believe in an invisible hand that solves all problems, like a divine or supernatural power, appear quite naive.[12]

It is particularly the last example that is cited countless times. According to Cremaschi (2002), interpreting it as an illustration of the harmony-of-interests thesis, a deterministic character of the cause-effect relationship, or that the hand's invisibility implies it being the Hand of God, is a common misunderstanding. Instead, he prefers the interpretation that people's actions can result in the same effect, whether the effect was intended or not part of the actor's intention.[13] Besides the different interpretations, the point is that a vast number of economists and social scientists in general have taken the figure seriously. Admittedly, some prominent economic theorists avoid its usage, e.g. the neoclassical theorists Jevons und Marshall, others refuse to accept it, and yet others use it to describe processes in their own framework, e.g. the Walrasian auctioneer, whose Smithian interpretation of the auctioneer then again is gainsaid.[14] Others

12 Besides these three prominent quotations, Mirowski points out that the "invisible hand" was already mentioned in a different context by Adam Smith – namely: in physics instead of economics: "heavy bodies descend, and lighter substances fly upwards by the necessity of their own nature; nor was the invisible hand of Jupiter ever apprehended to be employed in these matters" (Smith 1982 [1795], 49; cf. Mirowski 1989, 408).

13 No suggestion is made that the hand's invisibility implies it being the Hand of God, as was safely assumed by interpreters who used to read Adam Smith as a proponent of a dogmatically optimistic social theodicy centred on the harmony-of-interests thesis (Cremaschi 2002, 93–94).

14 Rothschild denies the Walrasian interpretation of Smith, where an auctioneer represents the invisible hand to ensure tâtonnement, adherence to Smith's understanding of the

see something theological (Oslington 2011) – especially in light of the distinct religious language in this era – naturalistic/evolutionary (cf. Brodbeck 2004, 17; Tiedge 2015), benevolent (cf. Samuelson and Nordhaus 2009, 665), progressive (Luhmann 1996b, 99–100) – but also progress inhibiting – (cf. Bronk 1998, 144–158), equilibrium compatibility (cf. Ingrao and Israel 1990) or romantic (cf. Bronk 2009) as a dominating notion of the figure.

The purpose of this part cannot be to completely present the variety of terminological interpretations, but rather to get a feel for the range of interpretation.[15] Most notably, the idea is to show that the power of fictions bears being highly compatible *because* of its ambiguity. Even if different fractions of interpretation evolve, which struggle for the sovereignty of their interpretation, they are still unified by a shared orientation towards a mutual fiction – *a fiction, which is to such an extent open for interpretation, that it seems to be unsurprisingly/surprisingly highly compatible at all times.*[16]

3.2 Impact on the economy: the IMF's and the other's "invisible hand" plodding through the world

As we will see in the following, such compatibility also plays a vital part concerning "invisible hands"-logics in the economy. There is a wealth of areas that could be mentioned, but due to the limits of this chapter, we will focus on the so-called SAPs of the International Monetary Fund, respectively, of the triad consisting of the IMF, the World Bank and the World Trade Organization (WTO). Therefore, the SAPs are a perfect example, because they not only show the so-called performativity of economic theory, as is well illustrated by the standard examples in economic sociology: Strawberry auction at Fontaines-en-Sologne (Garcia-Parpet 2008) and Black, Scholes and Merton's model (MacKenzie and

---

invisible hand: "The tâtonnement of general competitive equilibrium is a (blind) groping in the dark. Agents who are trying to interpret ambiguous protocols, or deciding whether to try to influence the rules of the game in which they are engaged, or 'groping for more efficient institutions', are much closer to the complicated merchants of Smith's theory" (Rothschild 1994, 322).

15 There is a lively debate about where Smith could have derived his figure from. The possible sources range from Macbeth to Newton (Cremaschi 2002, 101–102).

16 In the research area of the sociology of economic thoughts, these observations were usually made from a metaphoric point of view (see *Economics as a fictional genre*, in this chapter). The difference between a metaphor and a fiction perspective is particularly the narrative aspect. In this regard, it has to be emphasized that under the roof of a fiction like the "invisible hand", a wide range of narrations can be assembled.

Millo 2003). The example of SAPs goes much further in revealing the key role of economic policy and showing the extensive, worldwide influence of such an economic thinking, which is symbolized by the "invisible hand". The history of worldwide societal – and not only economic – transitions of nations has been much discussed (e.g., Vreeland 2006; Peet 2009; Copelovitch 2010; Stiglitz 2012; Giacovelli and Langenohl 2016a, 128–134). So, we can concentrate on the logical core of SAPs, and a few further illustrations, of how the "invisible hand" arouses.

The strategy of the triad (IMF, World Bank and WTO) has changed over the decades, since its founding in 1945, as a result of a multinational agreement in Bretton Woods 1944.[17] Initially, securing bank borrowings was the main focus of IMF activities. Concerning a brief outline of this change, in the temporal aspect, short-term and later mid-term economic-political interventions were replaced by long-term ones. And regarding the liabilities of the borrowing nations, it is observable that the structural provisions of the IMF, which are tied to lending, increasingly step more comprehensively and profoundly into economies (Peet 2009, 74–126). The fame of the IMF grew due to its capability to enable loan repayments for banks. Plainspoken, the IMF's role as a debt collector gave it authority. Particularly in the late 1960s, it is seen that the expanding lending initiatives of private investors to "Third World" countries were accompanied by highly insecure loan repayments. Initially, debtors had to take out further loans to meet the repayment claims of previous loan agreements. Thereafter, these payments also stopped. As a result, neither IMF interventions were doubted, nor was a decline in the direct influence of banks observable. Quite the opposite happened: The IMF was authorized to handle additional functions, with further possibilities to control increasingly dependent nations (Peet 2009, 83).

Against this backdrop, talking about the "invisible hand" in the context of SAPs points to conditions whereby the government reduces its influence on market structures and leaves the field open to free-market mechanisms, as we have seen only recently in Spain, Ireland and Greece. In this spirit, the three pillars of SAPs can be located: The first pillar aims at deflation of the economy by monetary measures. The second pillar consists of the application of market principles wherever possible – particularly by the liberalization of imports, reductions in subsidies, cost-covering the supply of public services and removal of price controls. And the third pillar targets governmental offtakes from the

17 Because of the world economy crisis and the Second World War, international trade relations broadly came to a halt. An option in the Bretton Woods Agreement sought to revive international goods traffic by providing an officially accepted and stable currency.

market, e.g. market-based instructed reforms of the areas of agriculture, energy, education, healthcare and finance (cf. Siebold 1995, 2). In a nutshell, liberated market forces should automatically break down the barriers erected by structural distortions. And the IMF clings to these core elements, even if this programme of privatization and deregulation is complemented by "social action programmes". Thus, the fight against inflation and reducing budget deficits, which should primarily be achieved by the manipulation of several monetary variables, still occupies centre stage. Growth enhancement, or maintaining an indispensable level of welfare spending, was subordinated, in the end, to macroeconomic stabilization by traditional IMF tools (Siebold 1995, 54). Finally, the market effect of highly esteemed self-interested company strategies, e.g., observable in the buyout of 14 Greek airports by the German company Fraport in the context of the IMF's austerity and privatization restrictions on the Greek government, is measured by selected macroeconomic variables.

This strategy of the IMF and its strategic partners does not only match on a structural level the aforementioned mainstream interpretations of the "invisible hand". Market players, politicians, economists[18] or IMF staff members refer to it in this way, too. Let's take a short look at some publications: Ahsan, the economist, asks for instance how a crash in the finance markets could happen, if the "invisible hand" works. He comes to the conclusion that Smith's idea of the "invisible hand" is still powerful, in the sense that: "Supervisory bodies need to focus on ensuring diversity in the marketplace, independence of opinion and conclusions that is free of manipulative and corrupting influence, decentralization of the market participants, and bottom up processes that aggregate information" (Ahsan 2012, 50). Furthermore, he mentions that the conflicts over Smith's "invisible hand" mainly result because of his "expansive rhetoric" (Ahsan 2012, 50).[19] Gorton (2010, 13), economist and consultant for, for instance, the US Board of Governors of the Federal Reserve System, also examines the financial crises of 2007, also in light of how the "invisible hand" could let this be possible – especially after a span of 75 years without any crisis – at all. His main explanation is that the triggering bank run was *itself invisible*, because it was

18 The reason why I also mention politicians and economists in this chapter, focusing on the economy, is that there is enough evidence for managers or politicians reproducing their academic knowledge from university in daily business (cf. Samuelson 1948, 36; Krell 2013).

19 Ahsan describes Smith's rhetoric style as inconsistent and exaggerating and refers to Warren Samuels, who lamented that: "I wish that Smith had had an editor" (Ahsan 2012, 50).

a bank run by banks and thus a run of firms on other banks. And these interbank markets were invisible to the public, journalists and politicians, who were only able to observe the effects of the run and often mistake them for the cause (Gorton 2010, 3). Basu (2016), an economist, and also Senior Vice President and Chief Economist of the World Bank, offers a new approach to economics that aims to overcome the idea of self-interested individuals, whose egoism leads to a greater good, as if orchestrated by an invisible hand, and pleads for collective action and fairness. He uses analytical tools to overcome mainstream economics and suggests, similar to Stiglitz (2012), that the ones who promote the idea that the current system is the only choice are solely serving the interests of those who benefit by it.[20] These few examples illustrate the significance of the "invisible hand" in the current debates of persons with high influence on changes to economic structures. Even if, in various passages, a scope of interpretation is addressed, these authors try to cling to an interpretation that is assumed to be commonly understood as appropriate.[21]

These illustrative insights into how the "invisible hand" is applied to the economy, and previously in economics, stress not only the ambiguity of the "invisible hand" and its adaptability, but also what progressive economists think of when they demand post-autistic economics. Devine (2006, 205) reminds us of autism on a psychological level. Here, autism originally consists of a lack of understanding of something like a society with its rules and conventions. In this meaning, mainstream economics was interpreted as being autistic, because of

20 Bronk's dissent as to the invincibility of "invisible hand"-logics is based on the case of externalities, because environmental costs were not reflected in market prices. And therefore, "individual decisions of self-interested market participants can no longer add up to an outcome which provides the maximum benefits to society as a whole" (Bronk 1998, 146).

21 Others use the "invisible hand" as a starting point, or more precisely as a contrast to different theoretical or empirical observations, which leads to modified phrasings that express differences to assumed common understandings. To name but a few: former IMF Managing Director Dominique Strauss-Kahn's contrast of the "invisible hand" to the "invisible fist" (IMF 2011); Shleifer and Vishny's (1999) "helping hand" and the "grabbing hand" mentioned by Quintyn and Masciandaro (2008), examining politicians orientated to a greater good or their self-interest; journalist Badger (2013), and also Sundararajan (2017), writes about companies like Airbnb or Etsy and, based on Smith's "invisible hand", distinguishes "visible work" from "invisible work". Adam Smith speaks himself about invisible hands on one side but also about the threatening hand of justice, which must be visible, therewith the invisible hand of the market operates properly (cf. Fritsch 2011, 9).

neglecting society and only accepting individuals, too. The "invisible hand" in this understanding seems to be the only way linking (more or less) observable action on the micro-level with macroeconomic measured outcomes.

3.3 Drawing a lesson from the "invisible hand": fictionality and its social impact

The basic model Ferguson, and shortly after him Smith, presented is not that complicated. Individuals do not have intended influence on higher social levels. This ability is reserved for God, fate or whatever higher form of existence is imagined – or just sardonically implied. And, just as McCloskey, Morgan and Mirowski point out, this simple framework needs a narration that explains what is precisely – in a specific context – meant by it, comparable to mathematical formulae (cf. Beckert 2016, 67–71). And as already mentioned, this structure offers an important advantage: Under the roof of this structure, as we have seen, a range of narrations can be assembled. But, just because it is simple, it does not mean that the structure of supplementary narrations is interchangeable at will.

The salient point of this chapter is that it is not structurally necessary that the mentioned proponents have to take the fiction as real: "Ever since Adam Smith, the central teaching of economics has been that free markets provide us with material well-being, *as if* by an invisible hand" (Akerlof and Shiller 2016 [emphasis added]). It is all about imagining a functionality. And if actors, particularly influential ones, build their expectations on the basis of such fictions, signal them and anticipate them reciprocally, then social structures emerge – and fictionality has real consequences. And this is more likely if Vaihinger (1924, 269) is right and: "Man's natural tendency is to take his thought for the direct expression of reality, to see in the forms of thought forms of existence". Besides, when Reich (2015, 191–192) calls the neoclassical actor a Laplacian demon ("Laplace'scher Dämon"), because he is equipped with a universal intelligence, so that he is able to draw conclusions today regarding the rest of all time, with the result that every market value can be precisely determined – then we have got to deal with a temporal consistent, "expectation maximize", and likewise a utopian (or dystopian, SG) outline of society.

What does an excursion to the neoclassical actor tell us? It tells us that if we formulate fictional, methodological, helpful exaggerations in such a way that we become better aware of them, then it is hopefully no longer that easy to take fictions at face value – or, even worse, as something like instruction for proper behaviour. So, if we ask ourselves about what we, as sociologists, can learn from the "invisible hand"-fiction, these are the *key findings* of this chapter:

First, we should profit from the benefits a fiction offers, but we must remain aware of not mixing them up with hypotheses or reality – as illustrated in *The "invisible hand" as consequential fiction*, in this chapter. In this sense, it is also a warning about dogmatization and the real consequences of powerful fictions.[22] And if we, as proposed above, complement Vaihinger's (1924) considerations about fiction and hypotheses, both equally shaping action, with Esposito's (2007) distinction, in the way that fictions are, in contrast to hypotheses, immune to empirical-based reality checks, then we can conclude that the fiction of the "invisible hand" is well prepared to be adopted for another 250 years, at least.

Second, it would be very wrong solely to demonize the application of strong fictions. A fiction like the "invisible hand" is a perfect example of how to use the current discussion in economic sociology not only for working on new theoretical approaches, but also for applying these considerations to the field of the sociology of economics. A plethora of contributions to economics and sociology are sprinkled with impressive images, e.g. Weber's "iron cage", and in combination with respective narrations these imaginations survive centuries without any loss of expression.

Third, switching to the sociology of economic thought, despite the mainly inner-economic controversy concerning either too many or too few mathematical methods, mathematical language has become widely accepted in economics. According to Porter (1994, 160; 1995; cf. Pribram 1998, 17), this is due to the abstract formalism of neoclassical mathematics that holds economics as an academic discipline together. Based on this assumption of Porter and the aforementioned, and also going beyond the assumed attractiveness of the "invisible hand" for methodological individualists (cf. Ullmann-Margalit 1978, 271), my hypothesis is that a strong narration like the Fergusonian/Smithian fiction of the "invisible hand" offers *a narration that holds economics, particularly with respect to its methodological individualism, together.* In other words: Economics is

22 Vaihinger (1924, 131) states that, concerning the dogmatization of the "invisible hand": "Linnæus and Smith built up their respective systems as purely artificial ones. Their followers either turned them into hypotheses or interpreted them as hypotheses (for it requires a high degree of mental training to recognize an idea as fictive), and then these hypotheses themselves at once became dogmas. Adam Smith's system was later regarded as an hypothesis, and since Buckle's convincing demonstration it has been treated almost universally as an artificial system built up on fiction. But the idea was regarded earlier so definitely as an hypothesis or dogma that it was believed not only that all actions were egoistic but that it was actually necessary so to act".

dependent on a dramatic, fictional story, which is far removed from the outward appearances of a strongly formalized, thoroughly mathematized discipline.[23]

But, fourth, its impact is not limited to economics – using at least the example of this volume. Even if – from a sociological perspective – an overemphasis on individualism and rationality is rarely observed in sociology, one of the few examples being Coleman (1990), the fiction at least provokes a methodological questioning. The findings should be interpreted as a stimulus for methodological reasoning and questioning concerning phenomena that are currently understood as not observable from a sociological point of view. In the not-too-distant past, there were phenomena regarded as not sociologically treatable, for instance when theoretical considerations about expectations were understood as the research domain of psychologists (cf. Giacovelli 2016a, 77, 85), or at times of Pax Parsonsiana, when a sociologically founded economic theory was almost unthinkable.

And the fifth point is that, in the same way that the future lies open in front of us, and regarding the fact that the unobservable part is always greater than the observable, fictions and also hypotheses will always determine our (scientific) life (cf. Giacovelli and Langenohl 2016b, 89–92). With this in mind, we should learn from Smith's scholars, who ignored the high status of sympathy and benevolence in *The Theory of Moral Sentiments* 1976 [1759] and raised self-interest from *An Inquiry into the Nature and Causes of the Wealth of Nations* (1976 [1776]) to a dogma. Against this background, we should self-critically take Vaihinger's (1924, 187) indication to heart, that the fictions of the masters could develop into the dogmas of their followers.

And, not least, there is a sixth point – rather an outlook than another systemization of the aforementioned arguments. The strong impact of the "invisible hand"-fiction sensitizes us to the fundamental importance of expectations as a key concept in sociology. According to these observations, fictions are able to shape expectations, which in turn shape communication and action – already exemplified by SAPs. These findings suggest, all the more, that it is advisable to work on a social theory of expectations – with a framing that goes beyond economic phenomena (cf. Giacovelli 2016a; 2017).

---

23 Concerning the scientific theoretical differences of mathematics in neoclassic economics and in pure mathematics, see Giacovelli (2016b). At least regarding the political economy, Vaihinger (1924, 20) concludes that by proceeding from the notion that all action is egoistic, Smith "succeeded in bringing the whole of political economy into an ordered system".

References

Ahsan, Mainul. 2012. "Where Was the Invisible Hand during the Crash?" *Economic Insights – Trends and Challenges* LXIV: 44–52.

Akerlof, George A., and Robert J. Shiller. 2016. *Phishing for Phools: The Economics of Manipulation and Deception*. Princeton: Princeton University Press.

Aydinonat, N. Emrah. 2008. *The Invisible Hand in Economics. How Economists Explain Unintended Social Consequences*. London and New York: Routledge.

Badger, Emily. 2013. "The Rise of Invisible Works." *Citylab*, October 31, 2013. Accessed November 5, 2017. https://www.citylab.com/life/2013/10/rise-invisible-work/7412/.

Basu, Kaishuk. 2016. *Beyond the Invisible Hand: Groundwork for a New Economics*. Princeton: Princeton University Press.

Beckert, Jens. 2013. "Imagined Futures. Fictional Expectations in the Economy." *Theory and Society* 42: 219–240.

Beckert, Jens. 2016. *Imagined Futures: Fictional Expectations and Capitalist Dynamics*. Cambridge: Harvard University Press.

Blaug, Mark. 1978. *Economic Theory in Retrospect*. Cambridge: Cambridge University Press.

Brodbeck, Karl-Heinz. 2004. *Die fragwürdigen Grundlagen des Neoliberalismus. Wirtschaftsordnung und Markt in Hayeks Theorie der Regelselektion*. Accessed November 5, 2017. http://www.khbrodbeck.homepage.t-online.de/hayek.pdf.

Bronk, Richard. 1998. *Progress and the Invisible Hand. The Philosophy and Economics of Human Advance*. London: Little, Brown and Company.

Bronk, Richard. 2009. *The Romantic Economist: Imagination in Economics*. Cambridge: Cambridge University Press.

Coleman, James Samuel. 1990. *Foundations of Social Theory*. Cambridge: Harvard University Press.

Copelovitch, Mark S. 2010. *The International Monetary Fund in the Global Economy: Banks, Bonds, and Bailouts*. Cambridge: Cambridge University Press.

Courtemanche, Eleanor, ed. 2011. *The Invisible Hand and British Fiction, 1818–1860. Adam Smith, Political Economy, and the Genre of Realism*. Basingstoke: Palgrave Macmillan.

Cremaschi, Sergio. 2002. "Metaphors in the Wealth of Nations" In *Is There Progress in Economics? Knowledge, Truth and the History of Economic Thought*, edited by Stephan Boehm, Christian Gehrke, Heinz D. Kurz, and Richard Sturn, 89–114. Cheltenham: B&T.

Devine, James. 2006. "Psychologischer Autismus, institutioneller Autismus und die Ökonomik" In *Die Scheuklappen der Wirtschaftswissenschaft: Postautistische Ökonomik für eine pluralistische Wirtschaftslehre*, edited by Thomas Dürmeier, Tanja von Egan-Krieger, and Helge Peukert, 203–216. Marburg: Metropolis.

Durkheim, Émile. 1982 [1895]. *Rules of Sociological Method.* New York: Free Press.

Eco, Umberto. 1976. *A Theory of Semiotics*. Bloomington: Indiana University Press.

Esposito, Elena. 2007. *Die Fiktion der wahrscheinlichen Realität*. Frankfurt am Main: Suhrkamp.

Esposito, Elena. 2011. *The Future of Futures. The Time of Money in Financing and Society*. Cheltenham (UK) and Northampton (MA): Edward Elgar.

Ferguson, Adam. 1767. *An Essay on the History of Civil Society*. Edinburgh: A. Miller & T. Caddel.

Fritsch, Michael. 2011. *Marktversagen und Wirtschaftspolitik: Mikroökonomische Grundlagen staatlichen Handelns*. München: Vahlen.

Garcia-Parpet, Marie-France. 2008. "The Social Construction of a Perfect Market: The Strawberry Auction at Fontaines-en-Sologne." In *Do Economists Make Markets? On the Performativity of Economics*, edited by Donald A. MacKenzie, Fabian Muniesa, and Lucia Siu, 20–53. Princeton: Princeton University Press.

Giacovelli, Sebastian. 2016a. "Changing Markets, Expected Expectations and Popitz's Objection." *Przegląd Socjologiczny/Sociological Review* 65: 75–90.

Giacovelli, Sebastian. 2016b. "Formelideal und Problemlösung – Über den Gebrauch mathematischer Formeln in der reinen Mathematik und der mathematisierten Ökonomik." *Forum Interdisziplinäre Begriffsgeschichte* 5: 115–124.

Giacovelli, Sebastian. 2017. "General and Economic Sociology Reunited? The Potential of Expectations." Paper presented at *New Economic Sociology and General Sociology: Where Do They Meet? Where Do They Diverge?*, May 22-23, 2017, Warsaw.

Giacovelli, Sebastian. 2018 forthcoming. "Neoklassische Formeln als Artefakte – Zur prägenden Kraft und temporalen Widerständigkeit." In *Zeit der Moderne: Regime, Logiken, Strukturen*, edited by Helmut Hühn et al. Hannover: Wehrhahn.

Giacovelli, Sebastian, and Andreas Langenohl. 2016a. "Zwischen Synchronizität und Gleichgewicht: Zeitformen im internationalen kapitalistischen System" In *Zeit und Form*, edited by Michael Gamper, Eva Geulen, Jens

Grave, Andreas Langenohl, Ralf Simon, and Sabine Zubarik, 111–136. Hannover: Wehrhahn.

Giacovelli, Sebastian, and Andreas Langenohl. 2016b. "Offshore-Finanzzentren zwischen Rückständigkeit und Avantgardismus" In *Inseln und Insularitäten. Ästhetisierungen von Heterochronie und Chronotopie seit 1960*, edited by Michael Ostheimer and Sabine Zubarik, 87–101. Hannover: Wehrhahn.

Giacovelli, Sebastian, and Andreas Langenohl. 2016c. "Temporalitäten in der wirtschaftswissenschaftlichen Modellbildung: Die Multiplikation von Zeitlichkeit in der Neoklassik." In *Die Innenwelt der Ökonomie. Wissen, Macht und Performativität in der Wirtschaftswissenschaft*, edited by Jens Maeße, Hanno Pahl, and Jan Sparsam, 33–54. Wiesbaden: Springer VS.

Gorton, Gary B. 2010. *Slapped by the Invisible Hand: The Panic of 2007.* New York: Oxford University Press.

Grampp, William D. 2000. "What Did Smith Mean by the Invisible Hand?" *Journal of Political Economy* 108: 441–465.

Hill, Lisa. 2006. *The Passionate Society: The Social, Political and Moral Thought of Adam Ferguson*. Dordrecht: Springer.

Husserl, Edmund. 2007 [1936]. *Die Krisis der europäischen Wissenschaften und die transzendentale Phänomenologie: Eine Einleitung in die phänomenologische Philosophie*. Hamburg: Meiner.

IMF. 2011. "Press Release: IMF Managing Director Dominique Strauss-Kahn Calls for New Global Approaches to Post-Crises World." *Press Release* 11/114. Accessed November 13, 2017. https://www.imf.org/en/News/Articles/2015/09/14/01/49/pr11114.

Ingrao, Bruna, and Giorgio Israel. 1990. *The Invisible Hand: Economic Equilibrium in the History of Science*. Cambridge: MIT Press.

Iser, Wolfgang. 1993. *The Fictive and the Imaginary: Charting Literary Anthropology*. Baltimore: Johns Hopkins University Press.

Jahan, Sarwat, and Ahmed Saber Mahmud. 2015. "What is Capitalism? Free Markets May Not Be Perfect, but They Are Probably the Best Way to Organize an Economy." *Finance & Development* June: 44–45.

James, William. 1890. *The Principles of Psychology*, vol. 1-2. New York and London: Holt and Macmillan.

Keynes, John Maynard. 1965 [1936]. *The General Theory of Employment, Interest, and Money*. New York: Harcourt.

Koselleck, Reinhart. 2004. *Futures Past: On the Semantics of Historical Time.* New York: Columbia University Press.

Krell, Gertraude. 2013. "Wie und mit welchen Machtwirkungen werden Wirtschaft(ende) und Arbeit(ende) fabriziert? Inspektionen von Ökonomie aus diskurs- und dispositivanalytischen Perspektiven" In *Ökonomie, Diskurs, Regierung: Interdisziplinäre Perspektiven*, edited by Jens Mäße, 213–239. Wiesbaden: Springer VS.

Luhmann, Niklas. 1976. "The Future Cannot Begin: Temporal Structures in Modern Society." *Social Research* 43: 130–152.

Luhmann, Niklas. 1996a. *Die Realität der Massenmedien*. Opladen: Westdeutscher Verlag.

Luhmann, Niklas. 1996b. *Die Wirtschaft der Gesellschaft*. Frankfurt am Main: Suhrkamp.

MacKenzie, Donald, and Yuval Millo. 2003. "Constructing a Market, Performing Theory: The Historical Sociology of a Financial Derivatives Exchange." *American Journal of Sociology* 109: 101–145.

Mäki, Uskali. 1990. "Practical Syllogism, Entrepreneurship, and the Invisible Hand: A Critique of the Analytic Hermeneutics of G. H. von Wright." In *Economics and Hermeneutics*, edited by Don Lavoie, 146–173. London: Routledge.

Mäki, Uskali, ed. 2002. *Fact and Fiction in Economics: Models, Realism and Social Construction*. Cambridge: Cambridge University Press.

McCloskey, Deirdre. 1985. *The Rhetoric of Economics*. Wisconsin: The University of Wisconsin Press.

McCloskey, Deirdre. 1990. *If You're So Smart: The Narrative of Economic Expertise*. Chicago: The University of Chicago Press.

McCloskey, Deirdre. 1994. *Knowledge and Persuasion in Economics*. Cambridge: Cambridge University Press.

Merton, Robert King. 1995. "The Thomas Theorem and the Matthew Effect." *Social Forces* 74: 379–424.

Mirowski, Phillip. 1989. *More Heat than Light. Economic as Social Physics, Physics as Nature's Economics*. Cambridge: Cambridge University Press.

Mirowski, Phillip. 1991. "Postmodernism and the Social Theory of Value" *Journal of Post Keynesian Economics* 13: 565–582.

Mirowski, Phillip ed. 1994. *Natural Images in Economic Thought: "Markets Read in Tooth and Claw."* Cambridge: Cambridge University Press.

Morgan, Mary S. 2012. *The World in the Model. How Economists Work and Think*. Cambridge: Cambridge University Press.

Oslington, Paul. 2011. *Adam Smith as Theologian*. New York: Routledge.

Peet, Richard. 2009. *Unholy Trinity: The IMF, World Bank and WTO*. London: Zed Books.

Pohoryles, Ronald J., ed. 2015. *Die Aktualität von Adam Smith.* Marburg: Metropolis.

Porter, Theodore M. 1994. "Rigor and Practicality: Rival Ideas of Quantification in Nineteenth-Century Economics." In *Natural Images in Economic Thought: "Markets Read in Tooth & Claw"*, edited by Phillip Mirowski, 127–170. Cambridge: University Press.

Porter, Theodore M. 1995. *Trust in Numbers: The Pursuit of Objectivity in Science and Public Life.* Princeton: Princeton University Press.

Pribram, Karl. 1998. *Geschichte des ökonomischen Denkens.* Frankfurt-am-Main: Suhrkamp.

Quintyn, Marc G., and Donato Masciandaro. 2008. "Helping Hand or Grabbing Hand? Architecture, Financial Structure and Market View." *IMF Working Papers* 8: 1–46.

Reich, Jens. 2015. "Zwischen Utopie und Heterotopie. Die Welt aus ökonomischer Sicht." In *Ökonomische Utopien*, edited by Sophia Ebert, Johannes Glaeser, 187–202. Berlin: Neofelis.

Reichspfarrer, Dominic, and Matthias Sulz. 2015. "Die unsichtbare Hand - eine missinterpretierte Metapher?" In *Die Aktualität von Adam Smith*, edited by Ronald J. Pohoryles, 43–65. Marburg: Metropolis.

Riles, Annelise. 2010. "Collateral Expertise: Legal Knowledge in the Global Financial Markets." *Current Anthropology* 51: 795–818.

Riles, Annelise. 2011. *Collateral Knowledge - Legal Reasoning in the Global Financial Markets.* Chicago: University of Chicago Press.

Rothschild, Emma. 1994. "Adam Smith and the Invisible Hand." *The American Economic Review* 84: 319–322.

Samuelson, Paul. 1948. *Economics.* New York: McGraw-Hill.

Samuelson, Paul, and William D. Nordhaus. 2009. *Economics.* Boston: Erwin Economics.

Schütz, Alfred. 1932. *Der sinnhafte Aufbau der sozialen Welt. Eine Einleitung in die verstehende Soziologie.* Wien: Springer.

Searle, John R. 1975. "The Logical Status of Fictional Discourse" *New Literary History* 6: 319–332.

Shleifer, Andrei, and Robert W. Vishny. 1999. *The Grabbing Hand: Government Pathologies and Their Cures.* Cambridge: Harvard University Press.

Siebold, Thomas. 1995. "Die sozialen Dimensionen der Strukturanpassung. Eine Zwischenbilanz." *INEF Report 13.* Accessed November 13, 2017. http://duepublico.uni-duisburg-essen.de/servlets/DerivateServlet/Derivate-29400/report13.pdf.

Smith, Adam. 1976 [1776]. *An Inquiry into the Nature and Causes of the Wealth of Nations*. Oxford: Oxford University Press.

Smith, Adam. 1976 [1759]. *The Theory of Moral Sentiments*. Oxford: Oxford University Press.

Smith, Adam. 1980 [1795]. *Essays on Philosophical Subjects*. Oxford: Oxford University Press.

Smith, Adam. 1982 [1795]. "The History of Astronomy." In *Essays on Philosophical Subjects*, edited by W. P. D. Wightman and J. C. Bryce, 33–105. Indianapolis: Liberty Press.

Stiglitz, Joseph. 2012. *The Price of Inequality: How Today's Divided Society Endangers Our Future*. New York: W.W. Norton & Co.

Sundararajan, Arun. 2017. *Sharing Economy: The End of Employment and the Rise of Crowd-Based Capitalism*. Cambridge: The MIT Press.

Thomas, William Isaac, and Dorothy Swaine Thomas. 1928. *The Child in America: Behavior Problems and Programs*. New York: Knopf.

Tiedge, Filip. 2015. "Mit Adam Smith die Beziehung des Menschen zur Natur neu bestimmen." In *Die Aktualität von Adam Smith*, edited by Ronald J. Pohoryles, 131–166. Marburg: Metropolis.

Tieffenbach, Emma. 2013. "Invisible-Hand Explanations: From Blindness to Lack of We-ness." *Social Science Information* 52: 450–470.

Ullmann-Margalit, Edna. 1978. "Invisible-Hand Explanations." *Synthese* 39: 263–291.

Vaihinger, Hans. 1924. *Philosophy of the 'as if'. A System of the Theoretical, Practical and Religious Fictions of Mankind*. London: Routledge and Kegan Paul.

Vreeland, James Raymond. 2006. *The International Monetary Fund: Politics of Conditional Lending*. New York: Routledge.

Karl-Dieter Opp

The Interdependence of Spontaneous Order and Institutional Design: Table Manners, Daylight Saving Time, Language and the Erosion of Institutional Design under Communist Rule

Abstract: This chapter aims at integrating two literatures that focus on different mechanisms of norm emergence: the spontaneous order tradition and the literature on human design. Spontaneous norm emergence and creation of norms by design are rarely separate processes; they are often concatenated in various ways. We explore their interdependence by analyzing in detail the following examples. (1) Why do table manners that are a spontaneous order evolve without intervention of some central authority? (2) Why does daylight saving time (DST), brought about by human design, not develop as a spontaneous order? (3) Why does the state interfere in the development of language – also a spontaneous order – by imposing spelling reforms in Germany and not in the US? (4) Why was institutional design undermined through the development of a spontaneous order in former communist states? We develop hypotheses that answer these questions.

Keywords: Spontaneous order; institutional design; conventions; table manners; daylight saving time; language reform

1 Introduction

The literature on the origin of norms and institutions (understood here as sets of norms) is divided into different schools. One is the *spontaneous order school*. It goes back to the Scottish moral philosophers, in particular to Adam Smith, David Hume and Adam Ferguson in the 18th century. This tradition was taken up by Carl Menger in the 19th century and Friedrich A. Hayek in the 20th century.[1] The *basic spontaneous order model* claims: an institution (e.g., a language) or some social pattern (behavior in a market) is an *aggregate* result of *numerous*

1 See Barry (1982); Hamowy (1987); Horwitz (2001); see also Schneider (1967).

discrete individual actions, and the individuals do not *intend* to create the aggregate result (see, e.g., Smith 2007 [1776], 349–350; Hamowy 1987, 3–4).

In the spontaneous order tradition, institutional design is of marginal interest, whereas in the public choice literature (e.g., Mueller 2003), it is center stage, and spontaneous order is rarely addressed in detail. This holds for the law and society literature as well (e.g., Roach Anleu 2000; Wagner 2010). Theories of norm emergence (e.g., Coleman 1990) do not distinguish these processes at all. The burgeoning literature on the new institutionalisms (e.g., DiMaggio 1998) does not provide systematic analyses about the conditions for the occurrence of these processes either.

In contrast to these literatures, in reality, we often find a *concatenation* of these processes. For example, spontaneous order such as a language may develop without state intervention. Then, at a certain time, a state introduces spelling rules as laws or ordinances. This may obstruct spontaneous order. There is thus often interdependence of spontaneous order and institutional design. This interdependence (or concatenation) is the major concern of this chapter.

We explore these processes by analyzing different examples of norms. We ask why *table manners* – a spontaneous order – evolved without human design. We further explore why *daylight saving time* was brought about by human design and did not develop spontaneously. A prime example of a spontaneous order is *language*. Why does the state sometimes interfere in the development of language by imposing spelling reforms and sometimes not? Under the communist rule, we find that institutional design was to a large extent *replaced by spontaneous order*. How can this be explained?

In what follows, we will use the following definitions. A *norm* is a statement that prescribes certain behaviors (see Opp 2015 for a discussion). An *institution* is defined as a set of norms (e.g., Hodgson 2006, 2). We use *order* synonymously with institution. Each of these concepts refers to oughtness. Regular behavior that does not involve oughtness is thus not a norm. We do not include "sanctions" as defining criteria of norms. These and other norm-related phenomena should be regarded as dependent or independent variables. The justification for those definitions is that they refer to the phenomena that we want to explain.

Institutional design is given if an actor (or a group of actors) decrees a norm or a set of norms that are supposed to hold for the members of a group. Examples of such actors are parliaments that make laws, firms that issue a dress code or fathers who give orders when to dine. In what follows, we are mainly concerned with state actors (governments, parliaments and administrations).

All other processes of norm emergence are subsumed under the concept of *spontaneous order.*

2 Processes of norm emergence and their explanation

2.1 Discontent, demand for change and regulatory interest

The basic spontaneous order model (see above) does not spell out why individuals perform the action that finally brings about the unintended collective outcome. To illustrate, assume people increasingly replace "Fris*eur*" with "Fris*ö*r" (both mean hairdresser) so that, finally, "Firs*ö*r" is adopted as the "correct" spelling in the society. "Fris*eur*" shows a French influence, whereas "Fris*ö*r" is German. Pronunciation of both words is identical.

Why would someone decide to write "Fris*ö*r" instead of "Fris*eur*"? There may be *discontent* with having words of foreign origin in the German language. This may lead to a *demand for change*. One could contribute to a change by replacing "eu" with "ö" in one's written documents.

However, discontent will not always lead to a demand for change. Assume, for example, one thinks that language or any other cultural item that evolved spontaneously is a cultural good that has to be accepted as it has developed. There is thus a preference for preserving spontaneous order, and no demand for change will originate. The low discontent and the preference for keeping the spontaneous order intact will not generate a *demand for regulation* or a regulatory interest that some authority should decree a change in spelling.

These arguments indicate that there are causal relationships between discontent, demand for change and regulatory interest (*fig. 1*): The higher discontent, the more likely is a demand for change, and the stronger this demand, the stronger is a regulatory interest. In addition, discontent has a positive causal effect on the latter variable.

It is plausible that there are *threshold effects*: only if discontent is relatively high, a demand for change and a regulatory interest will arise; only a relatively strong demand for change will bring about a regulatory interest.

The previous causal diagram is not complete. For example, if "Friseur" is the common spelling, using "Frisör" might elicit strong negative sanctions so that a person will not deviate from the common writing style. As has been said, a preference for preserving spontaneous order might neutralize the effects of discontent. We will address these factors later when we discuss the examples. At this point, it is important to note that the individual incentives for a behavior (such as adopting a new spelling) that brings about a spontaneous order might be different.

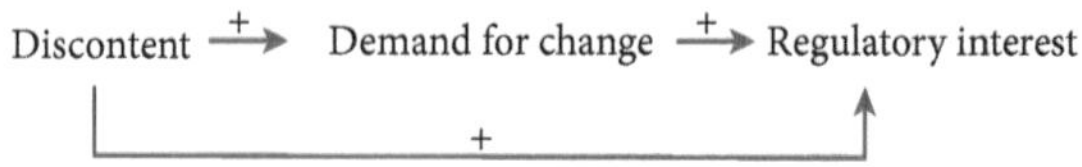

Fig. 1: Consequences of Discontent with Aspects of a Spontaneous Order

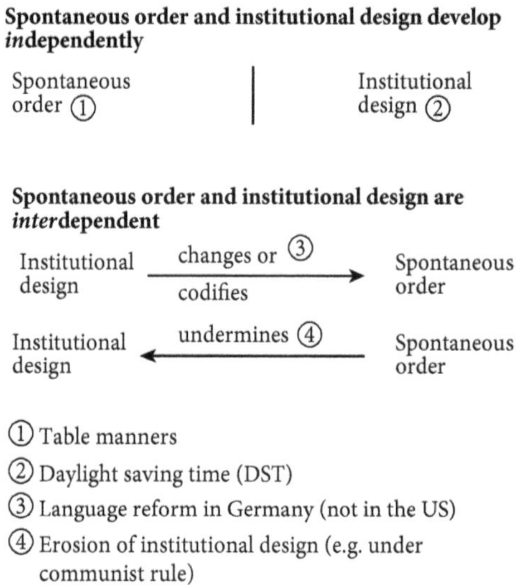

Fig. 2: Relationships between Spontaneous Order and Institutional Design

2.2 Spontaneous order and institutional design: kinds of relationships

There are spontaneous orders that develop without any interference of governments, and there is institutional design that does not encounter any spontaneous order. For example, table manners – our first case study – evolve without having been the subject of state action; DST – our second case study – originated by institutional design: setting the clock ahead or back is always decreed by some authority. The upper panel of *fig. 2* lists these two types of cases. There is thus *independence* of spontaneous order and institutional design.

Our next two cases refer to the *interdependence* of spontaneous order and institutional design. Case 3 refers to language that is originally a clearly spontaneous order (Keller 1994; 2014). The puzzling fact is that in some countries,

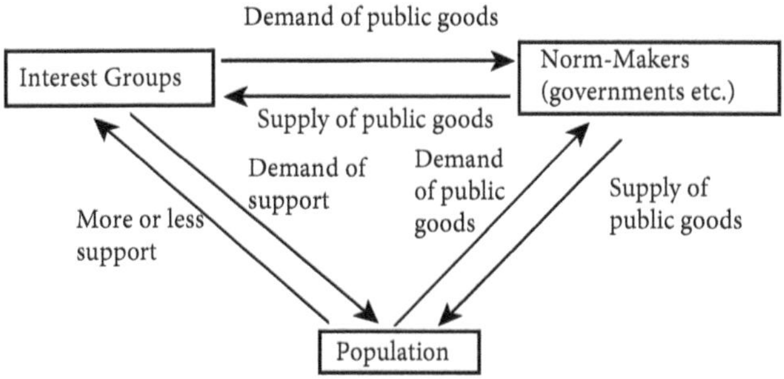

Fig. 3: A Multi-actor Model Explaining Spontaneous and Planned Emergence of Norms

language is a spontaneous order that resembles case 1 as in the US, but sometimes governments intervene as in Germany. We will discuss below why this is so.

Our final case 4 refers to communist regimes that regulated almost every aspect of the daily life. Over time institutional design eroded and was replaced with spontaneous order. The final section addresses the question how this can be explained.

There are many other examples that could have been analyzed. We selected examples that we found particularly interesting, that were not too complex for a single article and that illustrate the different possible cases.

2.3 The explanatory model

How can these different processes be explained? There are always at least two actors involved: the population on the one hand and governments (or any authority that is able to intervene) on the other. Even if there is only a spontaneous order, the state is a relevant actor for the possible decision to intervene. In many cases, there is a third actor involved: interest groups (*fig. 3*). Depending on the explanatory problems, these actors may be further partitioned. For instance, there may be different fractions in a population in favor of or against a law.

There are exchange relationships between these actors. For example, the norm-makers may be faced with a demand for a spelling reform (i.e., a certain kind of a public good) and satisfy this demand by making a law. This, in turn, may increase the support of the population in the next election. The kind of these relationships must be determined if explanatory problems are tackled.

The behavior of all actors is driven by preferences (goals) and constraints or behavioral opportunities. Among the constraints are the actions of the other actors. Actors "satisfice" (Simon 1997 [1945]), i.e. they maximize their subjective (not objective) utility.[2] There are a great variety of preferences or constraints of the actors in different situations, as our examples will indicate. Why actors make certain decisions has to be ascertained in the situation.

3 Table manners: the "primordial" spontaneous order

Table manners have spontaneously evolved since the human race exists. They refer to the kind of food that is allowed to be ingested under certain conditions and to the way the food is ingested. There are a great variety of table manners across countries and regions within a country (e.g., Visser 2012). So far there has been no state that has prescribed how, when and what to eat. How can this be explained?

3.1 The demand for regulation

Could there be discontent with the existing table manners in the population that might prompt state actors to intervene? To illustrate, the diffusion of western food in Japan had the effect that the exclusive use of chopsticks became impractical: eating spaghettis or steaks is easier with fork, spoon and knife (Wang 2015). This might have generated discontent with using only chopsticks.

What could be the options of a male person J in this situation? There are several *private strategies*. Those who want to ingest western food could order and buy cutlery in shops and use it at home. In restaurants, J might request cutlery or take it to the restaurant and use it there. If this happens often, restaurants will buy cutlery and offer it to customers. In this case, the basic spontaneous order model predicts that the exclusive use of chopsticks will attenuate and will be supplemented by the use of cutlery. There will thus be a peaceful coexistence of using both utensils.

Learning to use cutlery is costly. Perhaps these costs are higher than learning to eat the new western food with chopsticks. Thus, even if there is discontent with the use of chopsticks, the costs of changing to cutlery are still higher and people prefer to learn using chopsticks to ingest the new food. For many people, thus, there is discontent but no demand for change (see *fig. 1*).

It seems plausible that the example of the chopsticks holds for table manners in general. For example, it had been good manners in the old times to chop potatoes with a fork. This might have led to discontent because chopping potatoes with a knife, that is usually available at a table, is easier. Here switching to

2 We apply here a wide version of rational choice theory. For details, see Opp (1999; 2018).

Tab. 1: Payoffs for conformity to or deviation from table manners

Behavioral alternatives of the *traditionalist* A (chop potato with fork)	**Behavioral alternatives of the *modernist* B (cut potato with knife)**	
	(1) Traditional (use fork)	**(2) New (use knife)**
(1) Traditional behavior (chop potato with fork)	6, 4	5, 5
(2) New behavior (cut potato with knife)	5, 5	4, 6

First entry in each cell is the payoff for A, second entry the payoff for B.

the new "technology" incurs very low costs. But those who have learned to use forks might want to avoid these costs. Again, there might be some discontent but hardly a demand for change. Accordingly, one would expect a peaceful coexistence of different customs.

The spontaneous order model does not imply that everybody changes his or her behavior at the same time. In the present example, before everybody uses the knife to cut potatoes, there will be encounters between the *traditionalists* following the old rules and the *modernists* having adopted the new custom.

Encounters of people with different manners might cause *negative externalities* for each: modernists might be concerned about people who can't adapt to the new times, and traditionalists might denounce deviation from old cultural traditions. Even if those differences in behavior will not be regarded as world-shaking, people like it to be similar to other people. Which consequences will those interactions have? The payoffs are depicted in a game matrix (*tab. 1*).

It is first assumed that the payoff is always higher if one follows preferred custom. Similarity is rewarding: the payoff is higher if the other person one encounters follows the same custom as oneself.

Now let the traditionalist A observe a modernist B who engages, for whatever reason, in traditional behavior (*column 1*). A prefers to engage in traditional behavior as well. Let the payoff be 6. Using the knife would be an inferior payoff (namely 5), but the difference (6 vs. 5) is not large.

Next assume A observes that the modernist B performs his or her preferred behavior (*column 2*). Although A prefers traditionalist behavior (6 in *column 1*), the dissimilarity diminishes A's payoff by 1 (from 6 to 5). But if in this case A performs the new behavior, the payoff would still be lower because A is a traditionalist. For B, the situation is symmetric, as *tab. 1* indicates.

Note that there is an equilibrium in the upper right cell meaning that no actor has an incentive to choose another behavior, given the behavior of the other actor. Substantively, this means that it is best for the two actors if each acts according to his or her own preference. This concurs with the previous argument: there is some cost to switch to the other behavior, but the benefits are not large. Accordingly, one finds often peaceful coexistence of old and new manners.

The low costs of being different can be observed in foreign restaurants in western locations. In Japanese, Chinese and Vietnamese restaurants, chopsticks and cutlery are offered simultaneously. In Italian restaurants, one is relatively tolerant in regard to the way that spaghettis are eaten: whether one takes only the fork (which is "correct") or fork and spoon does not matter.

Even if the costs of eating differently would be larger, there is a clear opportunity to avoid diversity: one might choose *exit* when one observes diversity of eating, or one might choose restaurants that only offer one style of eating. So if diversity is regarded as an externality, there are ample opportunities not to be exposed to such externalities. This again reinforces peaceful coexistence of manners.

This situation that is modeled in *tab. 1* will result in a spontaneous order in which different eating customs coexist. This is what one can observe today in foreign restaurants in European countries and the US in which different utensils can be used.

Even if there is some discontent with existing table manners, the low costs of diversity make it unlikely that there is some regulatory interest: one will not incur the costs of advertising or organizing collective action to call for state intervention.

3.2 Are there incentives for institutional design?

It is difficult to see what the incentives could be that lead a state to prescribe table manners. Assume a law is passed prescribing to cut potatoes with the knife. State actors could expect to increase support. But this is unlikely because there is in general a strong *intrinsic aversion against regulation* in the population that can only be overcome by clear expected benefits through the regulation. Such a regulation changes habits, which is always costly. An intruding state is only accepted if the expected benefits are relatively large so that it pays to change a behavior. As was argued before, it is difficult to see what these benefits could be.

To conclude, in regard to table manners, there is thus in general no demand for state regulation, and there are in general no incentives for a state to supply regulation.

4 When spontaneous order does not work: the example of daylight saving time

Assume the time of day in a country is standardized so that all clocks show the same time. Due to the rotation of the earth and its orbit around the sun, it is darker in January than in, say, June. Daylight saving time (DST) is usually introduced in spring: the clock is advanced, mostly by one hour. This means that daylight can be enjoyed longer. If it is 6 pm and DST is implemented, it is then 7 pm. At the end of the summer, the clocks are again turned back an hour.

In 2016, 146 countries had DST, whereas it was absent in 170 countries. DST was first adopted in 1908 in Thunder Bay in Canada. Other Canadian locations followed. Germany was the first country where clocks were turned one hour on April 30, 1916. Other European countries adopted DST during World War I (July 1914 to November 1918). There is a varied history of adopting and repealing DST in Europe and outside Europe.[3] DST never evolved spontaneously; it was always implemented by institutional design. How can this be explained?

4.1 The demand for daylight saving time

Could DST have evolved spontaneously? A first condition is that there is some discontent in the sense that one would prefer longer evenings to enjoy daylight for leisure activities. This is only plausible if one knows how to fix this problem, namely by advancing clocks by, say, one hour. As a material benefit, one might consider saving energy costs. One could also reason that driving in the evening makes accidents less likely because one can see more in the light, and that crimes such as burglaries are less likely because such crimes mostly occur in the dark.[4]

However, DST has or may also have disadvantages. It might also lead to more road accidents: more people may drive due to the longer days, so the likelihood of accidents increases: the more cars on the road, the higher the likelihood of accidents. The question is whether on the whole accidents are more or less frequent. Due to increased driving, energy use increases. Again, the question is whether the increase of energy use through driving offsets the decrease of

---

3 For an instructive short overview of the history of DST, see http://www.timeanddate.com/time/dst/history.html (accessed April 14, 2018). See particularly, Prerau (2005).

4 For other advantages, but also disadvantages, see Prerau (2005, 198–204. See also 4–9 about the arguments Willett in his pamphlet in 1907 propagating the introduction of DST. Pp. 9–24 list the controversial arguments in the British parliament. Overall, it seems that the advantages of DST are greater than the disadvantages, but this discrepancy, if there is any, is small).

energy use due to more light. Furthermore, the switch to and from DST may lead to suffering from disrupted sleep schedules, which may lead to health risks. Because DST prompts people to spend more time outdoors, in some parts of the economy, revenues will decrease. For example, people may attend movie theaters less frequently. This short discussion suggests that the introduction of DST is in general a controversial issue. It is also plausible that the net effects of DST very much depend on the specific situation.

But assuming people expect more advantages than disadvantages of DST and know how longer days can be created, the question is how strong discontent with absence of DST is. Days become longer anyway in summer so that one can enjoy some of the advantages of more daylight even without DST. This suggests that discontent with the absence of DST will be low.

The fact that DST is a modern phenomenon supports this hypothesis. Benjamin Franklin's famous essay in the Journal of Paris 1784 is the beginning of the debate about DST. But the controversies about DST began much later, namely at the beginning of the 20th century when DST was first used in Canada in 1908. If the need for DST had been relatively intense, people would have thought more about how to extend the day and certainly would have gotten the idea that advancing the clock would be a simple solution to extend daylight.

If there is discontent with the absence of DST, this could be reduced by a *normative belief* that one should not disrupt a natural or divine order. When DST was discussed in the US in 1919, a Congressman said: "Repeal the law and have the clocks proclaim God's time" (Prerau 2005, 106).

When the controversy over DST began, advantages as well as disadvantages of DST were addressed. There were entrepreneurial figures, such as George Hudson in 1895 and William Willett in 1907 (see below) as well as groups such as farmers who propagated their opinions in favor of and against DST. Due to this controversy, it is also plausible that the citizen of a country had mixed feelings about DST. This supports the previous assumption that in the population discontent with the absence of DST has been weak, and, accordingly, there was no or little demand for change or regulation.

4.2 Could daylight saving time emerge by discrete individual action?

Assume there is some demand for change, i.e., for introducing DST. The basic spontaneous order model would suggest that a great number of individuals will decide to change the clock at a certain time in summer and then reset it at a certain time in the fall. The aggregate effect is a social pattern, namely DST, which is then normatively expected. Could DST originate in this way?

Tab. 2: Daylight Saving Time (DST) as a convention

Behavioral options of Person P	Behavioral options of others	
	Do not apply DST	Apply DST
Do not apply DST	5, 5	0, 0
Apply DST	0, 0	6, 6

First entry in each cell is the payoff for A, second entry the payoff for B.

Assume a male person P decides to advance his clock at a certain time by one hour and acts on this new time. This would bring about enormous problems. P will miss buses, trains or planes because he will always be late; P will be late at work and at other appointments. This holds for others as well who individually decide to advance the clock.

These problems arise because DST is a *convention* (Young 1996). This is the solution of a coordination problem such as driving on the right or left. Coordination originates if everyone behaves in the same way (such as driving on the right). Conventions are self-enforcing in the sense that non-compliance automatically generates high costs. This has been illustrated with creating one's own DST, in regard to driving on the "wrong" side consequences are perhaps more disastrous.

Tab. 2 models this situation. Let P consider what to do if all others do not use DST. In this case, it is best for P to comply. This yields a positive payoff of 5 vs. 0 if he unilaterally uses DST.

Now let P think about what to do if the others apply DST. In this case, it is best for P to follow suit. The matrix assumes that DST has some advantages over the old time – the payoff is 6 instead of 5 –, but doing what the others do is again clearly the best choice. Thus, there is no way that DST could emerge spontaneously by the decisions of separate individuals who set their clocks one hour ahead.

Tab. 2 assumes that advantages of DST only accrue to the population if *everybody* adopts DST. Perhaps, there is not such an all-or-nothing situation: if a very high percentage of others – say, 90% – use DST, those who have not yet adopted DST will incur particularly high costs and will switch immediately to DST. *Fig. 4* depicts this situation. There is a utility for P to adopt DST only if the overwhelming percentage uses DST. If this threshold is reached, then there is an advantage of sticking to DST for P.

4.3 Daylight saving time as spontaneous order in small close-knit groups

If the model of *fig. 4* holds, another mechanism of bringing about DST as a spontaneous order becomes more likely. P might *advertise* DST and convince others

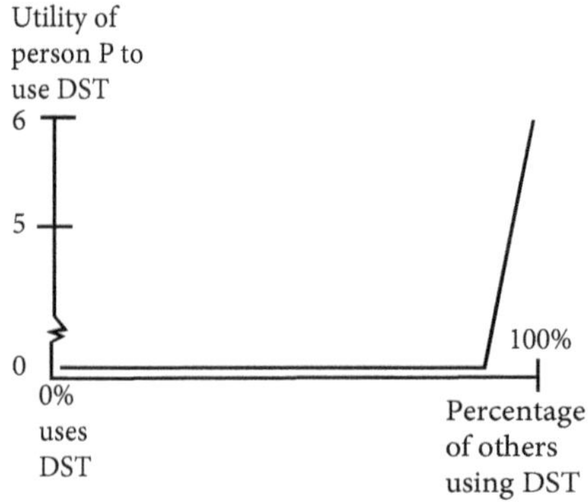

Fig. 4: Adopting Daylight Saving Time (DST) as a Function of Compliance of Others

of the advantages of DST. This is now more valuable for P than before because only a certain part of the population needs to switch to DST to generate DST in the society. P might suggest that the clock is advanced at a certain time and ask others to comply.

When will P advertise DST? One condition is that P would be relatively dissatisfied with the absence of DST and demand change or even regulation. If this is the case, P's proselytizing efforts will depend on the costs. They depend on the *size of the group*. The larger the group, the more time is needed to convince others to adopt DST. These costs are still higher if the group is heterogeneous.

When will P get promises? We assume in order not to complicate the argument unnecessarily that those who make promises keep them. Assume you are a member M of the group. One condition is that M's demand for change is relatively strong (in other words, M's benefits of DST are relatively high). However, M will only promise to adopt DST if he or she is relatively certain that the others do the same. There is thus a strategic interaction: one will choose DST if one expects the others to follow suit. But when will this be the case?

M expects others to adopt DST if they are supposed to demand change as well. The more members M knows who judge DST positively, the more M will expect others to join. This common knowledge about others' attitudes is to be expected if the group is relatively small. Thus, the larger the group, the less likely is M's trust that others will cooperate.

This trust will be particularly strong if members are highly connected in various social networks. In such close-knit groups, it will be likely that there is

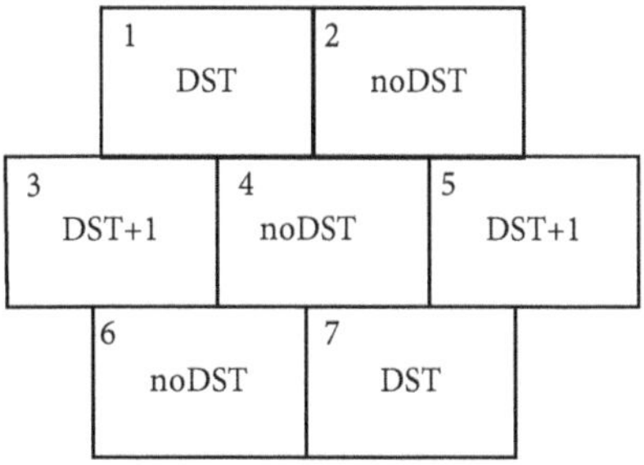

Fig. 5: Adjacent Groups with Different Daylight Saving Time (DST) Schedules

sanctioning for non-compliance: those who do not keep their promises will be punished by members of their group.[5]

M as a member of a small and close-knit group will be particularly confident that others will comply if the group is largely *independent of other groups*. In such a self-sufficient group, most of the daily interactions are between group members. For example, there might be several farms collaborating and producing almost everything that is needed. Appointments can thus easily be coordinated. Thus, if groups are largely independent, M will be relatively certain that others will comply: the costs of defecting are relatively low.

But even if in a small close-knit group there are some relationships to adjacent groups, this might not be problematic for M or other members. Assume there are seven groups that differ in regard to DST (*fig.* 5). Groups 1 and 7 have the normal one-hour DST, groups 2, 4 and 6 do not have DST and groups 3 and 5 advanced their clock by two hours. Now assume a member M of group 1 makes an appointment with somebody from 5. M needs to know the time schedule of the other group, the time when the appointment is scheduled and whether the time of group 1 or group 5 is relevant for the appointment. For example, let the member of group 5 suggest to meet at 2 pm at his place. Is it "local" time of group 1 or 5 and what is the local time of group 5 (DST, noDST or DST+1)?

Answering these questions is actually not very difficult in the present example: there are only seven groups and, we assume, they are relatively large. The required information for successful exchanges will easily spread. In the US, there are four time zones. Assume you live in Seattle and have a job interview

5 For the importance of social networks, see Coleman's (1990) theory of norms and Ellickson (1991).

in New York City at 1 pm. You know that it is three hours later in New York. If the potential employer writes you the time 1 pm, you know that this is the time in New York (which has become common knowledge as well). The worst case is that you ask the employer.

The conclusion is that under very special conditions, DST could evolve as a spontaneous order. But these conditions are hardly ever given, certainly not in modern industrialized societies. In the history of DST (Prerau 2005), there is no account of a case where DST came about as a spontaneous order.

4.4 Influencing institutional design by lobbying and collective action

So far it was assumed that discontent in the population about the absence of DST is low. Actually, in many contemporary societies (and in Britain around 1900), there were nonetheless single individuals and groups who had a strong regulatory interest in adopting or preventing the adoption of DST. This regulatory interest may bring about several kinds of action, ranging from writing letters to the government to organizing groups that lobby for DST (or try to prevent DST).

All these forms of behavior are contributions to providing a public good by putting pressure on those actors who can create the public good. DST is such a good in the sense that if it is provided, nobody can be excluded from its consumption. There is a vast literature about incentives for contributing to public goods provision, based on Olson's (1965) seminal book. We will not discuss or apply this theory. We take it for granted that sufficient incentives to contribute exist for certain individuals and interest groups. For example, in Britain around 1900, there were two prominent individuals who took various actions to get DST implemented: George Hudson in 1895 and William Willett in 1907 suggested a seasonal time shift to be introduced by the state (Prerau 2005, 1–24).

The motivations of such *political entrepreneurs* that include interest groups (in general see Frohlich, Oppenheimer and Young 1971) are often of a personal nature. Hudson had a shift-work job and collected insects. So having a longer day was attractive. Willett was an enthusiastic golfer, and a longer day would allow playing longer in the evenings.

Such entrepreneurs might bring about a critical mass that elicits a cascade of collective action in favor of DST. This might lead to incentives of a government to implement DST. However, lobbying and collective action are not the only possible incentives a government is faced with. Which incentives matter has to be analyzed in the special case, which will be done in the next section.

4.5 Incentives for institutional design

DST was highly controversial within the government and the parliament in Britain around 1900. If a government or parliament wants at least not to lose support of the population by taking action, it will try to make the issue less controversial. This could be done by setting up a committee and getting the opinions of experts in order to find an acceptable solution for all. The parliament met thirteen times and heard numerous testimonies. A special committee provided a favorable report that listed various advantages of DST (Prerau 2005, 19–20). However, a bill for launching DST did not have the support of the Prime Minister. His support was necessary for the bill to become a law. A second committee then rejected the bill. The debate continued.

The Prime Minister was a major opponent to DST. It seems that he did not want to yield to a controversial demand (Prerau 2005, 53). Perhaps he did not want to lose support or simply did not want to vote for a measure that might have negative consequences.

In general, thus, there is a controversial issue, and those who are in charge of a decision have controversial opinions as well. They probably believe that a non-decision at least for some time yields more popular support than adopting DST.

The situation changed radically after the outbreak of World War II. On May 17, 1916, the "Summer Time Act of 1916" established DST as a law in Britain. The controversies largely disappeared because launching DST seemed highly relevant for the war. The adoption of DST by other countries seemed to be seen as a signal for its usefulness. The advantages of saving energy became one of the major goals. One reason was that many miners fought in the war, and the production of coal was therefore declining (Prerau 2005, 56).

This belief of the advantages of DST was endorsed in September 1916. The Summer Time Committee explored the consequences of DST (Prerau 2005, 63). It concluded that it "could unhesitatingly say that the vast preponderance of opinion throughout Great Britain is enthusiastically in favor of summer time and its renewal, not only as a war measure, but as a permanent institution" (Prerau 2005, 68). The central goal to lower fuel consumption had been reached (Prerau 2005, 65). Other positive consequences were reported as well, and few negative ones (Prerau 2005, 65–66). In other countries, DST was regarded as a success as well (Prerau 2005, 68–70).

It is interesting that the controversial nature of DST ended when World War II broke out. To be sure, the consequence of saving energy was always regarded as an advantage of implementing DST. In times of war, this advantage became the major justification of DST. Thus, the controversies largely disappeared, and implementing DST clearly increased support of a government by the population.

Is there some incentive for countries to coordinate different DST schedules? These incentives are low because it is easy to get information about the time that is valid in a country. Thus, the transaction costs are probably too high. However, when countries form a union such as the European Union the bureaucracy might be inclined to coordinate different DST schedules. This happened in the European Union where in 1996 a standardized EU-wide DST (from last Sunday of March through the last Sunday of October) was implemented.

4.6 Conclusion

It was argued that it is not to be expected that DST will evolve as a spontaneous order, unless in very specific situations that have not occurred so far. DST is thus a product of institutional design. Its special feature is that it was (and still is) a controversial issue. It was illustrated mainly with the example of Britain around 1900 how a government makes a decision about adopting DST and, finally, seemed to gain support of the population. It would be interesting to investigate the process of implementing DST in other countries.

5 The obstruction of spontaneous order: why Germany has a spelling reform

Originally, language is a clear spontaneous order (see Keller 1994; 2014). Language is an interesting case because sometimes it is a "pure" spontaneous order, but there are countries in which institutional design has changed spontaneous order. There was a spelling reform in Germany in 1996. In the US, language remains a spontaneous order. Why is this so? This question is addressed in the next two sections. We begin with the orthography reform in Germany in 1996.

5.1 The demand for a spelling reform in the population

There is certainly *discontent* with spelling rules in most societies. Many German speakers are concerned about the numerous *inconsistencies* of the German language that make learning it difficult. Examples are the irregularities of the three articles that seem completely arbitrary: "der" is for male, "die" for female subjects and "das" for objects. However, there are numerous exceptions. For example, "future" (Zukunft) is an object, but has a female article ("die" Zukunft); the object "progress" (Fortschritt) has a male article ("der" Fortschritt). In English, there is one article only: the.

Will discontent lead to a demand for change? One might simply accept the situation that language has numerous exceptions and learn the rules. This is what typically happens every day when a language is learned. Language is accepted as a "natural" (cultural) phenomenon that is regarded as given.

Furthermore, language change would be costly because learning new rules of speaking and spelling is costly – as is every change of a habit. Accordingly, there will be an *aversion against change and regulation* of aspects of a language. One will bear these costs only if there are convincing justifications. These are difficult to come by. Most people will not care whether "Photo" (the old spelling) is changed to "Foto," even if that makes German more consistent.

If there would be a strong preference for consistency and low costs of re-learning, one would expect that the completely consistent artificial language Esperanto would have been generally accepted. But there are only few individuals who were willing to learn this language.

A demand for change or a regulatory interest could be brought about by *altruistic motivations:* one might have pity with lower-class people and immigrants who have particular problems with learning a language. A simplification would thus help them. It is, however, doubtful whether this motivation is so strong and common that this generates a strong demand for change or a regulatory interest. The argument might be that every normal member of a society is able to learn the language and should bear the costs of doing so.

The absence of a general demand for change and a regulatory interest in the population is endorsed by surveys: the overwhelming part of the population was against the spelling reform. For example, in October 1996, a representative survey showed that 75% of the population was against the reform, only 13% were in favor of it. This situation did not change later.

5.2 Could new language rules evolve spontaneously?

The basic spontaneous order model would suggest that discrete actions of individuals who prefer a new spelling simply perform the respective action that will lead then to a general change of language. The switch from "Fris*eur*" to "Fris*ör*" (see above) in one's writings illustrates this. In regard to changing grammar, a person might find it annoying that "future" in German is female ("*die* Zukunft") and decides to write (and say) "*das* Zukunft."

People would only act in this way if there is a demand for change, which is, as was said before, implausible. But assume there are some people who suffer from inconsistencies and use, for example, in a conversation "wrong" articles (such as "*das* Zukunft" instead of the common "*die* Zukunft)." Interaction partners would think the speaker has some inability to speak correctly. Accordingly, deviations from the common mode of speaking will be heavily sanctioned.

Some changes of a language seem to be *intrinsically aversive* although they may increase consistency. For example, "elaborate" means "aufwendig." This word is based on the noun "Aufwand," and the adjective was accordingly changed to "aufw*ä*ndig." For a German speaker, this looks simply ugly and is, accordingly, not generally accepted.

Nonetheless, there might be single spellings or words that change over time as the spontaneous order tradition suggests. For example, assume "Friseur" is common, and there is some hairdresser who wants to attract attention and posts a sign "Frisör" at his shop. Others might like this, and "Frisör" becomes generally accepted. The motivation here is not, however, changing inconsistencies but just getting some attention. This change is accepted because it hits the taste of the public and is thus not sanctioned negatively. In contrast, "*das* Zukunft" (instead of the common "*die* Zukunft") will be outside this taste.

Even if single changes of a language are compatible with the spontaneous order model, it is highly unlikely that all of a sudden simultaneously an entire language will change in the direction of consistency. This would be beyond the cognitive capacity of speakers in a society.

5.3 Interest groups and intellectuals as pressure groups for government intervention

In contrast to the population, the cultural elite in Germany does not reject language reform. But how to reform language is highly controversial. For example, in April and May 1998, there was a declaration of 600 professors of linguistics who opposed the reform of 1996.[6] Numerous other similar protests were enacted. So it seems that a majority or at least a great number of groups were against the reform. There was also an initiative "We Teachers against the Spelling reform" in 1997.

However, there was a part of the cultural elite who was in favor of the reform. Commissions made detailed suggestions about changes. Especially the Council for Orthography ("Rat für deutsche Rechtschreibung") was active in promoting

6 See http://schriftdeutsch.de/orthogra.htm, http://german.about.com/library/blreform.htm. Very informative is the report about a representative survey in 2008 of the German population: http://gfds.de/wp-content/uploads/2014/08/Umfrage_Rechts-_und_Verwaltungssprache.pdf (all accessed on April 14, 2018). See Eichhoff-Cyrus, Antos and Schulz (2009).

the orthography reform. The leader and advocate of the reform, Hans Zehetmair, was a former Bavarian Minister of State for Science, Research and Arts. The Council was commissioned to ensure further development of orthography and was, thus, a sort of state actor.

5.4 Language change by institutional design in Germany

Although spelling reform was rejected by the population and very controversial in the cultural elite, it came into effect in 1996, after about 20 years of preparations by several commissions. They took the initiative for the reform (Munske 2000; 2006). Then several modifications followed until the reform became effective in 2006. The new rules had to be taught in schools from 2007 onwards, and employees in the public administration were forced to adopt the new spelling.[7] Media in general adopted the reform, but they deviated in part from the new rules. There were no formal sanctions such as fines for not following the reform.

Language reform is not a matter of the federal state but of the single states (Länder). The normal procedure would have been to pass laws in each state. However, the reform was adopted at one of the conferences of the German education ministers (Kultusminister). It consisted of ordinances and not of laws. This means that the reform was not under parliamentary control but a decision by administrations. This did not violate the constitution (see the ruling of the constitutional court on July 14, 1998).

Given the widespread resistance to the reform, a puzzle is why it has been passed. Most of the population was against it, and it seems that the major part of the cultural elite rejected it as well.

One condition could have been that discontent with language inconsistency and thus a demand for change was much larger in the cultural elite than in the population. Maybe a linguistic professor really suffers from inconsistency? The goal of the reform was a *simplification by eliminating inconsistencies* in order to benefit learners of a language, especially members of the lower class and migrants. Thus, discontent with existing language and a regulatory interest were apparently strong in the elite.

Apparently, there were no incentives that discouraged the "law"-makers from implementing a reform. Language might have been regarded as an important *cultural public good* that has grown over centuries and that should not be

7 See the overview: http://german.about.com/library/blreform.htm). In German, see the more detailed overview: http://schriftdeutsch.de/orthogra.htm. (all accessed on April 14, 2018).

touched. It is striking that in principle, an encroachment upon the cultural heritage is legitimate. An exception is a resolution of the German federal parliament (Deutscher Bundestag 1998) stating: "The language belongs to the people. The state is restricted to determine procedures for recording the language as it exists." But this was only a declaration because the federal parliament was not in charge of the reform.

If language simplification was the major concern, why was the reform not much more radical? For example, it was discussed whether there should be no longer capitalization. This was rejected because of expected resistance (Munske 2000). One goal thus seemed to be to implement a reform that would not meet too much opposition. Perhaps, a more extensive reform was also due to some *moral threshold for encroachments.*

The question remains why the reform was implemented despite the strong opposition? Wouldn't governments expect to lose support of the population? Could one expect that fewer people would vote for the governing party or parties after the reform? This is unlikely for the following reasons. (1) The reform was a matter of the states and a joint decision. So no single party was in charge of the reform and could be blamed. Thus, there was a *diffusion of responsibility.* (2) There was no party that promised to cancel the reform. This could really lead to an increase of support of this party. However, the reform was the product of a compromise of the cultural ministers (Munske 2000) who regularly meet. There was no parliamentary control that would have led to an increase of the number of decision makers and, thus, perhaps changed matters. However, the reform was promoted by the cultural ministers. Deviating from the decisions of this cartel generates strong sanctions. It is very plausible that those who promoted the reform were aware of this situation.

5.5 Will spontaneous order overcome institutional design?

The ordinances were imposed by force on the school system and the public sector, and media and publishers subscribed to the reform. The major German dictionary "Duden" also propagates the new spelling. So, in the long run, the major ingredients of the reform will probably become accepted.

It is puzzling that despite general skepticism, that reform was voluntarily adopted by media and publishers. The general norm that supports such behavior seems to be that a decision that comes about in a legitimate procedure has to be accepted in a democracy.

Nonetheless, not every proposed change was accepted. Some changes were so much against the ingrained language habits that they are rejected. The old "überschwenglisch" (meaning lavish) will probably be kept and not the new "überschwänglisch." But some changes are widely accepted, such as writing "dass" instead of "daß."

What might impede general acceptance of the new rules is that people are still faced with the old spelling in literature written before 1996. So the new and old spellings will peacefully coexist, at least for a long time. My personal experience is that few people care about the new spelling, and negative sanctioning for "deviants" outside schools is not to be expected. But pupils will encounter the old spelling outside school and will regard it as equally legitimate. This speaks for a peaceful coexistence as well. Research will show to what extent the language reform is adopted in the future.

It is ironic that Hans Zehetmair who was a major driving force of the orthography reform expressed in an interview in 2015 (see the weekly DIE ZEIT, July 30, 2015) that the reform was "superfluous" and that "this should never happen again."

6 Leaving the spontaneous order untouched: why the United States does not have a spelling reform

The English language has many irregularities too. For example, in English, the plural for "house" is "houses," but for "mouse" it is not "mouses" but "mice." Emphases of words are inconsistent as well. For the *verb* "attribute" the emphasis is on the i, but the *noun* "attribute" is emphasized on the a. In one respect, the English language is even more complicated: the pronunciation is less similar to the written language in English than in German. However, English is easier in regard to the article: there is only one ("the"), whereas German has three. Anyway, the English language is irregular as well.[8]

As for the German language, a reform in the direction of simplification would have several advantages: learning the language for lower-class people and immigrants would be easier, and the more extensive use of English internationally would be encouraged. Those opposing reforms argue that disadvantages are, in short, that the cultural roots of a language would be obstructed. Nonetheless, there were efforts at reforms (see Hodges 1964). But these were proposals by individuals such as Benjamin Franklin with his "A Scheme for a New Alphabet and Reformed Mode of Spelling" in 1768) or Noah Webster (see his "American

8 The following is based on Hodges (1964). The classic book on the American language is Mencken (1919).

Spelling Book" of 1783, see Hodges 1964). Webster suggested various changes of the American language that were accepted.

Although it seems plausible that the dissatisfaction with English in the population is not stronger than in Germany, there is always a demand for change by the cultural elite (see the example of Noah Webster).

Wouldn't a government in the US have incentives to introduce a language reform? A major attempt was made by President Theodore Roosevelt who issued an order. The goal was to incorporate some spellings proposed by the Federal Printing Agency into governmental documents. "Criticism rose immediately from an outraged public, newspapers lampooned his order, and Roosevelt was forced to retract his edict" (Hodges 1964, 332). Later efforts failed as well.

How can the differences between Germany and the US be explained? Hodges (1964, 332) argues that "the decentralized system of educational control in this country precludes the possibility that a central authority can dictate spelling changes." But this system existed in Germany as well. However, the cultural ministers in Germany have formed a cartel, the cultural minister conference. Here the ministers meet regularly in order to coordinate their activities. So here it seems easier to arrive at a joint decision than in the US. However, such a cartel could have formed in the US as well.

So what explains why the US does not have a spelling reform? We can only speculate that a close-knit cultural elite as in Germany with a strong interest in language change did not exist in the US. It also seems plausible that the moral conviction not to change a long cultural heritage was stronger in the US.

A final hypothesis does not seem implausible. For a sociologist, including psychological characteristics in an explanation is suspicious. Everyday observations suggest that Americans have a much larger *tolerance for ambiguity* than Germans. For example, I often ask American colleagues whether it is correct to say "A" or "B." The typical answer is: either way. This is strange for Germans, because we always think that something must be right or wrong. Perhaps, one finds this low tolerance for ambiguity, especially in the cultural elite of Germany.

7 The power of spontaneous order: the erosion of institutional design

When a revolution has taken place, institutional design is at its height. Numerous laws are made that are supposed to realize the goals of the new elite. It is doubtful whether there is a demand for regulating all these matters in the population. The new power elite will nonetheless implement the new laws according to its ideology. These new laws are backed by a repressive sanctioning apparatus and by rewards for compliance (such as being promoted). Nonetheless, part of the population accepts these laws, especially those who subscribe to the new ideology.

However, over time law violation increases. This results in a decrease of acceptance of the (formal and informal) norms backed by the laws. A decline of informal and formal enforcement follows suit, along with a further attenuation of the norms and an increase of norm violation. Finally, the laws are repealed.

This process (*fig. 6*) is illustrated with the collapse of the communist regime in the GDR (German Democratic Republic, i.e., the former communist part of Germany) in 1989. There has always been some law violation. For example, workers did not report the true output numbers. Setting up private enterprises was prohibited, and there was a widespread barter economy where goods were traded without involving cash. Unconditional acceptance of orders by superiors was the norm, and violation was punished. Explicit criticism of the regime became more common as well.

In 1989, norm violation increased. For example, protests that were prohibited and crushed before became common; people did no longer blindly follow orders. Unification with West Germany in 1990 led to the replacement of the entire legal system with the system of West Germany.

What is the role of spontaneous order in this process? Institutional design was subverted by a spontaneous order. These "sub-institutional" rules were common knowledge, in part certainly remembered from the time before the revolution.

How can this process be explained? In the previous analyses, the first question always was whether there existed some discontent with the existing order. There can be no question that the central planning in an authoritarian setting generates great discontent, and there was a strong interest for regulating numerous behaviors in a different way.

At least for some legal rules, individual discrete behavior could establish spontaneous order. For example, instead of buying food in shops (that was often not available), people could try to barter with farmers. People could further set up illegally small firms. Such a large-scale individual deviation could have been an incentive for governments to change laws.

For the GDR, the emerging spontaneous order "from below" was certainly one incentive to change laws. Even an authoritarian regime is interested in support of the population. But why hasn't there been an increase in repression? It seems that in general the sanctioning capacities of the regimes decreased (for details see, e.g., Walder 1994). Especially in the GDR, Russian tanks were no longer available to suppress undesired behavior. In view of an increasing inefficiency of the economy and reforms in adjacent countries, the regime probably expected further loss of support and, thus, to a willingness to change institutional design.

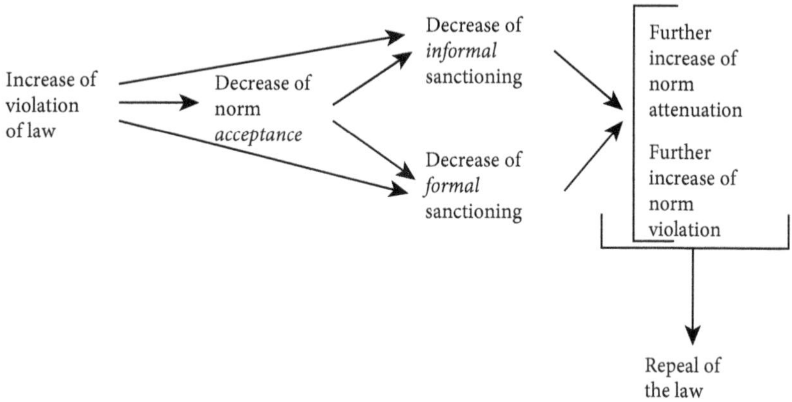

Fig. 6: A Process of Decreasing Norm Acceptance, Increasing Norm Violation and the Failure of Institutional Design

An example for such a process is China where economic problems of a central planning system led to stepwise changes to a "Capitalism from below" (Nee and Opper 2012). Had there been no unification of East and West Germany in which the entire East German law system was replaced by the West German system, a similar process could have occurred in the GDR.

8 Discussion

The basic idea of this essay is to integrate different literatures on spontaneous order and institutional design. These literatures focus mainly on one of these processes. However, often they are concatenated. We explored these interdependencies. We first looked at extreme cases where spontaneous order developed independently of institutional design (table manners and language in the US), and where institutional design was implemented independently of spontaneous order (daylight saving time). We discussed two other cases where both orders are concatenated: language in Germany and the breakdown of communist rule.

We found that the basic spontaneous order model claiming that the actions of separate individuals unintentionally bring about a norm or institution is rarely found in reality. There are political entrepreneurs (including interest groups) who intend change of the spontaneous order (such as Noah Webster in regard to language). There is further collective action that aims to influence spontaneous order.

Explanations of institutional design focus on the major goal to gain support in order to remain in power. We found, in particular in explaining language change in Germany, that state actors found a way to act against voter preferences by forming a cartel that diffuses responsibility. We also explored incentives to create institutional design de novo (daylight saving time) and a complex set of conditions that changed both types of order (collapse of communism).

Let us resume what was called the *basic spontaneous order model*: "An institution (e.g. a language) or some social pattern (behavior in a market) is an *aggregate* result of *numerous discrete* individual actions, and the individuals do not *intend* to create the aggregate result" (see before). This statement is a *definition*:

> Spontaneous order = df. an institution or social pattern that is an unintended outcome of discrete individual actions.

Such a definition allows to *identify* whether some collective phenomenon is a spontaneous order or not. In a similar vein, knowing how "man" is defined allows us to classify any object as being a "man" or not. A problem with the definition of "spontaneous order" is that it consists of a *causal hypothesis*. In order to classify some pattern as a "spontaneous order", one needs to know whether it was an unintended result of human action. Ascertaining a causal process is not necessary for categorizing some object as "man": here we only need to find out whether an object has some secondary sexual characteristics.

Let us look in more detail at this causal hypothesis (see *fig. 7*). The *explanandum* is some collective outcome such as the change of a language. The *causal factors* are the *intentions* of discrete individuals. They may aim at purely personal benefits such as avoiding the costs of learning new spellings or may want to bring about some collective outcome (such as a change of a language in a society). It is assumed that these intentions lead to some action of the respective individuals. The *explanatory question* is under what conditions those actions of individuals who have no intention to create some collective outcome bring about this outcome.

Fig. 7 shows that the basic spontaneous order model is only one possible model. Firstly, the actions of individuals may and often are motivated to bring about the collective outcome. Remember the example of the entrepreneurial figures mentioned before. Perhaps those actions are even more likely to bring about the collective outcome. Secondly, there are many examples where individual actions do not lead to a collective outcome. We mentioned the example of Noah Webster who wanted to introduce various changes of the American language but did not succeed. Thus, individual actions – whatever their intention is – are not sufficient to generate a social pattern (see the arrow with the question marks in *fig. 7*). Advocates of the spontaneous order model do not specify these conditions in detail.

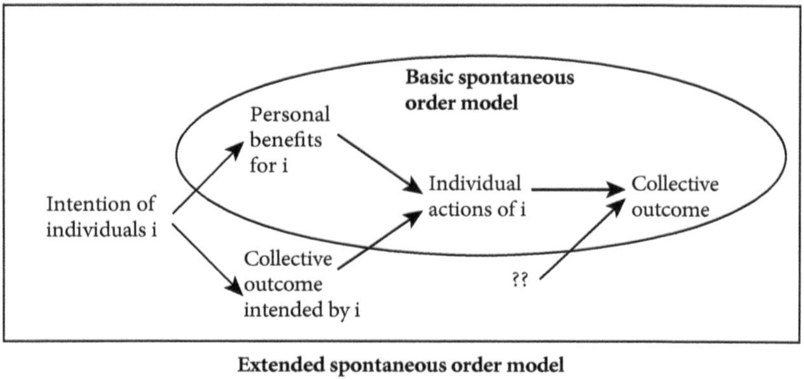

Fig. 7: The Structure of the Spontaneous Order Model

A model that includes those conditions and that also includes the intention to generate collective results could be called an *extended* spontaneous order model (*fig. 7*). It includes the *basic* spontaneous order model as a special case. A suggestion for future research is to specify such an extended model in more detail and test it. The present essay actually applies such an extended model.

The previous analyses confirm that one does not need different theories to explain spontaneous order or institutional design. The discrete individuals who often set in motion the origin of a spontaneous order as well as politicians or administrators act to achieve their personal goals by considering behavioral constraints and opportunities. This theory has been applied throughout this article. It is actually a wide social-psychological version of the theory of rational action (for details, see Opp 1999; 2018). It would be interesting to examine whether other institutions could be analyzed in a similar way. Examples could be dueling, female genital mutilation, equal rights of men and women, and adultery. The latter was a crime in Germany until September 1969. In regard to equal rights of men and women, it seems plausible that the process begins on the micro level as a spontaneous order: numerous women gain more rights from their husbands in private relationships. Some of these changes then became public through (female) political entrepreneurs and, finally, came on the political agenda to effect human design. These, then, further instigated private changes of women's rights. This would resemble process 4 in *fig. 2*: spontaneous order undermines and changes (the old) institutional design, which, in turn, changes spontaneous order (process 3 in *fig. 2*). However, it is not enough to recognize that interdependence exists but what is further required is a detailed analysis of the processes that change institutions.

One issue that is largely ignored in the literature and not fully solved in this essay either refers to the conditions that lead only to a *regular behavior* or to a *set of norms* (i.e., an institution). Take the example of the non-smoking norm. After it became increasingly apparent that smoking and being exposed to smokers lead to health hazards, people stopped smoking and increasingly sanctioned those who smoked in their presence. The effect was that smoking in the presence of others decreased. Was this only a regular behavior such as taking the subway instead of one's car to work or a norm? Or did a norm evolve that one *should not* smoke in the presence of others? Perhaps the initial stage of the emergence of a norm is a regular behavior that then changes to a norm. The "is" thus becomes an "ought." What are the conditions for such a process? Perhaps, there is a threshold effect: only if the externalities due to a behavior such as smoking reach a certain level "oughtness" originates (Opp 2002). To explore those conditions would be an important extension of the (basic and extended) spontaneous order model.

References

Barry, Norman. 1982. "The Tradition of Spontaneous Order." *Literature of Liberty* 5: 7–58.

Coleman, James S. 1990. *Foundations of Social Theory*. Cambridge (MA) and London: Belknap Press of Harvard University Press.

Deutscher Bundestag. 1998. *Drucksache 13/10183 vom 24.03.1998*. Accessed October 22, 2017. http://dip21.bundestag.de/dip21/btd/13/101/1310183.asc

DiMaggio, Paul. 1998. "The New Institutionalism: Avenues of Collaboration." *Journal of Institutional and Theoretical Economics* 154: 696–705.

Eichhoff-Cyrus, Karin M., Gerd Antos, and Rüdiger Schulz. 2009. *Wie denken die Deutschen über die Rechts- und Verwaltungssprache? Eine repräsentative Umfrage der Gesellschaft für deutsche Sprache*. Wiesbaden: Gesellschaft für deutsche Sprache (GfdS).

Ellickson, Robert C. 1991. *Order without Law. How Neighbors Settle Disputes*. Cambridge: Harvard University Press.

Frohlich, Norman, Joe A. Oppenheimer, and Oran R. Young. 1971. *Political Leadership and Collective Goods*. Princeton (NJ): Princeton University Press.

Hamowy, Ronald. 1987. *The Scottish Enlightenment and the Theory of Spontaneous Order*. Carbondale and Edwardsville: Southern Illinois University Press.

Hodges, Richard E. 1964. "A Short History of Spelling Reform in the United States." *Phi Delta Kappa International* 45: 330–332.

Hodgson, Geoffrey M. 2006. "What Are Institutions?" *Journal of Economic Issues* 40: 1–25.

Horwitz, Steven. 2001. "From Smith to Menger to Hayek. Liberalism in the Spontaneous Order Tradition." *The Independent Review* 6: 81–97.

Keller, Rudi. 1994. *On Language Change. The Invisible Hand in Language.* London and New York: Routledge.

Keller, Rudi. 2014. *Sprachwandel. Von der unsichtbaren Hand in der Sprache*, fourth edition. Tübingen: Francke Verlag.

Mueller, Dennis C. 2003. *Public Choice III*. Cambridge: Cambridge University Press.

Munske, Horst Haider. 2000. "Rechtschreibreform I: Von der Amtshilfe zum Protest." In *Germanistische Linguistik in Erlangen. Eine Bilanz nach 50 Jahren*, edited by Horst Haider Munske and M. Habermann, 129–139. Erlangen: Palm & Enke.

Munske, Horst Haider. 2006. "Die fragwürdige Herrschaft der Politik über unsere Sprache. Referat vor der Schweizer Orthographischen Konferenz." *Schrift & Rede* June 18, 2006. Accessed October 22, 2017. http://www.sprachforschung.org/index.php?show=news&id=477.

Nee, Victor, and Sonja Opper. 2012. *Capitalism from Below. Markets and Institutional Change in China*. Cambridge (MA): Harvard University Press.

Olson, Mancur. 1965. *The Logic of Collective Action*. Cambridge (MA): Harvard University Press.

Opp, Karl-Dieter. 1999. "Contending Conceptions of the Theory of Rational Action." *Journal of Theoretical Politics* 11: 171–202.

Opp, Karl-Dieter. 2002. "When Do Norms Emerge by Human Design and When by the Unintended Consequences of Human Action? The Example of the No-Smoking Norm." *Rationality & Society* 14: 131–158.

Opp, Karl-Dieter. 2015. "Instrumental, Axiological Rationality and the Explanation of Norms. Cherkaoui's (and Boudon's) Critique of Rational Choice Theory and Its Ability to Explain Norm Emergence." In *Theories and Social Mechanisms. Essays in Honor of Mohamed Cherkaoui*, edited by Gianluca Manzo, vol. 1, 183–206. Oxford: Bardwell Press.

Opp, Karl-Dieter. 2018. "Rational Choice Theory and Methodological Individualism." In *The Cambridge Handbook of Social Theory*, edited by Peter Kivisto, forthcoming. Cambridge: Cambridge University Press.

Prerau, David. 2005. *Seize the Daylight. The Curious and Contentious Story of Daylight Saving Time*. New York: Thunder's Mouth Press.

Roach Anleu, Sharyn L. 2000. *Law and Social Change*. London: Sage Publications.

Schneider, Louis. 1967. *The Scottish Moralists on Human Nature and Society.* Chicago: The University of Chicago Press.

Simon, Herbert A. 1997 [1945]. *Administrative Behavior. A Study of Decision-Making Processes in Administrative Organizations*, fourth edition. New York: The Free Press.

Smith, Adam. 2007 [1776]. *An Inquiry into the Nature and Causes of the Wealth of Nations*. Amsterdam: MetaLibri.

Visser, Margaret. 2012. *The Rituals of Dinner: The Origins, Evolution, Eccentricities and Meaning of Table Manners*. New York: Harper Collins.

Wagner, Gerhard. 2010. *Kraft Gesetz. Beiträge zur rechtssoziologischen Effektivitätsforschung*. Wiesbaden: VS – Verlag für Sozialwissenschaften, 35–63.

Walder, Andrew G. 1994. "The Decline of Communist Power: Elements of a Theory of Institutional Change." *Theory and Society* 23: 297–323.

Wang, Q. Edward. 2015. *Chopsticks: A Cultural and Culinary History*. Cambridge: Cambridge University Press.

Young, H. Peyton. 1996. "The Economics of Convention." *Journal of Economic Perspectives* 10: 105–122.

Part 2: Even Better Than the Invisible Hand

Helmut K. Anheier

The Principle of the Hiding Hand Revisited

Abstract: Introduced by Albert O. Hirschman in the 1960s to describe development programs at the time, the principle of the Hiding Hand describes the systematic discrepancy between what proponents propose when seeking permission for projects and what processes actually lead to certain outcomes. This chapter explores the recent renaissance of the principle and elaborates on its distinctness among related concepts in (organizational) sociology, organizational psychology and economics. By examining multiple combinations of two critical dimensions in project planning – estimation of complexity and overall awareness of planners – a typology of four hands is proposed: the Hiding Hand, the Protecting Hand, the Malevolent Hand and the Passive Hand. Each hand is associated with advantages leading to potential benefits, as well as disadvantages leading to potentially detrimental outcomes and unintended consequences. The Hiding Hand is offered as an argument in support of planning beyond purely rationalist approaches.

Keywords: Albert Hirschman; Hiding Hand; planning; rationalist approaches; unintended consequences

Hirschman's *Principle of the Hiding Hand* (1967a) is enjoying a remarkable comeback (Lepenies 2008; Adelman 2013; Offe 2013; Özcelik 2014; Flyvbjerg and Sunstein 2016). Yet similar to its initial reception some 50 years ago, two main deficits remain: first, the Principle is somewhat under-theorized and has not generated testable propositions or hypotheses that could be examined by systematic empirical tests; and second, despite its seeming face validity and indeed charm, its implications have yet to be explored in relation to other social science principles, and in particular the causes and other factors that might be implicated in the Hiding Hand phenomenon. The present chapter addresses both aspects.

The Principle of the Hiding Hand expresses a pattern Hirschman (1967b) observed when studying major development programs in the 1960s in countries as different as then East Pakistan, Uganda, Peru, Uruguay and (Southern) Italy. The perhaps best-known case is the Karnaphuli pulp and paper mill planned by the Industrial Development Corporations of East Pakistan to exploit the vast area of bamboo forest as raw material for industrial processing. Unexpectedly, after years of preparations, the mill lost 85% of its raw material due to a rare botanical event: the bamboo began to flower, which made it unusable for pulping. The mill's future was threatened because the planners had highly overestimated the steady supply of bamboo. Yet, they had also underestimated alternatives.

Instead of causing the closure of the mill, the bamboo flowering triggered the diversification of supply making the mill in fact more sustainable in the long term. Another example is the San Lorenzo irrigation project in Peru. Suffering from costly delays due to political changes and extensive project revisions, these challenges and subsequent revisions proved ultimately essential for the project's success. Indeed, the project served as the best practice for the reorganization of Peruvian agriculture (Hirschman 1967a, 11–12).

Looking for historical analogues, Hirschman discovered Sawyer´s analysis of US infrastructure projects undertaken during the first half of 19th century, a truly boom-and-bust era of economic history, and found similar patterns. Sawyer (1951, 199) concluded: "Had the total investment required been accurately and objectively known at the beginning, the project would not have begun".[1] Yet in the end, after periods of uncertainty, with many unanticipated consequences and innovative responses, the project turned out to be a success, Sawyer (1951, 200) writes, as "the error in estimating costs was at least offset by a corresponding error in the estimation of demand".

Most instructive for the empirical cases that lead Hirschman to formulate the Hiding Hand Principle is the following case:

> In 1851, construction began on one of the most important infrastructure projects in Massachusetts – the Hoosac Tunnel. Piercing through the Hoosac Mountain was the core part of the Greenfield and Troy Railroad, a vital addition to connect Boston to the Hudson River. Initially, James Hayward, a leading railroad engineer, expected the tunneling through the mountain's soft rock to be comparatively easy and cost-efficient. He estimated the construction would cost no more than $2 million. Almost 25 years later when the tunnel was finally completed in 1875, the total cost of the project had increased tenfold to $21 million. Digging through the Hoosac Mountain had turned out to be much more difficult and dangerous than expected. Had the funders known how challenging the project would be, most likely they would never have dared to invest in such a risky endeavor. Yet, the Greenfield and Troy Railroad was essential to the economic success of the factories of northwestern Massachusetts and, despite its high costs, benefitted the entire state long term (Gladwell 2013).

In such cases, Hirschman detected a systematic discrepancy between what project proponents "put on paper" when seeking permission or financing for projects, and the actual processes leading to some eventual outcomes that were in some ways more beneficial than promised. Often such projects were pushed by entrepreneurs or stakeholders and required some coalitions between technical

1 Sawyer focused on the Welland Canal built by entrepreneur W. H. Merritt to link Lake Ontario and Lake Erie (wellandcanal.com n.d.).

experts, usually engineers, finance, frequently banks and the public purse and political backing. He argued that if proponents, and especially planners and financiers, had known in advance all the seemingly insurmountable challenges that were lying in store, they would probably not have embarked on proposing any such projects in the first place, let alone push for realization.

Such challenges can involve technological, political, financial, economic or other factors, and often in some combination or another. For example, when digging a railroad tunnel, the geological formations of a mountain range may turn out to be different from what engineers assumed based on exploratory drillings and tests, and hence requiring extensive changes, as in the Massachusetts case above; when proposing a railroad project, nimbyism[2] may be stronger and more unpredictable than expected; or market conditions in digital communication may suddenly change due to technological advances or regulatory bans on roaming charges.[3] The key point is that proponents are typically unaware of such factors or may at best have some vague notion of the true challenges involved when embarking on projects.

But why did they forge ahead in the first place, when in hindsight the challenges encountered may frequently seem predictable, if not rather obvious? Put differently: why do some people – especially entrepreneurs, planners, financiers, politicians and philanthropists – take on tasks that seem near impossible, that carry high risks and involve huge costs of failure? That is where the Principle of the Hiding Hand comes in. Hirschman writes:

> Creativity always comes as a surprise to us; therefore we can never count on it and we dare not believe in it until it has happened. In other words, we would not consciously engage upon tasks whose success clearly requires that creativity be forthcoming. Hence, the only way in which we can bring our creative resources fully into play is by misjudging the nature of the task, by presenting it to ourselves as more routine, simple, undemanding of genuine creativity than it will turn out to be" (Hirschman 1967b, 13).

Indeed, Hirschman observed various projects being started that in retrospect looked unrealistic, over-ambitious, dilettante and even nearly deceitful. Such projects provided the impetus for the formulation of the Hiding Hand Principle.

---

2 NIMBY ("Not In My Back Yard") refers to a self-serving attitude among citizens to oppose any infrastructure measures in their immediate neighborhood. It is often associated with sentiments to protect rural and urban areas in the wider vicinity from any further developments. The massive rail project Stuttgart 21 in Germany is a good example of such nimbyism.

3 In September 2016, the European Commission agreed on a new approach ("Roam like at Home") to end all roaming charges in the EU in 2017 (European Commission 2016).

Examples included many of the infrastructure projects in the 19th-century America, or development projects in the 1960s' Africa or Asia. Current examples might well include the energy transition in Germany[4] ("if we shut down nuclear plants, we will get green energy"), re-energizing the idea of Europe[5] ("if we have a new narrative, the European project will move forward") and the Brexit referendum[6] ("if only we were to leave the European Union our domestic problems will be solved"). Other cases in point are private space travel[7] winning the war on drugs[8] and high-speed rail lines in California[9] among many other projects that are typically as ambitious as controversial and frequently populate the world's front pages and news websites.

For Hirschman, such ideas and proposals appear neither naïve or simply ill-conceived as such; nor are unlawful negligence, corruption, embezzlement, blackmail or any other wrongdoings involved. To the contrary, he sees great value in the aspirations and ambitions of the experts and the economic, political, social or cultural entrepreneurialism involved. Yet, he also points to the Principle of the

---

4 The German Energy Transition [*Energiewende*] is the shift from both nuclear and fossil energy to renewables and efficiency. It is Germany's largest postwar infrastructure project (http://energytransition.de/ [Accessed September 11, 2017]).

5 The New Narrative project was launched in 2013 to restore confidence in Europe and to revive a "European spirit". The project wants to create a European narrative beyond economic growth based on common culture and shared values (European Commission n.d.).

6 When Article 50 of the Lisbon Treaty was triggered in March 2017, both the United Kingdom and the European Union embarked on complex legal and political course with many unknowns. Hirschman would have assumed that many of the "Leave" voters had little ideal of such complexities, and had they known them might have changed their mind.

7 For example, Virgin Galactic, a spaceflight company within the Virgin Group, is developing a commercial space-line (http://www.virgingalactic.com/ [Accessed September 11, 2017]).

8 The term "war on drugs" was popularized during the Nixon Administration in the early 1970s and became a focus of the first Reagan Administration. The Obama Administration did no longer use the controversial term but embraced a strategy with the goal to prevent drug use, expand access to treatment, and reform the criminal justice system. In contrast, the Trump administration started rolling back these efforts, and Attorney General Jeff Sessions "re-declared" the war on drugs (Beckett 2017).

9 California is building the first high-speed rail system of the United States. By 2029, the system will run from San Francisco to the Los Angeles basin in under three hours. The system will eventually extend to Sacramento and San Diego, totaling 800 miles (http://www.hsr.ca.gov/ [Accessed September 11, 2017]).

Hiding Hand at work: by necessarily underestimating creativity or resourcefulness ex ante, proponents may well underestimate to a roughly similar extent the difficulties of the tasks itself. In a way, they trick themselves "by these two offsetting underestimates into undertaking tasks which we can, but otherwise would not dare, tackle" (Hirschman 1967a, 13).

The Principle was intentionally named such to insinuate not only intellectual gravitas but more importantly an almost playful proximity to Adam Smith´s "Invisible Hand" (see Mica, Wyrzykowska, Zielińska and Wiśniewski in this volume; Mica, Wyrzykowska, Wiśniewski and Zielińska in this volume; Samuels 2011). Indeed, he writes: "The principle is important enough to deserve a name: since we are apparently on the trail here of some sort of *Invisible or Hidden Hand* that beneficially hides difficulties from us, I propose 'The Hiding Hand'" (1967a, 13 [emphasis added]). The Principle also makes implicit reference to the notions of unanticipated consequences (Merton 1936; Meldolesi 1995, chap. 5; Mica, Arkadiusz and Winczorek 2011), consequentialism (Darwall 2003) and serendipity (Merton and Barber 2004; McDonald et al in this volume), among others, as we will see below.

What Hirschman labeled somewhat lofty "principle" was initially meant as a thought piece to reflect his experience with numerous large-scale projects in developing countries and occasioned by his work for the World Bank (Hirschman 1967a; Alacevich 2012).[10] The essay fit well into the emerging and mostly critical debate of *The Great Society*, addressing topics such as the expanding social security system, redistribution and taxation, the changing US class structure and race relations, among others.[11] It was also on early contribution to an emerging trope in the 1970s studies of economic development that signaled growing disillusionment with the planning optimism of the postwar years (see Bauer 1972 as among the most influential works).

In contrast to his many other contributions, however, the Hiding Hand Principle remained rather underdeveloped in Hirschman's thinking. Even though he made reference to it in some of his other writings (e.g., Hirschman 1982, 59, 95), it was less to elaborate and formalize the underlying idea, and

10 It was published in 1967 in *The Public Interest*, a neo-conservative journal run by Irving Kristol and Daniel Bell (Kristol 2005). Written in essay form rather than as a scholarly article, it aimed at a larger audience and, of course, the readership of *The Public Interest*.

11 Among the analytic challenges of the Hiding Hand Principle is the separation between concrete infrastructure projects (e.g., building dams and high-speed railroads) on the one hand, and policies on the other like social security reforms, economic development initiatives or urban renewal.

more to build a connection to the topic at hand. Whereas *Exit, Voice and Loyalty* (1970) and some of his other works have become classics of social science theorizing, and laid the foundation for further theoretical and empirical work, the Principle of the Hiding Hand remained somewhat of an intellectual orphan, at most a *petite idée* yet to be systematically connected to some broader theoretical framework (see Flyvbjerg 2001; Eiden-Offe 2013).

After its initial publication, the Principle was rarely taken up to inform further research in economics, political science or sociology. It remained closer to a witty wordplay by virtue of its implicit reference to Adam Smith than to becoming the testable set of propositions needed for theoretical advancement. Yet, what could be the contribution of the Principle of the Hiding Hand today? Is it indeed just an interesting idea yet to be developed? What would it mean to examine the Principle in today's context?[12]

1 Delineations

For placing the Principle, it is first of all necessary to position it relative to similar concepts and approaches. First and foremost among them is the "Invisible Hand", perhaps one of the most important foundational notions of economics, and associated with Adam Smith and Adam Ferguson. As Mica, Wyrzykowska, Zielińska and Wiśniewski (in this volume) describe, it depicts social institutions as the unintended consequence of individual action. It is an emergent institution, born of independence yet leading to interdependence; and it is not of human design or the result of purposive planning (see Samuels 2011).

The Invisible Hand Principle underpins the First Theorem of Welfare Economics: competitive markets tend toward an efficient allocation of resources. Under conditions of non-intervention, independent market participants will produce an interdependent outcome that is Pareto efficient, no one can be made better off without someone being made worse off. As Stiglitz (1994) has pointed out, many Pareto-efficient allocations of resources are possible, and not all of them may be equally beneficial to, let alone desirable by, society. For Hirschman,

---

12 One could argue that compared to the world of large-scale projects some 50 years ago, there are many more rules and regulations in place today, especially around transparency and accountability. Moreover, technology has advanced, and communication has become easier and quicker, making available information more plentiful and accessible. Is there still a place for the Hiding Hand in today´s world where things have become more unhideable?

however, the Hiding Hand seems to lead to beneficial outcomes even if different from the one´s initially intended or desired.

Yet, there are further and significant differences between the Invisible Hand and the Hiding Hand: the former is about independent actors creating an interdependent social institution as consequence, the market; the latter is about dependent actors seeking to realize some kind of project in jeopardy. The Invisible Hand is about achieving an unintended Pareto-efficient outcome and the Hiding Hand about finding solutions to encountered unexpected problems in achieving intended outcomes.

How different the two principles are becomes clear when we briefly recall the three conditions the First Theorem requires for markets to tend toward a competitive equilibrium that is weakly Pareto-optimal: no or minimal transaction costs as all participants have perfect information; entry and exit from a market is easy, i.e., low if any cost or regulatory barriers exist; and non-satiation of preferences, i.e., no two market allocations offer market participants equal satisfaction. By contrast, the Hiding Hand involves significant transaction costs, incomplete information, major sunk costs and lack of alternatives. In sum, the Invisible Hand is both normative ideal and axiomatic model, and the Hiding Hand an empirical generalization at best, and one that makes no systematic claims as to Pareto-efficiency but nonetheless posits the likelihood of some beneficial outcome resulting from coping with unanticipated adversity or problems generally.

The fundamental differences between the Invisible Hand and the Hiding Hand in arriving at an outcome point to consequentialism. With this term, philosophers refer to a set of normative ethical theories stipulating that the consequences or outcomes are the ultimate basis for any judgment about the rightness or wrongness – rather than the decisions and actions leading to them (Scheffler 1988). For consequentialist, a morally – though not necessary economically – right way of acting or not acting is one that will produce a beneficial outcome, or consequence for all stakeholders. It is an end that justifies the means approach if the end is superior to any other outcomes. As this seems to absolve amoral, unjust or illegal behaviors ex ante, rule consequentialism (Darwall 2003), a variant of the rather broad stipulations above, states that actions are not right or wrong simply because of their very own consequences; rather, rule consequentialism suggests that actions are only morally right when they are not in violation of accepted rules of behavior.

The Hiding Hand Principle does not explicitly specify the rule-boundedness of actions and inactions, nor does it necessarily assume beneficial outcomes for all stakeholders. Actors being tricked by the two offsetting underestimations of risks and resourcefulness to take on tasks they would normally not undertake, may or may not achieve positive outcomes for stakeholders or the focal community involved. Failure is a possible outcome, but the Hiding Hand makes success more likely. For Hirschman (1967a, 20), the Hiding Hand is "essentially a transition mechanism through which decision-makers learn to take risks" leading to outcomes including successes and failures but also many gradations in between. Thus, the Hiding Hand is about coping strategies first and foremost, and not about ex-post rationalizations and justifications of outcomes deemed beneficial in hindsight.

Closely related to the notion of the Hiding Hand is the concept of unintended consequences, going back to John Locke, Adam Smith and the Scottish Enlightenment philosophers, it was ultimately systematized by sociologist Merton (Merton 1936; see Mica, Peisert and Winczorek 2011). Unintended consequences arise from the likely gap between purposive action and control in the context of social complexity. In particular, acts aimed at social change confront other actors whose motives and consequently choices and actions may differ from what was initially intended. Underlying this thinking is the Burkian[13] fear that society, with its overwhelmingly complex tapestry of networks, institutions and organizations, its deeply embedded values and inert practices, lies beyond the reach of purposive change, and that even comprehensive and well-thought out plans to improve economy and society can have disastrous unanticipated consequences.

Merton (1936) identified several possible causes of unanticipated consequences that can be summarized under the headings of: ignorance; errors in analysis; short-termism; values, i.e., deeply embedded normative dispositions that favor one set of actions over others even though the latter would have been more rational; and self-defeating prophecy, i.e., the fear of some consequence that could propel actors to find solutions before or while the problem occurs leads to avoidance strategies.

In particular, the first and last cause are of interest, as the Hiding Hand "does its work essentially through ignorance of ignorance, of uncertainties, and of difficulties" (Hirschman 1967b, 35). But unlike in the case of self-defeating prophesies, where avoidance, indecision and inaction lead to the non-occurrence of uncertainties and difficulties, the Hiding Hand involves behavior closer to what social psychologists label self-fulfilling prophecy, i.e., "a *false* definition of the

---

13 Edmund Burke (1729-1797) was an English political philosopher and statesman who is often seen as laying the foundations of modern conservatism (see Lanford 1981-2015).

situation evoking a new behavior which makes the original false conception come *true*" (Merton 1948, 195) by virtue of positive feedback between belief and behavior.

What is more, value dispositions in place may facilitate behavioral trends toward self-fulfilling prophecies, be it in the form of entrepreneurial cultures with a "can-do-spirit" or planning ideologies suggesting however subliminal that "everything can be done". Hirschman (1967a, 20) saw parallels to Christianity´s "oft expressed preference for the repentant sinner over the righteous man who never strays from the part", and even referred to Nietzsche´s adage "That which does not destroy me, makes me stronger" in that context. Hirschman (1967a, 22) stressed, following George Sorel, the need for "myths" advocated by political, social or economics entrepreneurs to achieve change or realize complex projects, and saw merit in the "occasional need for exaggeration of prospective benefits", paraphrasing the philosopher Kolakowski. Thus, the Hiding Hand describes a special kind of behavioral outcome that is different from the notion of unanticipated consequences: not ignorance but ignorance of ignorance, and values favorable to entrepreneurialism, myth-making and self-fulfilling prophecies.

Related to the concept of unanticipated consequences is the notion of serendipity or lucky happenstance. Merton referred to it in the 1949 collection of essays *Social Theory and Social Structure* as serendipity patterns: seemingly isolated, unanticipated and ground-breaking discoveries that lead to further discoveries and innovations of many kinds. For Merton, such events are rarely isolated but patterned and facilitated by social structures that make such unexpected connections possible. The notion of serendipity is implicitly part of the Hiding Hand:

> While we are rather willing and even eager and relieved to agree with a historian's finding that we stumbled into the more shameful events of history, such as war, we are correspondingly unwilling to concede – in fact we find it intolerable to imagine – that our more lofty achievements, such as economic, social or political progress, could have come about by stumbling rather than through careful planning […] Language itself conspires toward this sort of asymmetry: we fall into error, but do not usually speak of falling into truth" (Hirschman 1967b, 13).

The Hiding Hand involves, as Hirschman states, ignorance of ignorance, which is different from what sociologists call the preventive power of ignorance.[14] The

14 The term "preventing power of ignorance" in this context describes the phenomenon that people underestimate the amount of norm violations; and this ignorance concerning the true number stabilizes the system of social norms (Popitz 1968).

basic idea is that there are advantages to not knowing or to being unaware by neutralizing behavioral impulses and patterns that would otherwise be evoked or emerge. For example, Popitz (1968) argues that the official under-reporting of crime statistics, as many crimes go unreported, actually reduces the number of law infringements: people would take social norms less seriously and begin to doubt them if they knew how often and repeatedly they are broken. Especially for minor offenses, the notion of "everyone does it" would undermine accepted norms underlying the law.[15] Yet the Hiding Hand Principle is different because preventive ignorance does not trigger creativity and does not lead to innovative behavior and subsequent changes. The ignorance about ignorance means continuity rather than change.

The Principle is also different from Weick's (1995) organizational psychology on the collapse of sense making under uncertainty. The central problem he poses is how to chart a way forward under conditions of extreme uncertainty. Weick uses a group lost on a mountain as an example of unconventional yet reasonable problem-solving: finding and using a map to escape – a map that turns out to chart terrain somewhere else, the group nonetheless manages to find safety – suggesting that any plan is better than no plan at all. Yet again, as in the case of preventive ignorance, the plan followed is conventional, routinized behavior, and more of an enactment of known patterns than the creative impulse the Principle entails.

It is also different from the "fantasy plans" sociologist Clarke (1999) writes about, i.e., unrealistic proposals made believable by the interplay of special interests and politics. For example, experience shows the near impossibility of containing and cleaning up massive oil spills on the open sea. Nevertheless, regulators and oil corporations continue to produce detailed contingency plans that serve symbolic rather than instrumental functions. They divert attention from the real environmental risks and, therefore, reflect the interests of influential political and economic actors. Plans may well be known as unrealistic but keep being propagated and treated as if they were indeed realistic. Again, there is

15 In German literature, the phenomenon of preventive ignorance has become known as "the ride across Lake Constance", after a famous 19th-century poem: in a clear and bitterly cold winter´s night, a lonesome rider in search of a ferry to cross the lake mistakenly thinks that the wide snowy expanse he crosses is the flat land leading to the shore, only to discover afterwards that he actually crossed the frozen lake itself. He dies from being shocked by the sudden awareness of the extreme dangers implied by his own ignorance (Schwab 1828).

no genuine creativity involved that seeks to overcome challenges and obstacles; rather it is an act of political salesmanship or even brinkmanship.

Moreover, the Principle is different from the explanations offered in economic and sociological studies of organizational failure that focus on incentives problems and bounded rationality (Garicano and Rayo 2016), where managers either face external constraints or make wrong strategic as well as operational decisions in triggering decline processes or even breakdowns (Mellahi and Wilkinson 2004). Often, explanations of failure rest on misalignments between organizational structures and decision-making on the one hand, and the demands of organizational task environments on the other (Anheier 1999; Mellahi and Wilkinson 2010). The Hiding Hand Principle, by contrast, is different as it addresses unknown or unlikely successes arising from conditions suggesting failure.

Indeed, it is also different from the notion of permanent failure advanced by Meyer and Zucker (1989). They suggest that organizations get locked in permanent failure when the reasons for their continued operations are separated from actual performance and attached to stakeholders that can block each other. For example, strong unions can stress the preservation of jobs irrespective of corporate performance, whereas management, stressing performance, seeks job cuts and reorganization, which the unions, in turn, block. As a result, the organization drifts into permanent failure mode. The Hiding Hand is different, as both management and unions are aware of the situation, both in terms of causes and likely implications – which involve neither unanticipated events nor consequences.

Put differently, the Hiding Hand involves processes toward some desired goal without fully knowing how to achieve it, nor being aware of all consequences of intermediary steps or achieving the actual outcomes. We may know some aspects of what is involved, be more certain about some facets or another, and we may even believe in the plans and metrics put forth, but we are engaging in a rather similar double underestimation. In other words, the Hiding Hand Principle means letting oneself be tricked by two offsetting underestimations: first, that it can be done within given means and in known ways, and, second, that it is not that difficult after all, and all can be achieved if only we try as best as we can.

2 The Hiding Hand and other hands

The dual underestimation embodied in the Principle of the Hiding Hand involves two dimensions: the state of knowledge at the start of the project, in particular, whether obstacles, challenges or difficulties likely to confront the project

Tab. 1: Typology of hands

Typology of Hands		STATE OF KNOWLEDGE	
		Ignorance	**Awareness**
TASK	**Underestimation**	*Hiding Hand*	*Malevolent Hand*
COMPLEXITY	**Overestimation**	*Protecting Hand*	*Passive Hand*

are known or unknown, including the possibility of not wanting to know. The second dimension refers to the under or overestimation of the complexity of the tasks ahead. These two dimensions yield four combinations, as presented in *tab. 1*. It becomes apparent that the Hiding Hand is only one of other possible outcomes of the relationship between knowledge and estimation. Specifically:

The Hiding Hand results from the combination of ignorance and underestimation of task complexity, as Hirschman suggests. Both are necessary conditions for the likelihood of stumbling into success, for finding solutions to seemingly insurmountable problems and for creativity to take hold. It is the equivalent of "Houston, we've had a problem here" in the Apollo 13 mission (Orloff 2004 [2000]). Referring to Merton´s (1968) distinction between latent and manifest functions, the latent function of the Hiding Hand is to make active problem-solving under conditions of ignorance possible[16] and to facilitate, as a coping strategy, the transitions from uncertainty to certainty. Its function is latent because actors must be unaware of the Hiding Hand when engaging to trick themselves by the two offsetting underestimates of knowledge and task complexity.

The *Protecting Hand*, by contrast, requires no latency but performs a manifest function of addressing ignorance by risk management and a planning approach that assumes worst-case outcomes. The Protecting Hand assumes its clearest expression in what has become known as the precautionary principle of policy-making and planning (Jordan and O'Riordan 2004). It states that threats of serious or irreversible damage *and* lack of full understanding are no reason for abandoning or postponing preventive measures. Awareness of a lack of full knowledge and an overestimation of complexity are the necessary conditions of the Protecting Hand to take hold.[17]

16 Latent functions are consequences that are neither recognized nor intended by participants in a relevant context. In contrast, manifest functions are consequences that are explicitly stated, expected, and understood by those involved (Merton 1968).

17 The precautionary principle is a main policy approach of the European Union (*Treaty on the Functioning of the European Union*, Article 191). Through preventive

Tab. 2: Hands, behavioral patterns and outcomes

Hands, Behavioral Patterns and Outcomes		TYPES OF HANDS			
		Hiding	**Malevolent**	**Protecting**	**Passive**
OUT-COMES	**Advantages**	Entrepre-neurialism	Gameful Unblocking	Precautionary principle	Planification
	Dis-advantages	Adventurism	Profiteering	Overregulation	Catastrophizing

The *Malevolent Hand* is, as Flyybjerg and Sunstein (2016) remarked, the "evil twin" of the Hiding Hand. With the awareness of fuller knowledge and willful underestimation of complexity as necessary conditions, it describes a kind of information asymmetry easily leading to profiteering and other kinds of planning and market failures. It is not about stumbling into error but an approach to capitalize on the greater ignorance of third parties such as investors who are tricked into believing that the project is sound and planned with care. There is no latency involved, but the manifest function of the Malevolent Hand is profiteering and would, in Merton´s terminology, be more properly labeled a manifest dysfunction.

The *Passive Hand* is about known and revealed knowledge that may lead to overly cautious approaches, even inaction. Here, planners overestimate the complexity of the task even though the state of knowledge is such that few unknowns should come as a surprise. What ought to be a steady state and routine is made problematic, even controversial. There can be a latent function involved, but in contrast to the Hiding Hand, it is not about triggering creativity but to stifle it, and compared to the Protecting Hand, it is not about risk management but risk avoidance, similar to the self-defeating prophecy, and likely dysfunctional.

Each hand is associated with characteristic advantages leading to potential benefits and disadvantages leading to potentially detrimental outcomes, as *tab. 2* summarizes. The Hiding Hand invites entrepreneurialism – the active problem-solving behavior under conditions of uncertainty, as was the case in Hirschman's example of the Karnaphuli pulp and paper mill in Eastern Pakistan, the Channel tunnel connecting the UK and France, or Sydney's Opera House. In each of these

decision-making in the case of risk, it aims at protecting the environment as well as human and animal health. For example, it can be invoked to withdrawal products from the marked if they might be hazardous – even if a complete evaluation of the risk is impossible (http://eur-lex.europa.eu/legal-content [Accessed September 11, 2017]).

cases, there was considerable risk-taking and uncertainty that required creative problem-solving. At the same time, the Hiding Hand can result in adventurism, i.e. seemingly daring but ultimately dilettante ways of approaching uncertainty.

The Malevolent Hand allows actors to take advantage of information asymmetries and other market and governance failures. It is essentially about profiteering and various forms of corruption. However, under some circumstances, and through successful gaming, the Malevolent Hand can help avoid planning obstacles and system blockages generally. In situations of what Crozier (1973) described as structures blocquées,[18] Malevolent Hands "play the system" not only for personal gain but to get things done somehow.

The Protecting Hand is the quintessential incarnation of the precautionary principle when facing a combination of unknown risks and latent risk communities. The rational calculation and management of risk is part of the "master narrative" of modernity, and at its best, a corrective of its optimism bias, i.e. the underestimation of costs and overestimation of benefits. At worst, the Protecting Hand can lead to overregulation and planning environments with high transaction costs and long gestation periods for even the most routine of projects.

Finally, the Passive Hand can lead to what could be called the planification syndrome, i.e., the notion that planning for more contingencies is the preferred option, even though many eventualities may either never materialize or with the lowest of probabilities. Its inherent risk avoidance implies slow and long-drawn-out planning and implementation processes that may, at high cost, nonetheless lead to acceptable results. Its negative version, "catastrophizing" by assuming worst-case scenarios as the base line can result in bureaucratization at best. At worst, with an emphasis on wanting certainty in controlling what may well be uncontrollable, the Passive Hand can trigger off tendencies toward a do-nothing approach.

Indeed, the four hands suggest rather distinct planning and policy-making cultures and even personality types. For the principle of the Hiding Hand to work, entrepreneurs, planners or policymakers require limited knowledge and underestimation of task complexity while letting themselves be tricked for creativity to kick in and for innovations to unfold. It requires a culture of accepting failure while rewarding, trying as much as success itself (see Hess 2012). The Malevolent

18 Crozier describes the 1960s France as a "blocked society". Overregulation and top-down bureaucratic rules create a system prone to stalemate, ultimately causing distrust and a system that can only change through crises rather than through some evolutionary development through compromise (Crozier 1973).

Hand, by contrast, expects and rewards gaming and cheating, creating a culture if not corruption then at least an acceptance of rule avoidance and "playing the system". The Protecting Hand suggests a culture of policy and technocratic foresight and caring, with an emphasis on risk anticipation and management. Finally, the Passive Hand connotes with a bureaucratic, administrative culture, stressing predictability and standard procedures.

3 Concluding thoughts

We suggest two ways forward: one, focusing on the development of testable propositions theoretically grounded in organization studies and approaches to risk behavior and information asymmetries under conditions of uncertainties in given infrastructure fields; the second, taking up a broader argument about rationality in infrastructure and development planning, an issue that has not been addressed in this chapter, but that certainly plays a role in the wider context of Hirschman´s work (see Meldolesi 1995, chap. 5) and more generally, too.

Perhaps, because Hirschman did not extend his treatment of the Hiding Hand to the other concepts and hands described above, and because he did not build a theoretical connection between the two dimensions of knowledge and complexity on the one hand and behavioral and cultural responses on the other, the Principle remained ultimately an underdeveloped insight of his rich oeuvre. As it stands now, and even having placed it into a family of hands, we are still some way off from a theoretically embedded argument and, subsequently, a set of testable propositions.

Of course, each of the combinations and resulting hands in *tab. 1* deserves much attention, and comes with many implications yet to be explored, as *tab. 2* illustrates. However, even the cursory discussion here has shown that Hirschman´s Hiding Hand is a rather special case, resting on a double conditionality that may limit its actual manifestation across the many infrastructure and development projects that have been and are taking place across different countries and fields.

Unfortunately, we do not know the relative frequencies of each of the four hands, nor do we have a systematic empirical base as to the extent to which advantages and disadvantages actually materialize. What is more, we do not know if hands can change into other hands, and under what conditions. Can Hiding Hands become malevolent, and protecting ones hiding, and could they be present simultaneously? What would such changes and co-presence mean for potential outcomes? Can some stakeholders be captive to, or lean toward, different hands?

Despite its "tongue in cheek" quality, the Principle of the Hiding Hand is not necessarily a benign principle where two necessary conditions coincide with a certain organizational and administrative culture that value individual dispositions such as taking initiative and risks, engaging experimenting and exploring. The entrepreneurialism and creativity embodied in the Hiding Hand Principle have a downside, a tendency toward adventurism and risky behavior. The Hiding Hand may well lead to failure.

As we have seen, the Principle is a part of a family of hands, with three other siblings. Yet, how does this family fare over time? Compared to some half a century ago when Hirschman formulated the Principle, large-scale infrastructure and development projects have continued to be planned and built. They remain numerous and also large in scale and scope. Experiences have been gained, and infrastructure and developments projects today are more and perhaps better regulated than in the past,[19] in part due to the impact of disasters and failures of many kinds such as Bhopal, Three-Mile-Island and Love Canal in the last decades of the 20th century, and the 2004 Indonesian earthquake and tsunami, Hurricane Katrina (2005), the Fukoshima Japan earthquake (2011), the 2010 blowout of Deepwater Horizon and the massive blackouts in India in 2012.

One could argue that consolidated, well-regulated fields are those in which awareness easily trumps ignorance and with lower probabilities of unanticipated events and consequences that would require the underestimation of complexity. Conventional air or road transport would be examples of such consolidated, well-regulated fields, as would be water and sewage systems. By implication, other hands become more important: the Malevolent Hand depending on the extent to which information asymmetries can be exploited; the Protecting Hand relative to the institutionalized practice of the precautionary principle; and the Passive Hand contingent upon the density of regulatory-administrative penetration of the field.

For newer or emerging fields such as digital infrastructure, transport systems for semi-autonomous vehicles or climate change adaption, the situation may well be different. The balance between awareness and ignorance favors the latter, and underestimation of complexity is more functional. In other words, such fields may offer more room for the Hiding Hand to work. The same would apply for

19 For example, Stern (2006) reports a significant growth in the number of infrastructure regulators, with over 200 created between 1995 and the mid-2000s, covering major fields like telecommunication, electricity, water and transport.

fields that are undergoing major changes, for example health care or even educational infrastructure.

Infrastructure policies and planning embody a strong belief in rationality, of the mastery of the world, to evoke a Weberian image, and in the sense that some form of orderly change is possible if planned and executed well for reaching better outcomes. For the planners and policymakers alike, action is better than no action; and any plan – however insufficient for navigating the complex and messy patterns of ever changing modern societies – is better than no plan at all. Policymakers can identify and grasp concrete facets of social causality, i.e., a "theory of change", and they can use them to achieve the desired outcomes. This seems to be the core premise of the rationalist approach to infrastructure planning.

One lesson the Hiding Hand Principle offers is that there is more to planning than a belief in rationality and the "best laid plans" that come with it. It can be a process involving trial and error rather than putting in place known procedures. It is also more than the intentional, systematic and rational pursuit of an outcome, and there may well be – and under some limited set of circumstances – other ways to increase the chances of meeting significant challenges: through the creative acts of "inventing and re-inventing the wheel" as we are "falling toward success", as Hirschman would have put it.

Yet falling into success out of ignorance of ignorance may be one way toward progress; another path is suggested by the consoling insight Tilly (1996) offers: learning from experience and past mistakes to find less failure-prone ways to approach complex and uncertain tasks, a phenomenon he labels the "invisible elbow". By yet another world play on the Invisible Hand, Tilly simply means that repeated tasks under anticipated, yet not fully known uncertainties allow actors to develop routines that increase chances of successful or at least satisficing performance. Perhaps, another way forward is to examine when the Hiding Hand Principle involves or invites learning, or if indeed, it applies to "one-shot", singular events only.

References

Adelman, Jeremy. 2013. *Worldly Philosopher: The Odyssey of Albert O. Hirschman*. Princeton (NJ): Princeton University Press.

Alacevich, Michele. 2012. "Visualizing Uncertainties, or How Albert Hirschman and the World Bank Disagreed on Project Appraisal and Development Approaches." Policy Research Working Paper 6260. Washington (DC): World Bank.

Anheier, Helmut K., ed. 1999. *When Things Go Wrong: Organizational Failures and Breakdowns*. Thousand Oaks (CA): Sage.

Bauer, P. T. 1972. *Dissent on Development*. Cambridge (MA): Harvard University Press.

Beckett, Lois. 2017. "How Jeff Sessions and Donald Trump Have Restarted the War on Drugs." *The Guardian*, August 21, 2017. Accessed October 24, 2017. https://www.theguardian.com/us-news/2017/aug/21/donald-trump-jeff-sessions-war-on-drugs.

Clarke, Lee. (1999). *Mission Improbable: Using Fantasy Documents to Tame Disaster*. Chicago (IL): University Of Chicago Press.

Crozier, Michel. 1973. *The Stalled Society*. New York (NY): Viking Press.

Darwall, Stephen. 2003. *Consequentialism*. Oxford: Blackwell Publishing.

Eiden-Offe, Patrick. 2013. "A Man, a Plan, a Canal. Der Ökonom und Sozialwissenschaftler Albert O. Hirschman." *Merkur* 6: 1104–1115.

European Commission. n.d. "New Narrative for Europe." Accessed September 11, 2017. http://ec.europa.eu/culture/policy/new-narrative/index_en.htm.

European Commission. 2016. "End of Roaming Charges in the EU in 2017: Commission Agrees on New Approach to Make It Work for All Europeans." Press release, Brussels, September 21, 2016. Accessed September 11, 2017. http://europa.eu/rapid/press-release_IP-16-3111_en.htm.

Flyvbjerg, Bent. 2001. *Making Social Science Matter: Why Social Inquiry Fails and How It Can Succeed Again*. Cambridge: Cambridge University Press.

Flyvbjerg, Bent, and Cass R. Sunstein, 2016. "The Principle of the Malevolent Hiding Hand; or, the Planning Fallacy Writ Large." *Social Research* 83: 979–1004.

Garicano, Luis, and Luis Rayo. 2016 "Why Organizations Fail: Models and Cases." *Journal of Economic Literature* 54: 137–192.

Gladwell, Malcolm. 2013. "The Gift of Doubt: Albert O. Hirschman and the Power of Failure." *The New Yorker*, June 4.

Hess, Edward D. 2012. "Creating an Innovation Culture: Accepting Failure Is Necessary." Guest post on Forbes, June 20, 2012. Accessed September 11, 2017. http://www.forbes.com/sites/darden/2012/06/20/creating-an-innovation-culture-accepting-failure-is-necessary/#613181a54e19.

Hirschman, Albert O. 1967a. *Development Projects Observed*. Washington (DC): The Brookings Institution.

Hirschman, Albert O. 1967b. "The Principle of the Hiding Hand." *The Public Interest* 6: 10–23.

Hirschman, Albert. O. 1970. *Exit, Voice, and Loyalty: Responses to Decline in Firms, Organizations, and States*. Cambridge (MA): Harvard University Press.

Hirschman, Albert O. 1982. *Shifting Involvements : Private Interest and Public Action*. Princeton (NJ): Princeton University Press.

Jordan, Andrew, and Timothy O'Riordan. 2004. "The Precautionary Principle: A Legal and Policy History." In *The Precautionary Principle: Protecting Public Health, the Environment and the Future of Our Children*, edited by Marco Martuzzi and Joel A. Tickner, 31–48. Copenhagen: World Health Organization.

Kristol, Irving. 2005. "Forty Good Years." *Public Interest* 159: 5–11.

Langford, Paul, ed. 1981-2015. *Writings and Speeches of Edmund Burke*, vol. 1-9. Oxford: Clarendon Press.

Lepenies, Philipp H. 2008. "Possibilism: An Approach to Problem-Solving Derived from the Life and Work of Albert O. Hirschman." *Development and Change* 39: 437–459.

Meldolesi, Luca. 1995. *Discovering the Possible: The Surprising World of Albert O. Hirschman*. Notre Dame (IN): Notre Dame Press.

Mellahi, Kamel, and Adrian Wilkinson. 2004. "Organizational Failure: A Critique of Recent Research and a Proposed Integrative Framework." *International Journal of Management Reviews* 56: 21–41.

Mellahi, Kamel, and Adrian Wilkinson. 2010. "Managing and Coping with Failure: Introduction to the Special Issue." *Group and Organization Management* 35: 531–541.

Merton, Robert K. 1936. "The Unanticipated Consequences of Purposive Social Action." *American Sociological Review* 1: 894–904.

Merton, Robert K. 1948. "The Self Fulfilling Prophecy." *Antioch Review* 8: 193–210.

Merton, Robert K. 1968. "Manifest and Latent Functions." In *Social Theory and Social Structure*, enlarged edition, 73–139. Glencoe (IL): Free Press.

Merton, Robert K., and Elinor Barber. 2004. *The Travels and Adventures of Serendipity: A Study in Sociological Semantics and the Sociology of Science*. Princeton (NJ): Princeton University Press.

Meyer, Marshall W., and Lynne G. Zucker. 1989. *Permanently Failing Organizations*. Newbury Park (CA): Sage.

Mica, Adriana, Arkadiusz Peisert, and Jan Winczorek, eds. 2011. *Sociology and the Unintended: Robert Merton Revisited*. Frankfurt am Main: Peter Lang.

Offe, Claus. 2013. "Getting Ahead by Trespassing – Adelman Jeremy, *Worldly Philosopher. The Odyssey of Albert O. Hirschman* (Princeton, Princeton University Press 2013)." *European Journal of Sociology* 54: 583–591.

Orloff, Richard W. 2004 [2000]. "Apollo 13 – The Seventh Mission: The Third Lunar Landing Attempt." *Apollo by the Numbers: A Statistical Reference*.

NASA History Division, Office of Policy and Plans, NASA History Series, 135-158. Washington (DC): NASA.

Özçelik, Emre. 2014. "Albert O. Hirschman: A 'Beamish' Social Scientist for Our Grandchildren." *Development and Change* 45: 1111–1133.

Popitz, Heinrich. 1968. *Über die Präventivwirkung des Nichtwissens. Dunkelziffer, Norm und Strafe*. Tübingen: Mohr.

Samuels, Warren J. 2011. *Erasing the Invisible Hand: Essays on an Elusive and Misused Concept in Economics*. Cambridge: Cambridge University Press.

Sawyer, John E. 1951. "Entrepreneurial Error and Economic Growth." *Explorations in Entrepreneurial History* 4: 199–204.

Scheffler, Samuel, ed. 1988. *Consequentialism and Its Critics*. Oxford: Oxford University Press.

Schwab, Gustav. 1828. "Der Reiter und der Bodensee." In *Gedichte. Erster Band*, 364–366. Stuttgart and Tübingen: Cotta.

Stern, Jon. 2006. "Evaluating Infrastructure Regulators - Developing UK and International Practice." CRI occasional lecture, Royal Society, September 26, 2006. Bath: University of Bath.

Stiglitz, Joseph E. 1994. *Whither Socialism?* Cambridge (MA): MIT Press.

Tilly, Charles. 1996. "Invisible Elbow." *Sociological Forum* 11: 589–601.

Weick, Karl E. 1995. *Sensemaking in Organizations*. Thousand Oaks (CA): Sage.

wellandcanal.com. n.d. "Brief History." Accessed September 11, 2017. http://www.wellandcanal.com/hist.htm.

Bruna Ingrao

Invisible or Visible Hands? The Image of Markets in Contemporary Macroeconomics

Abstract: The chapter deals with the association of the invisible hand metaphor with the Arrow-Debreu model of general economic equilibrium, exploring the conceptual ambiguities of such association and showing that it is ill conceived. In the second half of the 20th century, economic theory saw the paradoxical, complementary development of research programmes in macroeconomics inspired by the neo-Walrasian imagery, and the drastic decline of the neo-Walrasian research programme, due to technical and conceptual pitfalls. A puzzle in the sociology of science arises: why was the Arrow-Debreu model the reference metaphor for competitive markets in mainstream macroeconomics, notably in the rational expectations revolution and in real business cycle research, notwithstanding the visible dead ends of the neo-Walrasian research programme? In pursuing the dream of optimal equilibrium paths, the core of macroeconomic theory failed to deal with the many failures in the market coordination of private choices and intertemporal plans during periods of depressions and financial crises, as they emerged on the international scenery in well-known historical episodes. The chapter invites scholars to drastically abandon the imagery of the ghost auctioneer and intertemporal optimal equilibrium, to look at markets as institutional networks in changing environment, where market agents produce innovative change, with improved opportunities for orderly coordination, or with increasing risks of disequilibria, imbalances and conflicts. Partial coordination is achieved more or less effectively by the simultaneous effort of visible hands, which produce it purposively, within spheres of cooperative interaction, or as the intended result of profit-seeking activities.

Keywords: General equilibrium; macroeconomics; visible hands

1 The invisible hand metaphor in economics

In economics, the metaphor of the invisible hand has a long history, since Adam Smith introduced the phrase in various passages in his writings. The contexts in which the idea appears in Smith's two books and in his essays were extensively analysed and commented on in the literature on the history of economic thought in the 18th century, with a variety of conflicting interpretations (Ahmad 1990; Rothschild 1994; Ingrao 1998; 2013, 128–129; Grampp 2000; Khalil 2000). In the book *Erasing the Invisible Hand* (2011), Samuels systematically explored the widespread diffusion of the idea of the invisible hand in economic literature. In a life-long research project, this scholar collected and classified the many occurrences of the "invisible hand" in philosophical, economic and political discourse, both in academic writings and in the media. In his book, while examining the passages where the idea was mentioned or dealt with, he signalled a high number of ill-defined meanings attached to the concept. These include vague references to the working of markets, the operation of competition, the price mechanism, the principle of private property, the self-interest motive, the profit motive, entrepreneurship, the so-called unintended consequences' principle, philosophical ideas of the harmony of interests or of a self-regulating social order (Samuels 2011, chap. 3, 59 ff.). The invisible hand is a metaphor, and a powerfully evocative one. Surrounded by an aura of imagination, it invites the exploration of meanings. The power of metaphors, after all, resides in the open invitation to go beyond strict analogy, to cross borders, to freely connect distant experiences or ideas in imagination.

In this chapter, we shall deal exclusively with the association of the invisible hand metaphor with the theoretical idea of market equilibrium of Walrasian descent, and notably with the Arrow-Debreu mathematical model of general economic equilibrium. Ideas of general economic equilibrium are a recurrent topos in contemporary economic literature, and notably in macroeconomics, as it was developed since the mid-1950s and up to today. In what follows we shall explore the invisible hand imagery both in the Arrow-Debreu model, in its various interpretations, and in mainstream, mathematical models in macroeconomics. We shall try to assess the reasons for the persistent fascination of the invisible hand metaphor in economic discourse, more or less covert as it has been, and how its original meanings have been betrayed, although being reasserted. In the end, we shall suggest that it is time to radically let the invisible hand imagery fade out of the economic discourse on the market economy, to turn to the exploration of the many visible hands, which actively help markets work more or less smoothly, achieving coordination or, sometimes, failing to perform their coordinating, cooperative tasks. We shall discuss the networks of specialized activities, institutions, organizations and trades, which are the very visible hands that make market economies work, with no "as if" invisible hand pulling the strings. At the close of the chapter, we shall address the puzzle of why the visible hand imagery associated to the Arrow-Debreu general equilibrium was so persistent in contemporary macroeconomic theories.

In their classic book in 1971, Arrow and Hahn explicitly advanced the association of the Arrow-Debreu model, as it was perfected by Debreu in his book in 1959, with the invisible hand metaphor (Debreu 1959; Arrow and Hahn 1971, 1). Hahn (1982, 1), with explicit reference to Smith, evoked the "orderly and coherent disposition" of economic resources emerging in "a society of greedy and self-seeking people constrained only by the criminal law and the law of property and contract". The exact meaning of the association is controversial; it is not clear which of the visions of the invisible hand, among the many mentioned above or advanced in economic literature, is really relevant as far as the specific representation of markets in the Arrow-Debreu model is concerned. The mathematical model per se is a system of primitive concepts, axioms and equations and disequations. Does this axiomatic skeleton deal with markets, and with markets in which ideal market economy? The difficulty is quite serious, if the mathematical skeleton of the model is interpreted as a flexible, conceptual instrument to represent a variety of interactions and contexts, by changing the interpretation attached to the primitive concepts around which it is built. Debreu, defending a radical axiomatic methodology, suggested that the interpretation of the mathematical object that forms the core of an axiomatic theory should be flexibly adapted to the theoretical questions to be addressed (Debreu 1986). He maintained that such instrumental flexibility in interpretation is the true richness of the formal structure known as the Arrow-Debreu model, which is commonly known as the fictional image of perfectly competitive markets.[1] Among economic theorists, in widespread interpretation the Arrow-Debreu model deals with the coordination of optimal, independent choices by rational agents in that state of the world – the equilibrium of the economy – which clears the markets and has the properties of both feasibility and Pareto optimality.[2] This fictional state may be conceived as an ideal system of exchanges, and, consequently, as the ideal image of an abstract market economy, or, alternatively, as the normative image of a social mechanism achieving optimal coordination in the centralized allocation of resources, with no violation of principles of rationality in individual choices. The normative interpretation has been revived in recent literature both as a clue to historical reconstruction of the development of general equilibrium theory since the 1940s, and as a new path of research (Boldyrev and Ushakov 2015).

In widespread reading, the Arrow-Debreu model is claimed to be the formal representation of a system of complete spot and forward, interdependent, perfectly competitive markets coordinated in optimal, intertemporal equilibrium. In economic literature, the model was considered again and again as the image of a system of perfectly competitive markets, portraying the static, atemporal

1 Berta (2000) underlined the paradox of the low number of references to the notion of "market" in Debreu's writings that she explains in terms of his axiomatic epistemology.

2 For the full definition of the state of equilibrium, see Ingrao and Israel (1990, chap. 1).

image of interdependent exchanges or, in dynamic interpretation, the resting point towards which markets finally tend adjusting to equilibrium, or even as the dynamic image of intertemporal markets optimally adjusting, when shaken by unanticipated shocks. When conceived as the normative Utopia, the Arrow-Debreu model portrays the optimal state of resource allocation, which the far-sighted state planner might reach by rationally coordinating consumers and producers in the planned economy, without violating their rational maximizing plans. In all these versions, the invisible hand metaphor is at work as an underlying principle of coordination of rational, individual choices, either through the competitive price system or through some design mechanism simulating or replicating the price system. To this day, the Arrow-Debreu model of general equilibrium remains the most developed mathematical image that economic theory produced to portray the simultaneous working of a network of competitive markets, whether they be conceived as fictional images of markets properly as they should ideally be, or whether they be conceived as nuts and bolts in the allocation mechanism designed by a benevolent, rational planner.

Such equilibrium metaphors of markets have been dominant and persistent, although well-known difficulties persist in terms of mathematical results and economic interpretation in the neo-Walrasian model.[3] On the crucial questions of the uniqueness and the global stability of the neo-Walrasian general equilibrium, no major results have emerged that may radically question the critical comments Ingrao and Israel advanced since 1990, on the basis of the technical literature that had emerged since the late 1970s. The ambiguities associated with time, uncertainty and anticipations in general equilibrium models are further obstacles that have not yet been removed. They were repeatedly addressed in critical discussions on the many conceptual pitfalls in neo-Walrasian models. Since back in the late 1920s and in the 1930s, in seminal writings Hayek, Lindahl, Hicks and Morgenstern had anticipated the awkward coexistence of equilibrium and perfect foresight (or self-fulfilling expectations) in an environment of limited information and economic change. This difficulty finally imposed the adoption of the postulate of perfect farsightedness in framing the neo-Walrasian model in the 1940s and the 1950s. The perfect farsightedness by all maximizing agents operating in the markets could be postulated only by adopting the fictional

3 Both Kirman (1992, 2006) and Rizvi (2006) provided updated overviews of the technical literature on the subject, commenting extensively on the consequences of the negative results reached by Mantel, Debreu and Sonneschein. Kirman's articles critically addressed the many fallacies in neo-Walrasian general equilibrium theory that undermine its effectiveness as a conceptual tool for understanding how markets work.

device of complete forward markets for all traded goods, with the associated assumption of contracts specified for all possible contingencies in the given set of states of the world, so that no unexpected contingency might emerge, which might radically upset the rational expectations of agents and falsify their ex ante optimal plans.

A set of meanings are involved thus far: the axiomatic theory that is *per se* a mathematical object; the reading of such a mathematical object as the model of a fictional world of interactions (a fictional market economy), by imposing appropriate meaning to variables and equations; finally, the stories that are narrated by transfigurating the Chinese shadows moving in the puppetry theatre thus built into characters and situations that are related to actors and events in real markets. Does the equilibrium image of coordination conveyed by the stories told on the Arrow-Debreu general equilibrium model, conceived as the fictional image of competitive markets, fit with the invisible hand metaphor? Although the invisible hand idea was associated to it, many of the vague meanings of the invisible hand metaphor we listed above are poorly related, if at all, to its conceptual skeleton. Because of its peculiar structure, the story told on intertemporal, farsighted coordination in a general equilibrium economy fails to effectively portray the working of the invisible hand both at the metaphorical level, and in terms of a credible representation of how (and if) markets achieve coordination in environments of imperfect information and economic change. The assumptions postulated in reading the model are the perfect transparency of price and quality information; the rational, farsighted choices by all agents taking decisions; no violation of budget constraints; no social or institutional interactions among traders in the market, and the convention of instantaneous market coordination by some fictional auctioneer. These assumptions jointly exclude a whole set of competitive strategies that firms adopt in market societies, such as price competition and the choice of effective strategies of pricing, quality competition and the search for process and product innovation, advertising and the building of customer loyalty, the fight to eliminate competitors, the risk of insolvency or bankruptcy, the building of human capital, the establishment of cooperative networks with suppliers and so on and so forth. In general equilibrium, entrepreneurial profits are zero, by definition. Since 1912, Schumpeter (1912 [1934], chap. 1) had opposed the Walrasian "circular flow" in the allocation of resources to the dynamic process of destructive creation, where entrepreneurs compete to upset established markets, but also to earn entrepreneurial profits by product innovation or productivity gains. As Hayek (1990 [1978]) noted in a now forgotten article, competition is a discovery procedure whose value is in discovering what is not transparent knowledge a priori. The assumptions stated above jointly exclude the possibility of unintended consequences from intentional individual behaviour on collective social outcomes, such as those due to various externalities, innovation or bankruptcy. The hand is indeed invisible, and not even a hand, that is – if not a benevolent dictator – at least some social process of interaction that forces people to achieve coordination. The auctioneer is a concealed ghost, nothing more than a theorem of existence for a set of equations and disequations. The social consequences should be perfectly transparent once the goods, the technologies and the preferences are appropriately specified; but there is no proof of a unique optimal solution. On the other side of the coin, the constructive, normative interpretation of general equilibrium theory, which was proposed by various authors, turns the neo-Walrasian model into the intentional coordination mechanism operated by a paternalistic centralized authority, a visible hand allocating resources according to some "mechanical" procedure.

2 The consequences of the "palace revolution" in general equilibrium theory

In the light of the poor mathematical results and the persisting conceptual weaknesses, the Arrow-Debreu model was abandoned as an effective tool in economic research, though in a somewhat silent and covert way. A "palace revolution" had brought the edifice down, as Kirman (2006, 249–250) expressed it with witty humour.[4] Since the 1980s, theoretical research on neo-Walrasian models drastically declined, due to the absence of further technical results to be expected after the negative proofs reached by Mantel, Sonnenschein and Debreu in the 1970s. Many mathematical economists in the field, who could well appreciate the extent of the damage, refrained from explicit acknowledgement of what had happened; but it was well understood that scarce analytical progress was to be expected. For ambitious mathematical economists working at the edge of

4 "The warning bell was sounded by such authors as Donald Saari and Carl Simon […], whose work gave an indication, but one that has been somewhat overlooked, as to why the stability problem was basically unsolvable in the context of the general equilibrium model. The most destructive results were, of course, already there, those of Hugo Sonnenschein […], Rolf Mantel […], and Debreu […] himself. But those results show the model's weakness, not where that weakness comes from. Nevertheless, the damage was done. What is particularly interesting about that episode is that it was scholars of the highest reputation in mathematical economics who brought the edifice down. This was not a revolt of the lower classes of economists complaining about the irrelevance of formalism in economics; this was a palace revolution" (Kirman 2006, 249–250).

economic theory, general equilibrium theory lost its appeal; since the effort of research ceased to produce robust results, the field was progressively abandoned by the most innovative scholars. At the edge of research in mathematical economics, neo-Walrasian models lost pride of place in favour of game theoretic models. Having lost primacy in mathematical economics, research in the wake of the Arrow-Debreu model survived in a specialized niche of minor relevance to the current advancement of the economic discipline, while new fields of research opened up in behavioural and experimental economics.[5]

This loss of primacy signals that the general equilibrium research programme had come to a standstill in contemporary economics; it turned into a degenerative research programme. The major contribution it provided with its rigorous line of mathematical research was to help economists discover the intricacies and fallacies of the idea of general market equilibrium, when put to the test of axiomatic formalization. Notwithstanding the evidence that dead ends had been reached, testified by the practice of the most qualified professionals, no authoritative, mainstream scholar in economics certified the death of the neo-Walrasian family of models as a progressive research programme. The most authoritative scholars in the field were fully aware of the conceptual and technical difficulties. Both Arrow and Hahn, among others, explicitly dealt with the pitfalls and limitations of the Arrow-Debreu model.[6] There were a few brave critical voices; but no outstanding scholar in the economic profession ever proclaimed the failure of the line of research in the neo-Walrasian general equilibrium in achieving the goals it had pretended to achieve. The loose reference to the neo-Walrasian general equilibrium theory as the backbone of economic theory, or "the peak of neoclassical economics" to use Samuelson's (1952, 61) phrasing, did not decline, not only in popular literature, but in highly academic papers. Disappearing at the frontier of research by the late 1980s, in ample economic literature the Arrow-Debreu general equilibrium model stayed alive as the presumed image of the invisible hand that leads markets to equilibrium.

In the second half of the 20th century, economic theory saw the paradoxical, complementary development of apparently successful and well-accepted research programmes in macroeconomics inspired by the neo-Walrasian general equilibrium approach, and the parallel, drastic decline of the neo-Walrasian research programme, due to the insurmountable technical and conceptual

---

5 Rizvi (2006, 231) connected the emergence of new pluralism in microeconomics with the dead ends in general equilibrium research. The emergence of behavioural economics had, of course, older roots.

6 See e.g. Arrow (1974; 2009).

pitfalls mentioned above. This difficult coexistence proved possible because of the reticent summing up of the unsolved difficulties, but it was achieved thanks to a sophisticated technical trick. In macroeconomics, the general equilibrium approach, although being proudly vindicated, was radically supplanted by the widespread use and abuse of representative agent models, conceived as if they were general equilibrium models properly. For the reader not familiar with economists' technicalities, a representative agent model portrays the optimal, intertemporal choices of a single, rational agent, under various assumptions about the exogenous shocks that might affect the economy, the economy being resumed by the single agent's behaviour.

> The idea is to imagine that the economy is populated by the single immortal consumer, or a number of immortal consumers. […] For this consumer every firm is just a transparent instrumentality, an intermediary, a device for carrying out intertemporal optimization subject only to technological constraints and initial endowments. Thus any kind of market failure is ruled out from the beginning, by assumption. There are no strategic complementarities, no coordination failures, no Prisoners' Dilemmas. […] Inseparable from this habit of thought is the automatic presumption that observed paths are equilibrium paths (Solow 1988, 310).

The Chinese shadows moving on the puppetry theatre of markets are Hermits all alike, each one identical to the other ones. Under the representative agent assumption, the collective outcome is postulated to be effectively summarized by the optimal behaviour of the representative hermit (so to speak), which summarizes the optimal path they all will identically choose, under whichever shock might affect their isolated condition.[7] These models pretended to narrate stories about the optimal coordination of independent choices in market economies, although in their pieces only a single Chinese shadow was acting, moving with graceful rationality in optimally adapted, dynamic paths. It is, of course, hardly credible that the stories told in a representative agent scenery be interesting narratives about a market economy where millions of people interact in conditions of radical uncertainty, innovation and change. However, technically, representative agent models are more manageable than models with many agents and many goods; thus, within their simplified mathematical framework, they seemed to promise robust results and neat conclusions. They were marketed "as if" they could indeed narrate stories about complex, historical market

7 In his book on the history of contemporary macroeconomics, De Vroey (2016, chaps. 15, 16) provides an extensive survey on these hermit economies in macroeconomic modelling and their criticism.

economies. Unfortunately, the "as if" assumption that justified the shortcut was wishful thinking; an advanced technical literature clearly demonstrated that multi-agents, multi-goods, genuine general equilibrium models cannot be reduced by simplified aggregation procedures to fully equivalent representative agent models. In genuine general equilibrium theory, the crux of the difficulties was exactly that the underlying microeconomic assumptions did not impose enough structure on aggregate excess demand functions. There is no one-to-one mapping by aggregation from a disaggregated neo-Walrasian model into a fully equivalent representative agent model, unless exceedingly strong, simplifying assumptions are postulated. The interest of the theoretical exercises proposed by representative agent models is anyhow poor when we wish to deal with "strategic complementarities", "coordination failures" or "Prisoners' Dilemmas" in economic life. And the more so if we need to focus on market institutions, radical innovation and historical change. It is as if a representative car model would be chosen to study the frequency of car accidents; in the ideal experiment, poor conclusions are achieved, if it is postulated that there is no traffic, but a single car going on the roads, and not even traffic laws.

3 The delusion of optimal coordination in competitive markets in new classical macroeconomics

Since the 1950s and to the late 1970s, the crucial reference to the neo-Walrasian general equilibrium model inspired both the Keynesian scholars, who contributed to the so-called neoclassical synthesis and the scholars, on the opposite side, who promoted the so-called monetarist counterrevolution. In the 1970s and the 1980s, neo-Walrasian general equilibrium theory found enthusiastic supporters among the scholars, who promoted the rational expectation revolution in macroeconomics, building the theories and interpretations known as new classical macroeconomics. The statute of the neo-Walrasian general equilibrium model in macroeconomics is an open question even today, although meanwhile, as the evolution of research has shown, the neo-Walrasian programme is not just agonizing, but dead after a long while.

The theoretical effort of the macroeconomists in the so-called neoclassical synthesis was inspired by the effort at the reconciliation of microeconomics and macroeconomics and, notably, by the effort to adopt a general equilibrium approach in macroeconomic modelling. In 1963, Modigliani, considering the most advanced macroeconomic models of the mid-1950s, insisted on the advantage of the explicit reliance on the general equilibrium approach in macroeconomics.

> The mid-fifty model is explicitly structured in terms of markets, one for each commodity, with each market in turn described by (a) supply conditions, (b) demand conditions, and (c) clearing of market or equilibrium conditions, of which one is redundant (Walras' law). The main advantage of the general equilibrium framework is that it insures a systematic and, at least initially, symmetrical treatment of all markets (Modigliani 1963, 80–81).

In 1968, in his celebrated presidential address to the *American Economic Association*, "The Role of Monetary Policy",[8] Friedman (1968) introduced a loose reference to Walrasian general equilibrium in defining the concept of the natural rate of unemployment, a concept that dominated developments in macroeconomics in the 1970s and the 1980s, and it is still one of the basic conceptual tools in macroeconomics today.

> The "natural rate of unemployment", in other words, is the level that would be ground out by the Walrasian system of general equilibrium equations, provided there is imbedded in them the actual structural characteristics of the labor and commodity markets, including market imperfections, stochastic variability in demands and supplies, the cost of gathering information about job vacancies and labor availabilities, the costs of mobility, and so on (Friedman 1968, 8).

The implicit claim of this assertion was that such an extended model of general equilibrium equations existed, or that it could be easily produced by introducing appropriate changes in the existing system of Walrasian equations, with no major revision of its theoretical frame. It was mere wishful thinking, since such a refined version of the neo-Walrasian general equilibrium model did not exist; it was most dubious that it could ever be produced in rigorous mathematical language within the frame of the Arrow-Debreu model or other neo-Walrasian models. Moreover, the claim was predicated on the idea that real market forces could be freely disjointed from monetary ones in analysing the state of the economy.

> To avoid misunderstanding, let me emphasize that by using the term "natural" rate of unemployment, I do not mean to suggest that it is immutable and unchangeable. On the contrary, many of the market characteristics that determine its level are man-made and policy-made. [...] I use the term "natural" for the same reason Wicksell did – to try to separate the real forces from monetary forces (Friedman 1968, 9).

---

8 This address became a cornerstone in the campaign against Keynesian, active policies to curb unemployment. Friedman argued that monetary policy cannot control the rate of unemployment in the long run; the expansionary monetary policy aimed at curbing unemployment will end up promoting accelerating inflation.

Ample literature in the currents named conventionally new classical macroeconomics, which innovated macroeconomic theory since the 1970s, was built on the ambitious project to build on the general economic equilibrium approach to take into account fluctuations in business cycles. The Arrow-Debreu version of general economic equilibrium was the main source of inspiration for Lucas among the authors, who contributed to the innovative business cycle theories emerging in the 1970s. His models of equilibrium and business cycles, based on unanticipated monetary shocks, and the assumption of rational expectations, were framed in a pretended general equilibrium skeleton, with misperceptions due to local, limited information. These models were assumed to narrate stories relevant to understanding business cycles as going on in the global market economies, although the reception of such narrations was somewhat open to the free interpretation of both academic and non-academic audiences.[9]

In 1996, in his Nobel Lecture and in 2004, in recollections about the research path he had followed, Lucas explained that his research project had aimed at rebuilding macroeconomics on Walrasian foundations (Lucas 1996; 2004). He described his research project in the 1970s as inspired by the seminal book *Money, Interest, and Prices: An Integration of Monetary and Value Theory* (1965 [1956]), where Patinkin had tried to rebuild macroeconomic theory within the frame of Walrasian equilibrium theory. Although paying tribute to Patinkin, Lucas maintained that this scholar was not aware of the updated technicalities in general equilibrium theory. In facing the same task, Lucas underlined, his reference model had been the Arrow-Debreu, the neo-Walrasian version of general equilibrium, which he perceived as the most sophisticated device available to capture the working of a system of perfectly competitive markets, flexibly adaptable both to a static conception of equilibrium and to a dynamic one. This recognition was linked to Lucas's epistemological vision that progress in economic theory is primarily, if not exclusively, conquered, thanks to the advancement realized by the use of more refined instruments in mathematization or in statistical testing.[10] He wrote:

---

9 In his epistemological approach, Lucas maintained a degree of freedom in the stories about the real world that it is possible to narrate interpreting fictional mathematical models in macroeconomics. Rigorous assertions are allowed only about what is going on in the puppetry piece; any inference from the puppetry piece to the real world is just loose reasoning.

10 "And then I see [...] the progressive element in economics as entirely technical: better mathematics, better mathematical formulation, better data, better data-processing methods, better statistical methods, better computational methods. [...] more empirically founded, more powerful solution methods, and so on" (Lucas 2004, 22).

> I think Patinkin was absolutely right to try and use general equilibrium theory to think about macroeconomic problems. Patinkin and I are both Walrasians, whatever that means. I don't see how anybody cannot be. It's pure hindsight, but now I think that Patinkin's problem was that he was a student of Lange's, and Lange's version of the Walrasian model was already archaic by the end of the 1950s. Arrow and Debreu and McKenzie had redone the whole theory in a clearer, more rigorous, and more flexible way. Patinkin's book was a reworking of his Chicago thesis from the middle 1940s and had not benefited from this more recent work (Lucas 2004, 16).

Thus, Lucas placed neo-Walrasian general equilibrium models as the core theoretical foundation of his models of equilibrium and business cycles, much as he saw them as the conceptual skeleton of the family of real business cycles models, which were emerging as dominant macroeconomic theories since the early 1980s (Lucas 2013; Sargent 2015). Back in 1980, Lucas had justified the postulate of competitive equilibrium on methodological constraints, with the appeal to the economy principle that mandates to keep free parameters to the minimum in scientific explanation. To predict the collective outcome of the interaction of greedy, maximizing agents, only the rationality assumption in behaviour is required plus the idea of competitive equilibrium, as if the "invisible hand" were effectively at work at infinite speed.

> Economics is sometimes characterized as the working out of the implications of the idea that individuals pursue their self-interest, yet we have just observed how empty an idea this is, applied in isolation to even the most trivial animal experiment.[11] Can we imagine that it gains power in some mysterious way when applied to human societies with millions of participants? […] I have emphasized that it is the hypothesis of competitive equilibrium which permits group behavior to be predicted from knowledge of individual preferences and technology without the addition of any free parameters. This needs further illustration, in contexts closer to our interests than animal experiments. Employment and nominal wages are, in an immediate sense, determined by some very complicated labor market interactions involving employees and employers. It is possible, we know, to mimic the aggregate outcome of this interaction fairly well in a competitive equilibrium way, in which wages and manhours are generated by the interaction of "representative" households and firms (Lucas 1980, 710–711).

In 2004, Lucas attributed to the Arrow-Debreu formal frame, as applied to build models in macroeconomics, prodigious properties, underlying notably the

11 The argument started by the interaction of hungry apes catching bananas in a cage. No orderly collective outcome could be easily forecast as a result of the effort by each self-interest ape to catch as much pieces of bananas as possible.

possibility to convert it into all kinds of dynamic models, and even to reframe it to include monetary aspects, a hope later almost abandoned.[12]

> It got replaced by the Arrow-Debreu model, which shows how you can take what seems to be a static general equilibrium model and talk about markets for contingent claims, talk about any kind of dynamics you'd like, coming right out of the economics. No auctioneer, or the auctioneer works very quickly. Everything is accounted for in terms of preferences and technology in this model, and everything can include as much dynamics as you can get from a Tinbergen model or Slutsky's model (Lucas 2004, 22–23).

All these properties were predicated on the assumption that the Arrow-Debreu model might be simplified, reframing it into a representative agent model at no cost, either conceptual or technical. Lucas's approach is a shorthand: competitive equilibrium may be and has to be postulated "as if" no visible social arrangements to promote and reach coordination were relevant, or "as if" they could be "fairly well" summarized in "as if" wonderlands of representative agents to "mimic" markets economies. As if markets could be competitive a priori, irrespective of any institutional frame. This is a serious misconception, but it has been a dominant idea in contemporary macroeconomic modelling. In real business cycle modelling, the fictional wonderland attached to the mathematical skeleton is some hermits' economy, where, as we anticipated above, the single hermit's behaviour successfully replicates the macro variables. In such an autistic world, all hermits are identical replicants, and no social interaction affects their behaviour. In the stories attached to real business cycle models,[13] economic fluctuations of macro relevance are narrated as if they might be imagined to be due to the optimal adaptation of rational choices to unanticipated productivity shocks, instead of being narrated as if they were related to misperceptions due to monetary surprises.

A peculiar idea of the invisible hand is embedded in this vision. No auctioneer is needed, or "the auctioneer works very quickly". The prodigious ghost coordinating the fictional economy works at infinite speed and with no costs. It is

12 He had already expressed this judgement in 1980. "In particular, it is possible to construct systems in competitive equilibrium, in a contingent-claim sense, which exhibit a vast variety of dynamic behavior. The idea that an economic system in equilibrium is in any sense 'at rest' is simply an anachronism" (Lucas 1980, 708). On the contrary, in 2013, Lucas had turned sceptical on the hope to fuse monetary theory with existing macro models, which he recognized did not include money at all (Lucas 2013).

13 Their skeleton is basically a Solow's growth model with productivity shocks. For an excellent introduction to these models and their interpretation or criticism, see De Vroey (2016, chaps. 15, 16).

really invisible, since coordination in equilibrium is postulated a priori under the representative agent's assumption. No social relations are mentioned that should help the coordination job.[14] When we look at the core of the competitive equilibrium postulate, what it amounts to is to exclude any role for the legal and institutional arrangements, the political and social scaffolding or historical contingencies in the understanding of both successes and failures in coordination going on within market economies. They are not there in the picture, and the picture has been drawn from such an angle not to have them there.

It is a metaphor of the "invisible hand" powerful and concealed, far away from the ones Smith, Walras or Hayek had ever conceived. According to Walras, the *tâtonnement* process imagined in pure economics should replicate the forces of competition in an ideal way, as they operate on daily in the markets. There is ample historical debate on the balance between the normative approach versus the realistic interpretation in Walras's writings, but there is no doubt that Walras meant to portray effective forces working in competitive markets leading to the convergence to the equilibrium state, if just in an ideal way and under normative constraints. It is a conception far away from what Hayek meant by the unintended consequences rooted in custom, culture and institutions. As he underlined in his writings, the complex networks in the division of labour and knowledge in contemporary markets impose relations of trust among traders in transactions, under the dominance of social norms based on law and inner ethics, which facilitate in contemporary economies cooperation by exchanges.[15]

In 2009, Arrow wrote:

> I conclude by a speculation as to current and future developments. Economic analysis has tended to be based on individual behavior. There is assumed to be only one set of

14 "In the general equilibrium model, no 'organization' or specification of interpersonal relationships is assumed. The consistency of allocations in the sense that what individuals receive is just what they desire is achieved by an anonymous price system that all agents take to be given. Thus there is no need for any specification of the relationships within the economy; the only way in which agents communicate is through the price system. Indeed, to pursue their analyses, economists have stripped away all the institutional details and structures that were still very much present in the work of both Walras and Pareto and even more so in the work of Alfred Marshall" (Kirman 2006, 253).

15 In the years of totalitarian rule in many European countries, and soon after the end of World War II, Hayek was especially worried by the possible erosion of this cultural heritage in Europe, under the pressure of totalitarian ideologies (see Ingrao 2013, chap. viii).

> social institutions, namely, markets. Perhaps governments also matter when dealing with market failures, also called externalities. But clearly social institutions and social interactions among individuals also matter, and perhaps significantly (Arrow 2009, 14).

To scholars of social sciences, Arrow's remark sounds obvious as far as social and political life is concerned in interaction with the market economy; but this is not yet the core of the question. Social norms and institutional settings form, or course, the environment within which market activities go on, as large literature underlined in studies of economic history, development studies and political science, much as in institutional economics or in political economy.[16] The question is that the very notion of "markets" requires the reference to norms and institutions to frame the technologies used in transactions, and to establish the possibility of orderly exchanges. These institutional arrangements are part and parcel of the working of markets. In market economies, exchanges depend on relations of trust between people; on socially shared means of payments, trusted as such in the community; on networks of customers and suppliers sharing channels of communication; on labour services provided according to regulations by law or custom; on credit agreements trusted by borrowers and lenders; on property rights and regulations; on socially shared expectations regarding crime and punishment; on incentives or built-in enforcements not to violate contracts because of social norms or sanctions[17] and so on and so forth. Social norms and institutions are required to build trust and make the "many visible hands" work, which more or less make some orderly coordination possible in the exchanges, in the midst of continuous processes of innovation, change and social conflict, which go on in market societies.

---

16 Let's just remind the role Adam Smith assigned to a tolerable system of justice, or to agrarian contracts, and other institutional settings to promote the wealth of nations, on which ample historical literature exists. The historical studies on the industrial revolution gave relevant space to institutions, much as recent research in development studies. The field is too broad to be surveyed here. For two ambitious books focused on the interaction of political institutions and markets, see *Violence and Social Orders: A Conceptual Framework for Interpreting Recorded Human History* (2009) by North, Wallis and Weingast, and *Political Order and Political Decay: From the Industrial Revolution to the Globalization of Democracy* (2014) by Fukuyama. See also North, Wallis, Webb and Weingast (2012).

17 On the enforcement of contracts, see Bowles and Gintis (1993).

4 The unintended consequences of depressions and financial crises

In summary, an ample literature in new classical macroeconomics was built on the ambitious project to account for fluctuations in business cycles within the general economic equilibrium approach, and notably on the assumed foundation of neo-Walrasian models (or pretended neo-Walrasian models). The analytical and conceptual questions, which stand unsolved in existing neo-Walrasian models, were ignored or put aside; no mention at all of the "palace revolution" that had "brought the edifice down". The puzzle that this silence proposes will be dealt with in the last paragraph; but further legitimate questions arise. Whether fluctuations in a market economy be narrated as caused by real productivity shocks (as in real business cycles models) or by unanticipated monetary shocks (as in the earlier macroeconomic models in the 1970s), why was it considered so crucial to look at them as being just the optimal trembling of the invisible hand under exogenous shocks? Why should economists adopt, as Lucas argued, the equilibrium postulate looking at business cycles, instead of dealing with fluctuations in income and employment as serious disequilibrium phenomena in plans, and the flows of market transactions? Why should severe depressions be explained on metaphors evoking the optimal reaction of a perfectly coordinated system responding to exogenous shocks?

In principle, there is no immediate empirical evidence, whether based on historical events or on intuitive understanding of how the economy works, to justify such a presumption. Contrary to Lucas's argument, singular occurrences (to paraphrase Lucas's jargon) are in the essence of the business cycle phenomenon, so much so that Fisher (1933, 338) maintained that the business cycle does not exist as such in historical events, and Hicks (1982 [1981]) suggested that there is no standard business cycle. Each historical episode of boom and depression shows a peculiar sequence of events. Up to today economic historians discuss how the refusal by the Clearing Banks of New York to guarantee the liabilities of the Bank of United States precipitated its insolvency in 1930, or how conflicts on bailouts and monetary intervention among executives at the Federal Reserve Bank of Chicago and at the Federal Reserve Bank of New York precipitated banking panics in the worst phase of the Great Depression. In political history, crucial events are an essential part of the sequences of events that follow; they are notably so also in economic fluctuations, as far as historical episodes and not just theoretical exercises about wonderlands are concerned.[18]

18 In his book *Gli ultimi giorni: Stati che crollano nell'Europa del Novecento* [Last days. Collapsing States in 20th Century Europe] (2009), historian Macry studies the crucial

Lucas dealt with the Great Depression in the 1930s as an exceptional occurrence that is not to be explained by ordinary business cycle theories. He conjectured that its severity was the effect of the poor management of monetary policies, a thesis already advanced by Friedman. The villain of the piece was looked at outside the business world and its practices, to put the blame exclusively on the invasive or incompetent hand of the state. The central bankers' hands were, of course, poorly effective during the worst depression years: "a disaster of miscalculation and obduracy all around" (Eichengreen 2015, 166). However, economic historians debate on the complex roots of the disaster of failed monetary policies, with a diagnosis on the severity of the Great Depression that includes a full range of market failures in finance and the real economy, much as institutional frailties in the domestic and international monetary system, heavy debts in both the private sector and public administrations or the perverse spiralling down of world trade.

In major depressions, historical evidence converges to signal the failure in the coordination of both intertemporal and simultaneous choices, the widespread difficulties in balancing budgets, the widespread disappointment of anticipations, the erosion of trust in market transactions, all prominent market phenomena during depression times and acute during severe financial crises. In financial history, all financial crises prove that there were no perfect markets for contingencies that could cover the emerging risks with appropriate contracts. Families, firms, banks and financial institutions went bankrupt, or were seriously affected by the fall of their income and wealth. They had plainly not been able to buy at equilibrium prices the contingency claims that should have protected their balance sheets from the risks associated to the set of all possible states of the world over their decision horizon. Coordination failures in financial crises unleash severe unintended consequences from individual behaviour to collective outcomes, because of imitative expectations and herding behaviour in financial markets, liquidity traps, credit rationing and credit crunches or the domino effects of bankruptcies, all phenomena well known to scholars who studied recurring financial crises or major depressions, such as the Great Depression in the 1930s and the Great Recession in 2007–2009.

In pursuing the dream of optimal equilibrium paths, the core of macroeconomic theory failed to deal with the many gaps in the market coordination of

failures by public authorities to act effectively, which accelerate the sudden collapse of States, as it was the case of the tsarist Empire in 1917 or the Austro-Hungarian Monarchy in 1918.

private choices and intertemporal plans during periods of depressions and financial crises, as they clearly emerged on the international scenery in well-known historical episodes. In 2009, almost ten years ago, Leijonhufvud, monetary economist and historian of economic thought, reminded this uncomfortable truth.

> The efficient markets hypothesis of modern finance theory is incorporated as a component of dynamic stochastic general equilibrium theories. Its core assumption that future returns are normally distributed fits neatly into rational expectations models but has been proven false innumerable times. The repeated occurrence of financial crashes or crises hardly seems consistent with intertemporal equilibrium theory. A list covering only the last 20 years would include the October 1987 stock-market crash on Wall Street and the Norway banking crisis in the same year, followed by Japan (1990), Sweden and Finland (1991), the East Asian crises (1997), Russia (1998) and Brazil (1999), the US dotcom crash (2000), Argentina (2001), with the latest instalment being the on-going credit crisis centred in the USA (Leijonhufvud 2009, 749–750).

Financial crises evoke the question: why did a major systemic failure happen in saving plans, in portfolio choices, in insurance against risk, involving the diffusion of insolvencies and bankruptcies? Economic theory has been elusive on insolvencies and bankruptcies. Insolvencies and bankruptcies cannot occur in the ideal Arrow-Debreu economy: by assumption, each and every agent is committed not to violate his or her budget constraint and, by assumption, the intertemporal budgets constraints are coordinated ex ante by the invisible hand of the ghost auctioneer. What do insolvency or bankruptcy mean, in theoretical terms, as far as the working of markets is concerned?

The risk of insolvency signals the difficulty or the impossibility for an economic unit to meet the commitments for payments that were agreed on in contracts. The insolvent economic agent is at risk of violating his or her budget constraint; he or she has miscalculated the cash flows over the relevant time horizon of the budget. Unless the delinquency in payments at due times had been rationally planned ex ante, a situation that implies the voluntary break of the social rules of behavioural fairness in voluntary contracts, the agent has neither rationally planned nor rationally anticipated the inability to pay according to the outstanding contracts that he or she had signed. The expected cash flows did not materialize at the right time to balance the flows of payments, or they have been overvalued as far as market prices, incomes, sales or assets' values were concerned. The firm or family may become insolvent and turn bankrupt because of a long-term imbalance in the balance sheet or because of a liquidity crisis; in the latter case, the long-term balance sheet is balanced in terms of net wealth, but the timing of flows is not properly balanced. Payments are due, which cannot be postponed until the required cash flows to cover them become available.

Bankruptcy may be forced by a liquidity crisis even if the firm or the family might in principle dispose of positive net wealth over their intertemporal horizon. If they have none or limited access to credit, the liquidity crisis cannot be overcome by today's debt against future incomes or the future sales of assets. For the individual economic unit, insolvency may signal a cognitive deficiency in terms of rational, intertemporal planning; but it may also result as the unintended consequence of systemic conditions. The rational intertemporal planning of the single unit is disrupted by other agents' insolvencies and bankruptcies, due to the state of the macro economy at large, the loss of employment, the unexpected reversal of price trends and so on and so forth for unexpected shocks or systemic failures affecting private incomes or wealth. The perceived risk of insolvency affects the spending behaviour of families and firms and the availability of credit; credit rationing by banks or other financial institutions may result because of the higher perceived risks of insolvencies in the macro economy (Bernanke 1981; 1983).

A bankruptcy is a socially recognized impossibility by an economic unit to meet monetary commitments according to contracts; it involves the agreement to be reached among debtors and creditors according to the laws in force, after procedures of evaluation and negotiation. It requires costly legal controversies to settle the disorder it created in the flow of payments, and it affects the reputation of the bankrupt unit, with legal consequences. As far as systemic consequences are concerned, a bankruptcy may be of minor or major relevance according to the size of the bankrupt unit; if the agent going bankrupt is a large bank (e.g. "too big to fail"), the settlement requires complex agreements to be reached among many agents, with substantial losses to be more or less fairly attributed to some, or all, of them. To give but a historical example, the suspension of payments by the Credit Anstald Bank in 1931, a major Austrian bank and financial institution "too big to fail" in Europe at the time, opened the way to controversial negotiations, whose impasse and dead ends precipitated the financial crises in Europe and worldwide (Eichengreen 2015, 140–143). More recent examples, as the Lehman Brothers's collapse, are well known.

Insolvencies and bankruptcies are unintended and unanticipated consequences of both social interaction and individual choices. They signal a major failure in the coordination of economic choices by the single family or firm over the time horizon, but also a major failure in social interaction. The missing payments by one family or firm affect the balance sheets of other families or firms that had scheduled them in their cash flows, to discover they cannot cash them at all. When the invisible hand has, so to speak, gone bankrupt, visible agents in their social roles (executives, lawyers, courts, government officials, central bankers and so on and so forth) have to sit in visible meetings to see how debts and credits should be arranged, and finally agree on who should pay what to whom. Here the visible hands and brains making markets work come to light.

5 The many visible hands at work in the market economy

The efficacy of a metaphor is to open the mind to a novel conception, to illuminate or suggest by a powerful image a new world of meanings. Does the metaphor of the invisible hand, as it is embedded in the imagery of general economic equilibrium, invite us to explore how markets work? When we think of the "as if" ghost auctioneer in fictional competitive markets of the Arrow-Debreu type, do we open our mind to the deeper, intuitive understanding of social interaction in market transactions? Do we conquer a graphic picture of how hundreds of thousands or millions of people get to manage millions of markets transactions? The answer is plain: No. As far as contemporary market economies are in question, in their varieties in today's global world, the metaphor of the invisible hand is biased and ill conceived, whatever might have been its philosophical relevance in the history of economic ideas in the 18th, 19th or the early 20th century.

The main point is simple and straightforward: no auctioneer exists to make the complex network of market transactions, on which our lives depend, work in a smooth way, to reach that state of fictional, optimal coordination that is theoretically classified as an equilibrium state. Markets comprise a motley collection of intertwined social institutions, dealing with production and allocation of resources in time, in environments undergoing continuous innovation and change. No centralized authority exists, which might collect and spread the appropriate information, communicate and set prices, or have the power to impose whichever optimal allocation of resources in real time. No a priori, perfect coordination of agents' intertemporal choices is established through the flow of market transactions. There are even no optimal, intertemporal plans to coordinate, ex ante or ex post, in dynamic adjustment to unanticipated shocks. People's choices result from the strategies they have been able to devise in conditions of radical uncertainty; the strategies are forward-looking guidelines that have to be converted into sequences of choices by adapting choices facing surprises, innovation or constraints. People redesign their economic strategies anew by inventive imagination, conceiving new paths and opportunities; creative, constructive imagination is a powerful instrument, but economic agents operate with limited means, information and cognitive capabilities. A large literature exists on these limits and how they affect market choices and coordination in exchange. Economic strategies and their evolution in patterns of choices go on in path-dependent, irreversible time processes. In advanced market economies, each sensible person (not to speak of an intelligent, well-informed one) is aware of radical uncertainty, possible mistakes, deceptions, changes and irreversibility in economic strategies and market choices.

Sociologist Tilly (1996, 592) has suggested the metaphor of the "invisible elbow"[19] to underline that purposeful social action is subject to continuous disappointment as far as expected results are concerned, and that "all social interaction contains incessant errors, constantly corrected". According to his suggestion, durable order in social structures depends also on the socially shared correction mechanisms that people apply to their purposeful social action, such as they are set by culture and social ties, in an evolving pattern. He wrote:

> System inheres not only in available alternatives and patterns of choice among them, but also in orderly constraints on error-correction set by culture, social ties, their interaction, their change (Tilly 1996, 592).

The complex structure of institutions, which surround and structure market transactions, developed to reduce uncertainty on reciprocal commitments; to protect fairness, accountability, performance and to avoid violation of signed contracts. They include money, property rights, civil and penal law, government, the practices of financial institutions that manage the system of payments, the stock and commodities exchanges and so on and so forth. Markets comprise local, partial systems of coordination, special markets within markets, with staff and organization, which work to continuously adapt coordination in transactions, to smooth arising disequilibria in an environment that generates endogenous innovation and change. Not always the set of institutions is so established and well functioning to prevent or avoid financial crises, bankruptcies, unemployment, loss of human capital, extreme inequalities or conflicts. Neither the providential ghost auctioneer is there, nor the visible hand or powerful elbow of the benevolent (or perhaps malignant) dictator. It is time to abandon the metaphor of the invisible hand, in its multiple meanings, if we really wish to understand how market economies work to facilitate the encounter of so many needs and desires, to supply so many different producers and consumers with flows of goods and services, though voluntary contracts and payments.

19 The aid of the "elbow" (Tilly 1996), when the hands are full with loads, indicates a correction mechanism that helps to reach a certain aim (to open a door in the story) by the flexible adaptation of means to end under constraints.

Markets work, more or less smoothly, thanks to visible hands, bodies and brains and visible communication systems. While specific communication systems may be more or less centralized, many of them are decentralized and local. The active behaviour and dynamic strategies of single agents, or groups of agents, take care of partial coordinating activities, within evolving institutional settings, in processes of change over time. Whatever might be and is the relevance of the price system to facilitate the clearing of markets, markets clear, as far as they clear, thanks to more varied institutions and processes than the pricing mechanism. These include networks of logistics, marketing, transport, research, trade and finance that are not coordinated ex ante and a priori, now and forever; they operate by adjustment processes in time, which may succeed or fail. The actors of both the innovative and the adaptive changes going on are trained private people or trained public officials, accountable workers or executives in public and private organizations, who actively and purposefully create economic change. They act not simultaneously, now and forever, but in irreversible sequences in time. They act on expectations, in an uncertain environment that is subject both to external shocks and endogenous evolution.

In market economies, a rich set of social networks, professional activities and specialized agencies help to promote coordination in production and exchange, with more or less frail tools of communication, negotiation and enforcement. The orderly coordination, more or less effective, of millions of transactions allocating resources in current economic activity, or as far as future payments and commitments are planned, is neither the result of the instantaneous deliberation of whatever agency, visible or invisible, auctioneer or planner, nor the prodigious effect achieved by invisible social forces. Partial coordination is achieved by the simultaneous effort of visible hands, which produce it purposively, within spheres of cooperative interaction, or as the intended result of profit-seeking activities. Market agents themselves produce innovative change, with improved opportunities for orderly coordination, or increasing risks of disequilibria, imbalances and conflicts.

6 How is coordination achieved in markets with no visible or invisible auctioneer?

Let us think of the property markets. These are markets where highly differentiated goods are demanded and supplied by millions of potential buyers and sellers. No auctioneer exists to coordinate their desires, or to adjust their balance sheets to make ends meet for each of them, and finally to make demand meet supply for each specific good that is traded. Transactions in properties form a network of bilateral exchanges of non-standard goods, each of whom is to be priced before being put on the market.[20] Most often, potential buyers reach the final decision to buy in a process of sequential search, choices being adapted to emerging opportunities, or constraints. Thousands of real estate agents, privately or in real estate companies, work to locally collect and spread information, to advertise the selling or buying opportunities in the media or on the web, to price each different property according to good criteria for effective pricing, to help potential buyers and sellers bargain, to guarantee by appropriate procedures that regular contracts be signed and not violated, and to respect existing laws and regulations. The pricing of houses to be sold is a specific profession, and real estate agents are active promoters of the encounter between demand and supply, locally or within larger areas. Banks and financial institutions are also players in the property markets. They provide the payment systems without which most transactions could not be realized at all, and they assess the creditworthiness of the traders, who may access the market. After detailed, more or less sound inquiries, banks or other financial, private or public agencies finance potential buyers to overcome liquidity constraints, assessing their capability to incur debt and repay in the future. Technically, to provide the possibility of intertemporal substitution for each liquidity-constrained buyer, lot of trained staff in financial institutions have to design and market mortgage contracts, staff who must have the human capital to soundly assess creditworthiness. No transparent information is fully available, a priori; the risk of default is to be cautiously evaluated, with possible mistakes, as it happens. No all-knowing auctioneer will cover the risk for each and every possible contingency, as in theoretical intertemporal equilibrium with complete, forward markets. Private buyers may turn insolvent; real estate companies may go bankrupt; banks or mortgage companies collapse. Or, by sound prudential practices, sufficient information gathering and spreading, and intelligent rules of behaviour, they manage to achieve their visible hands' job (helping, e.g., a young couple get their first house with sustainable mortgage). Their joint work as professional market agents helps to bargain the equilibrium price, and clear the specific transaction, or stabilize the specific property market at reasonable disequilibrium conditions. Hundreds of thousands of trained, specialized employees and executives participate in these markets, assessing prices and creditworthiness, evaluating the risks, devising strategies to expand the pool

20 The retail insurance markets are similarly a network of bilateral exchanges of non-standard goods, each of whom is priced before being put on the market. Insurances are marketed by specialized agents.

of potential buyers or to capture new flows of funds from potential financers, innovating the services they offer to speed the encounter between buyers and sellers. They play a crucial role in helping demand meet supply over the time horizon of many years often needed to repay a bank loan, not to speak of the complex organization required to collect the funds flowing into the property markets, whose fragility in covering risks was so evident in the 1930s as in the 2007–2009 financial crises.[21]

Markets are extended networks of bilateral, monetary transactions regulated through voluntary contracts, whose design and rules depend on jurisprudence and custom. All market activities are regulated by civil and penal law and have to conform to administrative regulations; they are overviewed and sanctioned by various government agencies. The coordination of such an ample set of bilateral, monetary transactions requires the creative, daily presence of specialized traders, executives, employees and even down-to-the-street sellers, who sell out in street markets the residual goods no more apt to be sold through more formal channels of trade. In each trade, active strategies of process and product innovation aim at facilitating the coordination of exchanges in local or global markets. Their results are more or less effective in achieving the end, or nurture, by biases in the system of incentives and the building up of frail debts, the possibility of future failures and crises.[22] The multiple systems for the coordination of independent choices do not work just on the transparent signal of prices; they depend on a variety of communication networks, which work or fail depending on their resilience or fragility, on custom, on regulations and effectiveness of sanctions or investment in human capital for training. The many visible hands may fail to be effective in achieving some measure of orderly coordination, not only in front of major shocks, but as a result of poor leadership, educational gaps, lack of resources, excessive exposure to risk, misplaced regulations or other institutional

21 One of the dramatic aspects of the Great Depression was the bankruptcies of farmers who could not repay the mortgages on their farms due to the fall of agricultural prices; their insolvency had domino effects on the financial fragility of local banks. The foreclosures that followed caused social unrest (Hiltzik 2011). As it is well known, the miscalculation of risks in the mortgage markets was a crucial aspect in the sub-prime crisis in 2007–2009.

22 Soon before the Great Depression, aggressive strategies of selling equities to private subscribers had inflated the Stock exchange speculative bubble. Soon before the Great Recession, aggressive marketing strategies by real estate agents and financial institutions had inflated both prices and sub-prime mortgage financing in property markets.

failures. Since no auctioneer is acting at infinite speed to clear individual choices in market transactions, specialized workers and executives work daily to make demand and supply meet with no unsustainable disequilibrium, trying to monitor and adjust daily the disequilibria arising. The contingencies, when they arise, far from being included in advance in exhaustive ex ante contingency claims, have to be assessed carefully, evaluating their causes and effects, as it happens in the event of a car crash or a natural disaster.[23] The assessments, which estimate the terms of compensation necessary to adapt market prices to the specific contingency, through monetary payments, require teams of trained specialists in insurance contracts, not to speak of judges in courts or public servants in government offices when procedures require going to court or appeal to public administration. Markets could not have developed as they did in history had not the expansion of the private and government services they require been growing with the network of bilateral exchanges, thanks to investment in human capital and resources, or the expansion of public administrations.

In 1973, Leijonhufvud advanced the conjecture that it is known as "the corridor hypothesis". The conjecture suggests that the macroeconomic system will behave differently when it is disturbed by minor shocks that move it from its full employment equilibrium path, or when it is subject to major shocks. With perturbations within a certain range, counteracting tendencies will bring the system back, or at least near, full employment equilibrium, the stability band being named "the corridor". With severe perturbations, the macroeconomic system may go out of the corridor, entering a destabilizing path, where the counteracting forces do not bring it back to full employment equilibrium, and the deviations from equilibrium upset the coordinating mechanisms (Leijonhufvud 1973; 2009). Leijonhufvud's conjecture proposes a mixed biological and mechanical metaphor, referring to homeostasis; the invisible hand – to apply the older metaphor that is the subject of this chapter – is imagined as a homeostasis mechanism that works effectively only within limits, to keep the economy on

23 Historian Eichengreen (2015, 318), discussing public policies after the two major financial crises in the last 100 years, the Great Depression and the Great Recession, observed that in the 1930s the federal government had to hire 20.000 specialists to assess and oversee the mortgage restructuring needed to face the insolvencies in the repayments due by homeowners, achieving to help only one in ten homeowners at risk of insolvency. This was a major effort, and a similar effort did not materialize in the 2007–2009 crisis also because a larger commitment of manpower would have been required, at heavy cost, due to the greater complexity of mortgage finance and the higher number of homeowners at risk of insolvency.

its intertemporal, full employment equilibrium path. The macro economy may fall into destabilizing adjustment processes, which do not converge back to full-coordination equilibrium, for a significant period of time. Fisher had advanced a similar conjecture in formulating his debt-deflation theory of great depressions in the early 1930s. He had proposed the metaphor of "the 'capsizing' of a ship"; the ship, after being tipped beyond a certain angle by the waves, will show no tendency to return to equilibrium, and will sink (Fisher 1933, 339).

These conjectures are a precious reminder to avoid both extreme visions of market economies: the catastrophist one, seeing the always impending crisis, or the permanent instability of market societies, on one side of the coin; the invisible hand faith, on the other side, predicating the optimality of market equilibrium, and its self-adjusting, stable persistence. The corridor hypothesis, or Fisher's metaphor of the capsizing ship, are useful reminders that the vision of markets as mysterious, perfectly oiled, self-adjusting mechanisms should be radically rejected. Each severe depression, each financial crisis, needs the attentive study of myopic strategies adopted by actors in the business and financial world; of biased incentive mechanisms built-in in the existing market institutions; of poorly designed transaction technologies; of financial fragility in the balance sheets of families, firms and financial institutions; of the spreading of destabilizing, imitative expectations and of various regulatory failures. They call into question the choices made by governments and central bankers in acting as authoritative, visible hands to restore trust, support families at risk, bail out banks and firms, or lend as lenders of last resort.

The relevance of institutions and their architecture to the stability of market economies, the role of incentives and their possible biases in affecting economic behaviour and market coordination, the effects of limited information on the working of markets, the systemic effects of bankruptcies or of the perception of bankruptcy risk, the contagion of expectations, the bounded rationality in economic choices or other deviations from the paradigm of Olympian rationality have been widely explored and accounted for in economic literature, in the history of economic ideas and in economic theory properly. They have been explored in historical literature on the main episodes of depressions and financial crises, in theoretical and historical research on speculative bubbles in stock markets and property markets, in experimental and behavioural economics, in the field named economics of information, in models of macroeconomic disequilibrium, in models and theories addressing incomplete markets and asymmetric information, and so on and so forth. They have been addressed from a variety of perspectives, with interesting and fruitful results, which were not and could not have been encompassed within a unique, formal theory, not to speak of a unique, overall mathematical frame. We drove the inspiration for the summary overview attempted in this chapter from various pieces of these trends of research.

Still, the question remains open: why the invisible hand equilibrium imagery did not fade out? Why is it still the reference metaphor of markets, notably in macroeconomics? This question invites an exploration in the sociology of science more than in theoretical economics.

7 A puzzle in the sociology of science

The contemporary mainstream in economics, as various scholars have underlined, has a mixed and flexible core, which cannot be reduced to the old-style neoclassical paradigm. Today, "mainstream" economics covers a variety of fields of research and different families of models. Quite paradoxically, the neo-Walrasian imagery still seems to dominate as the economists' core metaphor on some hidden mechanism in the working of markets, although it is neither analytically sound, nor credible or reliable as the fictional story of how real markets work. The evolution of macroeconomics under the delusion of the great achievements of general equilibrium theory poses a major puzzle in the sociology of economics as a discipline. Why was the Arrow-Debreu model the reference metaphor of the invisible hand in standard macroeconomics just in the years when it was losing its appeal as an effective research engine among the mathematical economists, who had more actively promoted its development? This persistence, and the failure to openly acknowledge what should be considered the bankruptcy of this line of research, raises interesting questions about the sociology of the validation of theories in economics. In their recent book, Düppe and Weintraub (2014) carefully studied the attribution of scientific credit, and recognition, for the theorem of existence in general economic equilibrium theory, in terms of the social and interpersonal dynamics within academic communities at the time. They failed to see, or suggest, that a similar problem is open regarding the assessment of the global success or failure of the neo-Walrasian research program. On this, a curtain of silence prevails in the economic profession, although the question looks like being relevant, and disturbing.

Mathematical models in economics, as both theories and engines of formal research, are validated as instruments of research in processes of assessment by powerful academic communities, quite independently from the falsification against evidence associated to each specific model, or family of models. By the dominant criteria of assessment, mathematical models in economics do not need to be realistic representations of economic phenomena observed in reality;

they are conceived as thought experiments, parallel worlds of imagination, theoretical case studies or even economic fables (Ingrao 2015). In academic communities in departments of economics, the tendency prevails to freely explore fictional wonderlands embodied in mathematical models, "as if" they could capture some inner core of economic behaviour, or economic interaction, independently of any precise criterion of conformity to characteristics or real traits in observable market behaviour, or in market economies as we know them by contemporary evidence or by historical research and narration. The criterion of falsification of mathematical models against empirical evidence is absent in large part of economic theory. When it is taken into account, models are all the same conceived as depicting "as if" fictional worlds, which are acceptable, provided their simulations might somewhat replicate the trends of relevant economic variables. The degree of mimicry acceptable is blurred, and it may be manipulated by manipulating statistical techniques.

This modelization freedom is predicated and practised under a variety of epistemologies; it is rarely questioned in the profession, as far as theoretical economics is concerned. Academic scholars promote and validate the adoption of new families of mathematical models as opening fruitful fields of research, by crowning the presumed achievements they open up, mostly on the basis of shared ideologies, or on the perceived promises in terms of further formal results, that is by the production of academic papers according to conventional standards of scientific research shared within the dominant communities. Most academic communities in economic departments share the common aim to show up as hard scientists, affirming in their own and wider communities that their discipline is hard science, by imposing the strict adherence to the criterion of mathematization, and by the use of advanced statistical techniques in pursuing evidence. In the multi-faced mainstream in macroeconomics, the dominant aim of much of highly academic research is to pursue assumed scientific methods by the mathematization of the economic discourse, applying mathematical and statistical techniques already validated in the so-called hard sciences. Economic scholars compete in the game to emerge as advanced scientists in the eyes of their own colleagues of competing communities or versus larger communities of scientists. They compete by producing sophisticated mathematical models whose degree of technical sophistication is by itself considered a mark of scientific achievement as opposed to the use of less complex technical languages, or as opposed to the discursive languages of culture that are the domain of the humanities. These are considered tantamount to plain chatter by the overwhelming majority of professional economists, quite independently from the discerning insights that they might offer.

Thus, to address the puzzle of the persistence of the invisible hand imagery in mainstream macroeconomics, a sociology of science perspective should be adopted. As far as Lucas's ideology was concerned, back in the 1960s, the Arrow-Debreu model was perceived as the top achievement in technicality by the profession. The idea might be justified (with qualifications) in the early 1960s; it is certainly not justified today. A stubborn, myopic attitude was at stake as far as the postulate of rationality in behaviour was concerned, ignoring ample literature on bounded rationality (in its various meanings), and moreover ignoring creative, constructive intelligence in economic life. A strong element of ideology was dominant in the idea to portray the interdependent choices of millions, as if they were but the rational plan of a single representative agent. The idea, on which so many mainstream models in macroeconomics were built, defies even the common-sense intuition of the "invisible hand" metaphor. It is difficult to conceive why the social interaction of millions of diverse agents in millions of market transactions should be easily reduced to the farsighted, optimal plan of a single rational agent even in abstract theory! Whatever its ideological or sociological roots might be, to be explored in further historical research, the open puzzle signals the poor ability by authoritative scientific communities in economics to assess the validity of their research on a sound Popperian criterion of falsifiability, or even by the logical criterion of robust mathematical results.

References

Ahmad, Syed. 1990. "Adam Smith's Four Invisible Hands." *History of Political Economy* 22: 137–144.

Arrow, Kenneth J. 1974. "Limited Knowledge and Economic Analysis." *American Economic Review* 64: 1–10.

Arrow, Kenneth J. 2009. "Some Developments in Economic Theory Since 1940: An Eyewitness Account." *Annual Review of Economics* 1: 1–16.

Arrow, Kenneth J., and Frank F. Hahn. 1971. *General Competitive Analysis.* Amsterdam: North Holland.

Berta, Nathalie. 2000. "Le marché dans le modèles de Gérard Debreu." *Recherches Economiques de Louvain* 66: 303–308.

Bernanke, Ben S. 1981. "Bankruptcy, Liquidity and Recession." *The American Economic Review* 71: 155–159.

Bernanke, Ben S. 1983. "Nonmonetary Effects of the Financial Crisis in the Propagation of the Great Depression." *The American Economic Review* 73: 257–276.

Boldyrev, Ivan, and Alexey A. Ushakov. 2015. "Adjusting the Model to Adjust the World: Constructive Mechanisms in Postwar General Equilibrium Theory." *Journal of Economic Methodology* 23: 38–56.

Bowles, Samuel, and Herbert Gintis. 1993. "The Revenge of Homo Economicus: Contested Exchange and the Revival of Political Economy." *The Journal of Economic Perspectives* 7: 83–102.

De Vroey, Michel. 2016. *A History of Macroeconomics from Keynes to Lucas and Beyond*. New York: Cambridge University Press.

Debreu, Gerard. 1959. *Theory of Value. An Axiomatic Analysis of Economic Equilibrium*. New Haven and London: Yale University Press.

Debreu, Gerard. 1986. "Theoretic Models: Mathematical Form and Economic Content." *Econometrica* 54: 1259–1270.

Düppe, Till, and E. Roy Weintraub. 2014. *Finding Equilibrium: Arrow, Debreu, McKenzie and the Problem of Scientific Credit*. Princeton: Princeton University Press.

Eichengreen, Barry. 2015. *Hall of Mirrors. The Great Depression, the Great Recession and the Uses – and Misuses – of History*. Oxford and New York: Oxford University Press.

Fisher, Irving. 1933. "The Debt-Deflation Theory of Great Depressions." *Econometrica* 1: 337–357.

Friedman, Milton. 1968. "The Role of Monetary Policy." *American Economic Review* 58, Mar. 1: 1–17.

Fukuyama, Francis. 2014. *Political Order and Political Decay: From the Industrial Revolution to the Globalization of Democracy*. New York: Farrar, Straus and Giroux.

Grampp, William D. 2000. "What Did Smith Mean by the Invisible Hand?" *Journal of Political Economy* 108: 441–465.

Hahn, Frank. 1982. "Reflections on the Invisible Hand." *Lloyds Bank Review* 144: 1–21.

Hayek, Friedrich August von. 1990 [1978]. "Competition as a Discovery Procedure." In *New Studies in Philosophy, Politics, Economics and the History of Ideas*, 179–190. London: Routledge.

Hicks, John. 1982 [1981]. "Are There Economic Cycles?" In *Money, Interest and Wages, Collected Essays on Economic Theory*, vol. II, 332–346. Oxford: Basil Blackwell.

Hiltzik, Michael. 2011. *The New Deal: A Modern History*. New York: Free Press.

Ingrao, Bruna. 1998. "Invisible Hand." In *The Elgar Companion to Classical Economics*, edited by Heinz D., Kurz and Neri Salvadori, vol. I, A-K, 436–442. Cheltenham: Edward Elgar Publishing.

Ingrao, Bruna. 2013. *Portraits of European Economists*. Roma: Aracne editrice.

Ingrao, Bruna. 2015. "La pile instable d'assiettes. Contes économiques et récits romanesques." *Récit romanesque et modèle économique, Romanesque* 7: 67–85, Paris: Classique Garniers.

Ingrao, Bruna, and Giorgio Israel. 1990. *The Invisible Hand: Economic Equilibrium in the History of Science*. Cambridge (MA): MIT Press.

Khalil, Elias L. 2000. "Making Sense of Adam Smith's Invisible Hand: Beyond Pareto Optimality and Unintended Consequences." *Journal of the History of Economic Thought* 22: 49–63.

Kirman, Alan. 1992. "Whom or what does the representative agent represent?" *Journal of Economic Perspectives* 6, Spring: 117–136

Kirman, Alan. 2006. "Demand Theory and General Equilibrium: From Explanation to Introspection, a Journey down the Wrong Road." *History of Political Economy* 38: 246–280.

Leijonhufvud, Axel. 1973. "Effective Demand Failures." *The Scandinavian Journal of Economics* 75: 27–48.

Leijonhufvud, Axel. 2009. "Out of the Corridor: Keynes and the Crisis." *Cambridge Journal of Money, Credit and Banking* 33: 741–757.

Lucas, Robert E. Jr. 1980. "Methods and Problems in Business Cycle Theory." *Journal of Political Economy* 12: 696–715.

Lucas, Robert E. Jr. 1996. "Nobel Lecture: Monetary Neutrality." *Journal of Political Economy* 104: 661–682.

Lucas, Robert E. Jr. 2004. "My Keynesian Education." *History of Political Economy*, Annual Supplement, 36: 12–24.

Lucas, Robert E. Jr. 2013. "Introduction." In *Collected Papers on Monetary Theory*, edited by Max Gillman, pp. xvii-xxx. Cambridge: Harvard University Press.

Macry, Paolo. 2009. *Gli ultimi giorni. Stati che crollano nell'Europa del Novecento*. Bologna: Il Mulino.

Modigliani, Franco. 1963. "The Monetary Mechanism and Its Interaction with Real Phenomena." *The Review of Economics and Statistics* 45(1): 79-107.

North, Douglass, C., John Joseph Wallis, and Barry R. Weingast. 2009. *Violence and Social Orders. A Conceptual Framework for Interpreting Recorded Human History*. Cambridge: Cambridge University Press.

North, Douglass, C., John Joseph Wallis, Steven B. Webb, and Barry R. Weingast, eds. 2012. *In the Shadow of Violence: Politics, Economics and the Problems of Development*, Cambridge: Cambridge University Press.

Patinkin, Don. 1965 [1956]. *Money, Interest, and Prices: An Integration of Monetary and Value Theory*. New York: Row Peterson & Company.

Rizvi, S. Abu Turab. 2006. "The Sonnenschein-Mantel-Debreu Results after Thirty Years." *History of Political Economy* 38: 228–245.

Rothschild, Emma. 1994. "Adam Smith and the Invisible Hand." *American Economic Review* 84: 210–220.

Samuels, Warren J. (assisted by Marianne F. Johnson and William H. Perry). 2011. *Erasing the Invisible Hand. Essays on an Elusive and Misused Concept in Economics*. Cambridge: Cambridge University Press.

Samuelson, Paul A. 1952. "Economic Theory and Mathematics--An Appraisal." *The American Economic Review* 42, 2. Papers and Proceedings of the Sixty-fourth Annual Meeting of the American Economic Association, May: 56–66.

Sargent, Thomas J. 2015. "Robert E. Lucas, Jr.'s *Collected Papers on Monetary Theory*." *Journal of Economic Literature* 53: 43–64.

Schumpeter Joseph. A. 1934 [1912]. *The Theory of Economic Development: An Inquiry into Profits, Capital, Credit, Interest, and the Business Cycle.* Harvard: Harvard University Press.

Solow, Robert M. 1988. "Growth Theory and After." *American Economic Review* 78: 307–317.

Tilly, Charles. 1996. "Invisible Elbow." *Sociological Forum* 11: 589–601.

Zbigniew Szkop, Rafał Wiśniewski and Marta Sylla

Payment for Ecosystem Services as a Potential Remedy for Market Failures

Abstract: This chapter investigates "the invisible hand of the market", broadly understood as the description of unlimited social benefits resulting from individual actions, in the relation to environmental goods and services. The chapter illustrates the reasons why "the invisible hand of the market" does not work in many cases when it comes to environmental protection issues. The concept of externalities is described as an example of market failure which causes divergence between social costs/benefits and private costs/benefits. The chapter also sets out the background and methods of economic valuation from a utilitarian perspective. It explains why the valuation of ecosystem services plays an important role in creating markets for the conservation of biodiversity, for instance through Payments for Ecosystem Services (PES). Therefore, it describes the PES concept as a potentially effective way of achieving conservation. The chapter concludes by showcasing examples from across the world, suggesting that PES can work to protect the environment whilst also imposing the positive indirect socio-economic impacts.

Key words: Environmental economics; nature conservation; market-based mechanisms; Payments for Ecosystem Services

Any situation where societies and individuals manage limited resources can be described as economy. This finite amount of resources, defined in economics as scarcity, denotes a condition when human needs exceed the available resources. In reality, every human activity is connected with some kind of economic aspect because everybody has some unfulfilled needs such as more time for relaxation, more money, better healthcare and many other examples. Therefore, this situation of limited resources requires that we choose alternative resources which are available at the time. Economics is a science attempting to find answers to the question of how people make choices, together with making recommendations on how these choices should be made in order to maximise welfare (Żylicz 2004). Natural resources are limited as well and therefore the investigation into conditions of the optimal use of natural environment resources lies also within the scope of modern economy.

Natural environment issues are examined in the works of pioneers of the labour theory of value, such as Petty (1662) and Cantillon (2010 (1775)), as well as in physiocratic theories. However, the real interest in problems of natural environment lies only in the classical economist works of Smith (1776), Ricardo (1817), Mill (1859), Say [1971 (1803)] and Marx [1976 (1867)]. Nevertheless, it can be declared that a systematic advance in the field of combined economic-ecological research started at the end of the 1960s. It is connected with globalisation and the internalization of the modern ecological crisis (Michałowski 2013). Roughly around the same period, the development of environmental economics started, which is a subfield of the neoclassical economics theories examining static and dynamic conditions for the optimisation of natural resources and environmental qualities used (Słodowska-Hełpa 2015). Instruments for economic optimisation analysis are utilized here in order to designate means and methods applied later for environmental policy implementation. These tools are specifically used to minimalize the costs of achieving planned or desired environmental targets (e.g. the improvement of the natural environment quality) or the implementation costs of "ecologically sustainable growth" (usually expressed as investment costs). Within this framework, economization of the natural environment aids a more efficient use of limited assets and human resources pivotal for the implementation of environmental policy tasks. This way such optimisation limits an alternative cost of natural environment protection, which is a drain on the resources necessary for the achievement of other objectives co-defining the level of social welfare, especially those associated with the economic welfare (Borys 2013). Economists have been providing tools to increase efficiency for achieving conservation and therefore the level of social welfare. PES is an example of such a tool created in belief of the power of the invisible hand of the market.

1 Invisible hand of the market vs. environmental protection

Neoclassical economics refers to the idea of market as an efficient system of resource allocation. This comes from the notion of the "invisible hand of the market". The mechanism of action of the invisible hand of the market was first described by Smith in *An Inquiry into the Nature and Causes of the Wealth of Nations* (1776). Smith (1776, 15–17) argued that all market participants (producers and consumers) are motivated by a desire to fulfil their own private needs and care for their own best interest. At the same time, as each one of them is attempting, as an individual, to maximize their own private revenue, each also contributes to the increase of the overall capital. This situation can be illustrated as an equilibrium of supply (MC – marginal cost) and demand (MB – marginal benefit) resulting in an efficient allocation of resources (q*) [where p – price, q – quantity, p* – optimal price] (*Begg, et al. 2005*, 87).

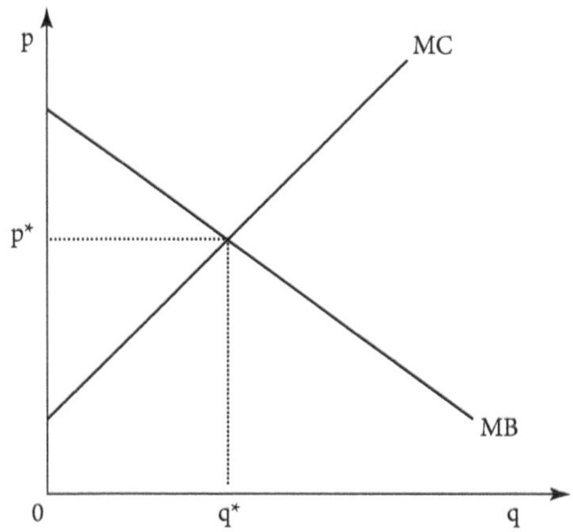

Diagram 1: Equilibrium on the perfect competition market (original from Begg, Fisher and Dornbush 2005, 87)

Nowadays, it is still acknowledged that the market provides efficient resource allocation, given the lack of any interference. Such a situation is referred to as a perfect competition market. The problem is that very rarely are conditions of such a market met.

Further analysis of market mechanisms sheds some light on the reasons for such a situation. The situation where the invisible hand is not working perfectly, i.e. when resources are not allocated efficiently, is called market failure. Economists working in the field of welfare economy describe three types of market failure: imperfect competition, social preferences and externalities (Samuelson and Nordhaus 2000, 71–75; Begg, Fischer and Dornbush 2005, 39). It was the discovery of the latter that was pivotal for the development of environmental economics.

Marshall [1920 (1890), 191] described for the first time the phenomenon of externalities, seen as the transfer of cost or benefit onto a party who did not choose to incur such benefit or cost, therefore affecting this party's welfare. Consequently, private costs or benefits are clearly different from overall social costs or benefits. The main idea of the invisible hand of the market mechanism is based on an assumption that every economic entity – producers and consumers – is concerned only for its own individual profit and tries to maximize its own private surplus of benefits over costs. The existence of externalities itself, understood as the difference between private and social costs or benefits,

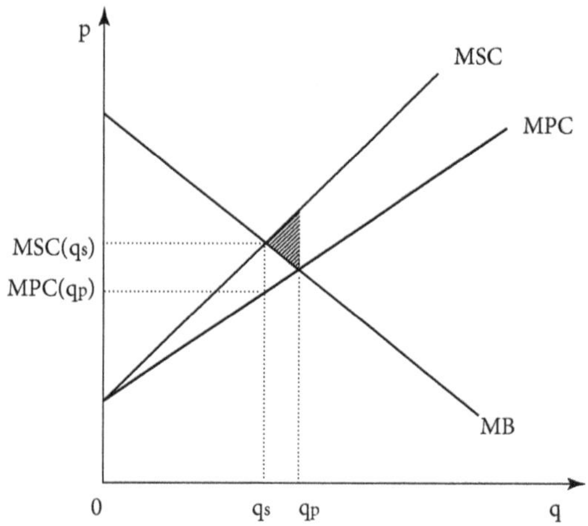

Diagram 2: Mechanism of externality (original from Żylicz 2004, 31)

means that market forces could endorse decisions which, albeit rational from the individual point of view, may be ineffective from the point of view of society as a whole (Begg, Fischer and Dornbush 2005, 86).

Market inefficiency associated with the occurrence of externalities can be graphically illustrated as an imbalance between supply and demand. The provision of goods, which results in a negative effect, is oversupplied, and the provision of goods resulting in a positive way is undersupplied in relation to Pareto optimal allocation. Taking this into consideration the application of externalities in the market analysis may be achieved through the modification of the supply or demand curve. If the supply of a good is associated with incurring an external cost, marginal external cost (MEC) must be added to marginal private cost (MPC). The sum called marginal social cost (MSC) shows the real cost of supplying the market with an additional unit of goods (Żylicz 2004) (*diagram 2,* where q – quantity, q_p – market quantity, q_s – social optimum).

Pigou was the first to formulate this method of defective market allocation amelioration, which was proposed in his book – *Economics of Welfare* (1920). The tax named for its initiator – the Pigou tax – is an asymmetrical price, which is charged to the party responsible for generating a negative externality equalling the MEC calculated for the optimal point. If an externality was a positive one, then the role of the tax would be taken by a subsidy. In case of an external cost associated with environmental degradation, the rule can be written in the form

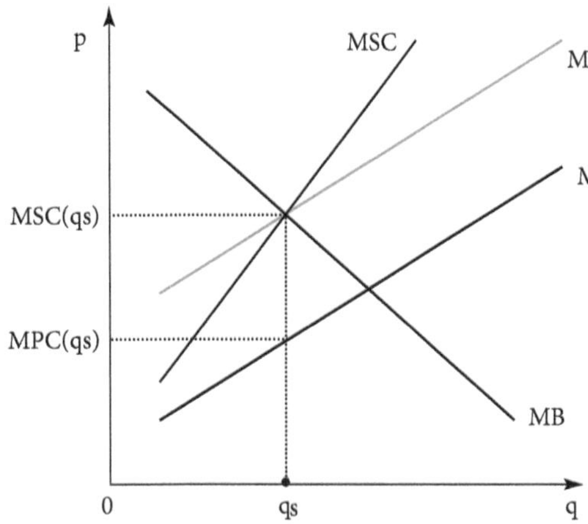

Diagram 3: Mechanism of action of the Pigou tax (original from Żylicz 2004, 56)

of the following equation: $PT(q)=MEC(q_0)(q-q_{threshold})$ (Pezzey 1992). In other words, levying the tax for a defined $(q-q_{threshold})$ unit of the emitted pollutant helps pollution producers to acknowledge the scarcity of environmental goods (precisely, the environmental ability for absorption of pollution) and creates incentives for more economical use of such goods. *Diagram 3* depicts the mechanism of action of the Pigou tax.

The introduction of the tax levies each unit of supply in such a way that the MPC increased by the addition of the tax equals the MSC in the optimal position (in other positions, it does not have to be the same). This means that producers charged with the tax will set the supply level at a level characterized by the maximum economic surplus (Pezzey 1992, 984–988).

Pigouvian taxes are central to understanding environmental policies because they set a standard for efficient regulation. They are the basis for evaluation of environmental taxes under monopoly (Barnett 1980, 172–181) and other forms of imperfect competition (Xepapadeas 1997), as well as the measuring point for second best taxes (Pang and Shaw 2011). Also, the efficiency of Pigouvian taxes is the starting point of comparisons of quotas and price regulation (Weitzman 1974; and more recently Kato 2011).

2 Economic valuation of ecosystem services

The Pigou tax, or appropriate subsidies, is often used in analyses of economics in the field of optimal management of natural resources and environmental qualities. A common example of externality, meaning a transfer of some costs resulting from one economic entity's activities onto another party without appropriate compensation, is environmental pollution. When one party emits pollution into the environment, therefore deteriorating its quality, then a third party suffers. In order to price the social cost of such negative consequence and, at the same time, to calculate the value of the Pigou tax chargeable to the producer of the pollution, economists estimate the value of incurred loss.

According to neoclassical economics, value as a basic economic category is expressed in market prices. It comes from a notion of utility, understood as benefits experienced by consumers through the increased consumption of a given good; thus, everything that does not serve to fulfil human needs is considered worthless. However, it needs to be emphasized that whilst this is an anthropocentric approach, it is not necessarily a materialistic approach (Żylicz 2004, 23). This is because economists acknowledge that total economic value (TEV) is an aggregation of many elements including also these intangible, nonmaterial ones, which nevertheless can be measured (Dzięgielewska et al. 2007, 10). Generally, TEV could be divided into two categories: use value (UV) and non-use value (NUV), sometimes called passive use value (PUV). Further, UV is usually further split into two types: direct use values (DUV) and indirect use values (IUV) (Żylicz 2015, 11–29). In order to estimate an external cost, it is necessary to examine how pollutants affect the environmental quality, and by doing this to assess the welfare of an individual who has lost an opportunity to use the environment and its qualities at the same level as before.

Economic values are appropriately reflected by their market price. However, sometimes a market for certain goods or services simply does not exist; this happens in the case of many environmental goods and services (Bellver-Domingo, Hernández-Sancho and Molinos-Senante 2016, 115–118). Hence, there are no market prices to serve as a basis to estimate the value of these goods and services. However, economists managed to tackle this problem by creating two methods of valuation of non-market goods: indirect and direct (Czajkowski 2010, 14–15). The first method is used to calculate economic value through the examination of surrogate markets, where people buy and sell goods complimentary to the good the value is sought. The second type of valuation refers to the hypothetical market, where a good could be bought and sold, therefore economists enquire respondents for their willingness to pay (WTP) for certain goods and services (Giergiczny and Kronenberg 2012, 74–89).

Indirect techniques of valuation are usually considered to be more plausible as they are based on preferences actually revealed. An example of this approach is a travel cost method (TCM) devised by Hotelling (Hotelling 1949, 45–56).

The basic premise is quite simple – the value of a certain place is expressed as the price a consumer is willing to pay to get there (Żylicz 2013, 10). According to the economic theory, the value associated with visiting the location should not be lower than the cost of travelling; it can even be higher for some travellers. Additionally, the analysis includes only a percentage of all people visiting the location. There are econometric methods allowing the creation of a visit curve on the basis of the travelling cost (Żylicz 2013, 9).

If it is not easy to identify a surrogate market, the value of the non-market good may be estimated directly, namely by asking respondents for their WTP for a good or service on a hypothetical market. This is called Contingent Valuation Method (CVM). The name refers to a situation where a respondent is given a hypothetical scenario regarding a good provision and his/her responses depend on the acceptance of the scenario (Fiedor 2002). The Arrow-Solow panel (special panel of social scientists formed to explicitly consider the criticisms of contingent valuation and make recommendations to NOAA (National Oceanic and Atmospheric Administration)) agreed that a properly designed CVM survey is accurate and may be used for the natural environment valuation taken as ecosystem services valuation (Arrow et al. 1993, 72–77).

3 Payment for ecosystem services

Ecosystem services are defined as benefits that people obtain from nature (Millennium Ecosystem Assessment 2005), and they can be assessed in biophysical and monetary terms. Ecosystem services contribute to human well-being (Haines-Young and Potschin 2010, 110) by regulating environmental conditions, providing recreational opportunities and supplying natural resources. Ecosystem services are only provided by nature; however, human input may enhance or hinder them. Natural ecosystems are complex, interrelated systems that depend on each other. An externality, e.g. in the form of water pollution, affects not only one ecosystem, but also threatens the biological diversity of plants and animals in proximity, which in turns has an impact on other ecosystems. The externality may hinder the provision of ecosystem service and thus decrease the benefits that people obtain from nature. The valuation of ecosystem services aims at having the incentive function, by helping different actors to change their behaviour (Ring et al. 2010, 21). The concept goes back to 1997. This, as it is commonly acknowledged, originated with the publication by Costanza et al. (1997, 253–260), where types of ecosystem services were described. There are three broad categories: provisioning (e.g. production of food and water), regulating (e.g control of climate and disease) and cultural services (e.g spiritual and recreational benefits). These three categories included seventeen types of services. The list was further extended and details were added. Currently the CICES list (Common International Classification of Ecosystem Services 2015) serves as a baseline for research and is recommended for the use of EU institutions.

Payments for Ecosystem Services (PES), also known as Payments for Environmental Services is a system of designed incentives offered to landowners or other natural resource owners for management of their land/resource in such a way that it provides a needed ecosystem service. PES underlying assumptions are based on the WTP of ecosystem service buyers and the willingness to accept by ecosystem service providers (Wang, Poe and Wolf 2017, 64). PES may create demand, which is a market force essential to address the imbalance threatening biodiversity and impeding sustainable development. PES may have different schemes depending on a socio-economic and environmental situation, as well as local, national or international scales (Rawlins and Westby 2013, 117–121). PES are therefore not taxes – it requires an agreement concerning voluntary transactions between a party receiving environmental benefits and a land manager who provides ecosystem services (Bennett and Gosnell 2015, 172). They are included here, however, because they resemble Pigouvian taxes in important ways. Specifically, user fees and Pigouvian taxes have the mechanism and potential functions: regulation of use and revenue generation. From that perspective, PES in a way can be seen as a case study for the Pigou tax.

The most common example of PES are the actions of governments around the world, which continuously create incentive programmes to support landowners producing ecosystem services and compensate them for the loss of income (Millennium Ecosystem Assessment 2005). This method is especially effective when there is no possibility of either purchasing the land so it could be excluded from the "normal" use to safeguard it or set up a protected area.

One of the most successful and long-term examples of PES implementation for ecosystem protection is the case of Costa Rica, which now serves as a good practice that many other countries have followed. We present the case study in order to provide description of the best-existing PES scheme mechanism that could become a potential remedy for market failure. We start with the ecosystem services which are the subject of the PES scheme. We discuss what economic instruments are used within the PES scheme. At the end, we describe the PES socio-economic impacts, concentrating on main actors taking part in the scheme.

4 Costa Rica case study

Costa Rica introduced the PES scheme protecting forest ecosystems in 1997. The regulations concerned four forest ecosystem services: "(1) mitigation of greenhouse gas (GHG) emissions; (2) hydrological services, including provision of water for human consumption, irrigation, and energy production; (3) biodiversity conservation; and (4) provision of scenic beauty for recreation and ecotourism" (Pagiola 2008, 712). Because of the fact that environmental services have been taken for granted for decades, it is difficult to operationalize the concept of ecosystem services. Even though people recognize the benefits they obtain from nature, they do not tend to pay for something that they did not have to pay for previously. Because the market did not cover these services before, they were considered to have been delivered for free.

The Costa Rica's PES programme included establishing the National Fund for Forest Financing – a designed economic instrument for financing the provision of ecosystem services mainly from the revenues from a fossil fuel sales tax. However, the underpinning assumption of the programme was creating a market for ecosystem services, where users would pay for the services they benefit from (Pagiola 2008, 713). Charging the users of ecosystem services was the most successful in terms of water provision. Water provision is the ecosystem service that has a market price, especially in the case of energy production. The operationalizing of PES became easier, when within the PES programme another economic instrument, i.e. environmental services certificates, was introduced (Pagiola 2008, 714). The certificates are standardised instruments enabling buyers to pay for the conservation of a specific ecosystem service in one hectare of designated forest area. This instrument was also promoted as a corporate social and environmental responsibility action, and therefore targeted at private companies (Porras et al. 2013, 13–14).

The introduction and management of the PES scheme in Costa Rica imposed relatively high transaction and compliance costs (Miranda, Porras and Moreno 2004, 33). The programme application required a lot of administrative work and technical support. Therefore, at the beginning of the PES in Costa Rica, the individual farmers joined the programme in cooperatives, bigger farmers joined as individuals and indigenous association were the minority participants (Porras et al. 2013, 20). In 2012, the proportion of indigenous groups increased significantly, as well as the legal entities that were established from cooperatives (Porras et al. 2013, 44). PES has also indirect socio-economic impacts in the form of improving social capital and diversification of economic activities, which in the case of Costa Rica was important for the indigenous people because it helped them to improve their living conditions, level of education and infrastructure (Porras et al. 2013, 46). PES is the economic instrument that draws from the beneficiary-pays principle rather than the polluter-pays principle (Engel, Pagiola and Wunder 2008, 663). The latter principle put the affected, very often poor, communities in the inferior position towards the polluter who provides compensations for the damages caused. PES puts the provider of ecosystem services in the superior position towards the beneficiaries. If the provider is a poor community that owns or manages the ecologically valuable land, PES may create synergies with poverty alleviation instruments (Pagiola, Arcenas and Platais 2005, 237). The experiences of Costa Rica's example are not easily transferrable to other local case studies. Successful PES programmes need to be adjusted to local demographic and socio-economic characteristics as well as land tenure arrangements and possible synergies between environmental and poverty reduction policies (Adhikari and Boag 2013, 73).

PES may also be implemented at a larger than local scale. There are several international PES schemes which address the ecosystem services that have a global significance (Farley et al. 2010, 2075). The Costa Rica example shows that international companies are mainly willing to invest in carbon sequestration, whereas local companies are willing to invest in watershed protection, biodiversity conservation, aesthetic services, and also carbon sequestration (Koellner, Sell and Navarro 2010, 2127). Carbon sequestration, as an ecosystem service, is also targeted by the international agreements on reducing global emission of greenhouse gases, which is a result of tropical forests vanishing and changes in the land use associated with this process. Preventing deforestation, forest planting and re-forestation can also protect services associated with biodiversity and ecosystems as well as preventing the climate change.

At the national level, PESs could provide a substantial contribution and support to the main aspect of the environmental conservation policy. The US government spends 1.7 billion dollars on direct payments to farmers on environmental projects (Kumar 2005, 15). Payments from the quality improvement programme of the Agriculture Department promote sustainable use of irrigation methods, nutrients and fertilizers, integrated methods of pest control and fauna and flora protection. The European system for the promotion of the environment-friendly agriculture and forestry, which is a part of the European Agricultural Programmes for Rural Development (European Commission 2005) is a similar solution. Its budget equals to roughly 4.5 billion Euros per year. In 2005, Environment and Agriculture programmes covered 36.5 million hectares in twenty-seven EU Member States (without Hungary and Malta) and were implemented through 1.9 million of contracts with farmers, each lasting from five to seven years (TEEB 2008, 49). PES in Europe is mainly implemented through the Common Agricultural Policy (CAP). The direct payments to farmers are supported by the EU budget, Member State budget and/or other private sources. PES offer communities a chance to increase their profits by opening new markets. The key to success is a "carrot-and-stick" method combining protective legislation with protection promoting incentives.

Wunder, Engel and Pagiola (2008, 834–852) conducted a comparative analysis of existing PES programmes and concluded that there is not one solution to fit all PES schemes, but user-financed PES programmes seem to perform better than government-financed PES programmes. Based on that, one may conclude that the invisible hand starts working when the market is created and it can bring better results than quasi-market situations. However, the Costa Rica case study shows that the initial external funds are crucial for building the capacity, institutional and technical background of the PES programme. Therefore, even the user-financed PES programmes are not purely governed by the invisible hand of the market because it is distorted by institutional interventions. In fact, this invisible hand very often wears a UN bracelet.

5 Discussion and conclusion

A decrease in the natural resources management efficiency results in a situation where problems of natural environment degradation together with environmental protection as a whole, gain more attention and significance. This situation requires a holistic approach, where economic processes should be tackled within the context disciplines which deal with the management of limited natural resources. Environmental economics is, without any doubt, such a field of knowledge. This subject area identifies and examines economic methods and instruments available in economic practices applicable and perhaps necessary in environmental protection. It also addresses the problems of researching economic implications of environmental policies. In this way, environmental economics, which stems from the neoclassical strand of economics, proves that the invisible hand of the market fails when it comes to environmental issues. One of the main reason is the existence of so-called externalities. Externality is the cost or benefit that affects a party who did not choose to incur that cost or benefit.

Pigou was the first to formulate the method of defective market allocation amelioration, the tax named for its initiator – the Pigou tax (Pigou 1920). It is an asymmetrical price, which is charged to the party responsible for generating a negative externality equalling the MEC calculated for the optimal point. If an externality was a positive one, then the role of the tax would be taken by a subsidy. The Pigou tax, or appropriate subsidies, is often used in analyses of economics in the field of optimal management of natural resources and environmental qualities. In practice, these taxes or subsidies may be introduced in the form of voluntary PES (Payment for Ecosystem Services). The idea behind PES is to create a market-based instrument for environmental goods and services to allow the invisible hand to work in the market. Economists have been providing tools (including economic instruments) to internalise environmental externalities and help the invisible hand to catch the broader effects of economic activities. PES is an example of such a tool that aims to support the positive externalities of producers of ecosystem services (Adhikari and Boag 2013, 72). PES offers the solution to market failure by creating the market. In that sense, PES is the economic instrument created in belief of the power of the invisible hand of the market. Because of that, PES receives a lot of criticism, especially in terms of commodifying nature (Kosoy and Corbera 2010, 1228). The article presents PES in order to provide general illustration of this instrument from the perspective of Adam Smith's ideas. However, we refrain from discussing the ethical and social implications of the commodification of natural resources and ecosystem services.

The number of PES applications on different scales is growing. We have presented case studies of PES schemes in the context of the invisible hand. All of them are solutions to the failure of markets to provide incentives to producers of PES. That failure creates environmental externalities – a situation where productive or consumptive activities inflict involuntary costs or benefits on others. It may be concluded that PES as an economic instrument is based on the belief that the invisible hand can take care of the environmental protection if only the market for such goods or services is created. It is also proven by analysing the existing PES examples that those PES schemes that imitate markets better are more effective.

One of the most representative PES local programmes is the Costa Rica PES scheme aiming at limiting deforestation and increasing four key ecosystem services. This well-designed PES scheme shares features of an efficient economic instrument in environmental protection, meaning it is informative, stimulating and generating income (Poskrobko and Poskrobko 2012). The Costa Rica PES scheme consists of several economic instruments, the environmental services certificates and the National Fund for Forest Financing being two of them. PES at a local scale also imposes the positive indirect socio-economic impacts which means that environment protection programmes may produce synergies resulting in both social and economic benefits. Costa Rica case study provides the example showing that PES is able to become the potential remedy for market failures.

References

Adhikari, Bhim, and Gemma Boag. 2013. "Designing Payments for Ecosystem Services Schemes: Some Considerations." *Current Opinion in Environmental Sustainability* 5: 72–77.

Arrow, Kenneth, Robert Solow, Paul R. Portney, Edward E. Leamer, Roy Radner, and Howard Schuman. 1993. *Report of the NOAA Panel on Contingent Valuation*. Report to the General Council of the US National Oceanic and Atmospheric Administration. Washington: Resources for the Future.

Begg, David, Stanley Fisher, and Rudiger Dornbush. 2005 [1984]. *Economics*. London 8th edition: McGraw-Hill Higher Education, Maidenhead.

Bellver-Domingo, Águeda, Francesc Hernández-Sancho, and Maria Molinos-Senante. 2016. "A Review of Payment for Ecosystem Services for the Economic Internalisation of Environmental Externalities: A Water Perspective." *Geoforum* 70: 115–118.

Bennett, Drew E., and Hanah Gosnell. 2015. "Integrating Multiple Perspectives on Payments for Ecosystem Services Through a Social-ecological Systems Framework." *Ecological Economics* 116: 172–181.

Borys, Tadeusz. 2013. "Nowe kierunki ekonomii środowiska i zasobów naturalnych w aspekcie nowej perspektywy finansowej Unii Europejskiej." *Ekonomia i Środowisko*1: 8–28.

Cantillon, Richard. 2010 [1755]. *An Essay on Economic Theory: An English Translation of Richard Cantillon's* Essai sur la Nature du Commerce en General. Translated by Chantal Saucier, edited by Mark Thornton. Auburn Ala: Ludwig von Mises Institute: 63.

Common International Classification of Ecosystem Services (CICES). 2015. "Towards a Common Classification of Ecosystem Services." Accessed October 13, 2017. http://cices.eu.

Costanza, Robert, Ralph d'Arge, Rudolf de Groot, Stephen Farberparallel, Monica Grasso, Bruce Hannon, Karin Limburg, Shahid Naeem, Robert V. O'Neill, Jose Paruelo, Robert G. Raskin, Paul Sutton, and Marjan van den Belt. 1997. "The Value of the World's Ecosystem Services and Natural Capital." *Nature* 387: 253–260.

Czajkowski, Mikołaj. 2010. "Nierynkowe metody wyceny." In *Wyzwania zrównoważonego rozwoju w Polsce*, edited by Jakub Kronenberg and Tomasz Bergier, 14–16. Kraków: Fundacja Sendzimira.

Dzięgielewska D., Tietenberg T., and Niggol Seo S. (Topic Editors), (2007), Total economic value, [in:] Encyclopedia of Earth, Ed. Cutler J. Cleveland (Washington, DC: Environmental Information Coalition, National Council for Science and the Environment). Accessed November 21, 2017, https://editors.eol.org/eoearth/wiki/Total_economic_value.

Engel, Stefanie, Stefano Pagiola, and Sven Wunder. 2008. "Designing Payments for Environmental Services in Theory and Practice: An Overview of the Issues." *Ecological Economics* 65: 663–674.

European Commission. 2005. "Rozporządzenie Rady 1698/2005 w sprawie wsparcia rozwoju obszarów wiejskich przez Europejski Fundusz Rolny na rzecz Rozwoju Obszarów Wiejskich (EFRROW)."*Oficjalny Dziennik Unii Europejskiej* L 277: 1–40.

Farley, Josh, Andre Aquino, Amy Daniels, Azur Moulaert, Dan Lee, and Abby Krause. 2010. "Global Mechanisms for Sustaining and Enhancing PES Schemes." *Ecological Economics* 69: 2075–2084.

Fiedor, Bogusław. 2002. "Podstawy ekonomii i zasobów naturalnych." Warszawa: Wydawnictwo C. H. Beck.

Giergiczny, Marek, and Jakub Kronenberg. 2012. "Jak wycenić wartość przyrody w mieście? Wycena drzew przyulicznych w centrum Łodzi." *Zrównoważony rozwój – Zastosowania* 3: 74–89. Kraków: Fundacja Sendzimira.

Haines-Young, Roy, and Marion Potschin. 2010. "The Links between Biodiversity, Ecosystem Services and Human Well-being." In *Ecosystem Ecology: A New Synthesis*, edited by David G. Raffaelli and Christopher L. J. Frid, 1–174. Cambridge: Cambridge University Press.

Hotelling, Harold. 1949. *An Economic Study of the Monetary Valuation of Recreation in the National Parks*. Washington DC: U.S. Department of the Interior, National Park Service and Recreational Planning Division.

Kato, Kazuhiko. 2011. "Emission Quota versus Emission Tax in Mixed Duopoly." *Environmental Economics and Policy Studies* 13: 43–63.

Koellner, Thomas, Joachim Sell, and Guillermo Navarro. 2010. "Why and How Much Are Firms Willing to Invest in Ecosystem Services from Tropical Forests? A Comparison of International and Costa Rican Firms." *Ecological Economics* 69: 2127–2139.

Kosoy, Nicolás, and Esteve Corbera. 2010. "Payments for Ecosystem Services as Commodity Fetishism." *Ecological Economics* 69: 1228–1236.

Kumar, Pushpam. 2005. "Market for Ecosystem Services." Winnipeg: IISD.

Marshall, Alfred. 1920 [1890]. *Principles of Economics*. London: Macmillan, 8th edition.

Marx, Karl. 1976 [1867]. *Capital*, vol. I. London: Penguin Books.

Michałowski, Artur. 2013. "Ekonomiczno-ekologiczne podstawy administrowania środowiskiem". *Administracja publiczna. Studia krajowe i międzynarodowe* 1: 1–14.

Mill, John, Stuart. 1859. *On Liberty*. London: Longman, Roberts & Green.

Millenium Ecosystem Assessment. 2005. *Ecosystems and Human Well-Being: Opportunities and Challenges for Business and Industry*. Accessed November 21, 2017. www.millenniumassessment.org/documents/document.353. aspx.pdf.

Miranda, Miriam, Ina T. Porras, and Mary L. Moreno. 2004. *The Social Impacts of Carbon Markets in Costa Rica. A Case Study of the Huetar Norte Region*. London: International Institute for Environment and Development.

Pagiola, Stefano, Augustin Arcenas, and Gunars Platais. 2005. "Can Payments for Environmental Services Help Reduce Poverty? An Exploration of the Issues and the Evidence to Date from Latin America." *World Development* 33: 237–253.

Pagiola, Stefano. 2008. "Payments for Environmental Services in Costa Rica." *Ecological Economics* 65: 712–724.

Pang, Arwin, and Daigee Shaw. 2011. "Optimal Emission Tax with Pre-existing Distortions."*Environmental Economics and Policy Studies* 13: 79–88.

Petty, William. 1662. *A Treatise of Taxes & Contributions*, London: Angel. Accessed November 21, 2017. http://www.hargaden.com/enda/wp-content/petty_taxescontributions.pdf.

Pezzey, John. 1992. "The Symmetry Between Controlling Pollution by Price and Controlling It by Quantity." *The Canadian Journal of Economics* 25: 983–991.

Pigou, Arthur C. 1920. *Economics of Welfare*. London: Macmillan Company.

Porras, Ina, David N. Barton, Miriam Miranda, and Adriana Chacón-Cascante. 2013. *Learning from 20 years of Payments for Ecosystem Services in Costa Rica*. London: International Institute for Environment and Development.

Poskrobko, Bazyli, and Tomasz Poskrobko. 2012. *Zarządzanie środowiskiem w Polsce*. Warszawa: Polskie Wydawnictwo Ekonomiczne.

Rawlins, Maurice A., and Leon Westby. 2013. "Community Participation in Payment for Ecosystem Services Design and Implementation: An Example from Trinidad." *Ecosystem Services* 6: 117–121.

Ricardo, David. 1817. *On the Principles of Political Economy and Taxation*. London: Murray.

Ring, Irene, Bernd Hansjürgens, Thomas Elmqvist, Heidi Wittmer, and Pavan Sukhdev. 2010. "Challenges in Framing the Economics of Ecosystems and Biodiversity: The TEEB Initiative." *Current Opinion in Environmental Sustainability* 2: 15–26.

Samuelson, Paul A., and William D. Nordhaus. 2000 [1985]. *Economics*, New York McGraw-Hill; Twelfth Edition.

Say, Jean-Baptiste. 1971 [1803]. *A Treatise on Political Economy; or the Production, Distribution and Consumption of Wealth*. New York: Augustus M. Kelley.

Słodowska-Hełpa, Małgorzata. 2015. "Interdyscyplinarna natura paradygmatu rozwoju – uwarunkowania i propozycje usprawnienia dialogu." *Nierówności Społeczne a Wzrost Gospodarczy* 41: 67–92.

Smith, Adam. 1776. *An Inquiry into the Nature and Causes of the Wealth of Nations*. Reprint. Oxford 1976: Clarendon Press. Accessed November 21, 2017. http://files.libertyfund.org/files/220/0141-02_Bk.pdf.

TEEB. 2008. *An Interim Report*. European Communities.

Wang, Pu, Gregory L. Poe, and Steven A. Wolf. 2017. "Payments for Ecosystem Services and Wealth Distribution." *Ecological Economics* 132: 63–68.

Weitzman, Martin. 1974. "Prices vs. Quantities." *Review of Economic Studies* 41: 477–491.

William Barnett. 1980. "Economic Monetary Aggregates an Application of Index Number and Aggregation Theory." *Journal of Econometrics* 14: 11–48.

Wunder, Sven, Stefanie Engel, and Stefano Pagiola. 2008. "Taking Stock: A Comparative Analysis of Payments for Environmental Services Programmes in Developed and Developing Countries." *Ecological Economics* 65: 834–852.

Xepapadeas, Anastasios. 1997. *Advanced Principles in Environmental Policy*. Cheltenham: Edward Elgar.

Żylicz, Tomasz. 2004. *Ekonomia środowiska i zasobów naturalnych*. Warszawa: PWN.

Żylicz, Tomasz. 2013. "Wycena usług ekosystemów leśnych." Paper presented at the Panel of Experts *„Wartość."* *"Lasy jako czynnik rozwoju cywilizacji; współczesna i przyszła wartość lasów"*, 15 October. Sękocin Stary: Instytut Badawczy Leśnictwa.

Żylicz, Tomasz. 2015. "An Economist Looks at Ecosystem Services." In *Towardsa Green Economy. From Ideas to Practice*, edited by Małgorzata Burchard-Dziubińska, 11–29. Łódź: Wydawnictwo Uniwersytetu Łódzkiego.

Part 3: The Invisible Hand, but Not of the Market

Francisco Fernandez de Castro and Raul P. Lejano

Program Implementation and the Invisible Hand of Community: The Experience of the Conditional Cash Transfer Program in Northern Mexico

Abstract: This chapter considers cooperative behavior during poverty program implementation in terms of informal norms and everyday practices. We argue that network interactions can stimulate other-regarding behavior embedded in socially and culturally constructed norms. The literature on cooperative behavior in social and economic development underlines cooperative arrangements in the context of formal institutional structures and rules. Less evident in the extant literature is how cooperation arises and evolves through more spontaneous and informal institutional processes in the policy arena. This study addresses this gap by exploring the implementation of the Mexican conditional cash transfer program and examining the working of the invisible hand of community – i.e., the non-formalized norms and everyday practices that work their own way to create cooperative arrangements and sustain the non-formalized institutional design that evolves.

Keywords: Cooperation; norms; networks; implementation; poverty

1 Introduction

The study of cooperative behavior underlying social and economic development has a long and varied tradition. It ranges from the study of fellow feeling or philanthropy in Aristotle's work (Berns 1994; Stanford Encyclopedia of Philosophy 2012) and the notion of sympathy in Smith's *Theory of Moral Sentiments* (1976 [1759]) to the vast literature on altruism and reciprocity (Andreoni 2006; Sugden 1982; Bekkers and Wiepking 2010; Brown and Ferris 2007), the study of self-interest-based cooperation in organizational settings (North 2005; Olson 1971 [1965]; Crozier and Friedberg 1980), and the well-documented framework of common-pool resources, according to which cooperation can emerge when individuals realize the long-term gain that can be obtained out of cooperative arrangements (Ostrom 1990; 2000; Agrawal and Ostrom 2001; Araral 2009). However, the literature, including that on common-pool resources, emphasizes formal cooperative arrangements that are translated into formal institutional structures and rules. Less evident in the literature is a description of how and why cooperation evolves through more spontaneous, non-deliberate, non-formalized institutions. This chapter addresses this gap by focusing on the "invisible hand of community" – i.e., those non-formalized norms and everyday practices that create cooperative arrangements, the social mechanisms that create and foster these norms and practices, and the non-formalized institutional design that evolves.

We apply the theory to the implementation of a poverty alleviation project. As we discuss, our theory also provides new ways to understand policy implementation. The extant literature on implementation discusses implementation styles (top down and bottom up approaches), institutional instruments, and models of administrative behavior (Howlett, Ramesh and Perl 2009; Hjern 1982; Pressman and Wildavsky 1984; Sabatier and Mazmanian 2005 [1979]; Barrett 2004; Sabatier 1986; deLeon 1999). In addition, there has been a move beyond the top down/bottom up debate to the extent that implementation scholars are developing models of policy actors behavior (e.g. game theory, principal agent theory) (O'Toole 2000; Saetren 2005) and examining policy tools or instruments for policy implementation, such as regulation, grants, policing, and advice, among others (Howlett, Ramesh and Perl 2009).

This scholarly literature has moved away from the organizational dimension of program implementation. As Bozeman (2013, 173) noted, "[…] many policy implementation studies are surprisingly ill-informed about organizations and organization theory, often unconsciously channeling ideas that have been longer and better developed in organization studies". The cost for poverty alleviation efforts is that governments have inadequate understanding of how informal organizational dynamics affect the programs' results. This chapter discusses the implementation of the Mexican Conditional Cash Transfer (CCT) program in order to illustrate how this informal and spontaneous organizational dimension works and helps the program achieve its goals.

The present study responds to another issue identified in the extant literature. The coordination and cooperation of actors to allocate and mobilize resources for the sake of economic growth and development is typically explained in terms of hierarchies, markets, and networks. Scholars advancing research on these areas have attempted to explain how the coordination and cooperation among different actors and organizational structures happens in the economic development process (Coase 1937; Williamson 2005; Powell 1990). Specifically, given that hierarchical coordination (hierarchy) can produce "losers", and deregulation (market) can lead to negative externalities (e.g.

poverty, environmental degradation, etc.), these explanatory frameworks lead to problems of efficiency (and legitimacy) in the context of public policymaking (Borzel 1998). The study of policy networks emerged as a response to these limitations (Rhodes 1990; Atkinson and Coleman 1992). Nonetheless, the analysis of networks in general, and policy networks in particular, have a strong emphasis on actors and structures of relationships with well-defined nodes and lines of interaction. Under these frameworks, there is little room to investigate complexities on the ground unfolding beyond the formal policy design. These frameworks are inadequate to understand the aberrations of informal and spontaneous mechanisms going on in the implementation stage. This study is a response to this gap.

2 Theoretical departure and approach

In our study *Norm, Network, and Commons: The Invisible Hand of Community* (Lejano and Fernandez de Castro 2014), we proposed a model of collective action that goes beyond individual rational actors and utility-maximizing behavior. The theory of our model suggests that communities act to solve collective action problems not only because of the presence of strategic advantage of cooperative behaviors but also because of other motivations such as other-regard, tradition, empathy, and others that do not translate into individual rationality. According to our theory, the individual, who might not initially have any reason to act in anything but an individual utility maximization (rational model), can encounter other persons or understand that they are part of a community of specific others. The individual recognizes her/his actions' effects on the welfare of these others and move from mere cognition of externalities, in general, to recognition of effects on specific persons. Her/his decision function includes now specific others welfare, which is another dimension, different from individual utility. While the rational model continues to provide powerful explanations for real-world situations, our theory suggests that there are cooperative behaviors that depart from this rational logic and are better understood in terms of other-regard, norms, scripts, social ties, etc. Thus, our proposition is that people can act out of regard for the other person, and interpersonal linkages can enable this inclination. In the aforementioned article, we formalize the model as one of networked interactions by actors making decisions according to sets of vector payoffs (also see Lejano and Ingram 2011). By "vector", we simply mean that each actor is influenced not just by a sense of their own individual utility but also others' utility, other norms such as cultural propriety, altruism, and others.

At the heart of our theoretical explanation is the working of shared norms and networks shaping cooperative dispositions. Accordingly, cooperative behaviors can be explained as a result of social ties (Wilson 2000), and are deeply embedded in community groups, their resources, and norms (Eckstein 2001; Bray 2009). Therefore, community and social context within which actors manage social problems are important factors to understand their cooperative course of actions. As we discussed in our aforementioned study, people's tendencies to cooperate are buried in their routines and are culturally and historically reproduced in the form of institutions. By institution we mean the social pattern that exposes a particular reproduction process. No enforcement or collective mobilization is needed to secure its reproduction (Jepperson 1991). Instead, its reproduction is possible given the enactment of cognitive scripts, moral templates, and symbolic systems (Amenta and Ramsey 2010; Meyer 2008) that define the appropriateness (March and Olsen 1989; Olsen 2010) of cooperative behaviors. The institutionalization of these cooperative behaviors means that there is a set of social reproductive synergies by which cooperation can attain specific properties of regularity. This regularity suggests the presence of self-reinforcing patterns of cooperative pre-dispositions in the form of *habitus* (Bourdieu 1990), which in turn shape people's socialization and the way they socially construct their reality. Thus, communitarian cooperative behavior can be embedded in constructed meanings of institutions.

In general, our theory addresses cooperation as a result not only of utility-maximizing strategic behavior but also as other-regarding dispositions through which people cooperate in terms of two mechanisms: (a) Fitting one's behavior to socially shared norms; and (b) the everyday interactions with individuals and groups (social ties), in a way that each person helps create and reproduce the beliefs or norms of others. It means that network interactions can stimulate other-regarding behavior embedded in socially and culturally constructed norms. For this to happen, no strategic deliberation or guiding action of any central authority or design is needed. There is no explicit oversight. This fact leads us to the notion of the *invisible hand of community* working its way and reproduced through the everyday practice without any central enforcement or monitoring mechanism. While the invisible hand of markets needs institutional structures that individuate, our notion of the *invisible hand of community* requires physical, virtual, or cognitive links among places, community members, or things along with the recognition through which one perceives them as the recipient of one's actions. This chapter builds on our previous work by exploring how this spontaneous mechanism works in the policy process.

3 The case study analysis

3.1 The paradox of an administratively lean poverty alleviation program

Conditional Cash Transfer (CCT) has evolved as a highly touted best practice in poverty alleviation (Fiszbein and Schady 2009; Adato and Hoddinott 2010; Levy 2006). The literature is vague, however, on the social and other mechanisms by which CCT programs achieve their results. Countries implementing a CCT program transfer money to disadvantaged families, through mothers, on the conditions that they invest in the education and health of their children. Although there is no conclusive evidence about the impact of CCTs on poverty, scholarly evaluations suggest that CCTs are improving school enrollment and health indicators, nutrition, and food consumption of recipients. See for example the research report by Hoddinott and Wiesmann (2010) examining the impact of CCTs on food consumption in Honduras, Mexico, and Nicaragua; the evaluation conducted by Maluccio and Flores (2005) intended to measure the impact of the Nicaraguan CCT program on school enrollment and the evaluation of the effect of the Mexican CCT on nutritional status of children and women of reproductive age in urban areas (Neufeld et al. 2005), to name but a few. In short, this body of research indicates that the CCT model has been improving the stock of human capital of the poor by increasing the level of education, health, and nutrition of beneficiary families.

But how is that possible? What, at the implementation level, makes this program a successful one in terms of human capital accumulation? What makes this program work on the ground? The CCT model is beyond its second decade, and there is still a question among scholars and international agencies (Adato and Hoddinott 2010) regarding the pathways through which CCTs actually affect education, health, and nutrition conditions of families. There have been important attempts in the CCT literature to investigate how this program works on the ground by examining different dimensions, such as views of beneficiaries and roles of family members (Adato and Roopnaraine 2004), beneficiaries' perception about the CCT program (SEDESOL-Progresa 1999), processes through which the CCT program certifies responsibilities (Escobar Latapi and Gonzalez de la Rocha 2001), or the effect of CCTs on intra-household relationships (Rivera, Hernández and Castro 2005). Our thesis is that CCT programs work because informal social and relational mechanisms create habituated processes of self- and other-oriented help. The present study contributes to this literature by exploring the spontaneous cooperative mechanisms that unfold in the implementation stage of the Mexican CCT strategy and affect its results.

We use the Mexican experience as a lens to understand how the CCT model works at the community level. According to the Mexican case, mothers receive the money; as a result, the family attends doctor visits and the beneficiary holder attends health talks. Their kids remain enrolled in the school and experience better health and nutrition conditions. Is it just the cash transfer along with the supply of education and healthcare services? What exactly happens between these service supplies and the results that CCTs achieve? During our fieldwork, we tried to explore the black box connecting the resources of the Mexican CCT model to its outcomes. However, instead of examining the black box *per se,* we found it relevant to focus on the arrow representing the resources that go into the box. For a discussion of spontaneous cooperative behaviors in the policy process, this decision was pertinent because our data show how beneficiary mothers bring informal resources into the program's implementation in order to keep the CCT model running in their community.

One salient resource is the cooperative disposition of vocales. In Mexico, a vocal is a beneficiary holder of the CCT program that is elected by other beneficiary holders, typically the mothers. A vocal is a community member that helps mothers to meet their program-related co-responsibilities and help program administrators coordinate with beneficiary families. In short, a vocal constitutes an essential link between the program and beneficiaries.

> We have thousands of recipients in this municipality. How can we coordinate these people in a face-to-face manner if we are just two persons in charge of the attention desk? It is impossible. We need people that help us attend and give beneficiaries the necessary assistance. Vocales' help is fundamental for these tasks. Vocales are the fundamental link [enlance fundamental] between us and beneficiaries. Were it not for vocales, it would be a chaos (Participant 1 – Administrator).
>
> Vocales became the pillars of the program. Vocales are organized through Community Development Committees (Comites de Promocion Comunitaria – CPC). They have been promoting the participation of beneficiary moms to achieve the program's goals in terms of education, health, and nutrition. For this purpose, vocales disseminate information and give orientation to beneficiary moms, visit health clinics and schools, and interact with beneficiaries, the program, and local institutions (Participant 2 – Administrator).
>
> Vocales help to establish better links between beneficiary families and the staff of health services, schools, and the program itself (SEDESOL 2008b, 11; PROSPERA-Comite Tecnico 2015, 11–12).

One paradox is that this essential linking role of vocales was officially conceived as voluntary, and the efficiency ethic would suggest such a role to be marginal. Instead, the program implementation relies on community resources that are informal and uncompensated, such as vocales' unpaid labor. According to the official documents (SEDESOL 2008b; PROSPERA-Comite Tecnico 2015), vocales should be willing to perform their linking role without receiving any salary. Interestingly, vocales' activities and responsibilities have been increasing over time.

> The program has been evolving during this sexennial administration and now, vocales have more things to do (Participant 3 – Administrator).
> In addition to my responsibilities as a vocal, I recently started my participation in the Adults Literacy Program. The program's staff wants me to spread the word in our barrios and invite beneficiary mothers to enroll in this literacy program. After our meeting with the program's staff, I needed to meet with moms in my barrio and share with them this information. **What was next?** I needed to prepare a list of names and contact information of mothers interested in participating in the literacy program (Participant 4 - Vocal).

These testimonies resonate with the fact that the program has been expanding in terms of both number of beneficiaries and components. The monitoring, attention, and information delivery tasks that the program administrators are responsible for have been increasing over time as a result of the program expansion. In Mexico, the enrollment of families went from five million families in 2000 to six million in 2016. In the city of San Luis Rio Colorado, the program started in 2002 with 1000 beneficiary families. Now, 5,000 families receive support from the program in this city. But the program has been increasing not only in terms of the number of beneficiaries but also in terms of its components. Since 2001, in addition to elementary and middle school, the program's support includes high school (SEDESOL 2001). In 2003, the program included a one-time cash transfer called "Jovenes con Oportunidades" (Youth with Opportunities) for students finishing their high school, in order to support the continuation of their studies (SEDESOL 2002). In 2006, the program started with a cash transfer for family members 70+ years old (SEDESOL 2005). In 2008, beneficiary families started receiving an additional financial support for electricity.[1] In 2009, the program included an additional amount of money to compensate the international increase of food prices (SEDESOL 2008a). Furthermore, during the present sexennial administration, the Mexican CCT has been encouraging beneficiary mothers to enroll in the literacy program in their municipality and submit proposals for productive projects (SEDESOL 2015). For a more detailed account on the program's evolution, see Ordoñez (2015) and González de la Rocha (2006).

---

1 Later in 2012, this support became part of the cash transfer for food. Food support has been part of the program since its early design in 1997.

Another paradox that runs counter to efficiency is that vocales' voluntary work has been increasing in a context of insufficient administrative structure. In San Luis Rio Colorado, the program is characterized by an increasing monitoring and desk service workload that only two administrators carry out in order to attend 5,000 families. The program is expected to grow in San Luis because this is a municipality with about 17,000 families living in poverty conditions. Out of these families, about 10,000 live in extreme poverty.[2] These administrators are called *Responsables de Atencion* (RA) and are in charge of the program's attention desk in this municipality.

According to the official description of the RA job position, the gross monthly income is about USD 440.00 (Mexican Pesos 7,660.00) and entails the following responsibilities (Prospera-DGAO 2015):

- Monitor and update the enrollment registry of the assigned micro-zone.
- Attend and guide beneficiary families regarding the paperwork of the program through personal attention or in groups at the program's office, local places, or beneficiary address.
- Deliver information about the status of beneficiaries in the program as well as possible additional benefits.
- Answer inquiries and complaints presented by beneficiaries.
- Register the actions executed in the field.
- Submit the resulting reports to the corresponding sub-state coordination unit in order to update the electronic records in the system.
- Help the program authorities with identifying suitable units for the execution of the program activities at the local level.
- Coordinate the orientation and training sessions with beneficiary holders and vocales' committees with the purpose of enhancing community development skills and public participation.[3]
- Give orientation and monitor the community oversight/surveillance [*contraloria social*] activities that take place during vocales' committees meetings.

In San Luis Rio Colorado, the RAs have temporary contracts [*contratos por honorarios*] with no employee benefits such as social security, medical plan,

2 Authors' estimate based on CONEVAL (2011).

3 In 2015, a third administrator was included for this city. This administrator is in charge of the training program for vocales and the organization of the community development committees.

life insurance, pension, paid vacation, and the like. In addition, their working conditions include intensive traveling schedules and field activities.

> Our situation is difficult. **Could you please be more specific?** On average, we earn about $7,000 pesos monthly, no retirement benefits, no health service coverage at all. We are officially temporary workers. I have been asking for a permanent contract and job security but the response that I got from the authorities is that "[…] given that poverty is going to end and it is a temporary situation, the program needs temporary operational staff only" [Participant 5 – Administrator].
> I have a temporary contract [*contrato por honorarios*] and no social security. No employee benefits at all. I needed to enroll in social security (what is called "seguro popular") on my own, not through my employer [Participant 6 – Administrator].

Under these precarious labor conditions that the RAs experience in order to manage an expanding program, vocales' help becomes decisive. Vocales help mothers to meet their program-related co-responsibilities and help street-level administrators to organize their interaction with mothers. During our fieldwork, vocales talked about "help" in terms of *facilitar* [facilitate]: facilitate the work of both beneficiary mothers and the program staff. Thus "help" becomes a natural cooperative disposition of vocales and is the main category in our data set. Vocales enact this category through different folk terms, according to the following arrangement:

Help/Facilitate (Main category)

(1) *Alentar/promover* [encourage]
(2) *Guiar/supervisar* [guide/advise]
(3) *Crear conciencia* [create awareness]
(4) *Informar* [disseminate information]
(5) *Supervisar* [inspect]
(6) *Coordinar* [coordinate]

Let us unpack these folk terms. Our data indicate that vocales encourage [*alientan/promueven*] healthy food consumption, school kids' enrollment, and meetings attendance. They give advice [*guian/asesoran*] to beneficiary mothers about how to check the accuracy of the information on the program's enrollment forms and cash transfer receipts, accomplish the program-related co-responsibilities, and prepare and submit funding requests for productive projects. Vocales create awareness [*crean conciencia*] of the importance of proper use of the cash transfer (purchase of healthy food and school supplies) and the importance of attending the program's meetings. Vocales disseminate information [*informan*] about the scheduled meetings, the program's requirements, beneficiaries' right to enroll family members in the health insurance program [called *seguro popular*], and the importance of enrolling in the adults literacy program. Vocales inspect [*supervisan*] the timely delivery of in-kind food support and supervise that the program's resources are not used for political proselytism, or that families really need the program's support. Finally, vocales help to coordinate mothers in different ways. They help to coordinate mothers' participation in meetings; they coordinate and often provide transportation for mothers' attending these meetings; and they coordinate and bring family resources for the program's operation including family assets, time, and labor.

Following Spradley (1979), we examined the semantic relationship between each folk term and the main category (help). The result is the following (Table 1):

Tab. 1: Semantic relationship between folk terms and main category

Folk Terms	Semantic Relationship	Main Category
(1) *Alentar/promover* [encourage] (2) *Guiar/supervisor* [guide/advise] (3) *Crear conciencia* [create awareness] (4) *Informar* [disseminate information] (5) *Supervisar* [inspect] (6) *Coordinar* [coordinate]	Is a way through which vocales	Help/facilitate the link between beneficiary mothers and the program

Last but not least, another paradox of this administratively efficient policy intervention is that vocales help beneficiary mothers to meet the program's requirements in a context of unrealistic assumptions in the policy design. Specifically, the program gives the cash transfer directly to mothers as beneficiary holders and takes for granted certain local conditions that mothers are supposed to control. First, households receive a cash transfer for food. Yet in addition to the presence of pricey food in the research setting, poor households experience a lack of food distribution infrastructure. Supermarkets are far away from disadvantaged neighborhoods, and public transportation is expensive and insufficient. Second, mothers are supposed to have control over their kids' school attendance. However, our data indicate that beneficiary holders experience difficulties in guaranteeing the school attendance of teenagers and older kids. In repeated instances, these kids preferred getting a job over having the program's scholarship. Third, mothers have to attend different meetings under the assumption that they have the time and resources to accomplish their meetings-related responsibilities, including doctor visits, health talks, and follow-up meetings with the program's attention desk. Data show that beneficiary holders do not necessarily have time to deal with multiple roles: mothers, workers (such as street vendors, housekeepers in wealthy homes, agriculture workers, or collecting recyclable materials on the street, etc.), home-based entrepreneurs, care givers for the elderly, etc., along with their co-responsibilities in the program. The inadequate public transportation, extreme temperatures during the summer and winter, and the fact that the average beneficiary mother does not have a car complicate the commuting of mothers to attend their multiple responsibilities.

> The program's meetings [MAPO - Mesas de Atención Personalizada Oportunidades] are far away from my home. The meetings take place at the Turtle Park [*Parque de las Tortugas*] where the municipal social development office is or at the City Forest Park [*Bosque de la Ciudad*]. The same situation happens regarding the doctor visits and health talks. They take place at the General Hospital, which is far away from my home. I have to borrow someone else's car or walk long distances with my kids. **Do you bring your kids to the MAPO meetings?** Yes, there is no other person at home able to take care of my kids during my meetings time. Taxi is not affordable. Public transportation is also expensive (Participant 7 – Beneficiary Mother).
>
> She (the deceased wife of the participant) used to experience difficulties re-organizing her time to do the program-related activities. She used to clean houses, and do the laundry and ironing work for wealthy families. She hardly had time for the program's meetings. The worse thing is that our kids were unattended most of the time. I do not know if I have to tell you this but … one day, my son … the one that is 15 year old now (11 year old at that time), was victim of sexual abuse … I regret that we had our kids unattended. (Participant 8 – husband of deceased beneficiary mother).
>
> There is no public transportation in this barrio. We have no supermarkets at all, no pavement, street lights do not work well, etc. If you live here and do not have car, then you do not have food unless you walk all the way down to the business district center and then walk back home with your grocery stuff. Taking a taxi is unaffordable (Participant 9 – Beneficiary Mother).

In sum, the unrealistic assumptions of the Mexican CCT program represent a gap between the program as envisioned by designers and the program that beneficiary holders experience in their everyday lives. The program takes for granted that beneficiary mothers, vocales, and street-level administrators have the resources to accomplish the implementation tasks of this widening program. Data contradict these assumptions and unveil structural factors at the local level running in the opposite direction. Under what conditions do vocales help and cooperate in the implementation process in order to fill this gap? The following section examines how the presence of close social ties and shared beliefs along with the notion of recognition discussed above explain instances of spontaneous cooperative moves intended to make the program work in this municipality.

3.2 Vocales make the Mexican CCT program work on the ground

According to the instrumental rationality framework, the poor are rational individuals that seek to maximize their utility or happiness[4] by making production and consumption choices (Duclos and Araar 2006). Within this framework, vocales might expect some gain that increases their individual utility given their cooperative moves in the implementation of the program. However, repeated instances in our data revealed that vocales, as beneficiary holders living in extreme poverty, display cooperative behaviors and narratives that deviate from this utility maximization drive.

Let us leave the instrumentalist framework, for a moment, and see what happens on the ground. Once beneficiary mothers and vocales participating in the CCT program are there, in the field, dealing with local constraints and unrealistic assumptions of the program, what happens exactly? In our previous discussion, we described how the program takes for granted the conditions under which mothers and vocales have to accomplish their program-related responsibilities. To recap, the program assumes that there is a limitless supply of women's time and energy. It also takes for granted that food availability/consumption is not problematic. The program assumes that mothers have control over kids' school attendance, or have control over resources such as transportation and/or urban environments that make the program's implementation challenging. The disagreement between these assumptions and the everyday life on the ground complicates further the burden on mothers, vocales, and street-level administrators. As a result, spontaneous but recurring instances happen. For example, kids and their friends suddenly emerge as local actors supporting vocales' work and the program's operation, family resources such as time and homes become part of the "assets" through which the program is sustained, and sometimes vocales use their church's support in order to help families accomplish their CCT-related co-responsibilities.

Kids' labor is one of the most intriguing informal resources that vocales bring to the program's operation. Vocales experience time and capability constraints that result in unexpected labor costs that kids help to deal with.

4 For a discussion on utility, happiness, and subjective well-being in the economic development literature, see Kimball and Willis (2006) and Fuentes and Rojas (2001).

When vocales have to disseminate information among beneficiaries, they use different ways, including posting announcements at schools and corner stores, texting, or emailing. Although the use of internet is not a program's requirement, it is becoming an increasing practice in the program implementation. The typical vocal in San Luis Rio Colorado has limited to no computer/internet knowledge and here is where kids and their networks come into action.

> My kids help me with my vocal-related activities … They are good at internet and computers. (They) have their own friends that also receive the program support. My kids send emails to their friends with the information that I want to spread among recipients in my colonia or help me post this information on Facebook. Their friends pass along this information to their parents and my kids receive a response from their friends confirming their parents' attendance to the meetings or confirming the receipt of the information (Participant 10 – Vocal).
> In order to spread the program-related information among beneficiary moms, I need internet. I do not have computer but I have cellphone. My cellphone does not have internet service but I can handle with this. **What do you do?** My kids do it. I do not have to pay for internet use. My kids know how to get into other people's internet accounts (hackers). So I have internet for free and I am able to spread information among moms (Participant 11 – Vocal).

Providing transportation is another spontaneous response of vocales. The typical beneficiary in San Luis Rio Colorado does not have a car. In the event that a beneficiary has a vehicle, on average, it is an old and malfunctioning one. In addition, beneficiary mothers who have cars can barely afford gasoline consumption. Furthermore, in disadvantaged barrios, public transportation routes are insufficient and sometimes beneficiary families cannot afford this service. So the necessary transportation to attend the program-related responsibilities is problematic, and there are communities in which vocales play an important role to handle with this situation. As this vocal declared:

> My husband has a car repair garage, and he normally has vehicles from different clients. Once we fix a car … **Do you also fix cars?** Yes, I do … we need to drive the car for short distances to make sure that the car is working well after the repair. As a vocal, I take advantage of those short trips to take moms from their home to our meetings and other program's activities. **Do you mean that you provide transportation for beneficiary mothers?** Yes. I need to coordinate with about 100 mothers in this colonia. Most of them do not have car. The existing public transportation routes are not enough and many people have to take more than one bus in case they can afford it. **How much does it cost?** It costs 10 pesos one trip per person. Families from this barrio have to take two buses in order to get the health clinic. **Then, the trip to the clinic cost is 20 pesos right?** Well … the round trip is 40 pesos per person but mothers have to take all the household

members to the clinic. It means that, if they have four kids, there will be six household members (including mom and dad) taking the bus. It equals 240 pesos (40 X 6). That is really difficult for low-income families (Participant 12 – Vocal).

Recurrent instances show how some vocales' activities might not be defined in the official guidelines but are relevant for beneficiary families. For example, the program defines a specific range of activities that vocales are supposed to do based on the different components of the program - health, education, nutrition, and adults literacy (SEDESOL 2008b). However, there are no guidelines about how to accomplish those activities. Then, vocales' improvisation, creativity, and cooperative disposition come into action when they are willing to help beneficiary mothers even when they (vocales) do not have the resources to do so. In situations like these, vocales manage the additional burden by looking for local or community support. This support typically comes from the municipality or local organizations such as the church, social activists, etc.

Let us take the example of vocales encouraging and supporting kids' school attendance. The typical tasks refer to vocales encouraging school attendance or interacting with school staff in order to address specific situations that beneficiary holders experience. Beyond that, there are circumstances imposed by the local context that deserve special intervention. Given that street-level administrators are not able to capture those contextual circumstances, vocales intervene voluntarily and create solutions for problems that are not always observable for the program's staff. The following quotations speak to this.

The school is far away. Most of the kids in this barrio attend the school during the afternoon. Kids have to walk about one kilometer to get to the school, then, later during the evening they have to walk back home the same distance. I always have water bottles for those kids. They stop here at my place, drink water, take a little break, and keep walking. **How do you get the water bottles?** I ask for help in our church. They supply the water bottles for those kids and I administer this water. **How does it relate to your role as vocal?** My vocal-related responsibilities do not include this task. However, I noticed how difficult it is for moms and kids to keep the school attendance because of both the extreme temperatures and the long distance between the school and their home. If kids do not attend the school, the program scholarship will be suspended. They need this money and I am glad I can help this way" (Participant 13 – Vocal).

I am illiterate. When I attend the health talks, I do not know how to take notes of the information we receive. I do not understand what the presenter shows in writing or the handouts we receive. I rely on my memory only. But I am not the only beneficiary with this limitation in my barrio. There are several persons in my colonia that are illiterate. My vocal already knows our problem and she is helping us. **How does she help you?** She knows the illiterate beneficiaries in our barrio. After each health talk, she calls us to make sure that we understood some relevant information delivered during the health talk. In addition, she is helping us to get enrolled in the literacy program of the city. I am thankful for having this vocal with us. I do not remember having a vocal like this in the past. **Could you please give me more detail?** In the past, nobody called me to see if I understood the health talk. In the past, nobody took care about how many illiterate persons are in our barrio. I do not remember a vocal visiting my home to see if I am doing well. This vocal does it (Participant 14 – Beneficiary Mother).

Both the activities that vocales perform and the strategies they use have different implications for vocales' personal and family time. During our interview with the vocal helping illiterate mothers (as described in the previous excerpt), we learned that she has a physical disability. She experiences mobility impairment in one of her legs. She cannot walk long distances. We also learned that she normally visits illiterate beneficiaries in order to explain important information that the program's administrators want to disseminate. When we asked about how she is organized, we became aware of the fact that her husband, who is a carpenter, provides transportation (and time) for her to visit beneficiary mothers. This is a five-person household: three kids, the vocal, and her husband. Two of the kids attend middle school and the older one is in high school. When the vocal's husband is busy and not able to help her, the older son, who is 17 years old, helps with the driving. This experience of husbands or partners providing time and transportation for vocales represents a typical situation in San Luis Rio Colorado. Out of 90 cases, 49 vocales are married or have partners. In these 49 cases, 41 vocales declared that the husband/partner spends some of his time helping vocales with the program-related activities. Transportation is a very common way through which husbands/partners help vocales. Some of these husbands/partners use their own old and malfunctioning car, others use a bicycle, some others borrow a car from a friend, etc.

As you can see, this leg looks different. I suffer from physical disability. I can walk short distances only, but my husband helps me a lot with my vocal-related tasks. He has an old pickup truck and drives me when I need to visit mothers' homes. Do you hear that hammer noise coming from that room? It is him (he is a carpenter). He is working now. **What happens when he is busy and you need transportation?** My older son helps me when he is available. Otherwise, my husband stops doing his work and helps me … Although he might lose money, he is willing to help me most of the time. But I also work. **What do you do?** I work in the agricultural sector, packing produces. I start at 4 am in the morning and get back home at 8 am. This is a seasonal job. **You said that you get back home at 8 am and what is next?** I sleep during the rest of the morning. Then, there is the cleaning of home and laundry, and food preparation for my kids and husband. **But how do you manage your visits to mothers' home?** When I have to visit moms or have other meetings, I simply do not sleep during the morning (Participant 15 – Vocal).

In general, a self-defined administratively lean and efficient program heavily relies on informal resources that vocales activate at the community level. Exploring the role of vocales helps the reader understand an informal organizational piece that makes the CCT model work on the ground. The way the CCT model is implemented in Mexico entails private costs that go beyond the formal structure of the program and unfold at the household and community level. In order to manage these costs, vocales bring informal community resources, which in turn help mothers attain their co-responsibilities. But where does vocales' cooperative behavior come from?

On the one hand, there are vocales confirming that they are willing to help mothers and program's administrators given the strategic advantage that they (vocales) perceive. Data show a common understanding about the collective gain of keeping the program running. Vocales want the program benefits in their communities, thus they are willing to bring voluntary work. Families (including vocales' families) can continue receiving the monetary and in-kind (food supplements) benefits of the program. Let us call them direct benefits. But vocales perceive indirect individual benefits that motivate their cooperation. These indirect gains range from reputation and leadership to political influence, first-hand information, and power.

> I have been a vocal for two years. I like being a vocal because I have political influence, and some sort of status or reputation [*somos alguien*] that is helpful when I have to negotiate with municipal authorities. Being a vocal improves my leadership [*me facilita lidear con las mamas y autoridades*] and gives me access to information that I would not obtain otherwise (Participant 16 – Vocal).
>
> I am a political activist who fights for the sake of women rights. I suffered from domestic, physical, and psychological violence for a long period of time. Now, I am helping moms in my neighborhood to escape from similar situations. When I learned that there is a program that gives money directly to the mothers, I realized that it was going to help women become stronger. Being a vocal gives me some power to actively participate in my barrio and municipality, so I am in a better position to help mothers escape from poverty and domestic violence (Participant 17 – Vocal).

On the other hand, motivations such as other-regard are important factors explaining vocales' help and do not necessarily translate into utility maximization. The presence of close social ties, local shared norms, and recognition emerge as a powerful explanatory framework to understand the cooperative dispositions of vocales in the context of the Mexican culture, which is discussed next.

3.3 The [o]ther-regarding disposition of Mexican women: culture, norms, social ties, and recognition

Although the conventional wisdom suggests a passive role of women in the Mexican society, there is evidence indicating the opposite. Studies report that

Mexicans regard women as an instrument, whether of the desires of man, or of the ends assigned by law, society, or morality. Prostitute, goddess, great lady, or lover, a woman transmits or preserves, but does not create the values and energies that nature or society entrusts to her (Paz 1992 [1950], 12, 13). In contrast, studies on Mexican culture show an active involvement of women in social development, motivated by other-regard inclinations historically engrained in women culture and their natural commitment for social change. For example, Sor Juana Inés de La Cruz (1651–1695) used the power of her verses to criticize the society of her time, to claim both public spaces and the rights to education and knowledge for women. Sor Juana broke the traditional scheme of women defending their intellectual work and claiming women's rights to education (Paz 1995).

Another salient example is Leona Vicario, one of the most prominent women of the Mexican War of Independence (1810–1821). Leona Vicario supported the cause of independence with all means at her disposal, exposing herself to a multiple risks and hardships. As Ramos Escandon (1996, 131) suggests, discussing Formoso de Obregon Santacilla (1939), Leona Vicario, "[…] with an enormous spirit […] felt the pain in which the colony had the Indian *criollos* humiliated [and] cruelly mistreated. [She] […] was heroically resolved to help the cause even at the cost of her own life […]." Others report that she acted as a messenger of the insurgents, sheltered fugitives, cooperated with the rebels by sending resources (money and medicines) to them as well as news and information of what happened in the vice regal court (Garcia 1979).

During the Mexican Revolution (1910–1920), the battlefield heroines called *La Soldaderas* were Mexican women, members of the poor, actively participating in this revolution. Why did they choose to participate in the battle? For *Soldaderas*, many of whom were mothers, they preferred to keep the family together and accompany their husbands to war rather than be forced to stay at home unprotected in the middle of an unrestrained revolution. While many *Soldaderas* were forced to join their husbands into the battle, many others decided to do it voluntarily (Poniatowska 1999, Reséndez Fuentes 1995). *Soldaderas* were not official female soldiers. They were the wives of poor male soldiers giving them everyday assistance. *Soldaderas*, while not fighting, would cook, serve as nurses, clean, carry critical supplies, and provide emotional support for the male soldiers, most of whom were usually their husbands. *Soldaderas* used to participate as smugglers who would bring ammunition, medicine, and other goods to Mexico from the United States. They were also journalists, propagandists, and political activists.

Soldaderas' cooperative inclination was decisive militarily and politically speaking. Their role was so crucial to the extent that Federal troops knew that the rebels' male soldiers heavily depended on *Soldaderas* for their most basic needs, so eliminating *Soldaderas* provided a great advantage to the Federal army.

Studies (Arrizón 1998) suggest that the Mexican Constitution was drafted with influence coming from prominent *Soldaderas*, though they would not officially be recognized as contributors because they were women. Others (Norris and Reiss 2006) argue that *Soldaderas*' legacy has contributed to several stereotypes of Mexican women today. For instance, modern Mexican women find identification in the strength and bravery of *Soldaderas*. In the United States, Chicanas have worked to reclaim the honor of these women who sacrificed their livelihood for their freedom and communities.

Soldaderas depicted other-regard motivations rather than individual utility maximization. For example, according to Norris and Reiss (2006), the *Soldadera* Beatriz González Ortega, a follower of Pancho Villa's army, served as a nurse to the soldiers and was able to contribute to their physical well-being. Regardless of her ties to the revolutionary group, she cared for both Villa's soldiers and Federal troops that had been captured. Beatriz used to burn the uniforms of all the wounded soldiers so that Villa would be unable to distinguish Federals from revolutionaries. She cared for the patients in an altruistic manner, setting aside the politics of the war. Unfortunately, her noble efforts were not recognized in such a favorable way. She was beaten and her life was threatened. As Norris and Reiss argue, Beatriz's ability to look beyond the uniform of a soldier and to show appreciation for humanity was inspiring. She exercised great compassion and strength in preserving the lives of the enemy, even if that meant sacrificing her own life. This *Soldadera* remains as respected today not only because of her role as a nurse but also because of her integrity and strength. To sum up, the *Soldaderas* legend represents a salient example of Mexican women's other-regard personalities deeply rooted in their history and culture.

Frida Kahlo (1907–1954) became a national and international representation of women endurance for the sake of social freedom and women's rights. Frida was three years old when the Mexican Revolution began in 1910. Later, she claimed that she was born in 1910 so people would directly associate her with the revolution. Frida maintained a great political activism in Mexico, trying to spread the national identity through the use of Mexican popular art and religious altarpiece [*retablos religiosos*] (Frida Kahlo Foundation 2016). Due to her lifestyle and activism, this Mexican woman is currently used as a symbol of the international feminist movement.

Nowadays, Mexican women keep demonstrating their willingness to help other people and promote social change. For example, the social movement "Women voices, stories that transform" [*Voces de mujeres, historias que transforman*] has been walking the country in order to collect examples of women who are making profound changes in their context. Members of this social movement have collected stories from mothers organizing themselves to mobilize their community against the long-lasting drug cartel war in Mexico and against the political repression of social mobilization. For further details, see the documentary *Porteando por la Paz* [Door Knocking for the Peace] (Voces de Mujeres 2016). This movement also captured stories of forgotten women such as *curanderas* [healers], who have been playing an important role in rural Mexico. *Curanderas*' work is very old. "More than work is a way of life, a way to resist, to continue revitalizing the practices of indigenous peoples, to continue to contribute from their space to the common good" (Voces de Mujeres 2015). One can see in this social movement's narrative an intriguing post that reads as follows: "Blood in the veins, milk in the tits, and love in the heart" [*Sangre en las venas, leche en las tetas y amor en el corazon*].[5]

Special attention deserves the case of a college student who has been internationally known as the "bravest woman in Mexico" who put her life under risk for the sake of her community's safety. Marisol Valles, a 20-year-old college student, is the former police chief of a Mexican town in the northern State of Chihuahua. In her rural town, Praxedis G. Guerrero, two rival drug cartels started fighting for controlling that region and made the State of Chihuahua one of the most dangerous areas in the world. In Praxedis G. Guerrero, the police chief was tortured and beheaded. After a year without police chief, Marisol Valles was the only person willing to step up and become the police chief in this town in 2010. She was dismissed from her position in March 2011. Unable to compete with the firepower of the drug cartels and after receiving personal threats, she failed to show up for work. She applied for U.S. asylum while in hiding (World Policy Institute 2013, Lavandera 2011, Llorca 2011). Marisol stood up against corruption and violence for the betterment of her community and attracted the attention of the international media as the "bravest woman in Mexico". Marisol is an outstanding example of courage and other-regard inclination of Mexican women.

Other-regarding preferences of Mexican women over their own payoff can be understood as a social norm culturally and historically reproduced in the form of institution. This other-regard institution is self-sustained through the everyday practice and the presence of close social ties and recognition. Let us go back to our discussion on vocales to illustrate how this institution works. Repeated instances in our fieldwork data indicate that vocales have close personal linkages with beneficiary families they serve. These community ties make vocales aware of their actions' effect on the well-being of other mothers. It is

5 See *Porteando por la Paz* documentary (Voces de Mujeres 2016).

not just the cognition of externalities. It is the recognition of effects on specific neighbors. As one vocal declared: "I was elected by my neighbors. I know my neighbors for 15 years. Some of them are my 'comadres'" (Participant 18 – Vocal). In Mexico, a *comadre* is the Godmother of a child with respect to the parents and Godfather [*compadre*] of this child.[6] In the city of San Luis Rio Colorado, *comadres* are typically close friends or relatives. They interact very often, organize gatherings, sometimes they are co-workers, and get together for soap opera time. Another vocal said: "because I am helping my comadres and friends, I am willing to help them whatever it takes. I want them to stay in the program" (Participant 19 – Vocal).

Social ties between beneficiary households and vocales also happen through their kids. For instance, another vocal's narrative shows that households' heads do not always know each other but their kids do it:

> Although this is a small barrio I do not know all the mothers very well. Yet our kids attend the school together and are friends. My kid brings his friends to our home and then, I realize who they are and where they live. One of my child's friends is shoeless. I know who his mother is but we seldom talk to each other. She works during the night and sleeps during the day. Most of the time, her kids are unattended. I realized that this family needs the program and I helped them with the enrollment information and paperwork. (Participant 20 – Vocal).

There are more specific norms working along with the other-regard institution discussed above. For example, the apparently trivial social practice of 'offering a glass of water to visitors' emerged as a relevant shared norm during our fieldwork. Recall the case discussed above, about the vocal bringing water bottles for kids in order to help them during their long walking from home to school. The way this vocal helps the kids becomes relevant given the extreme temperatures that pedestrians have to handle within this sandy city. This case depicts a cooperative mood of the vocal intended to help other families with their kids' school attendance. According to this vocal's narrative, she is willing to bring water for those kids because "nobody is denied a glass of water" [*a nadie se le niega un vaso de agua*]. According to this participant, she learned this saying from her grandmother and heard about it from other neighbors. In San Luis Rio Colorado (as somewhere else in Mexico), it is a common social practice. People at home offer a glass of water as a welcome sign without having the visitors to ask for it. This is a shared understanding. As the aforementioned vocal declared:

---

6 In addition to this social meaning, in San Luis Rio Colorado, "comadre" also refers to a woman who likes to gossip.

> When I realized that those kids needed to walk long distances in order to get the school, the first thing that came to mind was water. Then I thought to myself that offering water to kids that stop by my place would be beneficial for their long walking (Participant 20 – Vocal).

The willingness of this vocal to cooperate with beneficiary families in the way she does it follows a collective norm that has been transmitted from past generations and is reproduced through its everyday practice (the enactment of the saying: "nobody is denied a glass of water"). Interestingly, this apparently insignificant social practice emerged as a spontaneous and informal cooperative display that helps beneficiary families achieve the program-related co-responsibilities.

Furthermore, the notion of co-responsibility is a cultural disposition that became an institution within the framework of instrumental rationality and its symbol of efficiency. Instrumental rationality is derived from a subjective process of social construction based on symbols of modernity and efficiency (Dobbin 1994). Thus, with the institutionalization of instrumental rationality as a cultural system, this institution turns out to be inherent, imperceptible, and self-sustained.

Let us explore the example of the Mexican case. In Latin America, during the 1980s, the state was identified as a major cause of development failure and was also accused of cultivating a dependency culture. Molyneux (2006) contends that this situation explains the emergence of the principle of beneficiary responsibility along with related ideas of co-management or co-responsibility, self-help, or self-sufficiency, etc. At the same time, Molyneux continues, international organizations such as the World Bank became concerned with cost-sharing and efficiency, so that hitherto passive recipients of poverty programs became active participants in meeting the costs of development.

Nowadays, this discourse of co-responsibility is deeply set in the narratives of vocales participating in the implementation of the Mexican CCT program. During our fieldwork, recurring instances showed stories such as "we do not want the program's help for free" (Participant 21 – Vocal); "we do not have to seat down and wait for the government's solution to our problems" (Participant 22 – Vocal); "this program entails costs and we have to handle with those costs" (Participant 23 – Vocal); "we have to bring our part or contribution" (Participant 24 – Vocal); "if we want to escape from poverty, we have to pay what it takes" (Participant 25 – Vocal); "this program is for us…the minimum we can do is to put our own effort to accomplish our part" (Participant 26 – Vocal). In general, this notion of co-responsibility is a natural and spontaneous proclivity already embedded in vocales' stories through which they explain their inclination for helping beneficiary families and the program's staff.

4 Conclusion

After exploring 90 cases of vocales enacting their linking tasks in the implementation of the Mexican CCT program, we found that helping beneficiary mothers to meet the program's requirements emerged as a result of both: vocales' self-interest-driven cooperation and vocales' cultural pre-disposition to help. On the one hand, vocales' help is a cooperative behavior that conforms, in part, to utility maximization models of collective action due to the collective gain that vocales expect from keeping the program running in their community. Vocales' benefit includes not only the program's monetary and in-kind support but also indirect benefits such as reputation, political influence, and first-hand information that translate into power.

On the other hand, there are vocales whose narratives show cooperative inclinations that make sense in the context of the other-regarding institution deeply rooted in the Mexican culture and history. This other-regarding preference became a self-sustained practice due to factors such as close social ties between beneficiary holders and vocales along with shared beliefs at the community level. The institutionalization of the notion of "co-responsibilities" (that is a key component of the CCT model) became part of these shared beliefs and is inherent in the cultural system of efficiency underlying the implementation process of the CCT program. These shared beliefs triggered a spontaneous response of vocales inclined to help beneficiary families. Another factor explaining this cooperative move is the notion of recognition. What a vocal does can be seen (by the same vocal) to matter to specific beneficiary mothers. If what a vocal does has implications for the life of specific mothers and families (*comadres* and friends), then the welfare of these families matters for the vocal as well. Exploring the cases of vocales made the presence of recognition visible in the implementation stage of the CCT program.

But the working of the invisible hand of community also has its downside as long as it silences the voice options with respect to the Mexican CCT program. According to Hirschman (1995; 1970), when both exit and voice options are available in organizational settings, people would probably choose exit over voice in the event that a better alternative exists. In contrast, people would choose voice if they believe that the organization would seriously consider their voice. In the case of the Mexican CCT program implementation, spontaneous and informal cooperative arrangements help the program to manage the institutional mismatch between policy design and local context. As a result, the program keeps working the same way and beneficiary families do not voice public criticism strong enough to induce organizational change. Furthermore, exit is costly because the opportunity cost of leaving the program is huge. There is no substitute for the array of benefits that mothers get from the program. Mothers prefer paying the private costs that the program implementation entails over paying the opportunity cost of leaving the program. In short, the working of informal social mechanisms on the ground guarantees the implementation of the program, but at the same time, reinforces its weakness because those mechanisms quieten critical voice. Both costly exit and silenced voice can benefit a broader instrumental strategy of the CCT model.

The instrumental role of women in the CCT strategy is part of its institutional design. Molyneux (2006) contends that CCTs increase the burden for women as a way to secure the program's goals. The current poverty agenda is embedded in decentralization and privatization reforms and puts greater emphasis on participatory mechanisms in the delivery of social welfare. The role of poor women and participatory approaches became central to dealing with budget cuts, decentralization, and devolution of the state's responsibilities. Molyneux's argument coheres with the Mexican experience. As this chapter discusses, the role of women in general and the linking tasks of vocales in particular represent an essential part of the program implementation. Beneficiary mothers in Mexico are willing to manage this burden not only because of cooperative dispositions but also because of strategic gains such as receiving the cash transfer and enjoying increased autonomy. Both the gender perspective and the principle of co-responsibility work together, instrumentally, in the Mexican CCT program (cf. Chant 2008). This instrumental mood corresponds to an institutional framework in a way that normalizes the responsibilities of motherhood to secure the program's achievements. Once this social and policy practice is institutionalized, it becomes "normal" and "appropriate" in the context of the structure of meanings in which the CCT model makes sense.

Thus, the invisible hand of community in the Mexican CCT program implementation resembles the interplay between structure and agency (cf. Giddens 1984; Nicolini 2013; Feldman and Orlikowski 2011). As discussed in this chapter, the working of shared informal norms and meanings enable social interactions and ties (networks). Both norms and networks shape cooperative behavior, which is embedded in constructed meanings of institutions. Institutions exist and keep in existence through the recurrent people's performance. It means that social practices such as cooperation or help, co-responsibility, and motherhood at the service of the CCT model are reproduced through both material and discursive components of action. At the macro level, the everyday action explains the creation and evolution of social structures in which the policy script is enacted. If social structures evolve, cooperation also evolves through spontaneous, non-deliberate, non-formalized institutional frameworks. In short, informal norms within these frameworks and their enabling properties trigger self- and other-oriented help through social mechanisms and processes that make the CCT model work.

Our findings have policy implications because they help the reader understand the informal cooperative behavior that makes the CCT model work on the ground. Without a proper account of informal and spontaneous cooperative mechanisms through which the CCT model achieves its results, innovative poverty alleviation strategies such as CCT programs will become a policy practice without principles for success. The results of this study can be helpful to outline these principles and suggest a line of inquiry in the sociology of the invisible hand in general, and policy implementation scholarship in particular. The results discussed in this study are significant for developing a body of knowledge on how spontaneous cooperative mechanisms affect a poverty program's achievements in a context of unrealistic assumptions. Thus, policy practitioners and scholars should take into consideration not only the formal design of incentives, regulation, or enforcement instruments for program implementation, but also the working of shared beliefs, social ties, and recognition reproducing cooperative synergies that create opportunities for action, expand the program's impact, and help practitioners rethink program assumptions and late programming.

References

Adato, Michelle, and John Hoddinott. 2010. "Conditional Cash Transfers in the Second Decade: Current Debates and New Frontiers." In *Conditional Cash Transfers in Latin America*, edited by Michelle Adato and John Hoddinott, 351–372. Washington (DC): Institutional Food Policy Research Institute.

Adato, Michelle, and Terry Roopnaraine. 2004. *A Social Analysis of Red de Protección Social in Nicaragua*. Washington (DC): International Food Policy Research Institute.

Agrawal, Arun, and Elinor Ostrom. 2001. "Collective Action, Property Rights, and Decentralization in Resource Use in India and Nepal." *Politics Society* 29: 485–514.

Amenta, Edwin, and Kelly M. Ramsey. 2010. "Institutional Theory." In *The Handbook of Politics: State and Civil Society in Global Perspective*, edited by Kevin T. Leicht and J. Craig Jenkins, chap. 2, 15–40. New York: Springer.

Andreoni, James. 2006. "Philanthropy." In *Handbook of the Economics of Giving, Altruism, and Reciprocity*, edited by Serge-Christophe Kolm and Jean Mercier Ythier, 1201–1269. Oxford: Elsevier.

Araral, Eduardo Jr. 2009. "What Explains Collective Action in the Commons? Theory and Evidence from the Philippines." *World Development* 37: 687–697.

Arrizón, Alicia. 1998. "Soldaderas and the Staging of the Mexican Revolution." *The Drama Review* 42: 90–112.

Atkinson, Michael, and William Coleman. 1992. "Policy Networks, Policy Communities, and the Problems of Governance." *Governance: An International Journal of Policy and Administration* 5: 154–180.

Barrett, Susan M. 2004. "Implementation Studies: Time for a Revival? Personal Reflections on 20 Years of Implementation Studies." *Public Administration* 82: 249–262.

Bekkers, René, and Pamala Wiepking. 2010. "A Literature Review of Empirical Studies of Philanthropy: Eight Mechanisms That Drive Charitable Giving." *Nonprofit and Voluntary Sector Quarterly* 40: 1–50.

Berns, Laurence. 1994. "Aristotle and Adam Smith on Justice: Cooperation Between Ancients and Moderns?" *The Review of Metaphysics* 48: 71–90.

Borzel, Tanja A. 1998. "Organizing Babylon – On the Different Conceptions of Policy Networks." *Public Administration* 76: 253–273.

Bourdieu, Pierre. 1990. *The Logic of Practice*. Stanford (CA): Stanford University Press.

Bozeman, Barry. 2013. "What Organization Theorists and Public Policy Researchers Can Learn from One Another: Publicness Theory As a Case-in-point." *Organization Studies* 34: 169–188.

Bray, David Barton. 2009. "Collective Action and the Role of Community Norms." *Digital Library of the Commons*. Indiana University. Accessed August 25, 2011. http://dlc.dlib.indiana.edu/dlc/handle/10535/5942

Brown, Eleanor, and James M. Ferris. 2007. "Social Capital and Philanthropy: An Analysis of the Impact of Social Capital on Individual Giving and Volunteering." *Nonprofit and Voluntary Sector Quarterly* 36: 85–99.

Chant, Sylvia. 2008. "The 'Feminisation of Poverty' and the 'Feminisation' of Anti-poverty Programmes: Room for Revision?" *The Journal of Development Studies* 44: 165–197.

Coase, Ronald H. 1937. "The Nature of the Firm." *Economica* 4: 386–405.

CONEVAL. 2011. *Medicion de Pobreza en los Municipios de Mexico 2010*. Mexico: Consejo Nacional de Evaluacion de la Politica de Desarrollo Social.

Crozier, Michael, and Herhard Friedberg. 1980. *Actors and Systems: The Politics of Collective Action*. Chicago: University of Chicago Press.

deLeon, Peter. 1999. "The Missing Link Revisited: Contemporary Implementation Research." *Policy Studies Review* 16: 311–338.

Dobbin, Frank. 1994. "Cultural Models of Organization: The Social Construction of Rational Organizing Principles." In *The Sociology of Culture: Emerging Theoretical Perspectives*, edited by Diana Crane, 117–141. Oxford: Basil Blackwell.

Duclos, Jean-Yves, and Abdelkrim Araar. 2006. *Poverty and Equity: Measurement, Policy, and Estimation with DAD*. New York: Springer and International Development Research Centre.

Eckstein, Susan. 2001. "Community as Gift-giving: Collectivistic Roots of Volunteerism." *American Sociological Review* 66: 829–851.

Escobar Latapi, Agustin, and Mercedez Gonzalez de la Rocha. 2001. *Resultados de la Evaluación Cualitativa Basal del Programa de Educación, Salud y Alimentación (PROGRESA) Semiurbano. Septiembre – diciembre*. Mexico City: CIESAS-Progresa.

Feldman, Martha S., and Wanda J. Orlikowski. 2011. "Theorizing Practice and Practicing Theory." *Organization Science* (Institute for Operations Reserch and the Management Sciences) 22: 1240–1253.

Fiszbein, Ariel, and Norbert Schady. 2009. *Conditional Cash Transfers. Reducing Present and Future Poverty*. Whashington (DC): The World Bank.

Formoso de Obregon Santacilla, Adela. 1939. *La Mujer en la Organizacion Social del Pais*. Mexico: Talleres Graficos de la Nacion.

Frida Kahlo Foundation. 2016. *Frida Kahlo – The Complete Works*. Accessed December 30, 2016. http://www.frida-kahlo-foundation.org/biography.html

Fuentes, Nicole, and Mariano Rojas. 2001. "Economic Theory and Subjective Well-being in Mexico." *Social Indicators Research* 53: 289–314.

Garcia, Genaro. 1979. *Leona Vicario. Heroina Insurgente*. Mexico: Museo Nacional de Arqueologia, Historia y Ethnologia.

Giddens, Anthony. 1984. *The Constitution of Society. Outline of the Theory of Structuration*. Berkeley: University of California Press.

González de la Rocha, Mercedes. 2006. *Procesos Domesticos y Vulnerabilidad*. Mexico City: CIESAS.

Hirschman, Albert Otto. 1970. *Exit, Voice, and Loyalty: Responses to Decline in Firms, Organizations, and States*. Cambridge: Harvard University Press.

Hirschman, Albert Otto. 1995. *A Propensity to Self-subversion*. Cambridge: Harvard University Press.

Hjern, Benny. 1982. "Implementation Research: The Link Gone Missing." *Journal of Public Policy* 2: 301–308.

Hoddinott, John, and Doris Wiesmann. 2010. "The Impact of Conditional Cash Transfer Programs on Food Consumption." In *Conditional Cash Transfers in Latin America*, edited by Michelle Adato and John Hoddinott, 258–283. Baltimore: International Food Policy Research Institute.

Howlett, Michael, M. Ramesh, and Anthony Perl. 2009. *Studying Public Policy. Policy Cycles & Policy Subsystems*. Oxford: Oxford University Press.

Jepperson, Ronald L. 1991. "Institutions, Institutional Effects, and Institutionalism." In *The New Institutionalism in Organizational Analysis*, edited by Walter W. Powell and Paul J. DiMaggio, 143–163. Chicago (IL): University of Chicago Press.

Kimball, Miles, and Robert Willis. 2006. *Utility and Happiness*. University of Michigan, Department of Economics, Working Paper, March 3.

Lavandera, Ed. 2011. "'Bravest Woman in Mexico' Seeks Asylum in United States." *CNN*, June 6, 2011.

Lejano, Raul Perez, and Helen Ingram. 2011. "Modeling the Commons As a Game with Vector Payoffs." *Journal of Theoretical Politics* 24: 1–24.

Lejano, Raul, and Francisco Fernandez de Castro. 2014. "Norm, Network, and Commons: The Invisible Hand of Community." *Environmental Science and Policy* 36: 73–85.

Levy, Santiago. 2006. *Progress against Poverty. Sustaining Mexico's Progresa-Oportunidades Program*. Washington (DC): The Brookings Institution.

Llorca, Juan Carlos. 2011. "Marisol Valles, Young Mexican Police Chief Seeks U.S. Asylum." *The Associated Press*, March 11, 2011.

Maluccio, John, and Rafael Flores. 2005. *Impact Evaluation of a Conditional Cash Transfer Program: The Nicaraguan Red de Protección Social*. Washington (DC): International Food Policy Research Institute.

March, James G., and Johan P. Olsen. 1989. *Rediscovering Institutions. The Organizational Basis of Politics*. New York: The Free Press.

Meyer, John W. 2008. "Reflections on Institutional Theories of Organizations." In *The SAGE Handbook of Organizational Institutionalism*, edited by Royston Greenwood, Christine Oliver, Roy Suddaby and Kerstin Sahlin-Anderson, chap. 34, 788–809. Thousand Oaks (CA): Sage.

Molyneux, Maxine. 2006. "Mothers at the Service of the New Poverty Agenda: Progresa/Oportunidades, Mexico's Conditional Transfer Programme." *Social Policy & Administration* 40: 425–449.

Neufeld, Lynnette, Armando García-Guerra, Jef Leroy, María de Lourdes Flores López, Ana Cecilia Fernández Gaxiola, and Juan Ángel Rivera-Dommarco. 2005. *Impacto del program Oportunidades en Nutricion y Alimentacion en Zonas Urbanas de Mexico*. Mexico City: INSP.

Nicolini, Davide. 2013. *Practice Theory, Work, and Organization. An Introduction*. Oxford: Oxford University Press.

Norris, Laura, and Joseph Reiss. 2006. *Las Soldaderas. The Battlefield Heroines of the Mexican Revolution*. Ann Arbor: University of Michigan.

North, Douglass. 2005. *Understanding the Process of Economic Change*. Princeton University Press.

Olsen, Johan P. 2010. *Governing Through Institution Building. Institutional Theory and Recent European Experiments in Democratic Organization*. Oxford: Oxford University Press.

Olson, Mancur. 1971 [1965]. *The Logic of Collective Action. Public Goods and the Theory of Groups*. Cambridge: Harvard University Press.

Ordoñez, Gerardo. 2015. *Progresa-Oportunidades-Prospera: Avatares, Alcances y Resultados de un Programa Paradigmatico contra la Pobreza*. Manuscript presented at the 2015 Conference of the Mexican Network for the Study of Social Policy (REMIPSO).

Governing the Commons. The Evolution of Institutions for Collective Action. Cambridge: Cambridge University Press.

Ostrom, Elinor. 2000. "Collective Action and the Evolution of Social Norms." *The Journal of Economic Perspectives* 14: 137–158.

O'Toole, Laurence J. Jr. 2000. "Research on Policy Implementation: Assessment and Prospects." *Journal of Public Administration Research and Theory* 10: 263–288.

Paz, Octavio. 1992 [1950]. *El Laberinto de la Soledad*. Mexico: Fondo de Cultura Economica.

Paz, Octavio. 1995. *SorJuana Ines de la Cruz o las trampas de la fe*. Mexico: Fondo de Cultura Economica.

Poniatowska, Elena. 1999. *Las Soldaderas*. Mexico: CONACULTA.

Powell, Walter W. 1990. "Neither Market nor Hierarchy: Network Forms of Organizations." *Research in Organizational Behavior* 12: 295–336.

Pressman, Jeffrey L., and Aaron Wildavsky. 1984. *Implementation: How Great Expectations in Washington Are Dashed in Oakland*. Berkeley: University of California Press.

PROSPERA-Comite Tecnico. 2015. *Lineamientos Operativos de PROSPERA. Programa de Inclusion Social para 2015*. Mexico: Prospera-comite tecnico de la coordinacion nacional.

Prospera-DGAO. 2015. *Te Gustaria Formar Parte de Prospera?* Accessed July 7, 2016. https://dgao.oportunidades.gob.mx/siel/

Ramos Escandon, Carmen. 1996. "Quinientos afios de olvido: historiografia e historia de la mujer en Mexico." *Secuencia* 36: 121–150.

Reséndez Fuentes, Andres. 1995. "Battleground Women: Soldaderas and Female Soldiers in the Mexican Revolution." *The Americas* 51: 525–553.

Rhodes, R.A.W. 1990. "Policy Networks: A British Perspective." *Journal of Theoretical Politics* 2: 293–317.

Rivera, Leonor, Bernardo Hernández, and Roberto Castro. 2005. *Efectos del programa Oportuniades en las relaciones de pareja y familiares*. Mexico City: COLMEX.

Sabatier, Paul, and Daniel Mazmanian. 2005 [1979]. "The Implementation of Public Policy: A Framework of Analysis." *Policy Studies Journal* 8: 538–561.

Sabatier, Paul A. 1986. "Top-down and Bottom-up Approaches to Implementation Research: A Critical Analysis and Suggested Synthesis." *Journal of Public Policy* 6: 21–48.

Saetren, Harald. 2005. "Facts and Myths about Research on Public Policy Implementation: Out-of-fashion, Allegedly Dead, But Still Very Much Alive and Relevant." *The Policy Studies Journal* 33: 559–582.

SEDESOL. 2001. *Acuerdo por el que se establecen las reglas de operacion del programa de Educacion, Salud y Alimentacion (PROGRESA)*. Mexico City: Poder Ejecutivo Federal.

SEDESOL. 2002. *Acuerdo por el que se emiten y publican las Reglas de Operación del Programa de Desarrollo Humano Oportunidades, para el Ejercicio Fiscal 2003*. Mexico: Poder Ejecutivo Federal – Diario Ofical de la Federacion.

SEDESOL. 2005. *Acuerdo por el que se emiten y publican las Reglas de Operación del Programa de Desarrollo Humano Oportunidades, para el ejercicio fiscal de 2006*. Mexico: Poder Ejecutivo Federal – Diario Oficial de la Federacion.

SEDESOL. 2008a. *Acuerdo por el que se emiten las reglas de operacion del programa de desarrollo humano Oportunidades para el ejercicio fiscal 2009*. Mexico: Poder Ejecutivo Federal.

SEDESOL. 2008b. *Manual de Comites de Promocion Comunitaria*. Mexico City: Direccion General de Atencion y Operacion – Oportunidades.

SEDESOL. 2015. *Acuerdo por el que se emiten las Reglas de Operación de PROSPERA Programa de Inclusión Social, para el ejercicio fiscal 2016*. Mexico: Diario Oficial de la Federacion.

SEDESOL-Progresa. 1999. "Conocimiento de Progresa por Parte de las Mujeres Beneficiarias y Opinión sobre sus Apoyos." In *Más oportunidades para las familias pobres. Evaluación de resultados del Programa de Educación, Salud y Alimentación. Primeros avances, 1999*, 373–378. Mexico City: SEDESOL-Progresa.

Smith, Adam. 1976 [1759]. *The Theory of Moral Sentiments*. Indianapolis: Liberty Classics.

Spradley, James P. 1979. *The Ethnographic Interview*. New York: Holt, Rinehart and Winston,

Stanford Encyclopedia of Philosophy. 2012. *Aristotle's Political Theory*. Stanford: Stanford University.

Sugden, Robert. 1982. "On the Economics of Philanthropy." *The Economic Journal* 92: 341–350.

Voces de Mujeres. 2015. *Mujeres, Madres Andando*. Accessed December 28, 2016. http://masdemx.com/2015/12/20-mujeres-recorren-mexico-para-encontrar-historias-de-luchadoras-sociales/

Voces de Mujeres. 2016. *Antonia Zamora*. Accessed November 30, 2016. http://vocesdemujeres.mx/

Williamson, Oliver E. 2005. "Transaction Costs Economics." In *Handbook of New Institutional Economics*, edited by Claude Menard and Mary M. Shirley, 41–65. Netherlands: Springer.

Wilson, John. 2000. "Volunteering." *Annual Review of Sociology* 26: 215–240.

World Policy Institute. 2013. "The Plight of the 'Bravest Woman in Mexico.'" *World Policy Journal*, April 22.

Steve McDonald, Scott T. Grether, Kim S. Holland and Hannah McQueen

Serendipity in the Online Job Market*

Abstract: Serendipitous job finding occurs when people receive unsolicited job leads or are otherwise informally recruited into jobs via their personal connections. Most of the previous research on this topic has examined evidence that predates the rise of social media and Internet-based job finding. The present chapter draws on recent data from qualitative interviews with 32 human resource professionals and recruiters to shed light on how serendipity operates in the online job market. Results from these interviews show how job recruiters perceive online signals of worker quality and job mobility intentions in ways that are consequential for informal recruitment practices. Human Resources (HR) professionals use social media websites (especially LinkedIn) as critical tools to build, sustain, and recruit network contacts. In these ways, the Internet and social media has fundamentally transformed, rather than reduced, the experience of informal recruitment and serendipitous job finding.

Keywords: Hiring; recruitment; employment; Internet; social media

1 Serendipity in the online job market

Serendipity is an enduring feature in social life, even for the most routine activities. The job finding process is an ideal example. Economic theory describes the job search as a rational and intentional process of investing in information (Devine and Kiefer 1991). And yet, sociological research reveals that people commonly receive job information from unlikely sources in unexpected situations (McDonald 2010). The receipt of unsolicited job information via interpersonal connections often results in people being hired into new jobs. In fact, roughly one out of every four workers in the United States changes jobs without having engaged in a job search – among managers and supervisors, it is

* Authorship is alphabetical after first author. This research was supported by funds from North Carolina State University and the American Sociological Association's Fund for the Advancement of the Discipline. We are grateful for the advice and support provided by Amanda Damarin throughout the data collection process. We are also appreciative of the expert comments and recommendations from the editor and an anonymous reviewer. Much thanks to the HR community in the Research Triangle for their willingness to participate in this study.

nearly one out of every two (McDonald and Elder 2006). "Non-searching" into new jobs is a key indicator of serendipitous job finding and reveals the important role that social relationships play in facilitating access to hidden job opportunities (McDonald 2010). In order to better understand the hidden benefits of unsolicited job finding assistance, theorists developed the term "invisible hand of social capital" (IHSC), which refers to resources that individuals receive from their social network connections without active mobilization or solicitation (Lin 2000; Lin and Ao 2008; McDonald and Day 2010).

While previous studies revealed that the IHSC is common and beneficial for accessing high status jobs (McDonald 2015), much of the research draws on evidence that predates the rise of social media and Internet-based job finding. The implications of this technological transformation for the experience of serendipitous job finding remain uncertain. The Internet makes information on job seekers and job openings more available. How has the serendipitous job finding process been transformed by the Internet and social networking sites? What forms might serendipity take in the online job market? We analyze interview data from Human Resources (HR) professionals in order to address these questions. The interviews reveal several important insights. First, online social media platforms allow workers to passively transmit signals of quality and mobility intentions that may facilitate job recruitment. Second, online social media provides recruiters with a more effective means for developing, managing, and communicating with professional networks, thus facilitating opportunities for recruiting workers to fill job openings. Before presenting those results, we summarize the key concepts and issues related to serendipitous job finding.

2 Unsolicited assistance in the labor market

Individuals frequently engage in social actions that unwittingly result in future benefits. It is easy to imagine someone receiving information about a job opportunity while at the dog park or a bar or a high school reunion. Rather than being purely instrumental or intentional, motivations for engaging in the kinds of interactions that lead to these serendipitous encounters are both multiplex (involving multiple motivations simultaneously) and dynamic (changing over time: McDonald 2010). Much of the social capital that individuals generate comes from engagement in routine activities (Small 2009). For example, parents often develop important connections with other parents through their children's activities, like childcare and sports. The relationships that develop in these contexts are the unexpected byproducts of parental activities, which nonetheless can have a profound effect on the ways individuals live their lives (Small 2009).

Serendipity abounds in labor markets. Granovetter's (1995 [1974]) seminal monograph on *Getting a Job* was the first to point out that a substantial number of individuals report changing jobs without engaging in a job search. Survey data suggests that one-quarter of US workers were hired into their current job without engaging in a job search (McDonald and Elder 2006; McDonald 2015). People tend to "non-search" into new jobs when they hear about a job opportunity through their routine interactions or when they are directly offered jobs by contacts/employers (McDonald 2010). Estimates of the receipt of these unsolicited job leads vary, revealing that between 35% and 53% of the workforce heard about a job opportunity (without asking) during the last year as part of a casual conversation (McDonald, Lin and Ao 2009; McDonald et al. 2016).

According to Granovetter (1995 [1974], 36), "those who are searching [for work] would not if they didn't *have* to, and they wouldn't have to if they were good enough." Receiving an unsolicited job lead is partly due to a person's ability to signal their qualifications and fitness for a job opening to their network connections. These signals can be transmitted through previous experiences or direct interaction (Smith 2005; Marin 2012; Trimble O'Connor 2013). However, signals can also be discerned on the basis of individual characteristics. For example, employed workers and those who are working in high status positions (executive and managerial jobs) are significantly more likely than others to hear about employment opportunities through routine conversations (McDonald, Lin and Ao 2009) and are more likely to change jobs without engaging in job searches (McDonald and Elder 2006). Unsolicited job finding assistance also tends to be most common for members of dominant social groups (men and ethnic majorities) and for workers who are connected to people from dominant social groups (McDonald et al. 2009; McDonald 2011; McDonald et al. 2016). One study showed that women often "non-search" out of male-dominated jobs and into female-dominated jobs, with the reverse being true for men (Kmec, McDonald and Trimble 2010). In these instances, gender serves as a signal of fitness for a job and recruitment operates as a mechanism to better align worker signals with job characteristics.

Serendipitous job finding is fundamentally a social process, as personal intermediaries are almost always responsible when job opportunities "fall into your lap" (Granovetter 1995 [1974], 145). Receiving unsolicited job leads is therefore a positive function of the extensity of networks and the status of personal contacts (McDonald, Lin and Ao 2009). Well-connected individuals are most likely to learn about job opportunities without asking for them, even net of personal characteristics. Non-searching and the unsolicited receipt of job leads therefore illustrate the subtle and unique role that the IHSC plays in the job allocation process. Nonetheless, serendipitous job finding is studied almost exclusively from the perspective of the information receiver rather than the information sender. As such, the information diffusion processes that generate offers of unsolicited job finding assistance remain mostly obscured.

3 Serendipitous job finding in the online job market

Much of the empirical evidence on serendipity and the IHSC in the labor market predates the proliferation of the Internet and its expansive role as intermediary between workers and job openings. The Internet is fundamentally transforming the ways people are matched to jobs. Recent estimates suggest that roughly 80% of job seekers use the Internet to search for jobs (Green et al. 2012). Information about job openings is more readily available than ever, thanks to the emergence of job posting websites (e.g., Monster.com) and aggregators (Indeed.com). Email listservs and social media websites make it easier for employment opportunities to be transmitted *en masse* electronically. The Internet also allows for greater access to information about potential job candidates. Employers use information obtained via Google and social media websites such as LinkedIn and Facebook to screen job applicant pools and to find and recruit workers who might be willing to change jobs. According to the Equal Employment Opportunity Commission (EEOC), 75% of job recruiters are required to conduct online research on applicants (Roth et al. 2016). About 84% of employers reported they currently use social media to assist in their recruitment activities (SHRM 2016). The main reason for using social media is to recruit passive job candidates who might not otherwise apply for a job opening (SHRM 2016). The same survey showed that about three-quarters of the firms that used social media for recruitment said that social media allowed them to search for and contact passive job candidates (SHRM 2016).

These transformations are profound and may render moot our existing insights about the role the IHSC plays in the labor market. According to economic theory, lack of information about job candidates and job openings leads to inefficient job matching (Stigler 1961). A worker may not know that their ideal job is being advertised. Likewise, an employer may not be aware that their ideal candidate is looking for work. Workers and employers rely on personal connections to fill in those information gaps through informal job search and recruitment. Under conditions of perfect information, formal advertising will be enough to ensure high-quality matches between workers and employers. Using this logic, the proliferation of information is likely to lead to a much more formalized process of recruitment and screening, one that makes network connections less important for job matches (Freeman 2002). Consequently, actions of workers and employers may have shifted to more rationalized and purposive practices that routinize and streamline job finding, sidelining serendipitous experiences in the job market.

By contrast, others have suggested that Internet search and recruitment contribute to a "winner-take-all" market with increased demand for highly skilled workers and downward wage pressure for the rest of the workforce (Autor 2001; Nakamura et al. 2009). The premium placed on highly skilled workers might require recruiters to step up their efforts at informal recruitment to identify qualified candidates. Furthermore, social media platforms such as LinkedIn, Facebook, and Twitter may make it easier for workers and recruiters to build and sustain network relations that could eventually result in unanticipated employment opportunities.

The shift from a traditional to an online job market leads one to consider several important questions. Have serendipitous experiences receded into the background or do they still play a prominent role in job matching? What does the process of serendipity look like in online labor markets? How does online information impact the role of the IHSC in the online labor market?

To address these questions, we employ a unique approach. Most previous studies of serendipitous job finding examined the role of the individual who receives unsolicited assistance. By contrast, we attempt to unpack the serendipitous process by studying those individuals who are initiating this form of assistance: job recruiters. While the receipt of unsolicited job leads is often unexpected from the point of view of the information receiver, the actions taken by the source of that information can be instrumental and strategic. A focus on the actors that provide job information affords us with a view of the other side of serendipity – the heretofore hidden side of online job recruitment. By examining how job recruiters seek out potential job candidates, we can begin to unpack the hidden process of serendipity.

Our study emphasizes two aspects of online job recruitment. First, we examine how HR professionals interpret online information as signals of worker quality and fit for job openings. The Internet and social media are platforms for contemporary identity construction (Castells 1996; Rainie and Wellman 2012). Social networking sites maintain unique sociocultural frameworks through which individuals can project distinct identities to multiple audiences (Papacharissi 2009; van Dijck 2013). Job recruiters are often tasked with interpreting these online signals as part of their evaluation of potential job candidates (Bohnert and Ross 2010; Caers and Castelyns 2011). We therefore seek a deeper understanding of how these online signals might facilitate recruitment and selection of potential job candidates.

Second, we examine how job recruiters use Internet resources as part of their recruitment strategies. Previous research suggests that social networking sites (especially LinkedIn) are fundamental to the recruitment activities of HR professionals (Caers and Castelyns 2011; Davison, Maraist and Bing 2011; Bonet, Cappelli and Hamori 2013). However, the processes by which these activities occur remain opaque. Social media can serve as the modern day Rolodex, allowing HR recruiters to organize their existing professional connections, to expand their network by identifying potential candidates for job openings, and to contact workers whom they want to employ. Our investigation is aimed at illuminating these processes.

4 Data and methods

We analyze data from interviews with 32 HR recruiters collected from April to October 2014 in the Research Triangle of North Carolina (Raleigh, Durham, and Chapel Hill). Interviewees were asked about how the Internet and social media are used to advertise position openings, to "source" (i.e., fill) applicant pools, and to screen job candidates. They were recruited through participation in local HR professional organization activities and supplemented with respondent suggested referrals. While this is not a random sample, we used theoretical sampling techniques to enhance the heterogeneity of our sample. We conducted interviews with HR staff who work as generalists (who perform many HR functions, not just recruitment), recruiting specialists, staffing agents, and executive search consultants (headhunters). Our sample also derives from a wide variety of industries: real estate, law, finance, health care, engineering, manufacturing, private services, and education.

The semi-structured interviews centered on applicant recruitment and screening and averaged 1 hour and 8 minutes. The interviews were audio recorded (in all but one instance) and transcribed, resulting in nearly 800 pages of text. Data collection and analysis were guided by grounded theory, which allows for patterns to emerge inductively and reflexively from qualitative data. We used open coding procedures to assign elements of the text data to categories. We then examined the various themes and connections among the codes as part of a separate focused coding stage. Analytic memos were used to elaborate on the emergent themes. In this chapter, we describe several prominent themes that shed light on how serendipitous job finding operates in the online job market. All of the names presented here are pseudonyms to protect the anonymity of the interviewees.

5 Online signaling

Our data show that incorrect grammar, online pictures, and online activity can send signals to job recruiters about a person's work abilities, degree of professionalism, and interests in job mobility. HR professionals viewed grammar and spelling errors as indicators of a job applicant's professionalism and competence. For example, Kimberly, a generalist in the tech industry, used grammatical errors on cover letters as a way to narrow down her applicants:

> I've had people who just [had] glaring grammatical and spelling errors in their cover letter and they're applying for a sales position where they'd be writing proposals. Like, no. You can eliminate people right away (Kimberly).

Grammatical and spelling errors are perceived as signals that job applicants are not serious about work and are unlikely to be interviewed. Betty, a hiring administrator at a staffing agency, also said if people do not take the time to "proofread their own LinkedIn profile" this could translate into how they would proofread for a company: "If they were proofreading for a company and they haven't proofread their own LinkedIn profile, why would I give them a call?" Betty uses information obtained from online profiles to determine their work abilities. For other HR professionals as well, grammatical and spelling errors are but one type of signal they perceive from online profiles that can influence decisions about who they recruit for a job opening.

Online pictures also send signals to HR professionals. Most HR professionals interpreted online pictures as a signal that a job candidate either is, or is not, professional. For instance, Mark, a recruiter in a business-outsourcing firm, explicitly warned "college kids" about what they post online. He encouraged them to make sure their profile is "professional" and does not mention political or religious affiliations:

> There are people that are going to look at Facebook, or whatever, so I would be careful of what you do put out there. If you don't want people to know that you were at a bar partying on Friday night, then don't put that out there. If you're involved in some sort of political or religious organization, and you are looking for a job, I'd be careful because people have biases. I would definitely be careful. …Make sure you're not posting things on Facebook that somebody could view as inappropriate. Make your LinkedIn professional. I definitely think it reflects on you as a person. People, when they see that, make a mental determination of who you are (Mark).

This quotation reveals how information obtained from social media is viewed as a direct reflection of a person's character and competency. The "people" who might look at this information include potential future employers or recruiters who are looking to hire people who are "professional" and "appropriate." Online posts or photos that reveal drinking or partying can lead others to determine that a person is unprofessional or inappropriate to be hired. Mark also implied that recruiters can be biased against hiring workers whose online personas align with specific "religious or political organizations." The notion that this is something that others do (as observed in his comment, "There are people …") implies that Mark and recruiters like him do not evaluate potential job candidates based on this information, but that others might. Online information factored into the candidate evaluation process for the majority of the recruiters in our sample. These signals are also certain to impact which workers get recruited and which do not.

Lacking a profile picture on a social networking site can also send signals to HR professionals. Not having a profile picture can arouse suspicion among HR professionals as to why a job seeker did not include a picture. For example, Donna, who works as an HR consultant, wondered aloud about the absence of a LinkedIn profile picture:

> I wonder why. I wonder why. Why can't you – I mean, you have everything else up there. Why can't you put a snapshot of yourself? Are you afraid of discrimination? Do you not have a professional look about you? Are you – I just wonder, "Why?" Why would you not? If you're going to go to the trouble of putting a profile together, why don't you put a snapshot there, because that's the first thing that somebody's going to look at (Donna).

Donna's speculation echoed concerns among HR professionals about people who do not have a profile picture. Rather than focusing on the job seeker's work experience, level of education, references, and work history, profile pictures are "the first thing" people see. Picture-less profiles may signal "unprofessionalism" and can make someone a less appealing job candidate. As a generalist in the construction and infrastructure development industry, Kevin shared a similar view, saying, "If I'm looking at a LinkedIn profile, I'd like to be able to see the person's picture. Because if I don't see a picture, then I am wondering, 'What are they trying to hide?' " For Kevin, the absence of a photo raises his suspicion. He interprets this action of the job applicant as attempting to "hide" something and thus making that candidate less trustworthy and less appealing.

Some HR professionals said they intentionally excluded a profile picture because they did not want potential employers to judge them by their race or age. However, they also acknowledged that this can unintentionally signal "unprofessionalism." For example, Barbara, an older African-American woman working as a generalist in a science research laboratory was ambivalent about posting a picture of herself on LinkedIn. She was worried that displaying a profile picture could lead potential employers to make judgments based on her race or age.

> I do question my decision. I don't know if it was the right thing to do or not. A lot of people think, "Maybe I should wait until I'm in front of them, so they don't make any, judgments or decisions based on race or age." I am older, in my opinion, middle aged, I guess you could say. I'm not young. So, you know, does that make a difference? (Barbara).

Barbara's worries suggest that photos can send signals to potential employers and affect potential job offers. Kenneth, who worked in HR as a recruiter/consultant, expressed a similar concern, but as a person of color, he said he would rather be discriminated against before he started working at the job. When asked about why some people are hesitant to include a profile picture, he shared the following anecdote:

> Actually I've had this conversation with a friend of mine who didn't have a LinkedIn profile picture. I said, "Why don't you have a LinkedIn picture?" She said, "I don't want them discriminating based upon my gender or my race." I said, "Wouldn't you rather have them go ahead and discriminate against you now so you don't have to work for them? Than to get in there and start working for them and realize, they don't really like me, they like my skills, but they really don't like me as a person? They just hired me for my skill set? Is that the person you want to work for?" Well, no (Kenneth).

Kenneth stated that posting a picture may lead to discrimination. He acknowledged that this is a common dilemma faced by people from minority social groups. If we compare Kenneth's passage with Kevin's and Donna's above, we see that people can send signals to employers about fit for a job opening or a company regardless of whether or not they include a profile picture.

In addition to profile pictures, updating an online profile also sends signals to potential employers. HR professionals discussed how "tweaking a profile" on LinkedIn can signal that someone is passively searching for work. When asked about her interpretation of people updating their LinkedIn profile, Nancy, who specializes in long-term placements at a staffing agency, responded:

> When I see changes on somebody's LinkedIn profile that makes them more – for example, I'm connected with 1,000 people. Most of them I've never met in real life and most of them are targets that I want to meet [laughs] one day. If I see somebody has changed anything, I'm going to find a reason to talk to them. I'm going to assume that the reason why – if they have a new job, I'm going to call and congratulate them and see if I can work with their manager for their hiring needs. So, yeah, I follow all of the updates on the feeds [laughs]. If somebody had a very bland profile and then they update it, I'm like, "Okay, this person is looking to leave [laughs]" (Nancy).

Nancy's account shows that online activity can signal that someone is either looking for work or willing to change jobs. When someone alters their LinkedIn profile, that change is usually registered in the news feeds of their connections.

Nancy's comment also implies that workers are aware of this and, consequently, change their profiles to subtly signal their interest in changing jobs.

Lisa, who works as a generalist at a privately owned engineering company, said if she were to look for a job, right now, she would not post her resume on job sites. She would not want her current employer to see this online activity, because she knows that online activity can send signals to employers that she is unhappy and wants to quit:

> If I went to go look for a job right now, would I go post my resume on a job board? Heck no. Because I know what I do [sic]. I have [a subordinate] do a search regularly to see what employees we have posted. Because I can do a keyword search on [Company 4] and pull up everyone that's posted their resume on some type of social media and I know who's looking…I have a friend that's looking for a job right now and he went and made sure that his LinkedIn profile is updated because he started reaching out to people. Well, your employer, if you're connected to anyone at work, which most chances you are, they can see that activity (Lisa).

Lisa's account further shows that online activity, such as posting resumes online and making LinkedIn connections, may signal to your current employer that you are unhappy and willing to apply for new jobs. Job seekers have legitimate reasons for their reluctance to reveal their mobility intentions (their current employers might find out), so they must signal these intentions in a subtler way in order to attract the attention of recruiters.

6 Online recruitment via social media

The HR professionals that we talked to used social media networking sites to identify potential job candidates. LinkedIn was a clear favorite, in large part because it is specifically designed as a social media platform for professionals. Recruiters can also pay for LinkedIn services like Candidate Direct or Talent Solutions[1] to identify passive job seekers. Margaret, a recruiter at a consulting agency, was one professional who used Candidate Direct to maintain a database of potential hires:

> I would say that we do a search in LinkedIn and we have a program called Candidate Direct, which allows us to go into LinkedIn and come out with an Excel spreadsheet of a list of names, you know, based on certain criteria (Margaret).

1 Candidate Direct Marketplace® is an online staffing service for healthcare organizations that utilizes and advertises on LinkedIn. According to the website, the "marketplace" contains information about candidates, healthcare employers, and recruitment

Margaret explained that she does a keyword search in LinkedIn to identify potential job candidates who fit various skill criteria for new job openings. This approach is distinct from searching through job applications because she is attempting to identify people who might apply for a new job rather than those who have already applied. Her "spreadsheet" strategy demonstrates how LinkedIn can be used to locate passive talent who might be convinced to apply for a new job opening.

LinkedIn can also be used to find candidates who fill specific roles in competing companies. Nancy examined job titles and connections on LinkedIn and developed organization charts for different companies. This information was also used to identify qualified and/or passive job candidates.

> I am able to use it very quickly and get a lot of information and build org [organizational] charts for companies and see who knows each other because you get to see other people's connections (Nancy).

Nancy described searching LinkedIn by company name to find people who are currently doing the kind of work that she is attempting to recruit for in her own company. Information from LinkedIn can therefore be used to "poach" talent from competing organizations. Nancy's interest in "people's connections" also shows how she uses organizational information from LinkedIn as an entry point into a professional network of individuals who engage in similar types of work. Being connected with an established member of a professional network helps to signal that they are fit for employment in that type of job.

Recruiters explained that identifying passive job candidates is most important when filling higher-level positions (e.g., those in management) and jobs that require a specific skill set. Margaret approached this dilemma by joining LinkedIn groups in which people in similar occupations or fields connect. One of the "beauties" of LinkedIn is that even though there are fewer qualified candidates, "there's every passive candidate that there is, you know, and their profile doesn't say they're looking for a job, but you know, but they're out there … for the picking." Passive candidates are highly valuable when attempting to fill jobs with low labor supply. According to Margaret, LinkedIn is especially useful because it provides an active database of people who are doing work in specific

---

agencies. Employers can choose to hire through the site or use the resource to fill temporary positions.

Talent Solutions is a LinkedIn service that sells different packages to businesses depending on their needs. Some examples are: Recruiter Lite for recruiters who are looking for "top talent," job posts, referrals, and ads.

areas. Margaret likened these passive candidates to fruit, implying that they are ripe "for the picking." This metaphor suggests that recruiters view most workers as ready and willing to move to another job if given the right opportunity.

In addition to identifying job candidates, LinkedIn is also an important tool for reaching out to those candidates. Mary, a generalist in a real estate company, used LinkedIn informally to get the word out about job openings. She used InMails[2] to contact acquaintances in order to "tap" their networks and find potential candidates. According to Mary, the LinkedIn InMail feature serves as an ideal tool for communicating information about a job opening because it allows her to reach out directly to people in her professional network.

> If you're targeting something [sic], you can always send them a LinkedIn InMail. And, it's amazing how helpful people want to be. Especially when it comes to hiring and they may have a friend – "Oh, my friend's son, you know, he's been in the business for about 3-4 years and he would be a great candidate for you guys". People want to help other people and I really think that's a lot of the strategy of social media, in general, and especially when it comes to helping folks get jobs (Mary).

Mary's account highlights the indirect benefits associated with sending messages to her LinkedIn contacts. She relied on the fact that people tend to offer their own networks as potential job candidates. Her goal was not only to target specific individuals who might serve as job candidates, but also to allow her other contacts to refer people that they know who might fit well for the position opening. Mary framed this as a mutually beneficial connection; she found the type of target she's looking for and the candidates benefited from her personal networks.

Patricia, a recruiter at a large medical company, offered a more explicit example of how recruiters might reach out to someone. After evaluating their LinkedIn profile and deeming them to be good potential candidates or source of referrals, Patricia would contact a potential job candidate via email. Below, she described a hypothetical conversation that she might have with that person:

> "I noticed your skills and [your] experience could really match well to this job. You may not be interested, but I would love to have a conversation and network with you". So, I may do that in two emails or a phone call and an email. I might first email them and introduce myself. "Hey, saw your profile, just would love to chat with you. No pressure,

2 InMails is another LinkedIn sales feature that allows companies to send personal messages through the social media site. InMails are free to 1st degree connections, but members and businesses can purchase "credits" that allow them to send messages to anyone on LinkedIn, even if they are not directly connected.

just sharing information. You might know somebody". And then, if they're like, "Yeah that'd be fine, I'd be happy to talk to you", then I'd talk to them on the phone (Patricia).

Patricia described two different types of inquiries. A job opening served as the initiator to the first type of conversation, whereas the second involved a more ambiguous "just would love to chat" inquiry. In both instances, Patricia attempted to reduce the pressure that might be associated with this conversation. She indicated that she would still be interested in connecting even if the candidate is not interested in the job opening. The rationale is twofold. First, the target could be a potential recruit at a later date. Second, the candidate might be able to refer others who would be willing to apply for the position of interest (e.g., "you might know someone"). Patricia's description also refers to a mix of online (via LinkedIn) and offline (over the phone) communication. This hybrid approach of reaching out to potential job candidates reflects a broader sentiment among our interviewees that engaging in online social interaction is an essential strategy, but should be used in conjunction with other means of recruitment.

Similarly, Kevin used LinkedIn in a subtler way to find people to fill higher-level positions, like senior engineers or management. Kevin described how he can send out "feelers" in the form of InMail messages to signal his interest in a candidate. For Kevin and many other recruiters, the process of targeting a specific candidate was indirect. When contacting someone about a specific job opening, recruiters often avoided directly asking their target candidates if they were interested in the position. Instead, they tended to frame these inquiries in a way that suggested that the target might know someone else who might be interested. A more direct inquiry was perceived to be potentially uncomfortable for the target candidate to respond to. The indirect approach allowed the target candidate to express their own interest or to refer the recruiter to someone else who would be qualified for the position.

Recruiting potential job candidates involves perpetual networking. Donna said that she is constantly on the lookout for talent, even when she goes to a restaurant: "If I was looking for somebody in customer service and my service person was exceptional, maybe he or she would be interested in making a change." Managing online networks is an essential recruitment activity. As Robert (a recruiter at a public university) put it, "I'm on LinkedIn every day. It's just – it's just part of it. Like reading the newspaper." The quotations suggest that recruitment is not a discrete process that takes place only when a new job opening is posted to the Internet. Rather, recruitment is a process of continually reinforcing existing network contacts and identifying new connections.

Dan, a staffing agency recruiter, used LinkedIn as a resource to connect with people that he has never worked with or met in person:

> Some of these people may not be from conferences, they may just be people that I've worked with over the telephone, or I've worked with electronically. … I would say probably, maybe down to 50 percent, 40 percent, I would say would be those that I actually communicated with, and have worked with in some capacity … I have worked with clients for a decade that I have never met (Dan).

Dan described a very open strategy of building a broad online professional network comprised of many connections with whom he had limited previous contact. He appreciated the opportunities that online networking sites allow for expanding his network. This seemed especially important for his job as a staffing agency recruiter because his job duties involved filling candidate pools for a broad range of occupations.

By contrast, many of the people that we talked to placed limits on the extent to which they would accept LinkedIn requests. Robert maintained a personal policy of not accepting requests from random people. He has to have "met them, talked to them, or maybe have someone tell [him] about them" (Robert). He said it was "crazy" to simply add everyone who requested a connection.

> I don't really accept people randomly. And, I get hundreds and hundreds of people that I don't know. I'm not accepting them all into my network until I've either met them, talked to them, or maybe have someone tell me about them and I trust that person. Then I'll maybe invite them into the network. But, any random person, I'm kind of leery about that (Robert).

Robert expressed caution about his decision to accept someone as a connection. HR recruiters receive many requests to connect via LinkedIn, as workers know that recruiters are ideal sources of information about job opportunities. Robert's caution stemmed partly from concerns about connecting with someone who is only interested in asymmetric information exchange (obtaining job leads). Reticence to accept LinkedIn connections also derives from concerns about connecting with someone who has a bad reputation as a worker. A successful invitation therefore required a modest level of trust that could be gained through interaction or a referral by a friend. Edward, a recruiter in the medical services field, echoed Robert's preferences. Edward frequently accepted people into his LinkedIn network, but desired more than just a superficial "hello" in person before adding someone online. Edward also chose to limit his online network to people with whom he has already met.

Social media and online communication are also used to strengthen existing connections. Sharing information is one way that recruiters can find interested persons who may be converted into potential candidates.

> You know, so if I have a contact at a company, I'll know them, and then I'll send them an email and say look, here's some intelligence that I've gotten out there in the netherworld. So, again, it's just sort of using the tool there to identify someone, sort of make them from a cold connect to more of a warm connect that way, and that's done through recruitment as well (Dan).

When a job opening comes across his desk, Dan will go through his top prospect list and tell his connections about job opportunities. When he tells others what is happening on his end, they reciprocate his trust by sharing potential names that he might be interested in pursuing. A "cold connect" represents a weak connection that can be strengthened or turned into a "warm connect" by providing information about a job opportunity. Similarly, Nancy explained that she has a "LinkedIn Call Day" each week in which she contacts people in her professional network in order to enhance those connections. Part of her strategy involves sharing information about upcoming jobs and potential targets. She referred to these interactions as "schmoozing", which suggests that they are informal and gossipy. These examples reveal that building trust is an explicit goal of recruiters as they attempt to identify and recruit talented workers.

7 Discussion

Serendipity refers to the experience of unexpected discoveries. The increased availability of information about jobs, job candidates, and organizations on the Internet leaves open the possibility that serendipitous job finding has become a less salient feature of the job market. Our evidence casts doubt on this possibility. We examined how arbiters of job information use online social media as part of their recruitment activities. This is a novel approach. Whereas other studies of the transmission of unsolicited job information have focused on the experience of those who have received this information, we examine the source: HR recruiters.

Recruitment activities continue to play an important role in the job matching process. Our interviews with HR professionals yielded many important insights. Most HR professionals actively recruit individuals who might be willing to fill new job openings. The Internet and social media are central to this process. Recruiters scan websites to learn more about potential job candidates. They look for signals that indicate professionalism and appropriateness (or fit) for the position. These signals can be discerned from the language used in online profiles or the presence/content of online pictures. Signals are also important for determining the mobility intentions of a worker. HR professionals view subtle changes to LinkedIn profiles as indications that the person might be a passive job seeker and willing to apply to a new job. Interpreting these signals operates as a precursor to providing a job lead to a potential job candidate.

Social media (especially LinkedIn) provides a platform for HR professionals to identify and solicit potential job candidates. This is consistent with US survey data from HR professionals which show that nearly all HR recruiters (96%) who use social media for recruitment rely at least partly on LinkedIn (SHRM 2016). HR recruiters use LinkedIn to find potential candidates by searching for keywords, looking for workers in competing companies, and scanning members of professional groups. They often look for people who are well connected to professional networks. Recruiters are also looking for workers who might be dissatisfied enough in their current jobs to consider applying for a new one. LinkedIn contains a set of features that allow recruiters to make contact with individuals to provide them with information about job openings. The inquiries made by recruiters are often posed indirectly by asking their recruitment targets if they know someone who might be a good fit for the job opening. This indirect feature of the communication may make the receipt of information seem all the more serendipitous even when the actions that led to the inquiry are strategically employed.

Building recruitment networks and reaching out to contacts is a continual process that involves a mix of online and offline communication. HR professionals develop personal rules for deciding whom to add to their personal networks – rules that often hinge on the establishment of trust. Providing information about job opportunities helps to build trust and strengthen recruiting relationships. Trust is a valuable resource for convincing recruitment targets to apply for a new job. These activities also show how HR professionals not only work to expand their network boundaries, but also work to maintain their existing connections. In this way, the online activities of recruiters exceed those of most social media users who focus more on maintenance than expansion (Quan-Haase and Wellman 2004).

People often view the confluence of events that results in their receipt of unsolicited job leads as serendipitous (McDonald 2010). The interview data presented here suggests that the strategies employed by HR recruiters are mostly intentional. These two insights may seem counterintuitive, but they reveal an important social fact: processes that are perceived to be entirely random are often partially probabilistic (i.e., stochastic). Serendipity is a social construction that involves more than mere chance or providence (de Rond 2014). Unsolicited job leads can be solicited by signals conveyed online. In some cases, workers might intentionally send out these subtle signals (e.g., profile tweaks) in order to elicit job offers from recruiters. In other cases, signals are sent without full knowledge of their implications. Signaling ascriptive characteristics (e.g., race, gender, or age) is often outside of workers' control despite being consequential for the receipt of job leads (McDonald and Day 2010). People from disadvantaged social groups can attempt to hide these features from recruiters, but as the interviews showed, an absence of signals also tends to be viewed as detrimental.

The proliferation of online information about potential job candidates means that HR recruiters have more signals to review than ever before. Recruitment has emerged as a more salient feature in contemporary labor markets because the opportunity for recruiters to find ideal job matches has increased. Recruitment efforts are costly, though, which means that recruitment is often reserved for jobs that require a narrow set of skills (and thus a low labor supply) and managerial/ supervisory jobs (which are highly valued within organizations). The online job market appears to be most beneficial for people with highly specialized skills and those with supervisory experience. These features also served as the key predictors of "non-searching" in traditional labor markets (McDonald and Elder 2006) and they seem no less salient in the Internet era.

This study contains several important limitations. First, our analyses focus on a particular metropolitan area. The local economy of the Research Triangle is typical of many urban areas in the United States (especially Atlanta, GA; Austin, TX; Columbus, OH; Seattle, WA; Phoenix, AZ; and Silicon Valley, CA), although it does have a workforce that is relatively more highly educated and the local economy contains significant hi-tech and public sector (state government and university) employment. Online recruitment appears to be especially common for filling professional and managerial jobs (SHRM 2016), which makes the Research Triangle an especially good place to study these practices. However, we cannot rule out the possibility of variation across other cities or regions. Because job finding norms and practices vary widely across societies (Sharone 2013), cross-cultural replication is essential. Second, our study focused on how HR professionals utilize social media and online searching in their hiring decisions. As such, we cannot speak to the outcomes of these actions. Future research should explore the effect online recruiting has on the chances of being hired or promoted, perhaps as part of an audit study or experimental research design.

The serendipitous receipt of job leads is at least partly facilitated by the instrumental online recruitment activities of HR professionals. Our analysis therefore contributes to a "hidden-hands" explanation of serendipitous job finding – i.e., when a pattern emerges through conscious design but is perceived to be random (Nozick 1994). "Invisible-hands" explanations – in which patterns emerge in the absence of conscious design (Nozick 1994) – for serendipitous job finding are also possible. Whereas recruiters make conscious efforts to look for online signals, the way that they interpret those signals is often subconscious (cf., Fiske 1998). Furthermore, the processes that we described are by no means the only ways in which unsolicited job information is passed online. A lack of conscious intentionality is certain to be more apparent in circumstances where individuals receive unsolicited job finding assistance from their usual social media contacts (as opposed to recruiters for whom job sourcing is an explicit goal). Further delineation of these invisible and hidden aspects of serendipitous job finding is needed. Revealing that which is concealed remains the fundamental challenge of sociological inquiry (Portes 2000).

References

Autor, David H. 2001. "Wiring the Labor Market." *Journal of Economic Perspectives* 15: 25–40.

Bohnert, Daniel, and William H. Ross. 2010. "The Influence of Social Networking Web Sites on the Evaluation of Job Candidates." *Cyberpsychology, Behavior, and Social Networking* 13: 341–347.

Bonet, Rocio, Peter Cappelli, and Monika Hamori. 2013. "Labor Market Intermediaries and the New Paradigm for Human Resources." *Academy of Management Annals* 7: 341–392.

Caers, Ralf, and Vanessa Castelyns. 2011. "LinkedIn and Facebook in Belgium: The Influences and Biases of Social Network Sites in Recruitment and Selection Procedures." *Social Science Computer Review* 29: 437–448.

Castells, Manuel. 1996. *The Rise of the Network Society*. Oxford: Blackwell.

Davison, H. Kristl, Catherine Maraist, and Mark N. Bing. 2011. "Friend or Foe? The Promise and Pitfalls of Using Social Networking Sites for HR Decisions." *Journal of Business and Psychology* 26: 153–159.

Devine, Theresa J., and Nicolas M. Kiefer. 1991. *Empirical Labor Economics: The Search Approach*. Oxford: Oxford University Press.

van Dijck, José. 2013. "'You Have One Identity': Performing the Self on Facebook and LinkedIn." *Media, Culture & Society* 35: 199–215.

Fiske, Susan T. 1998. "Stereotyping, Prejudice, and Discrimination." *The Handbook of Social Psychology* 2: 357–411.

Freeman, Richard B. 2002. "The Labour Market in the New Information Economy." *Oxford Review of Economic Policy* 18: 288–305.

Granovetter, Mark S. 1995 [1974]. *Getting a Job. A Study of Contacts and Careers.* Chicago: University of Chicago Press.

Green, Anne E., Yuxin Li, David Owen, and Maria de Hoyos. 2012. "Inequalities in Use of the Internet for Job Search: Similarities and Contrasts by Economic Status in Great Britain." *Environment and Planning A* 44: 2344–2358.

Kmec, Julie A., Steve McDonald, and Lindsey B. Trimble. 2010. "Making Gender Fit and 'Correcting' Gender Misfits: Sex Segregated Employment and the Nonsearch Process." *Gender & Society* 24: 213–236.

Lin, Nan. 2000. "Inequality in Social Capital." *Contemporary Sociology* 29: 785–795.

Lin, Nan, and Dan Ao. 2008. "The Invisible Hand of Social Capital: An Exploratory Study." In *Social Capital: An International Research Program*, edited by Nan Lin and Bonnie Erickson, 107–132. Oxford: Oxford University Press.

Marin, Alexandra. 2012. "Don't Mention It: Why People Don't Share Job Information, When They Do, and Why It Matters." *Social Networks* 34: 181–192.

McDonald, Steve. 2010. "Right Place, Right Time: Serendipity and Informal Job Matching." *Socio-Economic Review* 8: 307–331.

McDonald, Steve. 2011. "What's in the 'Old Boys' Network? Accessing Social Capital in Gendered and Racialized Networks." *Social Networks* 33: 317–330.

McDonald, Steve. 2015. "Network Effects across the Earnings Distribution: Payoffs to Visible and Invisible Job Finding Assistance." *Social Science Research* 49: 299–313.

McDonald, Steve, and Jacob C. Day. 2010. "Race, Gender, and the Invisible Hand of Social Capital." *Sociology Compass* 4: 532–543.

McDonald, Steve, and Glen H. Elder. 2006. "When Does Social Capital Matter? Non-Searching for Jobs across the Life Course." *Social Forces* 85: 521–549.

McDonald, Steve, Lindsay Hamm, James R. Elliott, and Pete Knepper. 2016. "Race, Place, and Unsolicited Job Leads How the Ethnoracial Structure of Local Labor Markets Shapes Employment Opportunities." *Social Currents* 3: 118–137.

McDonald, Steve, Nan Lin, and Dan Ao. 2009. "Networks of Opportunity: Gender, Race, and Job Leads." *Social Problems* 56: 385–402.

Nakamura, Alice O., Kathryn L. Shaw, Richard B. Freeman, Emi Nakamura, and Amanda Pyman. 2009. "Jobs Online." In *Studies of Labor Market Intermediation*, edited by David H. Autor, 27–65. Chicago: University of Chicago Press.

Nozick, Robert. 1994. "Invisible-Hand Explanations." *The American Economic Review* 84: 314–318.

Papacharissi, Zizi. 2009. "The Virtual Geographies of Social Networks: A Comparative Analysis of Facebook, LinkedIn and ASmallWorld." *New Media & Society* 11: 199–220.

Portes, Alejandro. 2000. "The Hidden Abode: Sociology as Analysis of the Unexpected: 1999 Presidential Address." *American Sociological Review* 65: 1–18.

Quan-Haase, Anabel, and Barry Wellman. 2004. "How Does the Internet Affect Social Capital?" *Social Capital and Information Technology* 113: 135–113.

Rainie, Harrison, and Barry Wellman. 2012. *Networked: The New Social Operating System*. Cambridge (MA): MIT Press.

de Rond, Mark. 2014. "The Structure of Serendipity." *Culture & Organization* 20: 342–358.

Roth, Philip L., Philip Bobko, Chad H. Van Iddekinge, and Jason B. Thatcher. 2016. "Social Media in Employee-Selection-Related Decisions. A Research Agenda for Uncharted Territory." *Journal of Management* 42: 269–298.

Sharone, Ofer. 2013. *Flawed System/Flawed Self: Job Searching and Unemployment Experiences*. Chicago: University of Chicago Press.

SHRM. F2016. *Survey Findings: Using Social Media for Talent Acquisition: Recruitment and Screening*. Accessed October 29, 2017. https://www.shrm.org/ResourcesAndTools/hr-topics/talent-acquisition/Pages/Using-Social-Media-Find-Passive-Candidates.aspx.

Small, Mario Luis. 2009. *Unanticipated Gains: Origins of Network Inequality in Everyday Life*. Oxford (England): Oxford University Press.

Smith, Sandra Susan. 2005. "'Don't Put My Name on It': Social Capital Activation and Job-Finding Assistance among the Black Urban Poor." *American Journal of Sociology* 111: 1–57.

Stigler, George J. 1961. "The Economics of Information." *The Journal of Political Economy* 69: 213–225.

Trimble O'Connor, Lindsey. 2013. "Ask and You Shall Receive: Social Network Contacts' Provision of Help during the Job Search." *Social Networks* 35: 593–603.

Mikołaj Pawlak and Michał Kotnarowski

The Invisible Hand of Social Capital: Evidence from the Polish Labor Market*

Abstract: In the chapter, we demonstrate the conditions and effects of the invisible hand of social capital on the Polish labor market. The invisible hand of social capital is the effect of receiving unanticipated gains, thanks to the participation in social networks. It is another perspective on social inequalities. The empirical base for the study is quantitative survey data on representative sample of Polish employees who got a new job, in the July 2013–March 2015 period. The dataset allows analyzing various conditions of unsolicited social capital benefits and its consequences for the employees. According to the results of the study, a participation in the labor market improves the chances of receiving an unsolicited job offer, yet it is not improved by the size of the locality in which employee resides, human capital, and participation in religious practices. The invisible hand of social capital is correlated with larger income, better assessment of own material conditions, and better job satisfaction.

Keywords: Invisible hand; labor market; social capital; social inequalities; social ties

1 Introduction

The concept of the invisible hand of market is well known, and it is still focusing attention of social scientists. What economic sociology taught us in recent decades is that modern economic behaviors are not only to be understood within the market concept. Economic actions are embedded in networks of social relations (Granovetter 1985), and their proper explanation requires the study of not only impersonal exchanges (market approach) but also personal relations (networks approach). Recently, in studies of social networks, the concept of the invisible hand of social capital is getting some attention. As the concept of social capital makes our understanding of resources broader, similarly the concept of the invisible hand of social capital makes our understanding of gains won unintentionally, thanks to the participation in social structures broader as well. The

* This chapter was written in the framework of the project "What fills up the sociological vacuum? The reinterpretation of Stefan Nowak's thesis from a network perspective, as exemplified by the labor market behaviors", funded by the National Science Centre (DEC-2012/07/D/HS6/00977). We are very thankful for the critical comments of Marta Kindler and Steve McDonald which helped us in a better formulation of the arguments.

studies of the invisible hand of social capital focus on its presence on the labor market. It is usually studied in regard to the unsolicited job offers. People do not always search for jobs; jobs quite often also search for people, and usually they do through the networks of personal contacts. So the participation in the right social networks brings not only the advantage of having both access and possibility of mobilization of resources embedded in the networks, but it also has an advantage of receiving gains that were not intended. Thus, studies of the invisible hand of social capital broaden our understanding of the structure of social inequalities. The research questions of this chapter are: What are the conditions upon which the invisible hand of social capital emerges? And what are the effects of the invisible hand of social capital? In order to answer them, we use the quantitative study of newly employed Polish workers.

In this chapter, we demonstrate the conditions and effects of the invisible hand of social capital on the Polish labor market. We start with a brief conceptual discussion of the fuzzy concept of social capital in order to define the invisible hand of social capital in the social networks tradition of social capital studies. Then we present the current state of literature on the invisible hand of social capital. Following, we present the state of knowledge on network behaviors on the Polish labor market in order to describe the context for our study. Based on the literature review, we formulate six hypotheses regarding both the conditions for emergence and the correlates of invisible hand of social capital in Poland. Then we present the design of our quantitative replication of Granovetter's (1995) *Getting a Job* study, in which we collected nationwide sample of the newly employed. Then we present the results of our study, and we conclude with remarks about the invisible hand of social capital, its relation to social inequalities, and its relations to the concept of invisible hand of market.

2 Literature review

2.1 Social capital

The concept of social capital since the 1980s has received enormous attention in social sciences. In current serious analyses of market phenomena, not only financial but also social capital is taken into account as playing important role. Yet, as Portes (1998, 2) noted, "social capital comes to be applied to so many events and in so many different contexts as to lose any distinct meaning". Here we are not going to discuss all the understandings of the concept and avenues of its possible use in social analysis. In many ways, the social capital is a new term to describe the old sociological problems of social bonds and social cohesion being in the focus of social scientists since Marx, Durkheim, Simmel, Weber, and Parsons (Woolcock 1998). Conventionally, the introduction of the concept of social capital into the sociological mainstream is ascribed to Bourdieu (1986) and Coleman (1988), although it was already used by Loury (1977). The climax of the attention to the concept was reached, thanks to its use by Putnam (1993) in explaining the social basis for democracy.

For the purpose of this article, we use the social networks perspective on social capital. This line of theorizing about the social capital is derived from the seminal works of Granovetter (1973; 1995) on the strength of weak ties and the role of social networks for the labor market. The discovery of the role of social networks for the economic behaviors gave a new momentum for the economic sociology, which documents how the markets are socially embedded (Granovetter 1985). In this approach, social capital is understood as resources embedded in social networks (Lin 2001) or the advantage created by a person's location in a structure of relationships (Burt 2005). As Coleman (1988) described it in his seminal work, social capital allows actors to capitalize their position in social structure, so it is a resource for action. As we see, social capital is often understood as a mean for action, which requires mobilization by an actor. Yet, there are situations in which holders of social capital do not require to mobilize the social capital, because they receive the unanticipated gains of participation in social networks (Small 2009).

2.2 The invisible hand of social capital

As sometimes silently assumed and sometimes more openly expressed by authors presented above, social capital consists of resources that need to be mobilized. This means that beneficiaries of these resources need to be social actors: the capability of mobilizing constitutes their agency. Yet, contrary to other forms of capital, social capital quite often does not require purposeful mobilization of its holder. Yet, as studies on the labor market have documented, approximately a quarter to one-third of employees receive their jobs without prior search. A majority of them – 80% in the US studies (Granovetter 1995; McDonald and Elder 2006) – receive the information about job through personal contacts. So the participants of the social networks may gain advantage of the resources embedded in these networks without agentic mobilization (Lin and Ao 2008).

This phenomenon was named by Lin (2000, 792) "invisible hand of social capital", i.e., "embeddedness in resource-rich networks is associated with routine flow of useful information". Being connected to the social network means that actors encounter nearly endless number of small, routine interactions with other participants of the same network. They exchange various information not only purposively to achieve some kind of gains but also as an element of small talk. These information are by-products of participation in social networks. Actors who participate in the same social network on the basis of their work experiences usually pick up small-talk topics that are work related. So it is no surprise that information about new job openings and possibilities for job change almost "float unintentionally". Also, being connected to the right networks opens a possibility for being approached by employers intentionally looking for employees through personal contacts. The metaphor of the invisible hand comes from the fact that attainment in the labor market is less visible than in the case of purposive and visible search for jobs (Lin and Ao 2008, 113).

The invisible hand of social capital is strongly connected to the problem of social inequality (McDonald, Benton and Warner 2012). As we see, some people - thanks to the participation in the "right" networks - have larger chances of accessing the resources. Actually, in case of the invisible hand of social capital, the resources access the privileged actors. This sheds new light on the issues of inequality and constitutes the similarity between the metaphors of the invisible hand of market and the invisible hand of social capital. The invisible hand of market – at least in its original formulation by Adam Smith (1776) – brings effects that are not intended outcomes of aggregated, spontaneous actions of a larger pool of market participants but that from the outside look like orchestrated by some powerful actor "pulling all the strings". In case of the invisible hand of social capital, it is an aggregated consequence of multiple interactions of network participants, yet it seems from the outside that the network as a collective actor acts intentionally in order to secure the gains of its participants.

The invisible hand of market represents the outcome of non-coordinated individual actions' perception as orchestrated by a single omnipotent actor: emergent social structures seem to be designed. In case of the invisible hand of social capital, the gains received by some of the members of the network seem to be an effect of a kind of collective agency of the social group. Yet, it is an outcome of routine exchanges (such like small talks about employment opportunities) between members of networks with unequal access to the resources. So the second metaphorical meaning of "invisible" is connected to the hint that maybe the attainments of certain privileged actors are actually purposively achieved by their capabilities as collective actor. It seems that it was the line of Bourdieu's (1986, 249) thinking when he stated that "the backing of the collectivity-owned capital, a 'credential' that entitles them to credit, in the various senses of the word". The invisible hand of social capital is an interesting example explaining this problem: individuals interact and that creates "social capital" meaning access to the resources, which are then gained by individuals. Yet, for the external observer – the one excluded from this very network – it may seem that it is a planned strategic action of the whole group guarding its resources and purposively keeping it only for their members.

The invisible hand of social capital research usually focuses on the unsolicited job offers. Employment is a crucial resource in modern world, plus the research of network behaviors on the labor market are a very developed source of evidence (for recent reviews see McDonald et al. 2012; Trimble and Kmec 2011). Already, from the pioneer work of Granovetter (1995), we know that non-searchers are a quite substantial share of newly hired employees. According to McDonald and Elder (2006), in the United States (US), approximately 30% of jobs are acquired by non-searchers and unsolicited job offers are mostly transmitted through social networks.

The invisible hand of social capital has already its literature, and there are some characteristics of this phenomenon researched, yet the evidence comes mostly from the US. According to the study of Lin and Ao (2008), the invisible hand of social capital is correlated with the capacity of networks, human capital, and social participation. It means that receiving an unsolicited job offer is more likely for participants of larger and more resourceful networks, for individuals with larger human capital, and for individuals who more often participate in organizations.

According to several studies, non-searchers receive higher remuneration (Elliot 2000; Granovetter 1995; McDonald 2015). This is a particularly important aspect of the invisible hand of social capital as a manifestation of social inequalities. Participation in the so-called wrong networks in which there is only a handful of resources embedded does not bring benefits for their members (Fernandez and Fernandez-Mateo 2006). Non-searchers also more often take up managerial positions (Elliott 2000; Granovetter 1995). In the US, non-searching occurs more often among white men than women and minorities (McDonald and Day 2010), so the invisible hand of social capital is a mechanism feed-backing the privileged. Similar results were also obtained in Germany (McDonald, Benton and Warner 2012), Taiwan and China (Son 2013), and Singapore (Chua 2014).

2.3 Labor market in Poland

So far the phenomenon of the invisible hand of social capital was not researched in Poland. From the study of Pawlak and Kotnarowski (2016, 198), we know that in Poland 32.7% jobs are acquired by non-searchers. It is quite a large figure but comparable with the evidence from the US labor market. Poland recently (and during the time of the mentioned study) is in period of economy growth and significant decrease of unemployment. The unemployment is still recognized as one of the most troubling social problems in Poland. The unemployment rate is correlated with the size of cities (Tyrowicz 2011). In the largest cities of Poland, there is nearly no unemployment, while in smaller cities, it is a push factor of emigration.

The patterns of getting a job in Poland are similar to those in other countries, and there is no significant influence of the methods used on the income. This is confirmed by the International Social Survey Programme data (Słoczyński 2013) and the Study of Human Capital in Poland data (Jeran 2014). Individual social capital influences income attainment. This is confirmed by Polish Panel Survey (POLPAN) data (Słomczyński and Tomescu-Dubrow 2005) and Social Diagnosis data (Fałkowski and Łopaciuk-Gonczaryk 2010; Growiec and Growiec 2010). The personal resources that are embedded in the social networks of inhabitants of Warsaw improve their perceived chances of getting a new job (Filipek, Batorski and Bojanowski 2015).

3 Research problem: hypotheses

The aim of this study is exploratory. Being equipped with the conception of the invisible hand of social capital, we intend to learn the answer to two general research questions regarding the Polish labor market: What are the conditions for the emergence of the effect of the invisible hand of social capital? And what are the possible consequences of the invisible hand of social capital for individuals? Building on the literature review presented above, we formed six hypotheses.

First, we present the hypotheses regarding the conditions of the emergence of the invisible hand of social capital, namely what network characteristics of the respondents make it more likely that they will receive the unsolicited job offers.

Hypothesis 1: Non-searchers more likely participate in networks embedded with resources.

As we know from the number of studies (for review of the literature, see Granovetter 1995), the most relevant networks for job search are the networks developed in the context of work. This claim is also valid for the Polish labor market (Pawlak and Kotnarowski 2016). Therefore we formulated the following hypothesis:

Hypothesis 1a: Non-searchers more likely already have jobs.

In Poland, the unemployment rate is strongly negatively correlated with the size of the locality (Tyrowicz 2011). To phrase it as a stylized fact: the larger the city the lower the unemployment rate. Therefore, the assumption that workers living in larger localities will have access to the networks more embedded with relevant resources is worth testing. We formulated that claim as follows:

Hypothesis 1b: Non-searchers more likely reside in larger localities.

The connections between the different forms of capital lay at the base of the studies of social capital. Both the conceptualization of Bourdieu (1986) and Coleman (1988) stressed the correlation and transformability of human and social capital. This correlation was also found in the study of Lin and Ao (2008). Therefore we formulated the following hypothesis:

Hypothesis 2: Non-searchers more likely have a larger amount of human capital.

In order to operationalize the human capital and to test *hypothesis 2* in details, we took into account the conventional proxies of human capital, namely the tertiary education and the white-collar type of work.[1] Thus we formulated the following two partial hypotheses:

Hypothesis 2a: Non-searchers more likely have tertiary education.
Hypothesis 2b: Non-searchers more likely possess positions requiring higher qualifications.

After testing the hypotheses regarding the embeddedness of networks in resources and the connections between human and social capital, we decided to test the hypothesis regarding the size of the network. Although these are the resources in networks that matter, we also wanted to see if the size of the network makes the appearance of the invisible hand of social capital more likely. Unfortunately, due to the fact that our research was not primarily designed to study the issue of the invisible hand of social capital, we lack the proper measurements of the network size or the participation in organizations that are sites of network creation – like voluntary associations, sport clubs, etc. Therefore, the only proxy we could use is the participation in religious practices. By using this variable, we assume that people who participate in religious practices, which in the Polish context equals Sunday masses of the Catholic church, have access to larger networks formed in the context of the church as a kind of a third place (Oldenburg 1989).

1 One cannot forget that social capital and human capital are interconnected (Coleman 1988). The studies on the dual embeddedness demonstrate that institutional arrangements of certain occupations facilitate informal job acquirement and also unsolicited job offers, like in case of managerial positions (McDonald et al. 2012). So the tertiary education and white collar job most probably do not represent 'pure' human capital but are also influenced by the institutional conditions ameliorating the possibilities for achieving larger amounts of social capital too.

This assumption is in line with Lin and Ao's (2008) study, who showed that the invisible hand of social capital is correlated with social participation. Therefore, the third hypothesis states that:

Hypothesis 3: Non-searchers more likely participate in larger networks (regular participation in religious practices).

The following three hypotheses to be tested describe the effects brought by the invisible hand of social capital. It is always risky to propose claims about the causation, so the hypotheses are formulated in terms of correlations. Even if the mechanisms behind the correlations between the invisible hand of social capital and income, perception of material conditions, and job satisfaction are a mutual feedback, the presence of these correlations is a manifestation of social inequalities.

Obviously the most interesting is the question whether social capital brought by the invisible hand translates into the factual capital. According to several studies (Elliott 2000; Granovetter 1995; McDonald 2015) non-searchers receive higher wages. Therefore we formulated the following hypothesis:

Hypothesis 4: Invisible hand of social capital is correlated with larger income.

Next to the issue of income is the issue of the subjective perception of material conditions. The social inequalities that are manifested by the effects of the invisible hand of social capital are also associated with the self-perception of individuals. Therefore we formulated the following hypothesis:

Hypothesis 5: Invisible hand of social capital is correlated with better perception of material conditions.

The quality of job is not limited to the income, but it also consists of other factors, with job satisfaction as a very important one (Flap and Völker 2001). Therefore, we intended to test the following hypothesis on the association of the invisible hand of social capital with job satisfaction:

Hypothesis 6: Invisible hand of social capital is correlated with better job satisfaction.

4 Research design

4.1 Data collection

The analyses presented in this chapter are based on our original study conducted in Poland between 2014 and 2015. In the study, survey interviews were conducted with people who had started their current employment within the last 12 months. We constrained the period in which the subjects had gotten their jobs for two reasons.

Firstly, we wanted to control for effects related to long-term changes in the economic situation. During the last 25 years, Poland experienced many fluctuations in its economic situation, which were caused by factors such as the implementation of economic reforms at the beginning of the transformation away from the Communist system, crises in the world economy, or changes of public policies targeting the labor market. We wanted to control the possible effects from those fluctuations on phenomena under study. One has to keep in mind that we were not able to control for effects related to seasonal changes in the economic situation, since the data were collected over a period of ten months. Secondly, we were afraid that respondents would not be able to provide reliable answers about events that had happened in the distant past. Constraining the time period to the last 12 months was a solution to this problem. We assumed that respondents should not have problems in recalling circumstances related to getting a job if it happened within the last year.

In the study, the following situations were defined as cases of getting a new job: getting a job after a period of being unemployed, getting a first job after finishing education, and changing one's place of work in the case of people having been previously employed. What is important for the analyses presented below, we were interested in people who were actively looking for a job as well as people who received a job offer without having initiated any previous employment solicitations. Finally, we decided to look at a broad range of cases in order to include in the study a large possible number of situations in which personal contacts were used to get a job.

In the sampling procedure, we wanted to include representatives of the whole Polish population of people who got a new job within the last 12 months. To do this we needed to obtain a subsample of a representative sample of the Polish population. In order to meet the criteria mentioned above, we obtained a sample on the basis of the omnibus-type survey research conducted each month by the Public Opinion Research Center (CBOS).[2] The total sample size of each monthly wave of the CBOS omnibus study is roughly 1000 adult respondents. In each wave of the omnibus study, employed respondents received a filter question asking whether they had started the current job within the last 12 months. Respondents who answered positively on this question were selected for our study. The number of respondents selected for our study from a single omnibus wave varied from 16 to 66. The procedure of searching for people who got a new job in the last 12 months was repeated in subsequent waves of omnibus studies,

2 In each wave of the CBOS omnibus survey, a nationwide stratified random representative sample of adult residents of Poland was applied. Sample strata are defined as

until reaching 400 respondents. The process of data collecting took 10 months, from June 2014 to March 2015. During this period we obtained a national representative sample of 428 respondents who had gotten a new job in the 12 months before the interview.

4.2 Measurements

In the survey there was used a questionnaire, which was a Polish adaptation of a tool used in the seminal Granovetter's (1995) study. In order to determine which respondents were non-searchers, we included in the survey the question "Was there a period of time when you were actively searching for a new job, before you found the current job?" The respondents who answered "No" are treated in the analyses as non-searchers.

Participation in networks with larger amount of resources embedded was measured by the size of the respondents' place of residence. We distinguished three categories of size of residence, namely: a village, a town up to 100 thousand inhabitants, and cities having 100 thousand inhabitants or more. Since a size of residence is a categorical variable, this variable was presented as two technical dummy variables in a regression model. To use a size of the residence as a proxy for the accessibility to resources might seem coarse. Yet, in Poland there is a strong correlation between the size of the residence and the opportunities on the labor market (Tyrowicz 2011), so people who live in larger localities are usually tied with people with better access to resources.

The concept of human capital is operationalized as a higher level of education and level of qualifications required for the occupation. To represent the level of qualifications required for occupation, we used the variable type of occupation that has three values: manual worker, service worker, and specialist.

As an indicator of participation in larger networks, we used attendance at religious practices. Respondents who declared that they attended religious services at least every weak were qualified as possessing larger network. We are aware that

combinations of the Polish region and type of place of residence (large cities, small and medium towns, and villages) – altogether 65 strata were used in each wave of our survey. In each stratum, one or more smaller areas were selected (either group of streets in a particular city or a whole village). In each smaller area, nine respondents were selected randomly on the basis of the Polish National Identification Number (PESEL). The interviewer's aim was to conduct as many interviews as possible from the provided list. Replacements for the original sample were not allowed. The sampling procedure was repeated in the same way for each wave of the CBOS omnibus survey.

it is an imperfect proxy of participation in larger networks, but in our dataset we did not have a better one.

Subjective perception of respondent's material conditions took the form of a binary variable in which we distinguished between those who were satisfied with their financial situation and those who gave the other answer, i.e. neutral or negative. Similarly, we differentiated between satisfied with current job and respondents who gave the other answer (similarly as above: neutral or negative).

5 Results

Our sample consisted of 53.3% male and 46.7% female respondents. A total of 27.8% of the respondents had higher education. The average age of the respondents was 35.3 years. A total of 31.2% respondents resided in villages, 35.7% in towns up to 100 thousand inhabitants, while 33.1% in cities having 100 thousand inhabitants or more. A total of 32.7% of respondents were not actively searching for a job when they decided to take the new employment.

In the presentation of the results of empirical research, we will first refer to the first three hypotheses. First, we will present the results of the bivariate analyses in which we examine how the method of getting a job depends on the status on the labor market (*hypothesis 1a*), the size of place of residence (*hypothesis 1b*), education (*hypothesis 2a*), the type of occupation (*hypothesis 2b*), and the frequency of religious practices *(hypothesis 3*). In the next step, we will present the results of the multiple regression model. In these models, all variables corresponding to *hypotheses 1–3* are included in analyses as independent variables.

In the bivariate analyses referring to *hypothesis 1a*, we compare the frequency of methods of getting a new job in groups according to the status on the labor market at the time of getting a current job. We distinguish here between respondents who were previously employed and those who were not. Results of the bivariate analysis are presented as a contingency table in *tab. 1*. As can be observed, those who already had jobs more often got a new job without searching for it than those who were not employed – 29% of those who already had a job were non-searchers, while in the group of not employed 12% were non-searchers.

Moreover, respondents who were employed less often got a new job by active searching for it using formal and informal means than not employed. Formal means of getting a new job were used by 43% of respondents who were employed, and by 53% of those who were not employed. Similarly, informal means were used by 28% of employed and 35% of unemployed. The relationship between the method of getting a new job and previous status on the labor market is statistically significant. This is showed by the general chi-square test as well as

Tab. 1: Proportions of methods of getting a job in status on labor market groups

	other	employed
Non-searcher	0.12	0.29
Formal searcher	0.53	0.43
Informal searcher	0.35	0.28
Column Sum	1.00	1.00
Column N=	202	221

Overall test of independence Chi-square statistic=17.5, d.f.=2, p<0.001.

Test of independence Non-searcher vs. Formal searcher Chi-square statistic=14.4, d.f.=1, p<0.001.

Test of independence Non-searcher vs. Informal searcher Chi-square statistic=12.5, d.f.=1, p<0.001.

the chi-square tests comparing the non-searcher group with the formal-means group and the non-searcher with the informal-means group. The obtained result confirms *hypothesis 1a*, indicating that the non-searchers more likely already have jobs.

Let us now move on to the next hypothesis that the non-searcher is more likely to reside in larger localities. This hypothesis was not confirmed by the analysis. The share of non-searchers is the highest among the inhabitants of the largest cities - 24% of residents of cities with 100 or more inhabitants are non-searchers (*tab. 2*). However, the percentage of non-searchers among inhabitants of villages is only slightly lower (23%). Non-searchers are slightly less common among middle-town inhabitants (17%). According to the general chi-square test, the relationship between variables is statistically significant, but this is due to differences in the frequency of using formal and informal means in job searching between different types of residence areas. The larger the place, the more formal the way to find a job was, and the smaller the residence area, the more often the job was got using informal means. Statistical tests of the differences between non-searchers and the formal searchers show no statistical significance. On the other hand, a test on the differences between non-searchers and informal searchers indicates a statistically significant relationship, but the direction of the relationship (the lowest share of non-searcher among middle-towns inhabitants) does not follow the direction expected by *hypothesis 1b*. In conclusion, the results of the two-variable analysis did not confirm *hypothesis 1b*.

Tab. 2: Proportions of methods of getting a job in size of residence groups

	city 100th.+	town up to 100th	village
Non-searcher	0.24	0.17	0.23
Formal searcher	0.58	0.46	0.39
Informal searcher	0.19	0.37	0.38
Column Sum	1.00	1.00	1.00
Column N=	140	151	132

Overall test of independence Chi-square statistic=17.4, d.f.=4, p= 0.002. Test of independence Non-searcher vs. Formal searcher Chi-square statistic=2, d.f.=2, p= 0.368. Test of independence Non-searcher vs. Informal searcher Chi-square statistic=8.8, d.f.=2, p= 0.012.

According to *hypothesis 2a*, it is expected that getting a job without searching for it is more frequent among the better educated. According to the data presented in *tab. 3*, the percentage of non-searchers does not depend on the level of education. Among respondents with primary education, 22% are non-searchers, among those with secondary education 19%, and among respondents with higher education 24%. The general statistical significance test showed that the relationship between forms of job searching and education is statistically significant, but this relationship is due to the differences between respondents who get a new job using formal and informal means. The better educated were respondents, the more likely they formally got a job. Accordingly, the less educated they were, the more likely they got a new job using informal means. If we look at the results of the significance test comparing non-searchers with formal searchers and non-searchers with informal searchers, we do not record statistically significant relationships.

Hypothesis 2b concerns the relationship between the methods of getting a new job and the type of respondents' occupation. It is expected that getting a new job without searching for it is more frequent among people possessing positions requiring higher qualifications. This hypothesis is confirmed by the results of the bivariate analyses presented in *tab. 4*. The specialists found a new job without searching more often than service workers and physical workers. The share of non-searchers was equal to 29% among specialists, 16% among service workers, and 22% among physical workers.

Formal means for finding a new job was used most often among service workers (56%) and least among manual workers (39%). On the other hand, informal means were most frequently used by physical workers (39%) and least often by specialists (22%). Statistical tests indicate that the relationship among the analyzed variables is significant. It is shown by the general statistical significance

Tab. 3: Proportions of methods of getting a job in educational attainment groups

	primary	secondary	tertiary
Non-searcher	0.22	0.19	0.24
Formal searcher	0.36	0.54	0.51
Informal searcher	0.42	0.28	0.25
Column Sum	1.00	1.00	1.00
Column N=	124	183	116

Overall test of independence Chi-square statistic=12.7, d.f.=4, p= 0.013. Test of independence Non-searcher vs. Formal searcher Chi-square statistic=3.2, d.f.=2, p= 0.204. Test of independence Non-searcher vs. Informal searcher Chi-square statistic=3.1, d.f.=2, p= 0.214.

Tab. 4: Proportions of methods of getting a job in type of occupation groups

	manual workers	service workers	specialists
Non-searcher	0.22	0.16	0.29
Formal searcher	0.39	0.56	0.49
Informal searcher	0.39	0.28	0.22
Column Sum	1.00	1.00	1.00
Column N=	170	179	68

Overall test of independence Chi-square statistic=15.3, d.f.=4, p= 0.004. Test of independence Non-searcher vs. Formal searcher Chi-square statistic=7, d.f.=2, p= 0.03. Test of independence Non-searcher vs. Informal searcher Chi-square statistic=5.2, d.f.=2, p= 0.076.

test (significance level less than 0.01) as well as the test comparing non-searchers with formal searchers (0.03 significance level) and informal searchers (0.08 significance level). In conclusion, the results of the bivariate analyses confirm *hypothesis 2b*.

Hypothesis 3 indicates that non-searchers more likely belong to larger networks, which, in our analysis, is operationalized by participation in religious practices. The relationship between methods of getting a job and the frequency of religious practices is presented in *tab. 5*. Although the results indicate a statistically significant relationship between the two variables, they do not support *hypothesis 3*. Most often, finding a job without looking for it was found among two groups: regular practitioners and those who did not go to church at all (the share of non-searcher in both groups amounted to 25%). Least often were the non-searchers found among those who occasionally participated in religious practices (16%). It should also be noted that this group was most often

Tab. 5: Proportions of methods of getting a job in the religiosity groups

	no-goer	occasional	regular
Non-searcher	0.25	0.16	0.25
Formal searcher	0.44	0.52	0.45
Informal searcher	0.31	0.33	0.29
Column Sum	1.00	1.00	1.00
Column N=	71	193	157

Overall test of independence Chi-square statistic=6.3, d.f.=4, p= 0.176. Test of independence Non-searcher vs. Formal searcher Chi-square statistic=5.9, d.f.=2, p= 0.052. Test of independence Non-searcher vs. Informal searcher Chi-square statistic=4.2, d.f.=2, p= 0.119.

populated by persons getting a new job using both formal and informal means. In conclusion, a statistically significant relationship did not confirm *hypothesis 3*, according to which more frequent religious practices were associated with being a non-searcher.

Below we present analyses related to *hypotheses 1–3* that are carried out using the multiple regression model. By using this way of modeling, we are able to assess a unique impact of each of the variables related to our hypotheses on the method of getting a job. The dependent variable in the model is the method of getting a job. It is a categorical variable with three categories (non-searcher, formal searcher, and informal searcher). We analyzed relationships using a multinomial logistic regression model. Independent variables were all variables corresponding to *hypotheses 1–3*, i.e. the status on the labor market, size of residence, education level, type of occupation, and religious practices. All independent variables are also categorical, and for this reason, they appear in the model as sets of dummy variables. Multinomial logistic regression model results are presented in *tab. 6* below.

In the multinomial logistic regression model, the regression coefficients are estimated for each pair of dependent variable categories. Due to the specifics of the hypotheses tested in this chapter, we present the values of regression coefficients for non-searchers compared with formal searchers (values in *column A*) and informal searchers (values in *column B*). The value of the coefficients corresponds to the chances of being a non-searcher compared with the chances of being a formal searcher and an informal searcher, respectively.

The multiple regression model confirms *hypothesis 1a*. The chances of finding a job without searching for it are higher among people previously employed than not-employed. This relationship is statistically significant when we compare non-searchers with formal searchers (the regression coefficient is 1.17) and

Tab. 6: Multinomial logistic regression model – hypotheses 1-3

	Dependent variable:	
	Non-searcher vs. Formal searcher	**Non-searcher vs. Informal searcher**
	(A)	**(B)**
Status on labor market: employed	1.167	1.061
Reference category: not-employed	(0.290)***	(0.307)***
Size of residence: town up to 99th.	0.075	-0.905
Reference category: city 100 th. +	(0.336)	(0.376)**
Size of residence: village	0.465	-0.565
Reference category: city 100 th. +	(0.345)	(0.382)
Education: primary	0.009	-0.305
Reference category: tertiary	(0.454)	(0.481)
Education: secondary	-0.337	-0.064
Reference category: tertiary	(0.398)	(0.438)
Type of occupation: manual workers	0.174	-0.308
Reference category: specialists	(0.487)	(0.537)
Type of occupation: service workers	-0.427	-0.396
Reference category: specialists	(0.425)	(0.486)
Religious practices: no-goer	0.320	0.015
Reference category: regular	(0.384)	(0.414)
Religious practices: occasional	-0.536	-0.599
Reference category: regular	(0.302)*	(0.324)*
Constant	-1.284	0.145
	(0.427)**	(0.503)
Akaike Inf. Crit.	844.894	844.894

*Note: One-sided significance test: * p<0.05; ** p<0.01; *** p<0.001, values in the cells are regression coefficients together with standard errors in the brackets.*

non-searchers with informal searchers (the regression coefficient is 1.06). This relationship is also illustrated in *fig. 1*. It presents the predicted probability of being a non-searcher, formal searcher, and an informal searcher depending on the status on the labor market at the time of getting a new job. Values of these probabilities were calculated on the basis of parameters of multinomial logistic regression model for a typical respondent. By a typical respondent, we mean here a respondent for whom the other independent variables included in the model are equal to its mean values in the analyzed dataset. *Fig. 1* shows that probability of being a non-searcher is higher for the previously employed (0.29)

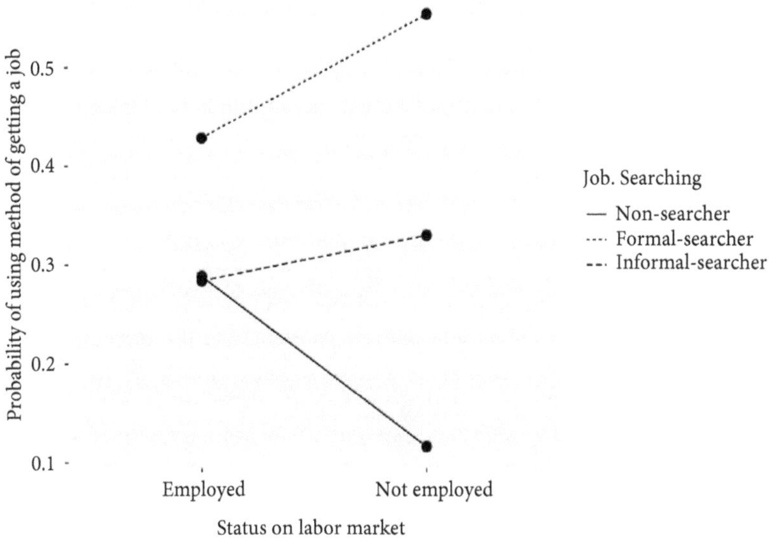

Fig. 1: Probabilities of using each method of getting a job in status on labor market groups. Note: Variable on horizontal axis (Status on Labor market) is a categorical one. For this reason, predicted probabilities for each category of Status on Labor Market are presented as points. These points are connected with dashed line in order to present differences between predicted probabilities for various categories of Status on Labor Market.

than for the not-employed persons (0.12). On the other hand, the probability of finding a job through formal search and informal search is greater among those previously not employed. Among the not-employed, the probability of finding a job in a formal way is 0.55 and the same number among the employed is 0.42. Likewise, the likelihood of finding a job using informal means is 0.33 among the not-employed and 0.28 among the employed. *fig. 1* shows one more information: Although there were differences in the probabilities of using the three methods of getting a new job, the probability of using formal means is the highest in both groups (employed and not-employed).

The results of the multinomial logistic regression model confirm, at least to some extent, *hypothesis 1b*. Accordingly, it is expected that non-searchers more likely reside in larger localities. It is confirmed when we compare the probability of being non-searchers with the probability of being informal searchers between large cities and small/medium-sized cities (up to 100,000 inhabitants).

If we compare the chances of getting a new job without looking for it with the chances of getting a job by searching it by informal means in larger cities, compared to middle-sized towns, the chances of getting a new job without searching are higher. However, we do not notice statistically significant differences between large cities and villages when comparing the probability of being a non-searcher with the probability of being an informal searcher. Additionally, for the comparison of chances of being a non-searcher and a formal searcher, we do not observe a significant difference between the sizes of place of residence.

The multiple regression analysis does not support *hypothesis 2*. This hypothesis indicated that the way of finding a new job depends on the respondents' resources, such as education and occupational status. *Hypothesis 3* is also not confirmed by the multivariate analyses. Religious practices are not connected with the modes of getting a new job as it is expected by the hypothesis.

The chances of finding a job without actively searching for it, compared to the chances of finding it through informal means, are significantly higher in the group of regular practitioners than in the group of occasional practitioners. However, there are no differences between regular practitioners and those who do not attend church. This result is the same as in the case of the bivariate analysis. In the multivariate model, we do not notice differences between groups distinguished according to the frequency of church attendance when we compare the chances of being a non-searcher with the chances of being a formal searcher.

Let us move on to the analyses related to the next group of hypotheses. *Hypotheses 4–6* are concerned on the potential link between the method of getting a new job and income (*hypothesis 4*), perception of personal economic situation (*hypothesis 5*), and job satisfaction (*hypothesis 6*). As we have mentioned earlier, we are investigating the potential impact of the method of getting a new job on various aspects of the respondents' economic and occupational situation. We do not argue, however, that the investigated relationships are of a causal nature.[3]

In the analyses related to *hypotheses 4–6*, the dependent variables are a respondent's income in the current work, subjectively expressed satisfaction with the material situation, and satisfaction with the current job. For each hypothesis, we estimated separate regression models. In each model, the independent variable of our interest was the method of getting a new job. In the same way as in the analyses presented above, the method of getting a new job has three possible

3 The set of data we have at our disposal does not allow for more sophisticated tests of causal relationships such as analysis with instrumental variables.

values: non-searcher, formal searcher, and informal searcher. However, one has to keep in mind that the material situation and job satisfaction may depend on a number of other factors than just the method of getting a job. Consequently, in the analyses related to *hypotheses 4–6*, we estimated multiple regression models in which we took into account control variables that are alternative explanations of the material situation and job satisfaction. Control variables were: age of the respondent, size of the place of residence, education, and type of occupation.

We start with the analyses related to *hypothesis 4*. We use a multiple regression model here, in which income is the dependent variable. Since income is defined on an interval scale, a linear regression model (estimated by ordinary least squares technique) is used. The result of the obtained regression model is presented in *column A* in the *tab. 7* below. According to the regression results, the way of finding a new job is related to the income of the respondents. Non-searchers' income is significantly higher than formal searchers' income (on average by Polish złoty (PLN) 271) and informal searchers' income (on average by PLN 267). The expected level of income in groups distinguished according to the methods of getting a job is shown in *fig. 2*. They were calculated according to regression model parameters for the respondents typical in the remaining independent variables (i.e., values of the remaining independent variables were set to their mean values in the sample). The average income for non-searchers is 2209 PLN, while the corresponding value for formal searchers is 1938 PLN, and for informal searchers is 1942 PLN. These results confirm *hypothesis 4*, according to which we expected non-searchers to have a higher income than people who were actively looking for a job.

The results of analyses related to *hypothesis 5* are shown in *column B* of *tab. 7*. The dependent variable was the subjectively perceived material situation of the respondents, which was described on a five-point scale, taking values from the definitely positive to the definitely negative. Because of the small number of negative assessments, this variable is recoded into a binary variable having values "negative or neutral" (value 0) and "good" (value 1). Due to the binary nature of the dependent variable, analysis was performed using the binary logistic regression model. The results of the model indicate that the assessment of respondents' economic situation depends on the method of getting a job. Non-searchers assessed their financial situation better than formal searchers and informal searchers. The result is visible in the middle graph in *fig. 2*. The likelihood of having a good financial standing among non-searchers is 0.66. The same value for the formal searcher group is 0.51, and for the informal searcher 0.52. This probability is calculated for the respondents that are typical in the values of other independent variables included in the model. Thus, the results of empirical

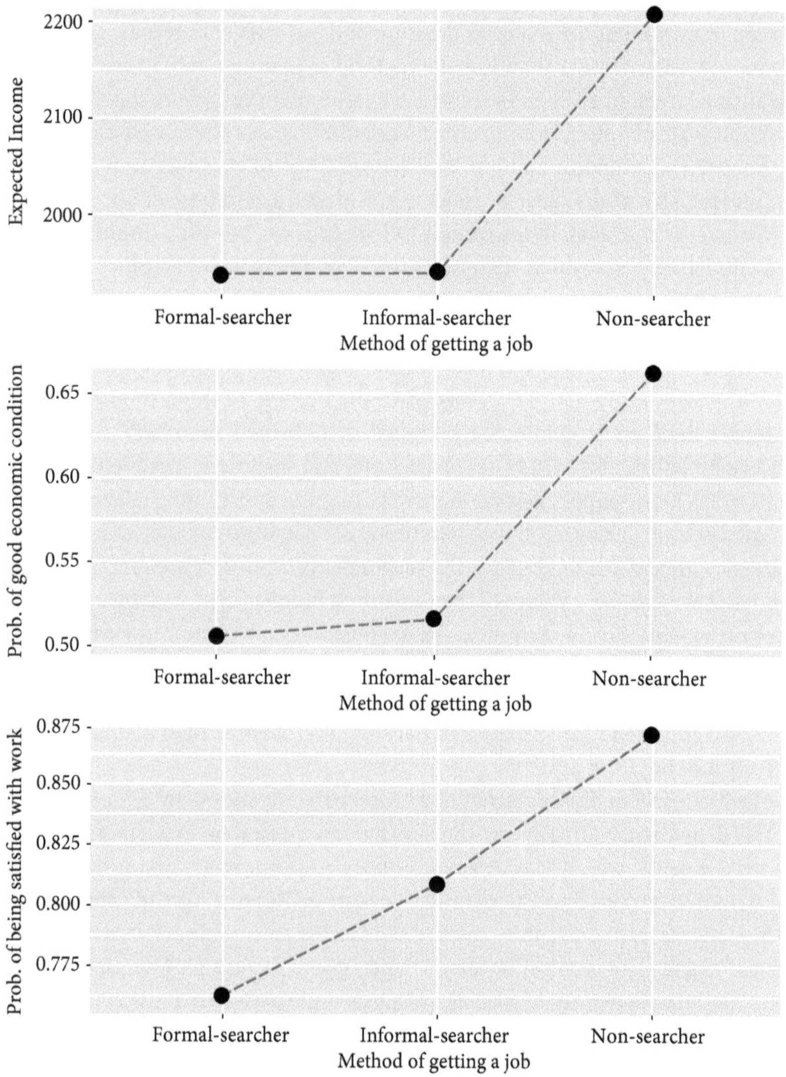

Fig. 2: Expected Income, probability of good economic condition, and probability of being satisfied with work in status on labor market groups – estimated by regression models. Note: The variable on a horizontal axis (Method of getting a job) is a categorical one. For this reason, predicted probabilities for each category of Method of getting a job are presented as points. These points are connected with dashed lines in order to present differences between predicted probabilities for various categories of Method of getting a job.

analyses confirm *hypothesis 5*, that non-searchers are more likely to have a good personal economic situation.

Let us now move on to the last of our hypotheses, which binds the way of getting a new job with satisfaction in it. Satisfaction is determined on a three-point scale: positive, neutral, and negative. Because of the low number of negative ratings, job satisfaction was transformed into a binary variable that received either negative or neutral (value 0) and positive (value 1). The analyses were performed using the binary logistic regression model. The values of the regression model coefficients are presented in *column C* in *tab. 7*. Job satisfaction is statistically significantly higher among non-searchers compared to formal searchers. When we compare non-searchers with informal searchers, the direction of dependence is consistent with the hypothesis: non-searchers are more satisfied with the job than informal searchers, but the difference between these groups in job satisfaction is not statistically significant. The results are also shown in the bottom panel of *Fig. 2*. We found that the highest probability of being satisfied with the work among the non-searchers group (0.87), slightly lower in case of the informal searcher group (0.80), and even smaller in case of the formal searcher (0.76). The results of these analyses confirm *hypothesis 6*, that getting a new job without active search is associated with greater satisfaction with it.

6 Discussion and conclusion

The presented data on the conditions of emergence and the outcomes of the invisible hand of social capital in Poland give another look at the social inequality in Poland. Participation in the labor market (*hypothesis 1a*) improve the chances of receiving an unsolicited job offer, so participation in networks embedded with resources is a valid condition of work of invisible hand of social capital. It means that a Polish worker who already has a job has larger chances of getting a useful information (useful in a sense that he or she took that opportunity) regarding new jobs. It is an analogy to Saint Matthews effect (Merton 1968): the ones who already participate in resourceful networks have larger chances of receiving fruits of this participation, which is strengthening their social position. Yet, the size of the locality of residence is not increasing the probability of receiving an unsolicited job offer (*hypothesis 1b* not confirmed).

To our surprise, the hypotheses on the influence of human capital on the invisible hand of social capital were not supported. Both tertiary education (*hypothesis 2a*) and work requiring higher qualifications (*hypothesis 2b*) are not significantly correlated with receiving unsolicited job offers in Poland. According to our data, we cannot say that inequalities in education and position on the

Tab. 7: Regression models – hypotheses 4-6

	Dependent variable:		
	Income	**Material situation**	**Job satisfaction**
	OLS	*logistic*	*logistic*
	(A)	(B)	(C)
Method of getting a job: Formal searcher	-270.674	-0.654	-0.740
Reference category: non-searcher	(146.245)*	(0.282)*	(0.367)*
Method of getting a job: Informal searcher	-266.699	-0.613	-0.463
Reference category: non-searcher	(155.002)*	(0.300)*	(0.387)
Age: 25-39 y.o.	189.970	-0.514	0.098
Reference category: 18-24 y.o.	(159.009)	(0.294)*	(0.357)
Age: 40-65 y.o.	419.430	-0.817	-0.478
Reference category: 18-24 y.o.	(165.906)**	(0.306)**	(0.353)
Size of residence: town up to 99th.	-88.292	-0.024	-0.358
Reference category: city 100 th. +	(135.407)	(0.257)	(0.316)
Size of residence: village	-94.918	0.296	-0.455
Reference category: city 100 th. +	(146.366)	(0.271)	(0.325)
Education: primary	-527.575	-0.706	0.014
Reference category: tertiary	(194.207)**	(0.363)*	(0.420)
Education: secondary	-59.624	-0.445	0.471
Reference category: tertiary	(166.435)	(0.310)	(0.374)
Type of occupation: manual workers	-526.464	-0.857	-1.604
Reference category: specialists	(208.527)**	(0.404)*	(0.621)**
Type of occupation: service workers	-746.275	-0.732	-1.688
Reference category: specialists	(185.247)***	(0.361)*	(0.581)**
Constant	2,757.484	2.173	3.454
	(226.328)***	(0.459)***	(0.685)***
Observations	342	417	413
R^2	0.137		
Adjusted R^2	0.111		
Log Likelihood		-268.918	-204.120
Akaike Inf. Crit.		559.837	430.240
Residual Std. Error	1,018.521 (df = 331)		
F Statistic	5.275*** (df = 10; 331)		

*Note: *p<0.05; ** p<0.01; *** p<0.001, values in the cells are regression coefficients together with standard errors in the brackets.*

labor market also translate into the inequalities in the chances of receiving unsolicited job offers. This finding is more meaningful in the context of the fact that the hypothesis regarding the participation in networks embedded with resources (*hypothesis 1a*) is supported. It means that in Poland the social characteristics, not the individual characteristics, of the participants of the labor market contribute to the inequalities. It is important to already have a job but education or the type of work (manual work, work in services, or position of specialist) does not influence the chances of receiving unexpected new job offers. We need also to remember that the level of education and type of occupation might also be connected with a social context of the labor market for a given occupation. If we treat human capital and type of occupation as characteristics of the social context of employment, we could speculate that the type of institutional arrangements of a given occupation are not making any difference in the chances of receiving an unsolicited job offer. What is important is to have an employment already – it is not that important what kind of a game one plays, it is important to play the game.

Unfortunately our data do not allow us to proper testing of the hypothesis about the influence of participation in larger networks on the invisible hand of social capital. We used as a proxy of participation in larger networks (consciously of its imperfection) the regular participation in religious practices (*hypothesis 3*). In this regard, the hypothesis was not supported, but the question about participation in other institutional settings enabling connection to larger networks remains open. For example, Gerber and Mayorova (2010) in the context of the Russian labor market claimed that the size of the locality of residence is a proxy of participation in larger networks. We believe that in the Polish context, it is rather the proxy of participation in networks more embedded with resources. There is no evidence that in Poland size of the locality is correlated with the size of the networks, yet there is a correlation between the size of the locality and the rate of unemployment and other indicators of economic performance. Regardless of this discussion, there is a need of further research about the size, composition, and capacity of networks in relation to the invisible hand of social capital.

On the side of the correlates of the invisible hand of social capital, all the three hypotheses were supported, so we are allowed to speculate that the invisible hand of social capital cumulates the positive outcomes for the holder of social capital by bringing: larger income (*hypothesis 4*), better assessment of one's own material conditions (*hypothesis 5*), and better job satisfaction (*hypothesis 6*). Unfortunately, we do not have statistical tools allowing to test the hypotheses about causation, but due to the fact that the hypotheses about correlation were supported, we are allowed to speculate about the influence of the invisible hand of social capital on income, perception of material conditions, and job satisfaction. So the invisible hand of social capital works in favor of the ones it touches. Receiving the unsolicited job offer most probably increases the likelihood of earning more money and being more satisfied (both with this particular job and with general material conditions). This outcome is intuitive. Non-searchers do not have any incentives to take jobs that are lousily paid and not bringing much satisfaction. Yet, this finding is important for our understanding of social inequalities, especially if we combine it with the findings about the conditions of the emergence of the invisible hand of social capital. Participation in more resourceful networks (*hypothesis 1a*) brings resources to the individuals (*hypotheses 4–6*) even if they do not mobilize them intentionally.

The similarity of the concept of the invisible hand of social capital and the invisible hand of market is twofold. The first aspect is the problem of intentionality. The complex social mechanisms behind the two invisible hands very briefly could be presented as follows. In case of the invisible hand of market, some individuals just intend to exchange some goods. As an unintended consequence of these exchanges, market and orchestration of prices emerge (Mica 2015). In the case of the invisible hand of social capital, some individuals by the virtue of participation in routine interactions, in which their preoccupation is limited to chatting or exchanging of gossip, benefit from the resources embedded in the network. Yet, as unanticipated gains, they receive access to resources that they do not need to mobilize by themselves.

The second aspect is that both the invisible hand of market and the invisible hand of social capital, being social mechanisms hidden behind the interactions of individuals, open for many the suspicion of intentional design. The social mechanism of the invisible hand of market looks like there is someone pulling the strings and intentionally orchestrating the prices. Similarly, in case of social capital, its invisible hand also opens possibilities for speculations that members of a particular network consciously support each other in an orchestrated way. The invisible hand of social capital is a social mechanism that brings gains to people connected to more resourceful social networks. No doubt it is sustaining and even increasing social inequalities. But it also opens a possibility for conspiracy theories in which social networks are ascribed with agency and treated as collective actors intentionally working for the purpose of increasing the gains of its members. It is not a case – regardless of the purposive gains brought by the mobilization of resources embedded in networks, they also bring gains that are unanticipated and the chances of receiving these gains are unequal.

6.1 Appendix: Construction of the variables used in empirical analyses

Method of getting a job:

Non-searchers – respondents who got a new job due to personal contacts without actively looking for it;
Formal searchers – respondents who were actively looking for a job and got it due to formal recruitment procedure;
Informal searchers – respondents who were actively looking for a job and got it due to personal contacts.

Previous employment status (respondent's status on the labor market at the time of getting a new job, values):

Employed – respondents were employed in another place;
Other – respondents not-employed: unemployed, respondents who finished education lately, respondents who had a break in their labor activities (e.g. parental leave).

Size of residence (size of the respondent's residence, values):

Village;
Town up to 100 th. inhabitants;
City with 100 th. inhabitants or more.

Education:

Primary;
Secondary;
Tertiary.

Type of occupation, (concerns job performed at the time of the interview, values):

Manual workers;
Service workers;
Specialists.

Religious practices (frequency of church attendance, values):

Non-goers;
Occasional (once a month or less);
Regular (at least once a week).

References

Bourdieu, Pierre. 1986. "The Forms of Capital." In *Handbook of Theory and Research of Sociology of Education*, edited by John G. Richardson, 241–258. New York: Greenwood Press.

Burt, Ronald S. 2005. *Brokerage and Closure: An Introduction to Social Capital.* Oxford: Oxford University Press.

Chua, Vincent. 2014. "The Contingent Value of Unmobilized Social Capital in Getting a Good Job." *Sociological Perspectives* 57: 124–143.

Coleman, James. 1988. "Social Capital in the Creation of Human Capital." *American Journal of Sociology* 94 (Supplement): S95–S120.

Elliott, James R. 2000. "Class, Race, and Job Matching in Contemporary Urban Labor Markets." *Social Science Quarterly* 81: 1036–1052.

Fałkowski, Jan, and Beata Łopaciuk-Gonczaryk. 2010. "Kapitał społeczny a dobrobyt materialny jednostki w Polsce – głos w dyskusji." *Zarządzanie Publiczne* 4: 59–69.

Fernandez, Roberto M., and Isabel Fernandez-Mateo. 2006. "Networks, Race, and Hiring." *American Sociological Review* 71: 42–71.

Filipek, Kamil, Dominik Batorski, and Michał Bojanowski. 2015. "Getting a Job: Resources and Individual's Chances on the Warsaw Labour Market." *Polish Sociological Review* 4: 475–492.

Flap, Henk, and Beate Völker. 2001. "Goal Specific Social Capital and Job Satisfaction: Effects of Different Types of Networks on Instrumental and Social Aspects of Work." *Social Networks* 23: 297–320.

Gerber, Theodore P., and Olga Mayorova. 2010. "Getting Personal: Networks and Stratification in the Russian Labor Market, 1985-2001." *American Journal of Sociology* 116: 855–908.

Granovetter, Mark. 1973. "The Strength of Weak Ties." *American Journal of Sociology* 78: 1360–1380.

Granovetter, Mark. 1985. "Economic Action and Social Structure: The Problem of Embeddedness." *American Journal of Sociology* 91: 481–510.

Granovetter, Mark. 1995. *Getting a Job: A Study of Contacts and Careers.* Chicago: University of Chicago Press.

Growiec, Jakub, and Katarzyna Growiec. 2010. "Social Capital, Well-Being, and Earnings: Theory and Evidence from Poland." *European Societies* 12: 231–255.

Jeran, Agnieszka. 2014. "Rodzina i znajomi – kapitał społeczny w znajdowaniu pracy." *Studia Humanistyczne AGH* 1: 43–58.

Lin, Nan. 2000. "Inequality in Social Capital." *Contemporary Sociology* 29: 785–795.

Lin, Nan. 2001. *Social Capital: A Theory of Social Structure and Action.* Cambridge: Cambridge University Press.

Lin, Nan, and Dan Ao. 2008. "The Invisible Hand of Social Capital: An Explanatory Study." In *Social Capital: An International Research Program*, edited by Nan Lin and Bonnie H. Erickson, 107–132. Oxford: Oxford University Press.

Loury, Glenn C. 1977. "A Dynamic Theory of Racial Income Differences." In *Women, Minorities, and Employment Discrimination*, edited by Phyllis A. Wallace and Annette M. La Mond, 86–153. Lexington: Heath.

McDonald, Steve. 2015. "Network Effects Across the Earnings Distribution: Payoffs to Visible and Invisible Job Finding Assistance." *Social Science Research* 49: 299–313.

McDonald, Steve, Richard A. Benton, and David F. Warner. 2012. "Dual Embeddedness: Informal Job Matching and Labor Market Institutions in the United States and Germany." *Social Forces* 91: 75–97.

McDonald, Steve, and Jacob C. Day. 2010. "Race, Gender, and the Invisible Hand of Social Capital." *Sociology Compass* 4: 532–543.

McDonald, Steve, and Glen H. Elder. 2006. "When Does Social Capital Matter? Non-searching for Jobs Across the Life Course." *Social Forces* 85: 521–549.

McDonald, Steve, S. Michael Gaddis, Lindsey B. Trimble, and Lindsay Hamm. 2013. "Frontiers of Sociological Research on Networks, Work, and Inequality." In *Research in the Sociology of Work: Networks, Work and Inequality*, edited by Steve McDonald, 1–41. Bingley: Emerald Group Publishing Limited.

Merton, Robert K. 1968. "The Matthew Effect in Science." *Science* 159: 56–63.

Mica, Adriana. 2015. "Unintended Consequences: History of the Concept." In *International Encyclopedia of the Social & Behavioral Sciences*, edited by James D. Wright (editor-in-chief), 24: 744–749. Oxford: Elsevier (2nd edition).

Oldenburg, Ray. 1989. *The Great Good Place.* New York: Paragon House.

Pawlak, Mikołaj, and Michał Kotnarowski. 2016. "Siła słabych powiązań na rynku pracy w Polsce." *Studia Socjologiczne* 2: 187–215.

Portes, Alejandro. 1998. "Social Capital: Its Origins and Applications in Modern Sociology." *Annual Review of Sociology* 24: 1–24.

Putnam, Robert D. 1993. *Making Democracy Work: Civic Traditions in Modern Italy.* Princeton: Princeton University Press.

Słoczyński, Tymon. 2013. "Wpływ sieci społecznych na zatrudnienie i wynagrodzenia w Polsce." *Wiadomości Statystyczne* 12: 42–55.

Słomczyński, Kazimierz M., and Irina Tomescu-Dubrow. 2005. "Friendship Patterns and Upward Mobility: A Test of Social Capital Hypothesis." *Polish Sociological Review* 3: 221–235.

Small, Mario Luis. 2009. *Unanticipated Gains: Origins of Network Inequality in Everyday Life*. Oxford: Oxford University Press.

Smith, Adam. 1776. *An Inquiry into the Nature and Causes of the Wealth of Nations*. London: W. Strahan and T. Cadell.

Son, Joonmo. 2013. *Social Capital and Institutional Constraints: A Comparative Analysis of China, Taiwan and the US*. London: Routledge.

Trimble, Lindsey B., and Julie A. Kmec. 2011. "The Role of Social Networks in Getting a Job." *Sociology Compass* 5: 165–178.

Tyrowicz, Joanna. 2011. *Histereza bezrobocia w Polsce*. Warszawa: Wydawnictwa Uniwersytetu Warszawskiego.

Woolcock, Michael. 1998. "Social Capital and Economic Development: Towards a Theoretical Synthesis and Policy Frameworks." *Theory and Society* 27: 151–208.

Loïc Wacquant

Crafting the Neoliberal State Workfare, Prisonfare, and Social Insecurity*

Abstract: In *Punishing the Poor* (2009a), I show that the ascent of the penal state in the United States and other advanced societies over the past quarter-century is a response to rising social insecurity, not criminal insecurity; that changes in welfare and justice policies are interlinked, as restrictive "workfare" and expansive "prisonfare" are coupled into a single organizational contraption to discipline the precarious fractions of the postindustrial working class; and that a diligent carceral system is not a deviation from, but a constituent component of, the neoliberal Leviathan. In this chapter, I draw out the theoretical implications of this diagnosis of the emerging government of social insecurity. I deploy Bourdieu's concept of "bureaucratic field" to revise Piven and Cloward's classic thesis on the regulation of poverty via public assistance, and contrast the model of penalization as technique for the management of urban marginality to Michel Foucault's vision of the "disciplinary society," David Garland's account of the "culture of control," and David Harvey's characterization of neoliberal politics. Against the thin economic conception of neoliberalism as market rule, I propose a thick sociological specification entailing supervisory workfare, a proactive penal state, and the cultural trope of "individual responsibility." This suggests that we must theorize the prison not as a technical implement for law enforcement, but as a core political capacity whose selective and aggressive deployment in the lower regions of social space violates the ideals of democratic citizenship.

Keywords: Bourdieu; citizenship; neoliberalism; prison; poverty; state; welfare; workfare

In *Punishing the Poor* (2009a), I show that the return of the prison to the institutional forefront of advanced society over the past quarter-century is a political response, not to rising *criminal* insecurity, but to the diffuse *social* insecurity wrought by the fragmentation of wage labor and the shakeup of ethnic hierarchy.[1]

---

* This chapter is adapted from Wacquant, Loïc. 2010. "Crafting the Neoliberal State: Workfare, Prisonfare, and Social Insecurity." *Sociological Forum* 25: 197–220. The reference system was adapted accordingly.

1 The fragmentation of wage labor and its reverberations at the lower end of the class structure are documented by Freeman (2007) for the United States and by Gallie (2007) for the European Union. Ethnic hierarchy is anchored by the ethnoracial division between whites and blacks in America (other categories finding their place in this dichotomous ordering through a process of triangulation) and by the ethno-national duality between citizens and postcolonial migrants in Western Europe. Massey (2007)

The punitive slant of recent shifts in both welfare and justice policies points of a broader reconstruction of the state coupling restrictive "workfare" and expansive "prisonfare" under a philosophy of moral behaviorism. The paternalist penalization of poverty aims to contain the urban disorders spawned by economic deregulation and to discipline the precarious fractions of the postindustrial working class. Diligent and belligerent programs of "law and order" entailing the enlargement and exaltation of the police, the courts, and the penitentiary have also spread across the First World because they enable political elites to reassert the authority of the state and shore up the deficit of legitimacy officials suffer when they abandon the mission of social and economic protection established during the Fordist-Keynesian era.

Punishing the Poor (2009a) treats the United States after the acme of the Civil Rights movement as the historic crucible of *punitive containment* as technique for the management of marginality and living laboratory of the neoliberal future where the convergent revamping of the social and penal wings of the state can be discerned with particular clarity. Its overarching argument unfolds in four steps. Part 1 maps out of the accelerating decline and abiding misery of America's social state, climaxing with the replacement of protective welfare by disciplinary workfare in 1996. Part 2 tracks the modalities of the growth and grandeur of the penal state and finds that the coming of "carceral big government" was driven, not by trends in criminality, but by the class and racial backlash against the social advances of the 1960s. Part 3 heeds the communicative dimension of penality as vehicle for symbolic boundary-drawing and explains why penal activism in America has been aimed at two "privileged targets," the black subproletariat trapped in the imploding ghetto and the roaming sex offender. Part 4 follows recent declinations of the new politics of social insecurity in Western Europe to offer a critique of the "scholarly myths" of the reigning law-and-order reason, prescriptions for escaping the punitive policy snare, and a characterization of the distinctive shape and missions of the neoliberal state.

Three analytic breaks proved indispensable to diagnose the invention of a new government of social insecurity wedding supervisory "workfare" and castigatory "prisonfare," and to account for the punitive policy turn taken by the United States and other advanced societies following its lead onto the path of economic deregulation and welfare retrenchment in the closing decades of the twentieth

---

and Schierup, Hansen and Castles (2006) display similarities and differences in ethnic stratification on the two sides of the Atlantic, including the massive overrepresentation of dishonored populations behind bars.

century. The first consists in escaping the crime-and-punishment poke, which continues to straightjacket scholarly and policy debates on incarceration, even as the divorce of this familiar couple grows ever more barefaced.[2] The second requires relinking social welfare and penal policies, inasmuch these two strands of government action toward the poor have come to be informed by the same behaviorist philosophy relying on deterrence, surveillance, stigma, and graduated sanctions to modify conduct. Welfare revamped as workfare and the prison stripped of its rehabilitative pretension now form a single organizational mesh flung at the same clientele mired in the fissures and ditches of the dualizing metropolis. They work jointly to invisibilize problem populations – by forcing them off the public aid rolls, on the one side, and holding them under lock, on the other – and eventually push them into the peripheral sectors of the booming secondary labor market. The third rupture involves overcoming the conventional opposition between materialist and symbolic approaches, descended from the emblematic figures of Karl Marx and Émile Durkheim, so as to heed and hold together the instrumental and the expressive functions of the penal apparatus.[3] Weaving together concerns for control and communication, the management of dispossessed categories, and the affirmation of salient social borders, makes it possible to go beyond an analysis couched in the language of prohibition to trace how the rolling out of the prison and its institutional tentacles (probation, parole, criminal data bases, swirling discourses about crime, and a virulent culture of public denigration of offenders) has reshaped the sociosymbolic landscape and remade the state itself.

A single concept sufficed to effect those three breaks simultaneously: the notion of *bureaucratic field* developed by Bourdieu (1994 [1993]) in his lecture course at the Collège de France in the early 1990s to rethink the state as the

---

2 A simple statistic suffices to demonstrate this disconnect and reveals the futility of trying to explain rising incarceration by escalating crime: the United States held 21 prisoners for every 1,000 "index crimes" in 1975 compared to 113 convicts per 1,000 crimes in 2000, for an increase of 438%; for "violent crimes," the jump is from 231 to 922 convicts per 1,000 offenses, an increase of 299%. This means that the country became four to five times more punitive in a quarter-century *holding crime constant* (a lagged index turns up the same trend). See Wacquant (2009a, 125–133) for further elaboration and Blumstein and Wallman (2000) and Western (2006, chap. 2) for different approaches leading to the same conclusion.

3 Garland (1989, 278) dissects the materialist (Marxist) and symbolic (Durkheimian) lineages in the study of punishment and proposes that they, along with Foucault, Weber and Elias, offer "resources to be drawn upon selectively rather than inviolable worldviews which can only be swallowed whole."

agency that monopolizes the legitimate use, not only of material violence (as in Max Weber's well-known capsule), but also of symbolic violence, and shapes social space and strategies by setting the conversion rate between the various species of capital. In this chapter, I extend Bourdieu's formulation to draw out the theoretical underpinnings and implications of the model of the neoliberal government of social insecurity at century's dawn put forth in *Punishing the Poor* (2009a). In the first section, I revise Piven and Cloward's classic thesis on the regulation of poverty via public assistance and contrast penalization as a technique for the management of marginality in the dual metropolis with Foucault's vision of the place of the prison in the "disciplinary society," Garland's account of the crystallization of the "culture of control" in late modernity, and Harvey's characterization of neoliberal politics and its proliferation on the world stage. In the second section, I build on these contrasts to elaborate a thick sociological specification of neoliberalism that breaks with the thin economic conception of neoliberalism as market rule that effectively echoes its ideology. I argue that a proactive penal system is not a deviation from, but a constituent component of, the neoliberal Leviathan, along with variants of supervisory workfare and the cultural trope of "individual responsibility." This suggests that we need to theorize the prison, not as a technical implement for law enforcement, but as a core organ of the state whose selective and aggressive deployment in the lower regions of social space is constitutively injurious to the ideals of democratic citizenship.

1 When workfare joins prisonfare: theoretical implications

In *The Weight of the World* (1999 [1993]) and related essays, Bourdieu proposes that we construe the state, not as a monolithic and coordinated ensemble, but as a splintered space of forces vying over the definition and distribution of public goods that he calls the "bureaucratic field".[4] The constitution of this space is the end result of a long-term process of concentration of the various species of capital operative in a given social formation, and especially of "juridical capital as the objectified and codified form of symbolic capital", which enables the state to

4 The concept is sketched analytically in Bourdieu (1994 [1993]), illustrated in Bourdieu (1999 [1993]), and deployed to probe the political production of the economy of single homes in France in Bourdieu (2005 [2000]). Several issues of the journal *Actes de la recherche en sciences sociales* offer further cross-national empirical illustrations, including those on "The History of the State" (1997, nos. 116–117), "The Genesis of the State" (1997, no. 118), the transition "From Social State to Penal State" (1998, no. 124), and "Pacify and Punish" (2008, nos. 173 and 174).

monopolize the official definition of identities, the promulgation of standards of conduct, and the administration of justice (Bourdieu 1994 [1993], 4, 9). In the contemporary period, the bureaucratic field is traversed by two internecine struggles. The first pits the "higher state nobility" of policymakers' intent on promoting market-oriented reforms and the "lower state nobility" of executants attached to the traditional missions of government. The second opposes what Bourdieu, riding off Hobbes's classic portrayal of the ruler, calls the "Left hand" and the "Right hand" of the state. The Left hand, the feminine side of Leviathan, is materialized by the "spendthrift" ministries in charge of "social functions" – public education, health, housing, welfare and labor law – which offer protection and succor to the social categories shorn of economic and cultural capital. The Right hand, the masculine side, is charged with enforcing the new economic discipline via budget cuts, fiscal incentives, and economic deregulation.

By inviting us to grasp in a single conceptual framework the various sectors of the state that administer the life conditions and chances of the working class, and to view these sectors as enmeshed in relations of antagonistic cooperation as they vie for preeminence inside the bureaucratic field, this conception has helped us map the ongoing shift from the social to the penal treatment of urban marginality. In this regard, *Punishing the Poor* (2009a) fills in a gap in Bourdieu's model by inserting the police, the courts, and *the prison as core constituents of the "Right hand"* of the state, alongside the ministries of the economy and the budget. It suggests that we need to bring penal policies from the periphery to the center of our analysis of the redesign and deployment of government programs aimed at coping with the entrenched poverty and deepening disparities spawned in the polarizing city by the discarding of the Fordist-Keynesian social compact (Musterd, Murie and Kesteloot 2006; Wilson 1996; Wacquant 2008a). The new government of social insecurity put in place in the United States and offered as model to other advanced countries entails both a shift from the social to the penal wing of the state (detectible in the reallocation of public budgets, personnel, and discursive precedence) and the colonization of the welfare sector by the panoptic and punitive logic characteristic of the post-rehabilitation penal bureaucracy. The slanting of state activity from the social to the penal arm and the incipient penalization of welfare, in turn, partake of the *remasculinization of the state*, in reaction to the wide-ranging changes provoked in the political field by the women's movement and by the institutionalization of social rights antinomic to commodification. The new priority given to duties over rights, sanction over support, the stern rhetoric of the "obligations of citizenship," and the martial reaffirmation of the capacity of the state to lock the troublemaking poor (welfare recipients and criminals) "in a subordinate relation of dependence and obedience" toward state managers portrayed as virile protectors of the society against its wayward members (Young 2005, 16): all these policy planks pronounce and promote the transition from the kindly "nanny state" of the Fordist-Keynesian era to the strict "daddy state" of neoliberalism.

In their classic study *Regulating the Poor* (1993 [1971]), Piven and Cloward forged a germinal model of the management of poverty in industrial capitalism. According to this model, the state expands or contracts its relief programs cyclically to respond to the ups and downs of the economy, the corresponding slackening and tightening of the labor market, and the bouts of social disruption that increased unemployment and destitution trigger periodically among the lower class. Phases of welfare expansion serve to "mute civil disorders" that threaten established hierarchies, while phases of restriction aim to "enforce works norms" by pushing recipients back onto the labor market (Piven and Cloward 1993 [1971], xvi and passim). *Punishing the Poor* (2009a) contends that, while this model worked well for the age of Fordist industrialism and accounts for the two major welfare explosions witnessed in the United States during the Great Depression and the affluent but turbulent 1960s, it has been rendered obsolete by the neoliberal remaking of the state over the past quarter-century. In the age of fragmented labor, hypermobile capital, and sharpening social inequalities and anxieties, the "central role of relief in the regulation of marginal labor and in the maintenance of social order" (Piven and Cloward 1993 [1971], xviii) is displaced and duly supplemented by the vigorous deployment of the police, the courts and the prison in the nether regions of social space. To the single oversight of the poor by the Left hand of the state succeeds the *double regulation of poverty by the joint action of punitive welfare-turned-workfare and an aggressive penal bureaucracy*. The cyclical alternation of contraction and expansion of public aid is replaced by the continual contraction of welfare and the runaway expansion of prisonfare.[5]

This organizational coupling of the Left hand and Right hand of the state under the aegis of the same disciplinary philosophy of behaviorism and

5 By analogy with "welfare," I designate by "prisonfare" the policy stream through which the state gives a penal response to festering urban ills and sociomoral disorders, as well as the imagery, discourses, and bodies of lay and expert knowledge that accrete around the rolling out of the police, the courts, jails and prisons, and their extensions (probation, parole, computerized data banks of criminal files, and the schemes of remote profiling and surveillance they enable). Penalization joins socialization and medicalization as the three alternative strategies whereby the state can opt to treat undesirable conditions and conducts (Wacquant 2009a, 16–17).

moralism can be understood, first, by recalling the shared historical origins of poor relief and penal confinement in the chaotic passage from feudalism to capitalism. Both policies were devised in the long sixteenth century to "absorb and regulate the masses of discontented people uprooted" by this epochal transition (Piven and Cloward 1993 [1971], 21).[6] Similarly, both policies were overhauled in the last two decades of the twentieth century in response to the socioeconomic dislocations provoked by neoliberalism: in the 1980s alone, in addition to reducing public assistance, California passed nearly one thousand laws expanding the use of prison sentences; at the federal level, the 1996 reform that "ended welfare as we know it" was complemented by the sweeping Violent Crime Control and Law Enforcement Act of 1993 (which stipulates the single largest increase in penal sanctions in US history) and bolstered by the No Frills Prison Act of 1995 (which funds the expansion of the prison system and eliminates incentives to rehabilitation).

The institutional pairing of public aid and incarceration as tools for managing the unruly poor can also be understood by paying attention to the structural, functional, and cultural similarities between workfare and prisonfare as "people processing institutions" targeted on kindred problem populations (Hasenfeld 1972). It has been facilitated by the transformation of welfare in a punitive direction and the activation of the penal system to handle more of the traditional clientele of assistance to the destitute – the incipient "penalization" of welfare matching the degraded "welfarization" of the prison. Their concurrent reform over the past thirty years has helped cement their organizational convergence, even as they have obeyed inverse principles. The gradual erosion of public aid and its revamping into workfare in 1996 has entailed restricting entry into the system, shortening "stays" on the rolls, and speeding up exit, resulting in a spectacular reduction of the stock of beneficiaries (it plummeted from nearly 5 million households in 1992 to under 2 million a decade later). Trends in penal policy have followed the exact opposite tack: admission into jail and prison has been greatly facilitated, sojourns behind bars lengthened, and releases curtailed, which has yielded a spectacular ballooning of the population under lock (it jumped by over 1 million in the 1990s). The operant purpose of welfare has shifted from passive "people-processing" to active "people-changing" after 1988 and especially after the abolition of AFDC in 1996, while the prison

6 Piven and Cloward (1993 [1971], 20 and footnote 23) acknowledge penal expansion and activism in the sixteenth century in passing in the rich historical recapitulation of the trajectory of poor relief in early modern Europe in which they ground their investigation of the functions of welfare in contemporary America.

has traveled in the other direction, from aiming to reform inmates (under the philosophy of rehabilitation, hegemonic from the 1920s to the mid-1970s) to merely warehousing them (as the function of punishment was downgraded to retribution and neutralization).

The shared historical roots, organizational isomorphism, and operational convergence of the assistential and penitential poles of the bureaucratic field in the United States are further fortified by the fact that the social profiles of their beneficiaries are virtually identical. AFDC recipients and jail inmates both live near or below 50% of the federal poverty line (for one-half and two-thirds of them, respectively); both are disproportionately black and Hispanic (37% and 18% versus 41% and 19%); the majority did not finish high school and are saddled with serious physical and mental disabilities interfering with their participation in the workforce (44% of AFDC mothers as against 37% of jail inmates). And they are closely bound to one another by extensive kin, marital and social ties, reside overwhelmingly in the same impoverished households and barren neighborhoods, and face the same bleak life horizon at the bottom of the class and ethnic structure.

Punishing the Poor (2009a) avers, not only that the United States has shifted from the single (welfare) to the double (social-cum-penal) regulation of the poor, but also that that "the stunted development of American social policy" skillfully dissected by Piven and Cloward (1993 [1971], 409) stands in close causal and functional relation to America's uniquely overgrown and hyperactive penal policy. *The misery of American welfare and the grandeur of American prisonfare at century's turn are the two sides of the same political coin.* The generosity of the latter is in direct proportion to the stinginess of the former, and it expands to the degree that both are driven by moral behaviorism. The same structural features of the American state – its bureaucratic fragmentation and ethnoracial skew, the institutional bifurcation between universalist "social insurance" and categorical "welfare," and the market-buttressing cast of assistance programs – that facilitated the organized atrophy of welfare in reaction to the racial crisis of the 1960s and the economic turmoil of the 1970s have also fostered the uncontrolled hypertrophy of punishment aimed at the same precarious population. Moreover, the "tortured impact of slavery and institutionalized racism on the construction of the American polity" has been felt, not only on the "underdevelopment" of public aid and the "decentralized and fragmented government and party system" that distributes it to a select segment of the dispossessed (Piven and Cloward 1993 [1971], 424–425), but also on the overdevelopment and stupendous severity of its penal wing. Ethnoracial division and the (re)activation of the stigma of blackness as dangerousness are key to explaining the initial atrophy and accelerating decay of the American social state in the post-Civil Rights epoch, on the one hand, and the astonishing ease and celerity with which the penal state arose on its ruins, on the other.[7]

Reversing the historical bifurcation of the labor and crime questions achieved in the late nineteenth century, *punitive containment* as a government technique for managing deepening urban marginality has effectively rejoined social and penal policy at the close of the twentieth century. It taps the diffuse social anxiety coursing through the middle and lower regions of social space in reaction to the splintering of wage work and the resurgence of inequality, and converts it into popular animus toward welfare recipients and street criminals cast as twin detached and defamed categories which sap the social order by their dissolute morality and dissipated behavior and must therefore be placed under severe tutelage. The new government of poverty invented by the United States to enforce the normalization of social insecurity thus gives a whole new meaning to the notion of "poor relief": punitive containment offers relief not *to* the poor but *from* the poor, by forcibly "disappearing" the most disruptive of them, from the shrinking welfare rolls on the one hand and into the swelling dungeons of the carceral castle on the other.

Foucault (1977 [1975]) has put forth the single most influential analysis of the rise and role of the prison in capitalist modernity, and it is useful to set my thesis against the rich tapestry of analyses he has stretched and stimulated. I concur with the author of *Discipline and Punish* (Foucault 1977 [1975]) that penality is a protean force that is eminently fertile and must be given pride of place in the study of contemporary power.[8] While its originary medium resides in the application of legal coercion to enforce the core strictures of the sociomoral order, punishment must be viewed not through the narrow and technical prism of

---

7 The catalytic role of ethnoracial division in the remaking of the state after the junking of the Fordist-Keynesian social compact and the collapse of the dark ghetto is analyzed in full in my book *Deadly Symbiosis: Race and the Rise of the Penal State* (Wacquant 2010). The depth and rigidity of racial partition is a major factor behind the abyssal gap between the incarceration rates of the United States and European Union, just as it explains their divergent rates of poverty (Alesina and Glaeser 2004).

8 Foucault's writings on incarceration are dispersed and multifaceted, comprising some 60 texts written over 15 years cutting across disciplinary domains and serving manifold purposes from the analytic to the political, and it is not possible to consider them in their richness and complexity here (these are captured by Boullant 2003). Instead, I focus on the canonical tome, *Surveiller et punir. Naissance de la prison* (Foucault 1977 [1975]). I give my own translation with page references to the original French edition, followed by the pagination in the US edition.

repression but by recourse to the notion of production. The assertive rolling out of the penal state has indeed engendered new categories and discourses, novel administrative bodies and government policies, fresh social types and associated forms of knowledge across the criminal and social welfare domains (Wacquant 2008b). But, from here, my argument diverges sharply from Foucault's view of the emergence and functioning of the punitive society in at least four ways.

To start with, Foucault erred in spotting the retreat of the penitentiary. Disciplines may have diversified and metastasized to thrust sinewy webs of control across the society, but the prison has not for that receded from the historical stage and "lost its raison d'être" (Foucault 1977 [1975], 297–298). On the contrary, penal confinement has made a stunning comeback and reaffirmed itself among the central missions of Leviathan just as Foucault and his followers were forecasting its demise. After the founding burst of the 1600s and the consolidation of the 1800s, the turn of the present century ranks as the third "age of confinement" that penologist Mathiesen (1990) forewarned about in 1990. Next, whatever their uses in the eighteenth century, disciplinary technologies have *not* been deployed inside the overgrown and voracious carceral system of our *fin de siècle*. Hierarchical classification, elaborate time schedules, non-idleness, close-up examination and the regimentation of the body: these techniques of penal "normalization" have been rendered wholly impracticable by the demographic chaos spawned by overpopulation, bureaucratic rigidity, resource depletion, and the studious indifference if not hostility of penal authorities toward rehabilitation.[9] In lieu of the *dressage* ("training" or "taming") intended to fashion "docile and productive bodies" postulated by Foucault, the contemporary prison is geared toward brute neutralization, rote retribution, and simple warehousing – by default if not by design. If there are "engineers of consciousness" and "orthopedists of individuality" at work in the mesh of disciplinary powers today (Foucault 1977 [1975], 294), they surely are not employed by departments of corrections.

In the third place, "devices for normalization" anchored in the carceral institution have *not* spread throughout the society, in the manner of capillaries irrigating the entire body social. Rather, the widening of the penal dragnet under neoliberalism has been remarkably discriminating: in spite of conspicuous

9 This is particularly glaring in the country's second largest carceral system (after the Federal Bureau of Prisons), the California Department of Corrections, in which grotesque overcrowding (the state packs 170,000 convicts in 33 prisons designed to hold 85,000) and systemic bureaucratic dysfunction combine to make a mockery of any pretense at "rehabilitation" (Petersilia 2008).

bursts of corporate crime (epitomized by the Savings and Loans scandal of the late 1980s and the folding of Enron a decade later), it has affected essentially the denizens of the lower regions of social and physical space. Indeed, the fact that the social and ethnoracial selectivity of the prison has been maintained, nay reinforced, as it vastly enlarged its intake demonstrates that penalization is not an all-encompassing master logic that blindly traverses the social order to bend and bind its various constituents. On the contrary, it is a skewed technique proceeding along sharp gradients of class, ethnicity, and place, and it operates to divide populations and to differentiate categories according to established conceptions of moral worth. At the dawn of the twenty-first century, America's urban (sub)proletariat lives in a "punitive society," but its middle and upper classes certainly do not. Similarly, efforts to import and adapt US-style slogans and methods of law enforcement – such as zero tolerance policing, mandatory minimum sentencing, or boot camps for juveniles – in Europe have been trained on lower-class and immigrant offenders relegated in the defamed neighborhoods at the center of the panic over "ghettoization" that has swept across the continent over the past decade (Wacquant 2009b).

Lastly, the crystallization of *law-and-order pornography*, that is, the accelerating inflection and inflation of penal activity conceived, represented, and implemented for the primary purpose of being displayed in ritualized form by the authorities – the paradigm for which is the half-aborted reintroduction of chain gangs in striped uniforms – suggests that news of the death of the "spectacle of the scaffold" have been greatly exaggerated. The "redistribution" of "the whole economy of punishment" (Foucault 1977 [1975], 7) in the post-Fordist period has entailed, not its disappearance from public view as proposed by Foucault, but its institutional relocation, symbolic elaboration, and social proliferation beyond anything anyone envisioned when *Discipline and Punish* (1977 [1975]) was published. In the past quarter-century, a whole galaxy of novel cultural and social forms, indeed a veritable industry trading on representations of offenders and law enforcement has sprung forth and spread. The theatralization of penality has migrated from the state to the commercial media and the political field *in toto*, and it has extended from the final ceremony of sanction to encompass the full penal chain, with a privileged place accorded to police operations in low-income districts and courtroom confrontations around celebrity defendants. The Place de grève, where the regicide Damiens was famously quartered, has thus been supplanted not by the Panopticon but by Court TV and the profusion of crime-and-punishment "reality shows" that have inundated television (*Cops, 911, America's Most Wanted, American Detective, Bounty Hunters, Inside Cell Block F*, etc.), not to mention the use of criminal justice as fodder for the daily news and dramatic series (*Law and Order, CSI, Prison Break*, etc.). So much to say that the prison did not "replace" the "social game of the signs of punishment and the garrulous feast that put them in motion" (Foucault 1977 [1975], 131). Rather, it now serves as its institutional canopy. Everywhere the law-and-order *guignol* has become a core civic theater onto whose stage elected officials prance to dramatize moral norms and display their professed capacity for decisive action, thereby reaffirming the political relevance of Leviathan at the very moment when they organize its powerlessness with respect to the market.

This brings us to the question of the political proceeds of penalization, a theme central to Garland's book *The Culture of Control* (2001), the most sweeping and stimulative account of the nexus of crime and social order put forth since Foucault.[10] According to Garland, "the distinctive social, economic, and cultural arrangements of late modernity" have fashioned a "new collective experience of crime and insecurity," to which the authorities have given a reactionary interpretation and a bifurcated response combining practical adaptation via "preventative partnerships" and hysterical denial through "punitive segregation" (Garland 2001, 139–147 and passim). The ensuing reconfiguration of crime control bespeaks the inability of rulers to regiment individuals and normalize contemporary society, and its very disjointedness has made glaring to all the "limits of the sovereign state." For Garland, the "culture of control" coalescing around the "new criminological predicament" pairing high crime rates with the acknowledged limitations of criminal justice both marks and masks a political failing. On the contrary, *Punishing the Poor* (2009a) asserts that punitive containment has proved to be a remarkably successful political strategy: far from "eroding one of the foundational myths of modern society", which holds that "the sovereign state is capable of delivering law and order" (Garland 2001, 109), it has revitalized it. This is true not only in America, where the leaders of both parties have reached complete consensus over the benefits of punitive penal policies targeted at the inner city (Chih Lin 1998), but also in Europe: Blair in England, Berlusconi in

---

10 Since its publication in 2001, Garland has engaged in extensive debates on the "culture of control" (e.g., Garland 2004), revising and qualifying his thesis on multiple fronts. For reasons of space and consistency, I concentrate on the model presented in the book and spotlight those elements that contrast Garland's portrayal of the crime-and-punishment duet in "late modernity" with the analysis of neoliberal penalization offered in *Punishing the Poor* (2009a) (I do not discuss, for instance, Garland's analysis of "shifts in private behaviors" spurred by cultural adaptations to the "high-crime society" by households, businesses, victims, etc., as these are irrelevant to the characterization of the penal state proper).

Italy, and Chirac and Sarkozy in France have all parlayed their martial images of stern "crime fighters" intent to clean up the streets into victories at the polls.[11]

By elevating criminal safety (*sécurité*, *Sicherheit*, *sicurezza*, etc.) to the frontline of government priorities, state officials have condensed the diffuse class anxiety and simmering ethnic resentment generated by the unraveling of the Fordist-Keynesian compact and channeled them toward the (dark-skinned) street criminal, designated as guilty of sowing social and moral disorder in the city, alongside the profligate welfare recipient. Rolling out the penal state and coupling it with workfare has given the high state nobility an effective tool to both foster labor deregulation and contain the disorders that economic deregulation provokes in the lower rungs of the sociospatial hierarchy. Most importantly, it has allowed politicians to make up for the deficit of legitimacy, which besets them whenever they curtail the economic support and social protections traditionally granted by Leviathan. *Contra* Garland, then, I find that the penalization of urban poverty has served well as a vehicle for the *ritual reassertion of the sovereignty of the state* in the narrow, theatricalized domain of law enforcement that it has prioritized *for that very purpose*, just when the same state is conceding its incapacity to control flows of capital, bodies, and signs across its borders. This divergence of diagnosis, in turn, points to three major differences between our respective dissections of the punitive drift in First-World countries.

First, the fast and furious bend toward penalization observed at the *fin de siècle* is not a response to *criminal* insecurity but to *social* insecurity. To be more precise, the currents of social anxiety that roil advanced society are rooted in *objective* social insecurity among the postindustrial working class, whose material conditions have deteriorated with the diffusion of unstable and underpaid wage labor shorn of the usual social "benefits," and *subjective* insecurity among the middle classes, whose prospects for smooth reproduction or upward mobility have dimmed as competition for valued social positions has intensified and the state has reduced its provision of public goods. Garland's notion that "high rates of crime have become a normal social fact – a routine part of modern consciousness, an everyday risk to be assessed and managed" by "the population at large," and especially by the middle class, is belied by victimization studies. Official statistics show that law-breaking in the United States declined or stagnated for 20 years after the mid-1970s before falling precipitously in the 1990s, while exposure to violent offenses varied widely by location in social and

11 See Shea (2009) for a comparison of the electoral success of law-and-order campaigns in France and Italy.

physical space (Wacquant 2009b, 144–147). Relatedly, European countries sport crime rates similar to or higher than America (except for the two specific categories of assault and homicide, which compose but a tiny fraction of all offenses), and yet they have responded quite differently to criminal activity, with rates of incarceration one-fifth to one-tenth the American rate even as they have risen.

This takes us to the second difference: for Garland, the reaction of the state to the predicament of high crime and low justice efficiency has been disjointed and even schizoid, whereas I have stressed its overall coherence. But this coherence becomes visible only when the analytic compass is fully extended *beyond the crime-punishment box and across policy realms*, to link penal trends to the socio-economic restructuring of the urban order, on the one side, and to join workfare to prisonfare, on the other. What Garland characterizes as "the structured ambivalence of the state's response" is not so much ambivalence as a predictable organizational division in the labor of management of the disruptive poor. Bourdieu's theory of the state is helpful here in enabling us to discern that the "adaptive strategies" recognizing the state's limited capacity to stem crime by stressing prevention and devolution are pursued in the penal sector of the *bureaucratic* field, while what Garland calls the "nonadaptive strategies" of "denial and acting out" to reassert that very capacity operate in the *political* field, especially in its relation to the journalistic field.[12]

Thirdly, like other leading analysts of contemporary punishment such as Young (1999), Zimring, Hawkins and Kamin, (2001) and Tonry (2004), Garland sees the punitive turn as the reactionary spawn of right-wing politicians. But *Punishing the Poor* (2009a) finds, first, that the penalization of poverty is not a simple return to a past state of affairs but a genuine institutional innovation and, second, that it is by no means the exclusive creature of neoconservative politics. If politicians of the Right invented the formula, it was employed and refined by their centrist and even "progressive" rivals. Indeed, the president who oversaw by far the biggest increase in incarceration in American history is not Ronald Reagan but William Jefferson Clinton. Across the Atlantic, it is the Left of Blair in England, Schröder in German, Jospin in France, d'Alema in Italy and Gonzalez in Spain that negotiated the shift to proactive penalization, not their conservative predecessors. This is because the root cause of the punitive turn is

12 The analytic and historical differentiation of the political from the bureaucratic field, and their respective locations inside the field of power is discussed in Wacquant (2005, esp 6-7, 14-17 and 142-146).

not late modernity but neoliberalism, a project that can be indifferently embraced by politicians of the Right or the Left.

The jumble of trends that Garland gathers under the umbrella term of late modernity – the "modernizing dynamic of capitalist production and market exchange," shifts in households composition and kinship ties, changes in urban ecology and demography, the disenchanting impact of the electronic media, the "democratization of social life and culture" – are not only exceedingly vague and loosely correlated. They are either not peculiar to the closing decades of the twentieth century, specific to the United States, or show up in their most pronounced form in the social-democratic countries of Northern Europe that have *not* been submerged by the international wave of penalization.[13] Moreover, the onset of late modernity has been gradual and evolutionary whereas the recent permutations of penality have been abrupt and revolutionary.

Punishing the Poor (2009a) contends that it is not the generic "risks and anxieties" of "the open, porous, mobile society of strangers that is late modernity" (Garland 2001, 165) that have fostered retaliation against lower-class categories perceived as undeserving and deviant types seen as irrecuperable, but the specific *social* insecurity generated by the fragmentation of wage labor, the hardening of class divisions, and the erosion of the established ethnoracial hierarchy guaranteeing an effective monopoly over collective honor to whites in the United States and to nationals in the European Union. The sudden expansion and consensual exaltation of the penal state after the mid-1970s is not a culturally reactionary reading of "late modernity," but a ruling-class response aiming to redefine the perimeter and missions of Leviathan, so as to establish a new economic regime based on capital hypermobility and labor flexibility and to curb the social turmoil generated at the foot of the urban order by the public policies of market deregulation and social welfare retrenchment that are core building blocks of neoliberalism.

13 Read the extended analysis of the sociopolitical foundations of the "penal exceptionalism" of Finland, Sweden, and Norway by Pratt (2008a; 2008b), in which the cultural commitment to social equality and welfare state security play a pivotal role, as they do in the sturdy resistance of Scandinavia to neoliberal nostrums. Another notable anomaly for the "culture of control" thesis is Canada, which is as "late modern" as the United States and yet has kept its incarceration low and stable over the past three decades (it even decreased from 123 to 108 inmates per 100,000 residents between 1991 and 2004, while the US rate zoomed from 360 to 710 inmates per 100,000).

2 Toward a sociological specification of neoliberalism

The invention of the double regulation of the insecure fractions of the postindustrial proletariat via the wedding of social and penal policy at the bottom of the polarized class structure is a major *structural innovation* that takes us beyond the model of the welfare-poverty nexus elaborated by Piven and Cloward just as the Fordist-Keynesian regime was coming unglued. The birth of this institutional contraption is also not captured by Foucault's vision of the "disciplinary society" or by Garland's notion of the "culture of control," neither of which can account for the unforeseen timing, steep socioethnic selectivity, and peculiar organizational path of the abrupt turnaround in penal trends in the closing decades of the twentieth century. For the punitive containment of urban marginality through the simultaneous rolling back of the social safety net and the rolling out of the police-and-prison dragnet and their knitting together into a carceral-assistential lattice is not the spawn of some broad societal trend – whether it be the ascent of "biopower" or the advent of "late modernity" – but, at bottom, an exercise in *state crafting*. It partakes of the correlative revamping of the perimeter, missions and capacities of public authority on the economic, social welfare, and penal fronts. This revamping has been uniquely swift, broad, and deep in the United States, but it is in progress – or in question – in all advanced societies submitted to the relentless pressure to conform to the American pattern.

Consider trends in France: in recent years, the country has eased strictures on part-time employment as well as limitations on night-time and week-end work. Its governments of both Left and Right have actively supported the development of short-term contracts, temporary jobs, and underpaid traineeships, and expanded the latitude of employers in hiring, firing, and the use of overtime. The result is that the number of precarious wage earners has risen from 1,7 million in 1992 to 2,8 million in 2007 – or from 8,6 to 12,4% of the employed workforce (Maurin and Savidan 2008). In June of 2009, France instituted the RSA (Revenu de solidarité active), set to gradually replace the RMI (Revenu minimum d'insertion, the guaranteed minimum income grant provided to some 1,3 million), a program designed to push public aid recipients into the low-wage labor market via state subsidies to poor workers premised on the obligation to accept employment (Grandquillot 2009). Simultaneously, the oversight of unemployment benefits is being farmed out to private firms that can terminate beneficiaries who reject two job offers and receive a financial bonus for each recipient they place in a job. On the penal front, accelerating the punitive turn taken by the Socialist government of Jospin in 1998–2002, the successive administrations of Chirac and Sarkozy have adopted sweeping measures of penal expansion (Bonelli 2008): intensified policing centered on low-income districts, youth night curfews, enlarged recourse to incarceration for street crimes (in sharp contrast to the depenalization of corporate crime), plea bargaining and accelerated judicial processing for low-level delinquents, mandatory minimum sentences for youth recidivists, annual targets for the expulsion of undocumented migrants, and the indefinite civil commitment of certain categories of sex offenders after they have served their sentence. The country's budget for corrections jumped from 1,4 billion euros for 22,000 guards confining 48,000 inmates in 2001 to 2 billion euros for 24,000 guards and 64,000 inmates in 2009.

Tracking the roots and modalities of America's stupendous drive to hyperincarceration opens a unique route into the *sanctum* of the neoliberal Leviathan. It leads us to articulate two major theoretical claims. The first is that *the penal apparatus is a core organ of the state*, expressive of its sovereignty and instrumental in imposing categories, upholding material, and symbolic divisions, and molding relations and behaviors through the selective penetration of social and physical space. The police, the courts, and the prison are not mere technical appendages for the enforcement of lawful order (as criminology would have it), but vehicles for the political production of reality and for the oversight of deprived and defamed social categories and their reserved territories (Wacquant 2008b). Students of early modern state formation, from Norbert Elias to Charles Tilly to Gianfranco Poggi, fully recognized that the monopolization of force, and thus the construction of a bureaucratic machinery for policing, judging, and punishing miscreants capable of minimally pacifying society, was central to the building of Leviathan. It is high time that students of the neoliberal era notice that the remaking of the state after the breakup of the Keynesian social compact has entailed not only renewed activity aimed at fostering international competitiveness, technological innovation, and labor flexibility (Jessop 1994; Streeck and Thelen 2005; Levy 2006) but also, and most distinctively, the forceful reassertion of its penal mission henceforth set in a pornographic and managerialist key.

Indeed, the second thesis advanced by *Punishing the Poor* (2009a) is that the ongoing capitalist "revolution from above" commonly called *neoliberalism entails the enlargement and exaltation of the penal sector* of the bureaucratic field, so that the state may check the social reverberations caused by the diffusion of social insecurity in the lower rungs of the class and ethnic hierarchy as well as assuage popular discontent over the dereliction of its traditional economic and social duties. Neoliberalism readily resolves what for Garland's "culture of control" remains an enigmatic paradox of late modernity, namely, the fact that "control is now being re-emphasized in every area of social life – *with the singular and startling exception of the economy*, from whose deregulated domain most of today's major risks routinely emerge" (Garland 2001, 165 [emphasis added]). The neoliberal remaking of the state also explains the steep class, ethnoracial and spatial bias stamping the simultaneous retraction of its social bosom and expansion of its penal fist: the populations most directly and adversely impacted by the convergent revamping of the labor market and public aid turn out also to be the privileged "beneficiaries" of the penal largesse of the authorities. This is true in the United States where the carceral boom has corralled (sub)proletarian blacks trapped in the bare hyperghetto. It is also the case in Western Europe, where the primary clientele of the expanding prison is composed of precarious workers and the unemployed, postcolonial migrants, and lower-class addicts and derelicts (Wacquant 2009b, 87–102).

Finally, neoliberalism correlates closely with the international diffusion of punitive policies in both the welfare and the criminal domains. It is not by accident that the advanced countries that have imported, first, workfare measures designed to buttress the discipline of desocialized wage work and, then, variants of US-style criminal justice measures are the Commonwealth nations that also pursued aggressive policies of economic deregulation inspired by the "free market" nostrums come from America, whereas the countries that remained committed to a strong regulatory state curbing social insecurity have best resisted the sirens of "zero tolerance" policing and "prison works".[14] Similarly, societies of the Second World such as Brazil, Argentina, and South Africa, which adopted superpunitive penal planks inspired by American developments in the 1990s and saw their prison populations soar as a result, did so not because they had at long last reached the stage of "late modernity," but because they have taken the route of market deregulation and state retrenchment.[15] But to discern these multilevel connections between the upsurge of the punitive Leviathan and the spread of neoliberalism, it is necessary to develop a precise and broad conception of the latter. Instead of discarding neoliberalism, as Garland (2001, 77) does,

---

14 In a major comparative study of the linkages between penal policy and political economy in twelve contemporary capitalist countries, Cavadino and Dignan (2006) find that the nations they characterize as neoliberal (as distinct from conservative corporatist, social democratic, and oriental corporatist) are consistently more punitive and have become much more so in the past two decades.

15 The international diffusion of "made in USA" penal categories and policies and its springs are treated at length in *Prisons de Poverty* (Wacquant 2009b). For further analyses of this near-planetary spread, read Jones and Newburn (2006) as well as Andreas and Nadelmann (2006).

on account of it being "rather too specific" a phenomenon to account for penal escalation, we must expand our conception of it, and move from an economic to a fully sociological understanding of the phenomenon.

Neoliberalism is an elusive and contested notion, a hybrid term awkwardly suspended between the lay idiom of political debate and the technical terminology of social science, which moreover is often invoked without clear referent. Whether singular or polymorphous, evolutionary or revolutionary, the prevalent conception of neoliberalism is essentially *economic*: it stresses an array of market-friendly policies, such as labor deregulation, capital mobility, privatization, a monetarist agenda of deflation and financial autonomy, trade liberalization, interplace competition, and the reduction of taxation and public expenditures.[16] But this conception is thin and incomplete, as well as too closely bound up with the sermonizing discourse of the advocates of neoliberalism. We need to reach beyond this economic nucleus and elaborate a thicker notion that identifies the institutional machinery and symbolic frames through which neoliberal tenets are being actualized.

A minimalist sociological characterization can now be essayed as follows. Neoliberalism is a *transnational political project* aiming to remake the nexus of market, state, and citizenship from above. This project is carried by a new global ruling class in the making, composed of the heads and senior executives of transnational firms, high-ranking politicians, state managers and top officials of multinational organizations (the OECD, WTO, IMF, World Bank, and the European Union), and cultural-technical experts in their employ (chief among them economists, lawyers and communications professionals with germane training and mental categories in the different countries). It entails not simply the reassertion of the prerogatives of capital and the promotion of the marketplace, but the close articulation of four institutional logics:

(1) *Economic deregulation*, that is, re-regulation aimed at promoting "the market" or market-like mechanisms as the optimal device, not only for guiding corporate strategies and economic transactions (under the aegis of the shareholder-value conception of the firm), but for organizing the gamut of human activities, including the private provision of core public goods, on

16 This is the common core one can extract from a vast (and uneven) literature on the topic across the disciplines, among which can single out the pointed analyses of Fligstein (2001) for sociology, Campbell and Pedersen (2001) for political economy, Comaroff and Comaroff (2001) for anthropology, Brenner and Theodore (2002) for geography, and Duménil and Lévy (2004) for economics.

putative grounds of efficiency (implying deliberate disregard for distributive issues of justice and equality).

(2) *Welfare state devolution, retraction, and recomposition* designed to facilitate the expansion and support the intensification of commodification, and in particular to submit reticent individuals to desocialized wage labor via variants of "workfare" establishing a quasi-contractual relationship between the state and lower-class recipients, treated not as citizens but as clients or subjects (stipulating their behavioral obligations as condition for continued public assistance).

(3) *An expansive, intrusive, and proactive penal apparatus* that penetrates the nether regions of social and physical space to contain the disorders and disarray generated by diffusing social insecurity and deepening inequality, to unfurl disciplinary supervision over the precarious fractions of the postindustrial proletariat, and to reassert the authority of Leviathan so as to bolster the evaporating legitimacy of elected officials.

(4) The *cultural trope of individual responsibility*, which invades all spheres of life to provide a "vocabulary of motive" – as C. Wright Mills would say – for the construction of the self (on the model of the entrepreneur), the spread of markets and legitimation for the widened competition it subtends, the counterpart of which is the evasion of corporate liability and the proclamation of state irresponsibility (or sharply reduced accountability in matters social and economic).

A central *ideological* tenet of neoliberalism is that it entails the coming of "small government": the shrinking of the allegedly flaccid and overgrown Keynesian welfare state and its makeover into a lean and nimble workfare state, which "invests" in human capital and "activates" communal springs and individual appetites for work and civic participation through "partnerships" stressing self-reliance, commitment to paid work, and managerialism. *Punishing the Poor* (2009a) demonstrates that the neoliberal state turns out to be quite different *in actuality*: while it embraces laissez-faire at the top, releasing restraints on capital and expanding the life chances of the holders of economic and cultural capital, it is anything but laissez-faire at the bottom. Indeed, when it comes to handling the social turbulence generated by deregulation and to impressing the discipline of precarious labor, the new Leviathan reveals itself to be fiercely interventionist, bossy, and pricey. The soft touch of libertarian proclivities favoring the upper class gives way to the hard edge of authoritarian oversight, as it endeavors to direct, nay dictate, the behavior of the lower class. "Small government" in the economic register thus begets "big government" on the twofold front of workfare and criminal justice. Between 1982 and 2001, the United States increased its public expenditures for police, criminal courts and corrections by 364% (from $36 to

$167 billion, or 165% in constant dollars of 2000) and added nearly 1 million justice staff. In 1996, when "welfare reform" replaced the right to public aid by the obligation to accept insecure employment as a condition of support, the budget for corrections exceeded the overall sums allocated to AFDC and food stamps, the country's two main assistance programs. That same year, corrections vaulted to third largest employment in the land after Manpower Incorporated and Wal-Mart (see Wacquant 2009a, 152–161). The results of America's grand experiment in creating the first society of advanced insecurity in history are in: *the invasive, expansive and expensive penal state is not a deviation from neoliberalism but one of its constituent ingredients.*

Remarkably, this is a side of neoliberalism that has been obfuscated or overlooked by its apologists and detractors alike. This blind spot is glaring in Giddens's celebrated reformulation of neoliberal imperatives into the platform of New Labour. In his manifesto for *The Third Way* (1999), Giddens highlights high rates of crime in deteriorating working-class districts as an indicator of "civic decline" and curiously blames the Keynesian welfare state for it (not deindustrialization and social retrenchment): "The egalitarianism of the old left was noble in intent, but as its rightist critics say has sometimes led to perverse consequences – visible, for instance, in the social engineering that has left a legacy of decaying, crime-ridden housing estates." He makes "preventing crime, and reducing fear of crime" through state-locality partnerships central to "community regeneration," and he embraces the law-and-order mythology of "broken windows": "One of the most significant innovations in criminology in recent years has been the discovery [sic] that the decay of day-to-day civility relates directly to criminality. […] Disorderly behavior unchecked signals to citizens that the area is unsafe" (Giddens 1999, 16, 78–79 and 87–88). But Giddens studiously omits the punishment side of the equation: *The Third Way* (1999) contains not a single mention of the prison and glosses over the judicial hardening and carceral boom that have everywhere accompanied the kind of economic deregulation and welfare devolution it promotes. This omission is particularly startling in the case of Britain, since the incarceration rate of England and Wales jumped from 88 inmates per 100,000 residents in 1992 to 150 per 100,000 in 2008, even as crime receded continually for the first ten years of that period (Hough and Mayhew 2004), with Anthony Blair presiding over the single largest absolute increase of the convict population during a prime ministership in the country's history – matching the feat of Clinton, his co-sponsor of the "Third Way" on the other side of the Atlantic.

A similar oversight of the centrality of the penal institution to the new government of social insecurity is found in the works of eminent critics of neoliberalism.

Harvey's extended characterization of "the neoliberal state" in his *A Brief History of Neoliberalism* (2005) is a case in point, which appositely spotlights the obdurate limitations of the traditional political economy of punishment that *Punishing the Poor* (2009a) strives to overcome. For Harvey, neoliberalism aims at maximizing the reach of market transactions via "deregulation, privatization, and withdrawal of the state from many areas of social provision." As in previous eras of capitalism, the task of Leviathan is "to facilitate conditions for profitable capital accumulation on the part of both domestic and foreign capital," but now this translates into penal expansion: "The neoliberal state will resort to coercive legislation and policing tactics (anti-picketing rules, for instance) to disperse or repress collective forms of opposition to corporate power […] *The coercive arm of the state is augmented to protect corporate interests* and, if necessary, to *repress dissent*. None of this seems consistent with neoliberal theory" (Harvey 2005, 2–3, 77 [emphasis added]).

With barely a few passing mentions of the prison and not one line on workfare, Harvey's account of the rise of neoliberalism is woefully incomplete. His conception of the neoliberal state turns out to be surprisingly restricted, first, because he remains wedded to the repressive conception of power, instead of construing the manifold missions of penality through the expansive category of production. Subsuming penal institutions under the rubric of coercion leads him to ignore the expressive function and ramifying material effects of the law and its enforcement, which are to generate controlling images and public categories, to stoke collective emotions and accentuate salient social boundaries, as well as to activate state bureaucracies so as to mold social ties and strategies. Next, Harvey portrays this repression as aimed at political opponents to corporate rule and "dissident internal movements" that challenge the hegemony of private property and profit (e.g., the Branch Davidians at Waco, the participants in the Rodney King riots in Los Angeles in 1991, and the anti-globalization activists who rocked the G-8 meeting in Seattle in 1999) (Harvey 2005, 83), when the primary targets of penalization in the post-Fordist age have been the precarious fractions of the proletariat concentrated in the tainted districts of dereliction of the dualizing metropolis who, being squeezed by the urgent press of day-to-day subsistence, have little capacity or care to contest corporate rule.

Third, for the author of *Social Justice and the City* (Harvey 1973), the state "intervenes" through coercion only when the neoliberal order breaks down, to repair economic transactions, ward off challenges to capital, and resolve social crises. By contrast, *Punishing the Poor* (2009a) argues that the present penal activism of the state – translating into carceral bulimia in the United States and policing frenzy throughout Western Europe – is an ongoing, routine feature of neoliberalism. Indeed, it is not economic failure but economic success that requires the aggressive deployment of the police, court and prison in the nether sectors of social and physical space. And the rapid turnings of the law-and-order merry-go-round are an index of the reassertion of state sovereignty, not a sign of its weakness. Harvey does note that the retrenchment of the welfare state "leaves larger and larger segments of the population exposed to impoverishment" and that "the social safety net is reduced to a bare minimum in favor of a system that emphasizes individual responsibility and the victim is all too often blamed" (Harvey 2005, 76). But he does not realize that it is precisely these normal disorders, inflicted by economic deregulation and welfare retrenchment, that are managed by the enlarged penal apparatus in conjunction with supervisory workfare. Instead, Harvey invokes the bogeyman of the "prison-industrial complex," suggesting that incarceration is a major plank of capitalist profit-seeking and accumulation when it is a disciplinary device entailing a gross drain on the public coffers and a tremendous drag on the economy.

Fourth and last, Harvey views the neoconservative stress on coercion and order restoration as a temporary fix for the chronic instability and functional failings of neoliberalism, whereas I construe authoritarian moralism as an *integral constituent of the neoliberal state* when it turns its sights on the lower rungs of the polarizing class structure. Like Garland, Harvey must artificially dichotomize "neoliberalism" and "neoconservatism" to account for the reassertion of the supervisory authority of the state over the poor because his narrow economistic definition of neoliberalism replicates its ideology and truncates its sociology. To elucidate the paternalist transformation of penality at century's turn, then, we must imperatively escape the "crime-and-punishment" box, but also exorcise once and for all the ghost of Althusser (1971 [1969]), whose instrumentalist conception of Leviathan and crude duality of ideological and repressive apparatuses gravely hamstring the historical anthropology of the state in the neoliberal age. Following Bourdieu, we must fully attend to the internal complexity and dynamic recomposition of the bureaucratic field, as well as to the constitutive power of the symbolic structures of penality to trace the intricate meshing of market and moral discipline across the economic, welfare, and criminal justice realms (Bourdieu 1994 [1993], 15–16; Wacquant 2005, 133–150).

3 Conclusion: penality in the building of a centaur state

In his meticulous comparison of eugenic measures in the 1920s, compulsory work camps in the 1930s, and workfare schemes in the 1990s in England and America, King (1999, 26) has shown that "illiberal social policies" that seek to direct citizens' conduct coercively are "intrinsic to liberal democratic politics" and reflective of their internal contradictions. Even as they contravene standards of equality and personal liberty, such programs are periodically pursued because they are ideally suited to highlighting and enforcing the boundaries of membership in times of turmoil; they are fleet vehicles for broadcasting the newfound resolve of state elites to tackle offensive conditions and assuage popular resentment toward derelict or deviant categories; and they diffuse conceptions of otherness that materialize the symbolic opposition anchoring the social order. With the advent of the neoliberal government of social insecurity mating restrictive workfare and expansive prisonfare, however, it is not just the policies of the state that are illiberal but *its very architecture*. Tracking the coming and workings of America's punitive politics of poverty after the dissolution of the Fordist-Keynesian order and the implosion of the black ghetto reveals that neoliberalism brings about, not the shrinking of government, but the erection of a *centaur state*, liberal at the top and paternalistic at the bottom, which presents radically different faces at the two ends of the social hierarchy: a comely and caring visage toward the middle and upper classes, and a fearsome and frowning mug toward the lower class.

It bears stressing in closing that the building of a Janus-faced Leviathan practicing liberal paternalism has not proceeded according to some master-scheme concocted by omniscient rulers. Nor does it spring mechanically from the systemic necessities of some grand structure such as late capitalism, racism, or panopticism (as in various neo-Marxist and neo-Foucauldian approaches as well as in the activist demonology of the "prison-industrial complex"). Rather, it arises from *struggles over and within the bureaucratic field*, aiming to redefine the perimeter, missions, priorities, and modalities of action of public authorities with respect to definite problem territories and categories. These struggles involve, crucially, not only battles pitting organizations stemming from civil society and state agencies, but also internecine contests between the various sectors of the bureaucratic field that vie to gain "ownership" of the social problem at hand and thus valorize the specific forms of authority and expertise they anchor (medical, educational, social welfare, penal, economic, etc., and within the penal domain, the police, courts, and confinement institutions and post-custodial means of control). The overall fitness of punitive containment to regulating urban marginality at century's dawn is a rough *post-hoc functionality* born of a mix of initial policy intent, sequential bureaucratic adjustment, and political trial-and-error and electoral profit-seeking at the point of confluence of three relatively autonomous streams of public measures concerning the low-skill employment market, public aid, and criminal justice. The complementarity and interlocking of state programs in these three realms is partly designed and partly an emergent property, fostered by the practical need to operations – with (sub)proletarian blacks from the hyperghetto figuring at the point of maximum impact where market deregulation, welfare retrenchment and penal penetration meet.

Whatever the modalities of their advent, it is indisputable that the linked stinginess of the welfare wing and munificence of the penal wing under the guidance of moralism have altered the makeup of the bureaucratic field in ways that are profoundly injurious to democratic ideals.[17] As their sights converge onto the same marginal populations and districts, deterrent workfare and the neutralizing prison foster vastly different profiles and experiences of citizenship across the class and ethnic spectrum. They not only contravene the fundamental principle of equality of treatment by the state and routinely abridge the individual freedoms of the dispossessed. They also undermine the consent of the governed through the aggressive deployment of involuntary programs stipulating personal responsibilities just as the state is withdrawing the institutional supports necessary to shoulder these and shirking its own social and economic charges. And they stamp the precarious fractions of the proletariat from which public aid recipients and convicts issue with the indelible seal of unworthiness. In short, the penalization of poverty splinters citizenship along class lines, saps civic trust at the bottom, and saws the degradation of republican tenets. The establishment of the new government of social insecurity discloses, *in fine*, that *neoliberalism is constitutively corrosive of democracy.*

By enabling us to break out of the crime-and-punishment box to relink welfare and justice while fully attending to both the material and symbolic dimensions of public policy, Bourdieu's concept of bureaucratic field offers a powerful tool for dissecting the anatomy and assembly of the neoliberal Leviathan. It suggests that some of the pivotal political struggles of this century's turn – if not the most visible or salient ones – involve, not the confrontation between the mobilized organizations representing subaltern categories and the state but battles internal to the hierarchical and dynamic ensemble of public bureaucracies that compete to socialize, medicalize, or penalize urban marginality and its correlates. Elucidating the nexus of workfare, prisonfare, and social insecurity, in turn, reveals that the study of incarceration is not a technical section in the criminogical catalogue but a key chapter in the sociology of the state and social inequality in the bloom of neoliberalism.

---

17 For a specification of the republican and liberal conceptions of democracy at stake here, read Held's *Models of Democracy* (1996).

3.1 Acknowledgements

This chapter is adapted from "A Sketch of the Neoliberal State," the theoretical coda to my book *Punishing the Poor: The Neoliberal Government of Social Insecurity* (2009a, "Politics, History, and Culture" series, Durham and London: Duke University Press). It is part of a transdisciplinary and transnational symposium, with responses by John Campbell, Bernard Harcourt, Margit Mayer, Jamie Peck, Frances Piven, and Mariana Valverde (published in English in *Theoretical Criminology* (2010, vol. 14, no. 1)), as well as critics from the corresponding countries, published in German in *Das Argument* (Berlin); in French in *Civilisations* (Brussels); in Spanish in *Sociographica* (Cordoba); in Brazilian in *Discursos Sediciosos* (Rio de Janeiro); in Italian in *Aut Aut* (Rome); in Portuguese in *Cadernos de Ciências Sociais* (Porto); in Norwegian in *Materialisten* (Oslo); in Danish in *Social Kritik* (Copenhagen); in Greek in *Ikarian Journal of Social and Political Research* (Athens); in Ukrainian in *Spilne* (Kiev); in Russian in *Skepsis* (Moscow); in Hungarian in *Eszmelet* (Budapest); in Slovenian in *Novi Plamen* (Ljubljana); in Romanian in *Sociologie Românească* (Bucharest); and in Japanese in *Gendai Shiso* (Tokyo). I am grateful to Mario Candeias and the Rosa Luxemburg Stiftung in Berlin for getting the ball rolling on this project, and to the editors of the journals listed above for their enthusiastic support of this project. This chapter benefited from reactions to presentations made at the 4th Conference on Putting Pierre Bourdieu to Work, Manchester, England, 23-24 June 2008, and to the Sociology Department Colloquium at Yale University, 26 February 2009.

References

Alesina, Alberto, and Edward L. Glaeser. 2004. *Fighting Poverty in the US and Europe: A World of Difference*. New York: Oxford University Press.

Althusser, Louis. 1971 [1970]. "Ideology and Ideological State Apparatuses." In *Lenin and Philosophy and Other Essays*, 127–186. New York and London: Monthly Review Press.

Andreas, Peter, and Ethan Nadelmann. 2006. *Policing the Globe: Criminalization and Crime Control in International Relations*. New York: Oxford University Press.

Blumstein, Alfred, and Joel Wallman, eds. 2000. *The Crime Drop in America*. New York: Oxford University Press.

Bonelli, Laurent. 2008. *La France a peur. Une histoire sociale de l'insécurité*. Paris: La Découverte.

Boullant, François. 2003. *Michel Foucault et les prisons*. Paris: Presses Universitaires de France.

Bourdieu, Pierre. 1994 [1993]. "Rethinking the State: On the Genesis and Structure of the Bureaucratic Field." *Sociological Theory* 12: 1–19.

Bourdieu, Pierre. 1999 [1993]. "The Abdication of the State." In *The Weight of the World: Social Suffering in Contemporary Society*, authored by Pierre Bourdieu et al., 181–188. Cambridge: Polity Press.

Bourdieu, Pierre. 2005 [2000]. *The Social Structures of the Economy.* Cambridge: Polity Press.

Brenner, Neil, and Nik Theodore, eds. 2002. *Spaces of Neoliberalism: Urban Restructuring in North America and Western Europe.* New York: Wiley/Blackwell.

Campbell, John, and Ove Pedersen, eds. 2001. *The Rise of Neoliberalism and Institutional Analysis.* Princeton (NJ): Princeton University Press.

Cavadino, Michael, and James Dignan. 2006. *Penal Systems: A Comparative Approach.* London: Sage Publications.

Chih Lin, Ann. 1998. "The Troubled Success of Crime Policy." In *The Social Divide: Political Parties and the Future of Activist Government*, edited by Margaret Weir, 312–357. Washington (DC): Brookings Institution and Russell Sage Foundation.

Comaroff, Jean, and John L. Comaroff, eds. 2001. *Millennial Capitalism and the Culture of Neoliberalism.* Durham and London: Duke University Press.

Duménil, Gérard, and Dominique Lévy. 2004. *Capital Resurgent: Roots of the Neoliberal Revolution.* Cambridge: Harvard University Press.

Fligstein, Neil. 2001. *The Architecture of Markets: An Economic Sociology of Twenty-First-Century Capitalist Societies.* Princeton (NJ): Princeton University Press.

Foucault, Michel. 1977 [1975]. *Discipline and Punish: The Birth of the Prison.* New York: Vintage.

Freeman, Richard B. 2007. *America Works: The Exceptional U. S. Labor Market.* New York: Russell Sage Foundation.

Gallie, Duncan, ed. 2007. *Employment Regimes and the Quality of Work.* Oxford: Oxford University Press.

Garland, David. 1989. *Punishment and Society: A Study in Social Theory.* Chicago: University of Chicago Press.

Garland, David. 2001. *The Culture of Control: Crime and Social Order in Contemporary Society.* Chicago: University of Chicago Press.

Garland, David. 2004. "Beyond the Culture of Control." *Critical Review of International Social and Political Philosophy* 7: 160–89.

Giddens, Anthony. 1999. *The Third Way: The Renewal of Social Democracy.* Cambridge: Polity Press.

Grandquillot, Dominique. 2009. *RSA Revenu de solidarité active*. Paris: Gualino Editeur.

Harvey, David. 1973. *Social Justice and the City*. London: Edward Arnold Publishers.

Harvey, David. 2005. *A Brief History of Neoliberalism*. New York: Oxford University Press.

Hasenfeld, Yeheskel. 1972. "People Processing Organizations: An Exchange Approach." *American Sociological Review* 37: 256–263.

Held, David. 1996. *Models of Democracy*. Cambridge: Polity Press.

Hough, Mike, and Pat Mayhew. 2004. "L'évolution de la criminalité à travers deux décennies du British Crime Survey." *Déviance et Société* 28: 267–284.

Jessop, Bob. 1994. "Post-Fordism and the State." In *Post-Fordism: A Reader*, edited by Ash Amin, 251–229. Oxford: Basil Blackwell.

Jones, Trevor, and Tim Newburn. 2006. *Policy Transfer and Criminal Justice*. Chichester: Open University Press.

King, Desmond. 1999. *In the Name of Liberalism: Illiberal Social Policy in the United States and Britain*. New York: Oxford University Press.

Levy, Jonah D. ed. 2006. *The State After Statism: New State Activities in the Age of Liberalization*. Cambridge (MA): Harvard University Press.

Massey, Douglas S. 2007. *Categorically Unequal: The American Stratification System*. New York: Russell Sage Foundation.

Mathiesen, Thomas. 1990. *Prison on Trial: A Critical Assessment*. London: Sage Publications.

Maurin, Louis, and Patrick Savidan. 2008. *L'Etat des inégalités en France. Données et analyses*. Paris: Belin.

Musterd, Sako, Alan Murie, and Christian Kesteloot. 2006. *Neighbourhoods of Poverty: Urban Social Exclusion and Integration in Comparison*. London: Palgrave Macmillan.

Petersilia, Joan. 2008. "California's Correctional Paradox of Excess and Deprivation." *Crime and Justice: A Review of Research* 37: 207–278.

Piven, Frances Fox, and Richard A. Cloward. 1993 [1971]. *Regulating the Poor: The Functions of Public Welfare*. New York: Vintage, expanded edition.

Pratt, John. 2008a. "Scandinavian Exceptionalism in an Era of Penal Excess. Part I: The Nature and Roots of Scandinavian Exceptionalism." *British Journal of Criminology* 48: 119–137.

Pratt, John. 2008b. "Scandinavian Exceptionalism in an Era of Penal Excess. Part II: Does Scandinavian Exceptionalism Have a Future?" *British Journal of Criminology* 48: 275–292.

Schierup, Carl-Ulrik, Peo Hansen, and Stephen Castles. 2006. *Migration, Citizenship and the European Welfare State: A European Dilemma.* Oxford: Oxford University Press.

Shea, Evelyn. 2009. "Elections and the Fear of Crime: the Case of France and Italy." *European Journal on Criminal Policy and Research* 15: 83–102.

Streeck, Wolfgang, and Kathleen Thelen, eds. 2005. *Beyond Continuity: Institutional Change in Advanced Political Economies.* Oxford: Oxford University Press.

Tonry, Michael. 2004. *Thinking About Crime: Sense and Sensibility in American Penal Culture.* New York: Oxford University Press.

Wacquant, Loïc, ed. 2005. *The Mystery of Ministry: Pierre Bourdieu and Democratic Politics.* Cambridge: Polity Press.

Wacquant, Loïc. 2008a. *Urban Outcasts: A Comparative Sociology of Advanced Marginality.* Cambridge (MA): Polity Press.

Wacquant, Loïc. 2008b. "Ordering Insecurity: Social Polarization and the Punitive Upsurge." *Radical Philosophy Review* 11: 9–27.

Wacquant, Loïc. 2009a. *Punishing the Poor: The Neoliberal Government of Social Insecurity.* Durham (NC) and London: Duke University Press.

Wacquant, Loïc. 2009b. *Prisons of Poverty.* Minneapolis: University of Minnesota Press.

Wacquant, Loïc. 2010. *Deadly Symbiosis: Race and the Rise of the Penal State.* Cambridge: Polity Press.

Western, Bruce. 2006. *Punishment and Inequality in America.* New York: Russell Sage Foundation.

Wilson, William Julius. 1996. *When Work Disappears: The World of the New Urban Poor.* New York: Knopf.

Young, Iris Marion. 2005. "The Logic of Masculinist Protection: Reflections on the Current Security State." In *Women and Citizenship*, edited by Marilyn Friedman, 15–34. New York: Oxford University Press.

Young, Jock. 1999. *The Exclusive Society: Social Exclusion, Crime and Difference in Late Modernity.* London: Sage.

Zimring, Franklin, Gordon Hawkins, and Sam Kamin. 2001. *Punishment and Democracy: Three Strikes and You're Out in California.* New York: Oxford University Press.

Adriana Mica, Katarzyna M. Wyrzykowska,
Rafał Wiśniewski and Iwona Zielińska

Invisible Hand in Sociology: Where Does It Take Us?

This edited volume started with the assumption that there is no such thing as a pure theory of invisible hand in sociology, not comparable with the analytical framework that is known to have developed in economics anyway. But that sociology has rather nourished an invisible hand-type approach.

The invisible hand-type undertaking is one of the main analytical frameworks for the study of unintended consequences in sociology. In general terms, this comes very close to the invisible hand in economics. As such, it presupposes that social institutions are researched in terms of unintended consequences of individual activities that were not purposively oriented toward implementing these outcomes. Yet, the sociological research is seldom openly presented in terms of the invisible hand theory; it comes usually in other flavors such as dialectical processes, effects of emergence, effects of aggregation, fallacies of composition, etc. With rare exceptions, such as Cherkaoui's (2007) invisible codes, these formulations do not go by the name of sociological invisible hand models. They are models of production of unintended consequences at systemic level that bear similarity with the invisible hand framing; the authors acknowledge this similarity, even legitimize these models with it, yet rarely call them as invisible hand patterns per se.

This state of affairs indicates that the invisible hand-type theory of unintended consequences in sociology is more than a noneconomic and pale counterpart of the traditional argument initiated by Adam Smith, or even earlier by Bernard Mandeville. The invisible hand-type model in sociology is not just the invisible hand's little brother, or not anymore. It might be less developed, that is true, but it is still a much more autonomous undertaking than it would occur at first sight, especially to someone who used to associate the invisible hand with economics. Looking from within sociology, the invisible hand-type research occurs as a rather fuzzy stream within the broader unintended consequences paradigm that sometimes self-proclaims itself in contrast with the invisible hand model from economics. This is a slowly-constituting-itself movement that challenges the original invisible hand model (by showing that this is neither the only nor the best-unintended model), and in many respects it even seems to have outgrown the rivalry with it.

The second assumption formulated in the introduction was that there is more than one analytical framework to study invisible hand processes in sociology. In the first type of context, the *related, but different from the invisible hand*, the focus is on the mechanisms of aggregation, emergence, and composition that work according to different rules than the invisible hand in economics. Elster's (1978, 107–108) counterfinality, for instance, differs from the mechanism of promotion of common good in several aspects. Just to give a sense of the discussion, the former depicts negative outcomes brought about by the fallacies of composition, whereas the latter is an unintended consequence of individual actions, but a desirable one.

In the second type of context, the *even better than the invisible hand*, the interest is in the mechanisms of error-correction, adaptation, and ignorance that are somehow complementary to the invisible hand, and which improve the prospect on the relation between the activities of individuals, the unintended consequences, and the reproduction of social structure. As in Tilly's (1996) example of bringing home the groceries, wherein the invisible elbow functions as an error-correction mechanism that – though not reducing the overflow from the bag per se – manages at least to coordinate the activity of coping with it.

In the third type of circumstance, the *invisible hand but not of the market*, the focus is on the mechanisms of emergence and smart aggregation, but which are attributed to other instances than the competitive market mechanism. This line of research has been particularly enriched lately with concepts such as the right hand and left hand of the state (Bourdieu 1999 [1993], Wacquant 2009 [2004]); the invisible hand of social capital (Lin and Ao 2008; McDonald and Day 2010); the invisible hand of race (Royster 2015); or the invisible hand of data flow (Harari 2017). The interest herein is in cunning, tricky, long-term processes that realize a certain finality. Unlike the first two streams, which somehow compete with the invisible hand model either by reducing it to the level of one of the many models of production of unintended consequences or by correcting and reformulating it, this stream reproduces the invisible hand type of framing because it justifies it by applying it.

With these two assumptions in mind, the edited volume aimed to gather contributions that would help circumscribe what is the potential of a would-be invisible hand-type model in contemporary sociology, as well as delineate more clearly the three research contexts in which the metaphor of the invisible hand is put to use. The chapters grouped into three main parts that reflect upon the three research contexts made a great contribution to illustrating and enriching these two initial assumptions. The added value, however, is that the collection of chapter presented together has revealed some tendencies that were not captured when this book project was embarked upon.

This concluding chapter of the book tries to show the manner in which the particular contributions advanced or falsified the initial two assumptions that the book rested on. Unlike our introductory discussion, which indicated the relevance of the chapters for justifying the typology of analytical frameworks advanced by this book, this analysis takes one step further in order to reveal how these chapters can also be interpreted as toppling the start-up assumptions, or as taking it in a completely different direction. This is an exercise very much in the genre initiated with Hirschman's (1995) *Propensity to Self-subversion*, wherein the author resumes after a few years his most important theses and gives them a critical kick in light of new empirical material or reinterpretations. Surely, in this very project on the invisible hand in sociology, the duration between the elaboration of the introduction and the writing of the concluding "subversive" chapter is much more reduced. Still, the convention initiated by Hirschman is maintained because we present the manner in which the thinking about sociology of the invisible hand evolved, thanks to the contributions gathered in this volume.

1 Related, but different from the invisible hand

The contributions gathered under this heading all show, one way or the other, that the invisible hand-like arguments employed in sociology are related to the original framing in political philosophy and economics, yet also nourish a certain specificity and autonomy. All chapters confirmed this finding, while also bringing some fresh insights.

Craig Smith's chapter focused on the impact of invisible hand arguments on political philosophy. It showed the role played by the invisible hand in advancing the debate on distributive justice. This chapter dealt mainly with the argumentative usage of the invisible hand explanations in political philosophy, and less with its explanatory potential. As indicated in *Three in One: Invisible Hand-Type Theories in Sociology* (Mica, Wyrzykowska, Zielińska and Wiśniewski in this volume), the direct benefit of this chapter was an enlightening collection of the multiple usages of the invisible hand arguments (argumentative, normative, explanatory, etc.). In other words, the chapter shows the distinctive manner in which the invisible hand is played out depending on the theoretical context.

In a more subversive manner, however, Smith's *chapter might be read as a suggestion that the attempt of this book is to link the sociological context with the invisible hand frame, demonstrating mainly its explanatory potential.* The distinctions operated in *Three in One* depicted the invisible hand-type theories in sociology in relation to phenomena of emergence of social institutions. Yet, these did not look at invisible hand-like arguments that can be stated to have moved the sociological imagination one way or the other, or to have challenged its main assumptions. And this prompts the question whether such an argumentative undertaking has ever taken place in sociology. The first answer that comes to mind is: Not too much. Although the unintended consequences concept was used by sociology to make some ethical arguments, the summative and aggregative accounts have rather focused on explaining the social phenomena. When it appeared, the normative component rather emerged in relation with the stream of *invisible hand, but not of the market*, especially in the context of the study of power. It is herein where the normative dimension, ethical message, and value commitment of the invisible hand explanations are the most visible.

Smith considered that the invisible hand explanations were a useful tool for advancing an alternative political theory to socialism in Hayek and a critique of the deliberate implementation of redistributive justice *à la* Rawls in Nozick. It is only in the chapters that relate to power that the same critical fervor and sense of manifesto is encountered. This means that the type of usage of the invisible hand explanations is also contingent upon the type of phenomenon that is being studied. *Hence, Smith's chapter takes us in the direction of weighing in more detail whether the distinctiveness of the sociological approach also manifests on levels others than the explanatory one.* The issue of power, for instance, belongs to the same normatively loaded phenomena such as justice. Meaning that irrespective of whether the approach appears in political philosophy or sociology, this will take a more argumentative turn. Hence, the modern sociological versions of the invisible hand argument are not so different when the explanation is targeting the normative.

Frederick Whelan's chapter had the aim to challenge the perception that the Scottish authors had a theory of unintended consequences that underlined exclusively the beneficial outcome. This showed that, in spite of a general perception that it was quite the contrary, the Scottish political philosophers also underlined the reverse and malignant part of the unintended. Whelan sketched the manner in which the invisible hand is perceived, and how, for instance, Boudon's perverse effects that result from the interaction differ from the "Humean analysis of mental operations" as well as "it is the direct opposite of Smith's invisible hand argument" about the unintended desirable outcome that results from the combination of social actions. As prefigured in *Three in One*, the merit of the chapter for the purposes of this volume was that it offered contextual evidence of the distinction between the invisible hand models in economics and the models in sociology that are similar, but not identical with these.

But Whelan's chapter also indicated that the view that the invisible hand arguments in economics look in one manner, while those in sociology in another one is part of the theoretical imagination. Reportedly, the distinction between the models rests partly on the value attached to the effect (desirable in economics vs. undesirable in sociology) and on the type of sources that are offered as explanation for the final outcome (aggregation in economics vs. aggregation–social interaction and interdependence in sociology). At closer scrutiny, however, the distinction between the models of unintended and combined effects of social actions in economics and those in sociology looks more like a tool for framing the identity of these than an irrefutable fact.[1] Hence, *the chapter by Whelan takes us in the direction that allows us to trace the sources of this rhetoric differentiating between the more traditional perspective in economics and the more modern sociological undertaking.*

Jocelyn Pixley's chapter reviewed distinct invisible hand models in economics and made an argument for the introduction of money in their framing. To the delight of sociologists of the invisible hand, the phenomenon of money is supposed to be interpreted as social relation, thus in the manner sociologists usually do. Yet, less gratifying, the models discussed by Pixley were rather loosely coupled, if at all, with relevant sociological models of the invisible hand. The inspiration for the reformulation of the models in economics came from sociological treatments of money, and not from sociological invisible hand-like models. To a certain extent, this can be taken to strengthen the argument of the volume that the invisible hand models in economics and the invisible hand-like models in sociology, although they intersected, have nevertheless evolved rather distinctively. Should the invisible hand-type models have been more visibly connected with the competitive market mechanism and the reach of equilibrium, they would have probably stood a better chance to be taken into account by Pixley. *Thus, Pixley's chapter opens the door to discuss further the impact of the*

1 Although this is not the place to develop this discussion further, it should be indicated that the framing of the invisible hand in distinct disciplines is not ad hoc. As indicated by Pixley, this is also contingent upon the general ideology and perspective on the world that the authors of these models aim to transmit. Accordingly: "The Elias version of self-control is an inspired 'solution' to Hobbes' terrifying state of nature seen too in *hopes* of Weber, Arendt and Durkheim for a 'happy' social order to *tame* so-called 'strong emotions' ([Editors: Helena] Flam […]). Smith's slightly similar hope in the 'invisible hand' has individual self-interest and empathy creating the greater good that Albert Hirschman […] criticizes" (Pixley 2012, 14–15).

invisible hand-type accounts advanced by modern sociology beyond sociology, and sociology of the invisible hand as such.

The second element that comes up in relation with this chapter is that unlike in *Three in One*, where the sociological discipline was presented as a bit of latecomer to the debate, *in Pixley's chapter, the power differential between the disciplines is inverted.* It is not as the sociological models are different, in the sense that these depart from the economic models of the invisible hand. But the economic models did not incorporate the intuition that money is a social relation, although these had the chance to do so. For instance, with the Polanyi argument of the mistreatment of money, land, and labor as commodities. Thus, one has to be more circumspect in presenting the relation between sociology and economics, where the former is always dominated by the latter. The chapter by Pixley evidenced situations when the economists borrowed from sociologists or when these should have incorporated what the sociologists are saying for some time already. This does not automatically suggest that the invisible hand-like models in sociology are "better" than the original framing. It would be also difficult to challenge economics in relation to a concept that was practically developed on its territory. But, it indicates that a step in this direction may not be as futile. *What differentiates the sociological models of aggregation, emergence, and fallacious composition is not only the logic of the mechanism and the type of outcome (bad vs. good) but also that these models are not applied to market situations. Three in One* missed this element when trying to capture the essence of the sociological types, yet it is fundamental.

Emma Tieffenbach's contribution synthetized the invisible hand explanation from various angles. This enlisted the various meanings that can be found in the literature (lack of foresight, lack of decree, nonprofit, etc.) and also analyzed the various arguments that hold that this kind of explanation has superior explanatory power in social sciences. After pointing to the weak point of each of these arguments one by one, the chapter concluded that the appeal of the explanation rests with the fact that it infuses the institutional kinds with a certain autonomy beyond the intentions and expectations of the agents who engage in purposive action. As stated in *Three in One*, in addition to the main argument, this chapter has the merit of capturing these nuances of meaning. The shifts or conflations of meaning constitute a recurrent yet not thoroughly developed subject in unintended consequences – such as, the risk of confusing the unanticipated with the undesirable, or the conflation of the unintended with the unexpected.

Yet, besides these observations regarding the shifts and conflations of meaning in relation with the unintended consequences, there was no attempt to analyze the variety of connotations of the invisible hand-like concepts that are present in sociology. What is more, when discussing their own concepts in relation with the original notion from political philosophy, the sociologists seem to have favored certain meanings (such as "lack of foresight", "lack of any sense of the aggregate shape of things", or the "spontaneous order"), while ignoring, or being unaware about others (such as the would-be "lack of decree," "profit motive", or "lack of theoretical knowledge"). *Tieffenbach's chapter paves the way for realizing that the invisible hand can be approached from many more angles than commonly ascribed in economics, and strives to enhance the discussion in sociology keeping this point in mind.*

Sebastian Giacovelli's chapter emerged as an anatomy of the approach to the invisible hand assumption that occurs in economics – that is, as a "fiction with real consequences". As stated in *Three in One,* this framing occurred as relevant for this edited volume because it pointed to a major distinction between the invisible hand perspective in economics and the invisible hand-type perspective in sociology. Namely, the latter does not appear to have ever been as successful as the original notion in economics, and to affect the behavior of social actors to such an extent – as, for instance, by influencing the logic underpinning the structural adjustment program of the international institutions, such as the International Monetary Fund. Although the performative turn in economic sociology started from studying the market, the truth of the matter is that sociologists do not take the invisible hand so seriously as economists do. *What emerges from Giacovelli's chapter quite clearly is that although the sociologists did study the invisible hand, this has never turned into a test of the legitimacy of its theoretical models.* Unlike class or social capital, the invisible hand metaphor has never become a key concept in sociology. From this point of view, it might seem a little risky to claim that the sociology of invisible hand really offers an alternative to what and how the invisible hand is being researched in economics. But the present volume takes this risk anyway. Because the difference is not only in what is researched, but also in the approach to it and in what is at stake for the discipline as such.

Karl-Dieter Opp's chapter discussed and illustrated the spontaneous order and the institutional design as explanatory models of emergence of institutions. Subsequently, the work introduced an extended spontaneous order model (that also includes elements of institutional design) and drew attention that it is important not only to realize the concatenation of the two models, but also the manner in which this concatenation plays out in practice. In other words, it is one thing to say that any model of emergence and development contains elements of spontaneous order and institutional design combined, and another thing to get to the bottom of the process as such.

Observably, Opp's chapter addressed the spontaneous order and not the invisible hand idea. Although this finds its cues in the XVIII formulation of the invisible hand, it is actually rather different. Typically, the notion of the invisible hand presupposes representatives of the Scottish enlightenment such as David Hume and Adam Smith, and even Bernard Mandeville. This is a particular type of explanation that reveals a concrete mechanism of emergence of an institution, usually market related but not necessarily, as an unintended consequence. On the other hand, the notion of spontaneous order entails a particular idea developed in principal by Karl Menger and Friedrich A. Hayek. This model is usually traced to Scottish moral philosophers (Adam Smith, David Hume, and Adam Ferguson in the 18th century) and seems to be restating the invisible hand argument. Namely, that various institutions (division of labor, social wealth, common law, market, liberty, language, etc.) emerge spontaneously as system level unintended consequences of social actions and interactions that were not coordinated or designed to bring about these institutions in the first place (see Whelan in this volume).

But, in comparison with the invisible hand, the spontaneous order idea is traced to, and not associated with, Adam Smith. Further, the spontaneous order explains the emergence of norms and institutions in contrast with the model of institutional design. Whereas, in the case of the invisible hand, the theoretical antonym is not so obvious, or it is more fuzzy. Furthermore, the spontaneous order seems to beneficiate of a more delineated theoretical cannon and methodological assumptions. But, in the case of the invisible hand, the metaphor part of the story is more poignant and seems to keep the whole theoretical approach together.

The spontaneous order framing is the terrain where the framing of economics, history of ideas, and sociology actually meet. When using the invisible hand idea, however, the conceptual distance between the models is more difficult to bridge, or this can be bridged by way of pointing to symmetrical differences (good vs. bad outcomes, social actions vs. social interaction, etc.). *Thus, Opp's chapter makes evident that the paradigm of spontaneous order is a "space of exception" (see Pixley on money) wherein various disciplines do meet and overlap to a certain extent. Although the invisible hand concept and the spontaneous order notion are quite similar, the former is less egalitarian than the latter.* There is something regarding the invisible hand that renders it as a specific notion that can be owned by distinct disciplines, but only exclusively.

The contributions regarding the *related, but different from the invisible hand* proved the general point made in the start-up discussion of this volume. The sociological take on the invisible hand-like phenomena is so clearly different from the one in economics that this does not even try to claim otherwise. But these chapters also indicated the following things. First, not all invisible hand-type explanations in modern sociology claim to be distinct from those in economics. But mainly those that have explanatory valences. Second, the distinction between the profile of the invisible hand theory in economics and the invisible hand-type theory in sociology is not so much an element that turned out to be this way, but it is the manner in which the identity of these disciplines is defined. Third, the sociological invisible hand-type theory had mainly worked with the meaning of the invisible hand as this is defined in economics (such as "lack of foresight", "lack of any sense of the aggregate shape of things", or the "spontaneous order") while ignoring other possibilities. Fourth, regardless of the level of sophistication achieved, the invisible hand-type theory in sociology is not so closely linked with the manner in which this discipline self-defines itself, as this is the case in economics. Fifth, closely connected, the impact of invisible hand-type theories beyond sociology is miniscule, or this just began to be exerted. And sixth, related concepts, reformulations, conceptual substitutions of the invisible hand may turn up to be more universal bridges between disciplines than the traditional concept. This notwithstanding, the fascination exerted by the invisible concept is imbattable.

2 Even better than the invisible hand

The contributions gathered under this heading are illustrative of treatments that, more or less indirectly, upgrade or rectify the original invisible hand argument. These do not propose an alternative to the invisible hand in economics, as the one framed within sociology for example. But they improve the general model. As can be expected, in the majority of cases, such upgrade starts from the fact that there are serious doubts whether the invisible hand, as customarily depicted, is really working. Furthermore, it also happens for the revision of the original concept to behave quite radically. As when the invisible ends up to be considered as partially visible, or even as visible, for example.

Helmut K. Anheier's chapter dealt with the principle of the hiding hand. Originally advanced by Hirschman (1967), this is one of the most acknowledged conceptual refinements of the invisible hand, and it happens to be intensively revised these days actually. The chapter explored its conceptual position in relation with similar notions in sociology, organizational psychology, and economics. Further, this integrated the hiding hand in a broader typology containing three more manifestations: the protecting hand, the malevolent hand, and the passive hand. The drawing of boundaries between the specific models validates the overall assumption that there is theoretical awareness of the characteristics of the invisible hand model, and of the fact that various sociological terms are related, but also quite different from the original formulation. As in the case of Whelan's chapter, the discussion by Anheier supported the image that the invisible hand is perceived in relation to beneficial outcomes, yet this also introduced further clarifications, as the relation between this model and consequentialism.

Anheier's chapter suggested that the creation of new concepts as reformulations of classical ideas is tricky. In the short run, this association may help promote the concept. In the long run, however, it may lead to its perception as a main theoretical upgrade to the initial concept, that besides being a sort of reinterpretation does not really have autonomy in its own right. This certainly occurs plausible, and the career of the principle of the hiding hand seems to confirm this hypothesis. However, this does not necessarily have to be the case. As indicated by Tilly's (1996) concept of the invisible elbow, the theoretical advancement may happen. Anheier rightly made the point that for the sociological discussion of the hiding hand to mature, it is necessary to develop various concepts together and delineate their profile in analytical and conceptual terms. *In other words, the introduction of new reformulations should be backed up by the systematization of the existing ones and by cumulative knowledge.*

The second important observation made by Anheier in relation with the rather slow implementation of the model of the hiding hand is that the connection between this model and other theories has not been sufficiently developed. This means that in addition to being coupled with other similar concepts within the unintended field, the upgrades to the invisible hand should also cherish brokerage with other domains. Anheier did just this when pointing to the connection with the ignorance and complexity literature. And the development of the invisible hand notion also seems to have confirmed to this pattern. *Thus, it can be inferred from Anheier's chapter, as far as the models that are even better than the invisible hand will be confined to the field of invisible hand and unintended consequences solely, these risk of being denied the possibility to deliver a more ample sociological message.*

Bruna Ingrao's chapter corrected the model of the invisible hand more on the visible side. This showed that it is not one invisible mechanism, but rather many visible hands that are operating. The chapter revealed that, in spite of its acknowledged failure as a research tool or agenda in mathematical economics, the invisible hand is further the dominant and most attractive "fictional story" of how the markets work within macroeconomics. It thus can be concluded, that irrespective of continuation, reformulation, or criticism, the invisible hand metaphor continues to remain a point of reference. Not being a sociologist, Ingrao lets this problem to be solved by sociology of science. Yet, this act of delegation is rather symbolic because in the next paragraph she launched what can be regarded a one hundred percent sociologically valid hypothesis explaining the process. Namely, that the reference to the invisible hand model functions as a sort of legitimacy provider because it testifies the level of mathematization of the theory, which is a token of its scientific character. Indeed, this seems as a quite valid and understandable hypothesis that could be quickly put to use by sociologists.

But what is perhaps not as obviously advanced as a direct hypothesis but it can be easily noticed *in Ingrao's chapter is that the fascination and renewed reference to the invisible hand metaphor has also changed what this metaphor stands for.* Ingrao pointed that in macroeconomics, for example, at some point the invisible hand model became reduced to representative agent models, and thus that the interaction aspect of the original notion was lost. Although not abstracted in a clear sociological statement, this observation is essential because it indicates that the dominant position of the invisible hand fictional story is actually the dominant position of a theory that changes in time. Thus, what the invisible hand stands for also undergoes change. But if this happens in economics, then it is also to be expected that the change takes place in sociology too. To a certain extent, we touched upon this aspect in *Three in One.* Wherein we showed, for instance, that inside the *related, but different* stream, there was a change of vocabulary from very specific concepts with theoretical overload (perverse effects (Boudon 1982 [1977]), social contradictions (counterfinality and suboptimality Elster 1978), etc.) toward more general terms with implications for everyday life or macroprocesses (see externalities (Elster 2007), mechanisms of emergence (Cherkaoui 2005; 2007)). While in relation with the *even better* stream, we discovered a tendency in the adaptation of notions such as the invisible elbow or the hiding hand to accentuate more the issue of power (see Auyero 2010a; 2010b; Flyvbjerg and Sunstein 2016). Still, more research is needed in order to understand the general semantic dynamics, and the manner in which changes in the meaning of the invisible hand in one theory are related, or not, to what is going on in the framework of others.

Zbigniew Szkop, Rafał Wiśniewski and *Marta Sylla's* chapter approached the invisible hand in the meaning of allocation of resources by the market. This chapter looked at the development and refining of tools for ameliorating the faulty allocation of resources by the market, and in relation with environmental goods in particular. This is one of the not-so-many instances in this volume wherein the invisible hand assumption goes beyond theoretical framing and conceptualization. Herein, the invisible hand is taken as denoting allocation of resources, and it has addressed frontally the problem of what to do in a situation of market failure. Thus, the discussion of the invisible hand is not carried out in terms of theory but of public policy.

In relation to *Three in One,* this chapter is revealing because *it sustains that it is not that the invisible hand is not working at all (as in Joseph E. Stiglitz's famous statement "the reason that the invisible hand often seems invisible is that it is often not there"). Rather, this needs a deep institutional foundation in order to work proper.* A shallow foundation would simply not do it. Although it does not provide directly a concept that would substitute for the invisible hand (as the preceding two chapters did), Szkop, Wiśniewski, and Sylla's chapter emerges in the genre of the *even better,* because the invisible hand of the market is shown to be contingent on other hands or supportive interventions. Drawing from the example of the Pigou tax, the chapter clearly indicates that the institutional foundation works in the sense of a supportive and error–correction structure as well. Thus, although not stated straightforwardly, this chapter goes in the direction of an invisible hand of deep institutional structures and more or less purposive error–correction mechanisms.

To conclude, the contributions gathered in relation with *even better than the invisible hand* have taken us in the following directions. First, the invisible hand metaphor is not a static concept. A semantic dynamic can be observed not only in economics, but also in sociology. Which means that the phenomenon of change of meaning is quite pervasive and we should be aware of, and try to understand it. Third, the specification of alternatives to the invisible hand is important, but equally important is also to spot the relation between various hands and the invisible-type of hands. Fourth, any theoretical exercise that proposes as its goal to bring together all these models that compete or offer to substitute the invisible hand should be aware that systematization alone does not suffice. The conceptual installments delivered by sociology of unintended consequences, and the sociology of the invisible hand, only confirm this fact. The treatments of invisible hand-like processes had always had a stronger impact when this came in a bigger theoretical package, in relation with other theories (such as functionalism, structuration theory, risk society, etc.). This is why the recent connection with the substantive issues of power is so important. This brokerage, as the one with the literature on ignorance and complexity, has the potential to propel the theory even further.

3 The invisible hand, but not of the market

What the chapters regarding the *invisible hand, but not of the market* have in common is the fact that these put the mechanisms in relation with other instances than the one we are commonly accustomed too. Whether traced to the community or social capital, in all these cases the invisible hand is presented in a nonconventional situation. Thus, unlike the *even better than the invisible hand*, in this case the working of the invisible hand is not substituted with a smarter kind of hand or code. The invisible hand remains, but the manner in which this is related to the market changes. Certainly, in terms of theory, this is a quite important feature because at least at the outset, this third analytical stream is not as critical as the other two streams are. This is also due to the fact that herein the invisible hand notion is more of a metaphor and the chapters are not really framed within the invisible hand literature. The metaphor was borrowed, but this happened for the sake of public policy, social capital, or job seeking literature, and not for that of the invisible hand.

Francisco Fernandez de Castro and *Raul P. Lejano's* chapter analyzed the implementation of programs against poverty in Mexico. This investigated how spontaneous mechanisms work in the process of policymaking. The main goals and resources of poverty reduction projects are set by social actors operating on macro level (like politicians and public institutions), while implementation is delegated to local communities. Yet, because of shortages, the implementation, or at least parts of it, falls on the shoulders of some of the local actors, such as women and parties committed to the success of the program. As a result, in the process of implementation, spontaneous cooperative processes occur, in order to make these programs work – that is, the invisible hand of community. By focusing on these informal norms and everyday practices, Fernandez de Castro and Lejano's chapter shows how the invisible hand metaphor is also useful to investigate phenomena that operate on micro levels of the social and economic life.

But the input of the chapter goes beyond providing an illuminating illustration. In a similar vein to Szkop, Wiśniewski and Sylla's contribution regarding the importance of the deep institutional structure, this chapter aspires to *uncover the backstage of the invisible hand*. Just as in the case of the invisible hand of the market, the backstage is the institutional structure, while in the case of the invisible hand of the community, the backstage is the links (such as physical, virtual, or cognitive) that guarantee the reproduction of certain institutions, public policy reforms, and organizational practices.

Steve McDonald, Scott T. Grether, Kim S. Holland and *Hannah McQueen's* chapter dealt with the problem of serendipitous job finding and online job market. The chapter indicated that nowadays it is almost impossible to fully investigate the modality in which the invisible hand operates without taking Internet and new media technologies into account. This showed that the invisible hand of social capital on the online job market is not so spontaneous as at first blush this seems to be. This is actually structured and "manipulated" by HR professionals in search for potentially new employees. Similarly to Fernandez de Castro and Lejano's work, or Szkop, Wiśniewski and Sylla's contribution, this chapter allows us to take a peep behind the curtain *of the invisible hand.* This makes us realize that there are certain categories of actors who take up, or are delegated, the role of securing that things go smoothly and that the invisible hand stays invisible.

Mikołaj Pawlak and *Michał Kotnarowski's* chapter further analyzed the job market, focusing on social inequalities in this area. This spotted the presence of the invisible hand of social capital highlighting the importance of social networks in the process of searching and finding a job. One of the main findings is that having already a job places the individuals in a privileged position in the social networks on the labor market and – in consequence – it makes it easier for these to get a new job (or an unsolicited job offer). Thus, the invisible hand ends up reproducing the problematic mechanisms that the social structure this is embedded in is known to manifest – such as social inequality.

Certainly, this is a reading that comes quite close to the one by McDonald, Grether, Holland and McQueen. As a matter of fact, the invisible hand of social capital that is illustrated by Pawlak and Kotnarowski builds on earlier interpretations developed, among others, by McDonald and the authors associated with him. Yet, *at closer look, it can be noticed that the framings of the invisible hand implemented by these two chapters, although seemingly similar, are in fact distinct.* The study by Pawlak and Kotnarowski might be catalogued as the good, old-fashioned invisible hand work (*à la* Nozick 1994), in which a social institution that seems to be guided by purpose or collective agency (in this case, job-search fragmentation and exclusion) is shown to be the outcome of processes of social interactions or interplay of social actions. Whereas the study by McDonald, Grether, Holland and McQueen seems akin to the more recently developed framing wherein the effort is to show how the apparently spontaneous and neutral invisible hand is in fact partly structured or connected with other hands.

Thus, the two "finding a job" type of chapters published in this volume depict two distinct framings of the invisible hand. One, more classical, in which the scope is to uncover the invisible hand. And the other, more recent, in which the aim is to indicate the relation between various visible–invisible types of hands and the ensuing dynamics. Noticeably, this is akin to the framing encountered in some of the other contributions listed in this volume (see Anheier, Ingrao, Opp, as well as Fernandez de Castro and Lejano, and Szkop, Wiśniewski and Sylla). The invisible hand (be it of market, community, or social capital) might be invisible, but this does not mean that this is decoupled from other phenomena, or that it operates in isolation.

Loïc Wacquant's chapter reformulated Bourdieu's initial model of the left hand and right hand of the state by rendering more obvious the police, the courts, and the prison as essential aspects of the right hand in addition to fiscal and economic governance. This was important in the context of this volume because it directly legitimized the idea to speak about concepts that trace invisible hand mechanisms to domains other than the market. Observably, however, the trademark of the hands of the state model is not only that the right hand and left hand are of the state, but also that these two hands are only distinguished by the fact that one is the right and the other is the left, with no additional elements regarding their visibility. Thus, the right hand and left hand of the state is a model liable to be included in both the *invisible hand, but not of the market*, and in the *even better* stream.

Wacquant's chapter pointed to the hands of the state that jointly, but also concurrently, orchestrate the management of inequality and marginality. Even if Wacquant rethought the Bourdieu model as to draw attention to the penal policy in addition to the market-related one, in fact in this model, the invisible hand of the market and the hands of the state (its right hand actually) are connected, or "wed" to use the more specific term of this author. *This chapter leaves us puzzling about the manner in which distinct types of hands that can be traced to instances other than the market – pre-existing patterns of influencing social life – interact, and shape each other.*

To sum up, the contributions gathered in relation with the *invisible hand, but not of the market* take us in two connected directions. First, there is a certain backstage or dirty work of the invisible hand. This pertains to the classical invisible hand of the market, but also to the invisible hand of community or to the invisible hand of social capital. This backstage includes elements as different as: institutional structures, patterns of error-correction, informal arrangement, and even millipede-like visible hands. Second, and this resonates with one of the findings of the previous section, it makes more sense and more relevant to research the relations between the invisible hand (be it the one of other instances than the market) and similar types of mechanisms. The invisible hand interacts with the working of other hands, while also being contingent on the institutional and cultural context, as well as on the more or less discrete operation of other actors, or of other hands, as in the case of Part II, where the focus moves from the invisible hand as such to its relation with other parties. Just that one essential difference remains. This last stream does not aim to replace or upgrade the invisible hand metaphor. The discussion takes place outside the invisible hand debate entirely.

4 Conclusions

As we have seen in this chapter, the discussions brought by the authors invited to contribute to this volume appear to conform to two logics. On the one hand, as envisaged in *Three in One* and revised herein, these confirm the typology of the three analytical streams that apply the invisible hand metaphor in sociology. On the other hand, however, they also seem to point in the direction of different kind of findings. These new elements, certainly, do not deconstruct the manner of systematization of the sociology of the invisible hand advanced herein. They do, however, move the discussion to a completely new level. To give an idea of the general debate that seems to be provoked by the contributions in this volume, let us point to the three main important conclusions that stand out.

First, the theoretical imaginary about the invisible hand identifies this concept with economics. It might be that this is the reason why the approaches that occur in the other fields are almost automatically presented as different. In the case of the discipline that constitutes the focus of this book, for instance, the invisible hand in economics is depicted as looking at desirable outcomes, while the framing in sociology as concerning the undesirable ones.

Still, although the association between the invisible hand and economics is indeed strong, this does not mean that the modalities of researching the invisible hand in other disciplines is so different, or that the disciplines are so polarized on the issue. Furthermore, there are other closely related concepts to the invisible hand (such as spontaneous order) wherein the theoretical distance between sociology and other disciplines (such as organization studies and political philosophy) is not that big. So that the bridging between sociology and other disciplines may be more facile. On the other hand, there is perhaps nothing more fortune when trying to bring together theoretical variations than claiming how different these are when coming, practically, to the same issue.

Second, irrespective of the stream the contributions belong to (*related, but distinct from the invisible hand*, the *even better than the invisible hand*, or the *invisible hand, but not of the market*), what emerged quite clearly is that the contemporary point of interest is rather the relation between the invisible hand and other types of hands, or the institutional and cultural infrastructure. This means that it is not the invisible hand alone, or the mechanism that works even better than the invisible hand that does all the magic. But it is actually the interaction of various, more or less, (in)visible hands.

Certainly, it could be further speculated, depending on the domain, the input of the other hands is more or less visible. For instance, the market seems to be naturally associated with the invisible hand because of its high level of individualization and approach to phenomena in terms of aggregation, while the political domain renders visible the interaction of various hands because this is used to explain social phenomena in terms of power-games, negotiation, or other type of relation. This suggests two things. The emergent interest in the interdependence between various hands is the extension of the investigation in the direction of uncovering new territories. But this might also be due to the generalization of the finding that the invisible hand is not as strong as to do everything by itself and thus a new formula in which the metaphor makes sense should be found.

Second, a theoretical enterprise that aims to launch the study of invisible hand in itself is likely to be less successful than in the case when this is associated or identified with another theory. The invisible hand of the market in economics was probably so successful because this offered a pure, general, and flexible theory of the market. In the case of sociology, however, the invisible hand – although linked with the theory of mechanisms of emergence or of interdependence – had not yet become a complex theory of society. For economists, at least as can be established from the discussions subsequent to the outburst of the 2008 economic crisis, the invisible hand is the main mechanism, this being tantamount to market actually. Whereas, in sociology, the invisible hand-type processes, although important, are just one of the many mechanisms that can be spotted. The sociological stream is not only different, but it is also much less engaged emotionally. Unlike economics, sociology does not stand to lose anything if the theory of the invisible hand is falsified or proven shaky.

Hence, the questions arise: What does it take to show that the invisible hand is indeed essential for the explanation of society? How could the sociology of invisible hand be more palpably linked with the paradigm addressing this problem?

It is evident that the contributions to this volume discuss the elements central to sociology – the study of the reproduction of social inequality and social structure, power, social capital, agency, negotiated order, and conflict. These provide useful explanations and offer tools to further enrich the field. For this reason, while sociology might not have invented the term of invisible hand, it definitely provides a rich and meaningful framework for deciphering it further. This formulates a useful explanatory narrative by taking into account the specificity of contemporary social processes. The contributions to this volume, for instance, have shown that in order to fully accomplish its interpretive possibilities, it is essential to adapt the invisible hand to current reality. First of all, it is crucial to go beyond traditional institutions and processes associated with the invisible hand metaphor (i.e., market, state, global economy). It is also important to reveal the phenomena occurring on meso and micro scale, like informality, everyday life, local job market, and local communities' actions. Furthermore, nowadays it seems almost impossible to investigate social, economic, political, and cultural processes without taking into account the Internet and new technologies. The inclusion of research on new media platforms is one of the promising paths for the development of the invisible hand metaphor, and sociology, as can be expected, has a lot to say in this regard.

Of course, at the end of the day, we return to the central question: Is the invisible hand a determining theory and how can we prove that it can dominate among so many competing ideas? Without recourse to a clear, positivist certainty, can it ever rise above its competitors? Does the invisible hand theory give solutions to real-life problems or offer definitive theorizing that enables perfect understanding, or is it simply another evocative and stimulating explanation, initially inspiring that, ultimately, rubs along with every other similarly interesting and exciting narrative that has yet to be disproved?

Perhaps instead of posing questions that cannot be answered, we should accept the invisible hand as it is in a nebulous, fuzzy field, working in and between other theories its dynamic presence, as an offspring to economics married to other disciplines – one of which happens to be sociology. We should not expect the theory to stand on its own in its pure form, because, if we do, then it renders it useless to provide any explanation to the complexity of life and leaves it handy only as a utopian model in academic musings.

References

Auyero, Javier. 2010a. "Chuck and Pierre at the Welfare Office." *Sociological Forum* 25: 851–860.

Auyero, Javier. 2010b. "Visible Fists, Clandestine Kicks, and Invisible Elbows: Three Forms of Regulating Neoliberal Poverty." *European Review of Latin American and Caribbean Studies* 89: 5–26.

Boudon, Raymond. 1982 [1977]. *The Unintended Consequences of Social Action.* London: Macmillan.

Bourdieu, Pierre. 1999 [1993]. "The Abdication of the State." In *The Weight of the World: Social Suffering in Contemporary Society*, authored by Pierre Bourdieu et al., 181–188. Cambridge: Polity Press.

Cherkaoui, Mohamed. 2005. *Invisible Codes: Essays on Generative Mechanisms.* Oxford: Bardwell Press.

Cherkaoui, Mohamed. 2007. *Good Intentions: Max Weber and the Paradox of Unintended Consequences.* Oxford: Bardwell Press.

Elster, Jon. 1978. *Logic and Society. Contradictions and Possible Worlds.* Chichester and London: John Wiley & Sons.

Elster, Jon. 2007. *Explaining Social Behavior: More Nuts and Bolts for the Social Sciences*. Cambridge: Cambridge University Press.

Flyvbjerg, Bent, and Cass R. Sunstein. 2016. "The Principle of the Malevolent Hiding Hand; or, the Planning Fallacy Writ Large." *Social Research* 83: 979–1004.

Harari, Yuval Noah. 2017. *Home Deus: A Brief History of Tomorrow*. London: Harvill Secker.

Hirschman, Albert O. 1967. "The Principle of the Hiding Hand." *The Public Interest* 6: 10–23.

Hirschman, Albert O. 1995. *A Propensity to Self-subversion*. Cambridge (MA) and London: Harvard University Press.

Lin, Nan, and Dan Ao. 2008. "The Invisible Hand of Social Capital: An Exploratory Study." In *Social Capital: An International Research Program*, edited by Nan Lin and Bonnie H. Erickson, 107–132. Oxford: Oxford University Press.

McDonald, Steve, and Jacob C. Day. 2010. "Race, Gender, and the Invisible Hand of Social Capital." *Sociology Compass* 4: 532–543.

Nozick, Robert. 1994. "Invisible-Hand Explanations." *The American Economic Review* 84: 314–318, Papers and Proceedings of the Hundred and Sixth Annual Meeting of the American Economic Association, May 1994.

Pixley, Jocelyn. 2012. "Introduction: New Perspectives on Emotions in Finance." In *New Perspectives on Emotions in Finance: Sociology on Confidence, Betrayal and Fear*, edited by Jocelyn Pixley, 1–22. London: Routledge.

Royster, Deirdre A. 2015. *Race and the Invisible Hand: How White Networks Exclude Black Men from Blue-Collar Jobs*. Berkeley, Los Angeles and London: University of California Press.

Tilly, Charles. 1996. "Invisible." *Sociological Forum* 11: 589–601.

Wacquant, Loïc. 2009 [2004]. *Punishing the Poor: The Neoliberal Government of Social Insecurity*. Durham (NC) and London: Duke University Press.

About the Contributors

Helmut K. Anheier is President of the Hertie School of Governance and Professor of Sociology. He also holds the Chair of Sociology at Heidelberg University and serves as Academic Director of the Centre for Social Investment. His research centers on indicator systems, social innovation, culture, philanthropy, and organizational studies.

Francisco Fernandez de Castro is Executive Director of the School of Government for Senior Management of Public Policy in Mexico. He is a scholar and practitioner. His major fields of interests are sustainable development and poverty eradication, program evaluation, policy design, and implementation.

Sebastian Giacovelli is a postdoc at Justus Liebig University Giessen. His interests concern social theory of expectations, economic sociology, sociology of economic thinking, and (energy) markets.

Scott T. Grether is a PhD candidate at North Carolina State University. His research centers on studying the reproduction of gender, racial, and class inequality in social interactions.

Kim S. Holland is a domestic violence housing advocate at a nonprofit organization in Seattle. Her bachelor's and master's degrees are both in Sociology, and her areas of interest have focused largely on inequality.

Bruna Ingrao is former Full Professor of economics at the University of Rome La Sapienza. She is a historian of economic thought. Her present research interests are in economics and literature and in the history of 20th century macroeconomics.

Michał Kotnarowski is Assistant Professor at the Institute of Political Studies of the Polish Academy of Sciences. He specializes in voting behavior, comparative politics, and political methodology.

Raul Lejano is Professor in the Steinhardt School of Culture, Education, and Human Development at New York University. His research centers around people's relationship with the environment, recently employing narrative research to explain movements for and against environment.

Steve McDonald is Professor of Sociology and University Faculty Scholar at North Carolina State University. He studies social networks and job finding processes, with focus on race, class, and gender inequality in access to employment opportunities.

Adriana Mica is Assistant Professor and Head of the Research Unit on Action and Consequences at the University of Warsaw. Her interests concern unintended consequences of social action, failure, diffusion of innovations, and ignorance.

Hannah McQueen is a sociology PhD student at North Carolina State University. Her interests concern the consequences of financialization, higher education, student loans, and the life course.

Karl-Dieter Opp is Professor Emeritus at the University of Leipzig and Affiliate Professor at the University of Washington (Seattle). His fields of interest are social theory, political participation, social norms and institutions, and the philosophy of the social sciences.

Mikołaj Pawlak is Assistant Professor at the University of Warsaw and Vice-President of the Polish Sociological Association. His interests concern new institutionalism, labor market, migration, and sociology of knowledge.

Jocelyn Pixley is an economic sociologist. In addition to her Honorary Professorship in Sociology at Macquarie University, she is Fellow at the Global Policy Institute at London Metropolitan University. She studies heterodox economics and public policy with specific interest in central banks, full employment, and social integration.

Craig Smith is Adam Smith Senior Lecturer in the Scottish Enlightenment in the School of Social and Political Sciences at the University of Glasgow. His research focuses on the moral and political thought of the Scottish Enlightenment.

Marta Sylla is a PhD candidate at the Wrocław University of Environmental and Life Sciences. Her interests concern the ecosystem service assessment and valuation, with special focus on economic valuation and environmental-economic accounting.

Zbigniew Szkop is a PhD student at the University of Warsaw. His main field of experience is assessment and valuation of urban ecosystem services.

Emma Tieffenbach is an independent researcher who earned a PhD in philosophy at the University of Geneva. Her works in philosophy of social sciences deal with a variety of topics, such as invisible-hand explanations, the limits of rational choice theory, social metaphysics, and the ethical boundaries of economic exchanges.

Loïc Wacquant is Professor at the University of California in Berkeley and Researcher at the *Centre européen de sociologie et de science politique* in Paris. His interests include comparative marginality, ethnoracial domination, the penal state, incarnation, and social theory.

Frederick G. Whelan is Professor Emeritus of political science at the University of Pittsburgh. His research has been in the area of political theory, especially the political thought of 18th century, and on democratic theory.

Rafał Wiśniewski is Associate Professor at the Cardinal Stefan Wyszyński University in Warsaw. He specializes in the sociology of culture, intercultural communication and environmental sociology. He is the Director of the National Centre for Culture in Poland.

Katarzyna M. Wyrzykowska is Assistant Professor at the Institute of Philosophy and Sociology of the Polish Academy of Sciences and Secretary of the Sociology of Arts Section of the Polish Sociological Association. Her research focuses on the sociology of music, music market research, and the methodology of qualitative research.

Iwona Zielińska is Assistant Professor at the Maria Grzegorzewska University. She is interested in science controversies and the public engagement with science and technology.

www.ingramcontent.com/pod-product-compliance
Ingram Content Group UK Ltd.
Pitfield, Milton Keynes, MK11 3LW, UK
UKHW011005120926
8556IPUK00027B/14

9 783631 672327